Claudia Jennings

An Authorized Biography

Claudia Jennings

A Biography

Eric Karell

Midnight Marquee Press, Inc.
Baltimore, Maryland, USA; London, UK

Copyright © 2018 Eric Karell
Interior layout: Gary J. Svehla
Cover design: Aurelia Susan Svehla
Copy editor: Janet Atkinson

Without limiting the rights under copyright reserved above, no part of this publication may be reproduced, stored in or introduced into a retrieval system, or transmitted, in any form, or by any means (electronic, mechanical, photocopying, recording or otherwise), without the prior written permission of the copyright owner or the publishers of the book.

ISBN 13: 978-1-936168-80-4
Library of Congress Catalog Card Number 2018952717
Manufactured in the United States of America

First Printing by Midnight Marquee Press, Inc., November 2018

Dedication

For Claudia's many friends and fans, but most of all to her family.

*Age cannot wither her, nor custom stale
Her infinite variety. Other women cloy
The appetites they feed, but she makes hungry
Where most she satisfies.*

Antony and Cleopatra II.ii., William Shakespeare

Table of Contents

8	Foreword by Roger Corman
9	Author's Introduction
20	Acknowledgments
22	Chapter 1: American Gothic 1949-1966
30	Chapter 2: Evanston 1966-1970
40	Chapter 3: Hugh Hefner and *Playboy* 1969-1979
64	Chapter 4: Fairy Tale 1970-1975
171	Chapter 5: It's Snowing in Los Angeles 1975-1977
180	Chapter 6: Utopia to Dystopia 1977-1979
216	Chapter 7: Summer of 1979: The Small Screen

227	Chapter 8: The Morning of October 3, 1979 and the Aftermath
238	Chapter 9: The Good is Oft Interred With Their Bones
251	Chapter 10: Claudia's Career in Perspective
268	Chapter 11: Connie's Poem
270	Chapter 12: Author's Notes
271	Filmography
274	A Completely Arbitrary Rating of Claudia's Films... from Best to Not-So-Best
275	Bibliography
278	Index
291	About the Author

Foreword

Many people in the film industry call me the master of the exploitation and fantasy film genres. But to paraphrase a great poet, in filmmaking, no man is an island. Over the years, I have worked with countless performers, artists and craftsmen whose hard work has contributed greatly to the success of my pictures.

This book is about one special actress who contributed much to that success, yet sadly has faded from the memories of many fans. Claudia Jennings was my favorite leading lady and single-handedly changed how women were viewed in cult cinema.

Claudia was a true professional. She took direction exceptionally well and hit her marks for the cinematographer without fail. These are not minor things in the movie business. But more importantly, the camera always found a way to capture her astonishing beauty. Audiences couldn't take their eyes off of her.

On screen, Claudia never portrayed the "good wife," "damsel in distress" or "helpless female." She epitomized toughness yet always remained sexy. Few actresses could combine these two traits, but Claudia did so effortlessly. Her expressions, poise and, most of all, her incredible eyes always made her stunning presence felt.

Claudia starred in four movies for me: *Unholy Rollers*, *The Moonshine County Express*, *The Great Texas Dynamite Chase* and *Deathsport*. If she had not been taken from us on October 3, 1979, I'm positive we would have made more films together. I have no doubt that such a talented, beautiful woman was well on her way to being an A-list star. Everyone who worked with her misses her dearly.

If you are a fan of Claudia Jennings, you will undoubtedly enjoy this well-researched, fascinating portrait by Eric Karell. I first spoke to Mr. Karell almost two years ago and immediately perceived his remarkable passion for horror and cult movies. His knowledge of Claudia Jennings and her place in the cinematic universe is unrivaled.

Enjoy this book, and cherish the opportunity it gives you to be with Claudia for a while.

—Roger Corman
January 1, 2018

Author's Introduction

In the 38 years since Claudia Jennings (née Mary "Mimi" Eileen Chesterton) died on the Pacific Coast Highway in Malibu, California, no one has fully chronicled her fascinating life and career. I was shocked when I first started my project that so little had been written about her. There were a few articles here and there, but for the most part Claudia's legacy had been preserved by the modeling she did for *Playboy*, not her acting—and more pointedly, not for her qualities as a human being.

Even after the full generation that has passed since her death, there are many reasons that Claudia Jennings deserves recognition. She defined the 1970s—a decade, it can be argued, that was more culturally explosive than the 1960s. Claudia burst upon the entertainment world during this tumultuous era. Her status as the top model for *Playboy* during that time gained her the attention of the country, and her unquestioned dominance of the drive-in movie market earned her the title Queen of the Bs.

Every notable person is a product of their times, as well as their upbringing. Claudia's life happened to intersect with one of the most significant portions of America's social history. Claudia was born in the post-World War II period, the second "war to end all wars" in a 30-year span. With many opposing forces pulling at one another, American morale was already under duress. The reintegration of our returning veterans to limited opportunities, racial discrimination, the role of women in the workforce with a newfound sense of independent thought and an economy geared to function best in times of total war all exerted pressure on a fragile nation.

This state of unease gave way to a much more depressing and dangerous environment: The hot war in Korea and then the Cold War. When the Soviet Union developed nuclear capabilities, every individual in the United States had the indelible anxiety of an atomic holocaust imprinted on his or her psyche. It was not a constant worry, yet there were moments when the world seemed bent on destroying itself. Then the 1960s brought our society a sea change it was ill prepared for. The decade started out with great hope, as Camelot thrived and a new dawn of progress and promise seemed on the horizon. Despite unparalleled prosperity, disillusion and sorrow quickly followed with the assassination of a sitting president, the escalation of a war in Southeast Asia and growing racial acrimony.

Even though it was a time of great social and cultural change, there was a distant thunder in the air. Unfortunately, while music and art broke out of their boxes, tensions that had remained under the surface erupted. Politics became a blood sport, and soon, American cities were burning, with the sad result that absolutely nothing changed for the better. Illegal drugs began to flood the country, appearing innocuous at first and many saw LSD and marijuana as beneficial substances. Soon, pharmaceuticals poisoned millions of lives as more lethal and addictive products became available. Their use was considered hip and cool by some Americans, despite their dangerous qualities. Claudia fell into this trap, as you will read later.

In the meantime, America's third major war in three decades created misery and a climate of violence at home. By the end of the decade, the excess resulted in a right-wing backlash, putting men in power that the vast majority of the nation would eventually regret. There was a malaise among the American people. We will probably never know whether the dark light with which we currently view our country had really been there all along.

When Claudia was 19, she witnessed—along with the rest of the world—the Democratic Convention in Chicago turn into a pitched battle. Millions watched on television as demonstrators hurled bricks at policemen, who then pummeled the guilty and innocent alike with truncheons. Members of the news media and bystanders were tear-gassed and Claudia's future employer, Hugh Hefner, was beaten by a police officer. These events occurred only a few miles from Mary Eileen Chesterton's home in Evanston. This toxic climate worsened as political assassinations only fueled the sense of anger and helplessness in American society. The country made a hard right turn politically, while at the same time Hollywood was becoming more liberal.

When news of the Watergate break-in first hit the papers, it was just another minor news story. Later, the incident forced our president Richard Nixon to resign, and we were left asking as a people, "Is this who we are?" Were our perceptions that our culture was decent, honest and responsible authentic, or were these perceptions carefully cultivated, groomed and manufactured by the media, our educational system and our leaders?

Once movie audiences could tell the difference between the bad guys and the good guys. Although *Mr. Smith Goes to Washington* gave us a disturbing view of our government, the happy conclusion destroyed the true message of the film. It was as if time had stood still since the making of that movie—until the 1970s. Our political system was failing us, and there was no boy senator riding to the rescue.

A cloud of cynicism soon descended upon America. People began to distrust each other in a country bitterly divided by generation, race, politics and even lifestyle. The military, once the pride of the United States, was now viewed with suspicion, as some saw it as a repressive and occupational entity. In Vietnam—the first war seen live on television—Americans watched with despair, anger and heartbreak, as the intervention seemed to offer no end. Our armed forces had lost their innocence, along with our government and the courts, as all were now seen as corrupt and prone to break the laws they were suppose to uphold.

The films of the 1960s and 1970s decided for the most part we were in truth a hypocritical, greedy, violent lot, led by individuals, authorities or large corporations that killed, robbed and raped us literally and metaphorically. The movies of this era taught us not to trust each other, because each stranger, family member or friend we met might be a psychotic killer. Cinema, which has always to some extent been the conscience of society, started to reflect a more nihilistic view. We saw the rise of the anti-hero, who typified the idea that each of us contains elements of darkness, selfishness, questionable ethics and violence. Claudia would play many characters that fit this description. The motion picture industry as a whole began to shift from purely a medium of entertainment with an occasional satire or social commentary to a reflection of all the historical events, cultural changes and psychological fears of the period. Along with the urge to exercise freedom of artistic expression, censorship laws relaxed, allowing films to show graphic violence and sex. Movies began to represent the perceived suppressed fantasies from all strata of American society. Naturally, one man's art became another's trash as images and actions never seen in mainstream movies became the norm.

The 1970s were also a decade that sent mixed signals to its generational mix. Where the 1960s touted hedonism and increased social awareness, the 1970s added a hard-edged mixture of anarchy and sexual violence. The role of women in society, and in cinema, was changing, but this metamorphosis was literally a double-edged sword. One faction of our country insisted women remain in their traditional roles as wives and mothers, while others demanded women be granted the same rights as men. This led to a clash between the two groups in the streets, courts and film.

This was the world Claudia Jennings was born into, an innocent young lady blissfully insulated from some of the terrible things surrounding her. Intellectual and naturally kind, she was never a cynic or a militant. She had a keen political mind, but it never veered toward extremism. The films she appeared in were contrary to her true nature, as you will read; however, the movies she starred in overwhelmingly reflected the new cinematic aesthetic.

Mary Eileen or Mimi, as family and friends called her, was aware of the cultural upheavals surrounding her life, and was sensitive to them. Politics and countercultural pursuits came in a distant second to Mimi's aspirations to be a movie star. The events of the 1960s and 1970s helped mold her into the glamorous and enigmatic celebrity she became, simultaneously materialistic and socially aware.

While doing research for her story, I came across many unfair and untrue statements made about Claudia in the years after her premature death. Of course, she was not there to defend herself or answer her accusers. I recognized a responsibility to provide a response to her critics, and it became an essential component of the work. There were things written and said about Claudia that provided a compelling motivation for me to investigate more thoroughly in order to provide the reader with as much detail as possible. She dated some of the wealthiest men in Hollywood and the music industry, but was not a gold-digger. Claudia was a trophy girlfriend or mistress in some cases, but she always kept the relationships equal. In her last interview for *Playboy*, she said she did not have boyfriends, but "great love affairs." This was a sign of her independence—something Claudia placed high in her value system. She did not want to be kept, owned or shackled, no matter how much her cage was gilded.

I read an article last month listing the 40 most beautiful women of the 1970s. Incredible as it seems, Claudia was not included among the starlets, actors and models on the list. Without denigrating the other women mentioned, since articles like these are obviously subjective, it seems to me that Claudia should have ranked higher than Erin Gray, Shelley Hack and many others who were mentioned. Unfortunately, this is another indication that time has faded the memory of her beauty, along with thoughts of her splendid career and the extraordinary humanity she possessed.

Claudia owned the 1970s as the Queen of the Bs, was *Playboy*'s most popular model and a symbol of cult chic, sex and Hollywood glamour. She was a rare combination of beauty and intelligence, a so-called sex goddess but also a feminist in an age when they were rare. Claudia was a role model for smart, independent women. The well-toned body that made her a frequent nude model also contained courage, self-confidence, a brilliant mind and empathy for her fellow human beings. She did not inherit wealth from a famous father or rely on a dubious set of talents for her notoriety. Claudia earned her success through hard work and an abundance of physical courage. Claudia was one of our society's true icons, but unfortunately one that is in danger of being forgotten. When I spoke to her friends, phrases like "heart of gold," "she loved people" and "she loved to have fun" came up frequently. This book is meant to be a celebration of her

Claudia Jennings on the cover of *Playboy*, June 1970, as the Playmate of the Year

life, not just her art. We should all cherish the memory of such a person and take joy in the spirit she brought to us. In my book I found it impossible to separate the person from the movie star, so while ample attention is given to her screen career, equal emphasis is accorded to her private life.

What prevents many people seeing Claudia in a true, non-judgmental light was her sex. If we compare her lifestyle with any number of her male contemporaries, the only difference is that none of them appeared nude in *Playboy*. Her association with the magazine created a conscious or subliminal prejudice concerning her morals and abilities as an actress, which followed her career until she died.

How I came to be the one to write her biography is an odd story, as well an improbable one. Truth be told, depending on how one looks at things, it can be interpreted as fate, a series of unusual circumstances or even something spiritual.

After coming home from work, my usual habit was to pour a large single malt scotch and watch a cult or horror film to relax. As I browsed the possibilities on *YouTube* one evening four years ago, *The Great Texas Dynamite Chase* caught my attention completely at random, simply because I noticed it starred Claudia Jennings. Up to that point in my life, unbelievable as it sounds, I had never seen any of her films despite being a student of horror, B and cult movies. I had only vague memories of her initial *Playboy* pictorial, and in addition, I was completely ignorant of any facts concerning her career and private life. I believe this indicates how far Claudia had disappeared from the public's view. On this particular night though, only one of her films would satisfy my curiosity.

The movie was brilliant; it spurred my amateur research project on Claudia, during which I became fascinated with her. However, it took one particular article, "But She Was a Cheerleader," published in the *Chicago Reader*, written by Albert Williams, that changed the project into a professional quest. The article was simultaneously touching, infuriating and heart-crushing. It instilled in me the overwhelming magnificence, sense of tragedy and loss that was the life of Claudia Jennings. The word "tragedy" is used frequently on our grim planet, where there are daily reports of despair and cruelty. Considering the Shakespearean aura surrounding her death, tragedy is an appropriate term.

Therefore, it was again surprising to find no one else had told her full and accurate story before then. The closest was a lengthy article in *Femme Fatales* magazine penned by Ari Bass. There were a few other paragraphs and pages in assorted books, magazines and websites dealing with cult films and cult stars, but nothing comprehensive. Moreover, certainly no written explanation could be found of how a beautiful, innocent young woman from the Midwest ended up being killed on the Pacific Coast Highway shortly before her 30th birthday.

As I found out, along with the good written about Claudia, there was much about her so-called promiscuity and her use of drugs. We can dismiss the accusations of promiscuity immediately. The word is an anachronistic term for a double standard that dishonestly shames women for multiple partners, yet idolizes men for the same behavior. Some media described her life as scandalous, which is pure rubbish. Claudia's life was much less scandalous than a 100 of her contemporaries and even greater amounts in present-day Hollywood. (I might add there are probably many more indiscretions about which we can only speculate.)

I imagine the very nature of her story, which seemed to have been more fiction than fact, shocked most people. It would have been a challenge to Jacqueline Susann or Harold Robbins to invent a more imaginative tale. Claudia's life was haunting: the rise of a beautiful, talented girl to stardom, then her brief fall to a dissolute and desultory period, only to see just before an anticipated second rise a cruel twist of fate end it all.

For those who read this book expecting to see nude photos of Claudia or hear the most intimate details of her private life, I'm afraid you'll be disappointed. The purpose of this book is to tell the story of her life, her career and her place in entertainment history. Her association with *Playboy* is an essential part of the Claudia's life needing clarification and explanation; therefore, a significant section of the book deals with Hugh Hefner and his empire. However, I believe it is important to tell the story of a Playmate without relying upon the crutch of pictures that are available all over the Internet. You did not have to see Claudia nude to realize what a beautiful woman she was.

Likewise, the book does not dwell on the tabloid aspects of her fatal accident. Once again, those that are interested can easily find pictures and articles that document the event.

Although she was angelic, Claudia was not an angel, as her sister Constance told me. She was the kind of human being that most of us would want in our lives: a loyal, true and honest friend. As all humans do, she had flaws. Claudia's missteps are common knowledge, yet they are a minor distraction to her overall story. I have not warped any facts, deliberately mischaracterized her or anyone else in the book, or rationalized her behavior. It would be easy to sanitize Claudia's story, but it would also be disingenuous. In my opinion, the difficult times she went through only serve to enhance all the noble aspects of her life.

When I state Claudia was innocent, it is not meant to imply she was pure and unsullied physically. I refer to her belief in the inherent kindness of fellow human beings and the overwhelming positive view of life that drove her spirit. She really *was* the honor student, cheerleader and All-American girl from St. Paul, Minnesota.

Claudia's career certainly had its highs and lows. She never seemed to break out of the B-movie/drive-in mold, with the exception of some small parts in large studio productions. She ironically missed the two biggest roles she auditioned for on television,

despite having performed well as a guest star on a dozen series. Still, shortly before she died, Claudia seemed poised to finally win that key movie role or land a spot on a first-rate television program.

As a prerequisite to understanding Claudia's place in movie history, I'm going to take you back to a film produced in 1958, a low-budget B-film called *Attack of the 50 Foot Woman*. The producers wanted the film to ride the wave of the atomic-bomb anxiety-induced giant creature films of the 1950s. To say the movie was not a hit when it premiered is an understatement, but the film has since attracted a well-deserved cult following, inspiring several remakes. I wonder how many people who watched the film in 1958 are aware of its messages about the role of women in society, or how it explores the morbid fear of females that the typical male has subconsciously, or consciously, feels.

To recap this gem, we meet our unfortunate heroine (Allison Hayes)—a wealthy, beautiful, mentally unstable alcoholic—right after her release from the local sanitarium. Unfortunately, her domestic situation is not supportive, and she starts getting progressively worse. The main problem is her husband, who is trying to have her committed to an insane asylum so he can get her money. He is also engaged in an affair with the town floozy Honey Parker (Yvette Vickers). Naturally, our heroine has a nasty case of poor self-esteem as a result.

Unfortunately for this lovely woman, things are about to get worse. While out one night on a joyride, she bumps into a spaceship inhabited by a rather large alien, who steals her diamond necklace. (The diamond is also the biggest one on the planet, or something to that effect.) Cue subplot: Mr. Spaceman needs the diamonds to power his ship back to the heavens. Of course, when she reports this encounter to the authorities, they scoff, figuring it is merely another booze-induced hallucination.

Cutting to the chase, the brief contact between alien and Earth woman causes our girl to sprout up to a robust 1,524 centimeters. As a treat to the male viewers, the hospital staff has to fashion a bikini for her to wear made out of hospital bed sheets. She is soon romping about town because, let's face it, no one likes hospitals. (She probably saw her bill.) The townspeople start to believe that poor Allison might indeed have had some kind of alien close encounter, but it's a little too late for them to say "sorry." Understandably, she's fed up with everyone's crap by this point, and decides to take a little me-time. Well, next thing you know, Ms. Allison is looking for her no-good husband, and finds him and his doxy in a rustic diner. She lifts the roof off as easily as opening a shoebox and, in a bad break for Honey Parker, Allison crushes her with a large beam, ending her role in the film.

Our statuesque protagonist is now really pissed off, and grabs her husband (Harry is his name, by the way; we know, because we hear her scream it about 100 times during the course of the movie) and starts to go…well, I guess, nowhere in particular. That turns out to be an unwise choice, as she saunters up to a power transformer that the local sheriff blows up with his riot gun, killing the enormous wife after she squishes the puny husband like a grape with her less-than-authentic-looking papier-mâché hand.

What is the audience to make of this grand cinematic adventure, an otherwise schlocky film that hides a plethora of social truths behind its veneer of cheesy special effects and broad acting? We see the poor woman go from a vulnerable, powerless brat to a figure of strength, capable of controlling her environment and the men who torment her. Allison is undone because, although she merely wants to be a faithful wife, her own weakness and her husband's evil plot makes this impossible (that and the small problem of her being 44 feet taller than everyone else). The husband, by contrast, is a manipulative, immoral jerk who would rather lock his wife away in a mental institution and steal her money than show any true love or empathy for her.

By the end of the movie, the husband and wife have switched roles. She is the dominant figure, which was very much against the cultural norms of the 1950s. Harry, conversely, diminishes in size, by contrast and in importance, since he is the weak one in the family—the non-provider, unable to function in any capacity as a "real man." Of course, the ultimate arbiter of this depressing domestic situation is the government, intervening to bring balance back to the community by violence, justified by the magnitude of the threat.

We have two conflicting views of the woman herself. She is repellant because of her size and the threat she poses, but she also exudes sexual attraction because of her beauty and provocative dress. Therefore, we have a strong woman, who despite the fact she is not responsible for her condition, poses a powerful and direct danger to men. The weak failure of a husband, likewise the town Jezebel, must also die, the fate of all deviant characters in a strict moral society.

What the filmmakers had done—unwittingly—was to set the table for the powerful B-movie queens to come. Many males have a difficult time reconciling the sexual side of women with their preconceived notions that they should be chaste and virginal. This psychological theory, commonly known as the Madonna/whore complex, puts women in a no-win situation, since they must now manage the worst aspects of both images. If she gives in to her own healthy sexuality and sleeps with a man who is more than a willing partner, the female has lost her moral and motherly aura. She is a "fallen" angel and cannot retrieve her purity. She is considered a slut, and she invites men in general to sleep with her regardless of whether their advances are welcome or not. Therefore, what attracted man to her in the first place has been replaced by disgust—and sometimes hatred. On the other hand, a woman who retains her virginity is considered a prude, and is a likely target for seduction or worse. A chaste female is therefore considered too big a prize for most men to resist.

Claudia Jennings, by contrast, was a 50-foot woman condensed to 5-foot-6-inches. Her most memorable characters were tough, savage and sexy. In her films, she flipped audience identification and turned common prejudices upside down. The directors of her films invited the audience to anticipate viewing a ravaged, naked Claudia, but during the course of the films she became the true hero and had audiences cheering for her to kill her antagonists. Claudia had gorgeous features and a perfect body, but she never came across as an unintelligent damsel in distress. She was never a "scream queen," although she would wrench screams out of the men who crossed her. Claudia used her form the same way she used her fists, a shotgun or a knife. She did not allow men to use her body; she allowed her body to use men.

Anne Francis as private detective Honey West

When she hit the screen, Claudia attacked with all the strength of the 50-foot woman—never as a freak or repulsive in any manner, but the psychological effect was the same. Men desired her but then became quickly disillusioned when she shot, castrated (literally and figuratively) and dispatched them in a variety of ways. She was the first female action star, and the most prolific, even in her short life.

Several women in the 1960s paved the way for Claudia and others. Anne Francis as the private detective on television's *Honey West* was beautiful and more than capable of defending herself. Diana Rigg as *The Avengers*' Emma Peel was the consummate female hero, brave, intelligent, beautiful and superior to men in the lethal arts. Yvonne Craig as Batgirl was as brainy and tough as she was sexy. Julie Newmar as Catwoman on the *Batman* television show combined glamour and evil in an intoxicating mix. Tura Satana, while not a hero, was as brutal and savage as any male character. Starring in Russ Meyer's *Faster, Pussycat! Kill! Kill!*, she displayed her martial arts expertise and did her own stunts. We can draw a direct line from Ms. Satana's acting career to Claudia's. Both were fiercely independent and had no problem with shedding their clothes. On the big screen, however, powerful women heroes were not prevalent, with one exception being Monica Vitti in *Modesty Blaise*.

The leading ladies of today's Hollywood owe Claudia and these other trailblazers of the 1960s and 1970s a debt, for showing that action heroes and villains can be women. Claudia would also survive and thrive in most of her roles, unlike the unfortunate 50-foot woman. It is perhaps fitting that her most amoral, sadistic character died at the end of the film.

Claudia's features and her abilities as an actress set her apart from her contemporaries. Almost all successful actors have a certain quality, a style and bearing which makes them unforgettable; their success is not always defined by their looks, but by their ability to connect

Diana Rigg as Emma Peel, the consummate female hero, in *The Avengers*

with the audience. Certain actors, known by a trademark gesture, a general bearing or charisma. Claudia possessed these tangible and intangible qualities.

No one will ever know whether Claudia would have succeeded in making that push into stardom beyond the exploitation genre. She gave us glimpses with her fine stage work, and surprisingly, in some of her television roles. Claudia showed tremendous promise as an actress—immensely talented, as you will read—but it seemed she was holding something back emotionally in her performances. At times, it almost seemed as if she was afraid to penetrate that crucial level of emotion—peeling back that last layer of onion, so to speak—for fear of releasing some deep, buried secret. I, for one, believe she would have attained stardom beyond the B-movie and drive-in fare that was her initial path to recognition. She was a diamond in the rough with all the potential of a superstar, needing only a bit of polishing to make her perfect.

Film critics were not kind to Claudia. I think there may have been a conscious or subliminal prejudice against her because of her *Playboy* appearances. The fact she appeared in bad movies didn't help her either. Very few great actors can rise above

Yvonne Craig as Batgirl, brainy and tough

the weight of two hours of celluloid detritus. There seemed to be an effort by critics to marginalize Claudia as an actress and a person; in addition, the reviews for her performances were generally better than the films themselves. Unfortunately, the poor reviews outnumbered the good.

Looking at the progression of her career, I have no doubt that if she had continued with her drama lessons, her performances would have become more nuanced and complete. We know that she did resume those lessons shortly before her death.

For your consideration and amusement, I have included synopses and reviews of Claudia's films—at least all the ones I have been able to find. In the interest of full disclosure, the reviews contain spoilers, so please watch the films you have not seen before reading the reviews. Also, be aware, I have an unusual style of film criticism, which uses humor and sarcasm and is intellectually relaxed. Claudia's films were fun, and I've treated them as such. I am not using my reviews to attack the filmmakers but to better equip the audience to enjoy the work.

One thing I want to stress is that though I may be rough on the films, I have nothing but respect for Claudia's acting and the efforts of the cast and crew. It isn't easy to make a film, especially one with a small budget, a tight shooting schedule and inadequate equipment. Remember, for the most part, Claudia appeared in independent films shot in the 1970s, with antiquated cameras and poor production values. Then again, money wasn't everything; for a laugh, watch *The Love Machine*, which cost millions to produce, and then watch *Unholy Rollers*, which was filmed at a fraction of the cost. Decide for yourself which movie was better.

Please note: Although I adore Claudia's films, we're not reviewing *Citizen Kane*, *The Godfather* or *Spartacus*. To give you a convenient parallel, I'm in the culinary business, where a restaurant experience can be judged in a similar fashion as a movie. I would not review a Burger King by the same standards I would Tavern on the Green. In fact, I would say evaluating a dining experience is more akin to reviewing a film than one might think.

There is one component in my book that adds a totally fresh perspective to Claudia's story; a spark of humanity comes from Claudia's sister, Constance. She supplied many facts and stories, and most importantly, a sense of who Claudia was as a sister and human being. This book marks the first time the Chesterton family has participated in telling Claudia's story, as they refused the opportunity previously for fear of seeing their dear Mimi's reputation sullied further.

Tura Satana in *Faster, Pussycat! Kill! Kill!* She was one of the early B-movie queens who did her own stunts and was a martial arts expert.

I believe that the true appeal of Claudia Jennings was her ability to convey a genuine empathy with her audience. She was a real person, an honest-to-God girl next door, not only a movie star or a diva. When viewing a film, it is all too easy to confuse the character with the actor. In order to understand Claudia it was necessary to learn about her life away from the lights, booms and set. The differences between Claudia Jennings the Playmate/movie star and Claudia Jennings the individual were astonishing.

I should add at this point that I was cautioned to remain detached emotionally from my subject. I wish I could say that was the case. I wrote this book as fairly and honestly as possible, yet I must confess that there were junctures where sentimentality fought against my ability to remain impartial. Although I was careful not to let my personal feelings disrupt the narrative, I soon became Claudia's champion. If my candidness brings forth some discomfort, and you feel this makes me unqualified to write her story, *mea culpa*.

The last thing to take with you is this important fact. Although Claudia's death was a tragedy, her life was not. She was a woman who lived in the moment, loved to laugh and always wanted to help others. She brought joy to her friends and family. She was a beautiful soul and is missed terribly, even now.

When I first came across Claudia's story, I recognized it was imperative that she be remembered. For her family and friends, this was my attempt to keep this exceptional woman's beauty, kindness, loyalty and love alive forever.

—Eric J. Karell
Johns Creek, Georgia

Acknowledgments

I would like to express my sincere gratitude and appreciation to the following people who were so essential in writing Claudia's story.

Above all, to Constance Chesterton and the Chesterton family. Without their belief in my determination to tell Mimi's story accurately and sincerely, I could not have completed the work.

Thank you to Roger Corman, who gave me his time for an interview and then wrote the foreword of this book. I don't know if the fans of his movies, and the entertainment community at large, truly understand his contributions to the art and science of the motion picture. My appreciation to Mr. Corman's assistant Cynthia Brown, who I'm sure, works just as hard as the Cormans.

To author, producer, distributor and director Ari Bass, who could not have been more helpful. He generously allowed me access to his original interview tapes from his *Femme Fatales* article on Claudia, and put up with my insufferable naïveté. He was Claudia's first biographer, helping to keep her memory alive with his hard work and sincere affection for the cult films of the 1960s and '70s.

To Claudia's other family in Los Angeles: Bobby Hart, Keith Jennings, Paige Millard and Keith Allison. They accepted me as a friend on blind faith, always offering me encouragement, support and their honest suggestions for the book.

To Barry Richards, in particular, who helped me from day one and became a friend as well as a contributor.

To Bobby Hart and Glenn Ballantyne, authors of *Psychedelic Bubble Gum*, for their generosity in sharing their work.

To all of Claudia's friends and associates, and others who shared their memories and were so kind in the process: Simone Boisseree, Sharmagne Leland-St. John-Sylbert, Victoria Hale, Gayle Gannes-Rosenthal, Deborah Chenoweth, Susan Miller, Barbara Leigh, Debra Jo Fondren, Skip Taylor, Lew Fideler and all of her friends in Evanston and Richmond, who participated in the book.

To the marvelous Dr. Jack Garfield, for his insights and honesty.

To Beverly and Ferd Sebastian, who loved Claudia unconditionally and now work tirelessly to make the world a better place.

To author Chris Koetting, who provided that spark of inspiration which enabled me to start working on the book.

To all the greats of the entertainment business who gave me some of their precious time—and something more valuable, the thrill of a lifetime: Si Litvinoff, Nic Roeg, Robert Emery, Mark Irwin, Sally Kirkland and her assistant Christine Torreale, Jesse Vint, John Saxon, Mike Greenfield, Michael Brandon and Johnny Crawford.

To Dr. Steven Watts for allowing me to cite his incredible book on Hugh Hefner.

My thanks to those at the *Los Angeles Times*, NBC Universal and the *Chicago Reader* for making their archives available.

Last but not least, my sincere appreciation for the guidance and patience shown by my publishers, Gary and Susan Svehla of Midnight Marquee Press. All I can say is that it's fortunate for me they are used to dealing with horror.

My sincerest thanks to those who supplied photographs used in the book: American International Pictures, New World Pictures, Columbia Pictures, Borsari Images, LT Productions, The Chesterton Family, Barry Richards, Dr. Jack Garfield, Keith Jennings, Harry Langdon, the *Chicago Reader*, Ari Bass, Si Litvinoff, Beverly and Ferd Sebastian, Roger Corman, Simon Boiseree, Paige Millard, Paramount Television, Dimension Pictures, Duque Films, Magic Eye of Hollywood Productions, DeVille Films, Quinn Martin Productions, Quadrant Films, Sujac Productions, Columbia Pictures, British Lion Film Corporation, D'Antoni/Weitz Productions.

Chapter 1: American Gothic 1949-1966

It was a cold day in St. Paul, Minnesota on December 20, 1949 when Mary Eileen Chesterton came into the world. St. Paul and Los Angeles, where Claudia Jennings would first enter the picture and then finally leave us, were half a continent apart geographically, and much further than that culturally. The character traits of the Midwest that fired her soul—the discipline, religious conservatism and traditional American morals—would be in sharp contrast to the ostentatious habits Claudia Jennings had acquired by early 1979 in Hollywood.

I stand at the edge of the Pacific Coast Highway, or PC1, as the residents of California refer to it. It is a beautiful and enduring symbol of our West Coast, specifically of Malibu. This gold and diamond-crusted slice of the American dream is so unlike St. Paul, and so unlike Mary Eileen; yet as I gaze at the upscale restaurants, luxury cars, expensive shops and palatial homes, it ultimately seems very much like Claudia.

I chose "American Gothic" as the chapter name to start her story for several reasons. After I researched her life, the image of Grant Wood's famous painting and the trappings of that unique genre of literature both came to mind. The portrait represented Claudia's origins in the Midwest, and was also somewhat representative of her relationship with her parents. The writings of Poe, Hawthorne and others were evocative because the themes explored in their stories seemed to uncannily predict her life.

Claudia's story is one straight out of the tradition of modern American Gothic, because her life was not ordinary and certainly did not appear to be real. Indeed, Claudia seemed to be a character out of a writer's imagination, with a narrative as improbable as any work of fantasy. Among the many themes of this story would be nightmare and dream in opposition and interaction, the beauty of sorrow and despair and the breakdown of the family unit, leading quite literally to the sins of the fathers. There is a theme of abjection, or being cast out, running through Claudia's life, as well as her rejection of the logical despite her high intelligence, leading to actions that would certainly cause harm.

Of course, the true tragedy of Claudia's life is not that a beautiful Playmate or a gifted actress was taken from us at so young an age. The true horror of her end was that she was, from childhood to the moment she died, an innocent—a kind and gentle soul who deserved better. Every human spirit must live in a world filled with iniquity, but Claudia should never have been surrounded by so much temptation and corruption. Somehow, these forces seduced her, and once surrounded, she decided to embrace them. Yet despite being beset by darkness and perdition, Claudia was able to fend off these dark impulses by virtue of her innate and unshakeable decency. Unfortunately, the inescapable nature of fate—a significant part of American Gothic literature—caught up with Claudia. This is where American Gothic and Shakespeare intersect, as our tragic hero is compelled toward her doom.

Parallels can be made between Claudia's life and one of American Gothic's classic works, Herman Melville's *Moby Dick*. The pursuit of fame by Claudia—for a variety of reasons as you will read—is similar to Ahab's quest for the great white whale. Ahab had a complex set of motivations—revenge being the primary one—and Claudia's goals were a mixture of the noble and the selfish (although she was selfish for noble reasons).

The notion of being far from home and at the mercy of elements beyond one's control also fit into the themes of destiny and impossible accomplishments. Claudia chased her dream of being a movie star and being wealthy beyond her dreams. The problem arose—would she be equipped to handle Hollywood when her gross appetites began to dominate her common sense?

Mimi at age 11, already owning the camera

Just as Ahab discovered, once one begins an obsessive pursuit, the hunter becomes the hunted. Quite literally, Claudia moved faster than the life she thought she wanted. When she finally slowed enough to examine her motives and achieve some clarity, it was too late. The tidal wave of her pursuits nearly drowned her.

Claudia's life was a struggle between her parents' strict Roman Catholic notions of shame and guilt and her own notions of happiness. American Gothic writings reflect the influence of Puritanism, a parallel concept to her parents' interpretation of Catholic doctrine. As she grew older, these conflicts would grow worse. Claudia's own rejections of these religious dogmas were obviously reflected through her association with *Playboy*.

Although American Gothic thought did not often focus on the woman's oppressed place in the home and society, a few writers, such as Charlotte Perkins Gilman, brought attention to their problems in works such as "The Yellow Wallpaper." In the story, a young bride is sequestered in one room of her home for health's sake. However, metaphorically and physically deprived of any stimulation, work, intellectual pursuits and the like, she slowly descends into madness. The woman becomes fascinated with the pattern of the wallpaper, believing she's become trapped within it like a maze. Life was very difficult for everyone in the 1800s, but more so for women, who were disenfranchised and often the victims of persecution, as witnessed by the earlier Salem witch trials. Claudia also felt that Hollywood, despite all of its rewards, was a dead zone intellectually.

Robert Louis Stevenson's *Strange Case of Dr Jekyll and Mr. Hyde*, while not American Gothic, certainly influenced many writers on this side of the Atlantic. Stevenson claimed his book was an allegory, and we can assign many of its characters' qualities to

Claudia. In the novel and in Claudia's story, there is the inevitability of fate. The fact that a dark side of human nature is released through the use of a drug can be compared to Claudia's use of cocaine and its destructive effects. Naturally, the duality of humankind emphasized in the work implies that there is saint and sinner, man and monster, God and Devil within us all. These are the themes that resonate within Stevenson's work and Claudia's story as well. Unlike Dr. Jekyll, Claudia was able to reverse the chemical's effect, so Mr. Hyde did not triumph. Despite her better efforts, Claudia's story still ended in tragedy.

The painting *American Gothic* can be interpreted in ways that seem to resemble Claudia's early life. The severe expressions on the two people mirror the tension present at times in Claudia's home. The feminine figure, generally accepted as a daughter, looks somewhat fearfully at the father. The single curl of hair dangling down from the rest of her severe style might be a sign of defiance or rebellion. Wood was always coy about sharing what the picture meant, and it is generally considered his way of satirizing the house that inspired the work. As most critics point out, there is always truth behind satire. One coincidence is that the house is located in Iowa, where Claudia, while still a child, resided for a short time.

Finally, although Claudia's life seemed like an American Gothic *roman a clef*, it was breathtakingly real and her death was shattering. Forgotten by the public for the most part, her memory still lives in the hearts of her friends and the appreciation of her fans.

It is only when we go back to Claudia's childhood beginnings that we can truly see the American Gothic origins of her story. There, when she was newly born, is the first stage set for our story.

She was the first child of Jerry and Joan Chesterton, two very intelligent and very Catholic individuals. Gerard Alfred Chesterton was from Brooklyn, and Joan Marie Houle hailed from Hutchinson, Minnesota. Jerry, as he was called, was fairly conservative and the epitome of the term "straight-laced." Joan was more liberal and open-minded. When Mary Eileen was a child learning to speak, she pronounced her name in a manner that sounded like "Mimi." The nickname caught on, and from that time on, her parents, sisters and friends all called her by that sobriquet.

Being the oldest child, Mary Eileen benefitted from a generous amount of attention from her grandparents and parents. She was a happy baby with beautiful

Mimi at age 15, during her sophomore year in Richmond (1966)

features and a lovely smile. Mimi was also an expressive toddler who would stand up in her crib and sing or chatter away with the adults.

Mimi grew up to be an extroverted and friendly child. By the time she was three, the Chestertons had moved to Milwaukee, the second of five states Mimi would live in before she was 16. Joan Chesterton, sensing Mimi's outgoing nature and natural flair for drawing attention to herself, enrolled her in acting classes at Marquette University. The four-year-old redhead was smitten with the theater. She would pull in friends around her neighborhood to help paint background scenes, fashion props and assist in putting on improvised plays in her parents' garage and backyard. Later on that year, with the encouragement of her mother Joan, she appeared in *The King and I* performed by the theater department at Marquette.

At the time, this was Mimi's breakout role. The production, performed before a large crowd with top-notch production values, was no backyard make-believe. Mimi, although quite young, had to rehearse, memorize lines, take direction and perform as if she were an adult.

The young girl was a natural performer. Looking at this portion of her life, one would have expected her to go on to fame on Broadway, Hollywood or television. Perhaps—and it was not far-fetched to believe so—she would have been successful in all three media. Claudia did have a taste of fame here and there; however, the question remains why a woman of such beauty, intelligence and talent took the path she did to achieve her goals.

In retrospect, Claudia's infatuation with the stage is not unusual. More often than not, most actors became enamored of the profession at an early age, instinctively recognizing a life in the theater as their destiny. Many in the profession are drawn

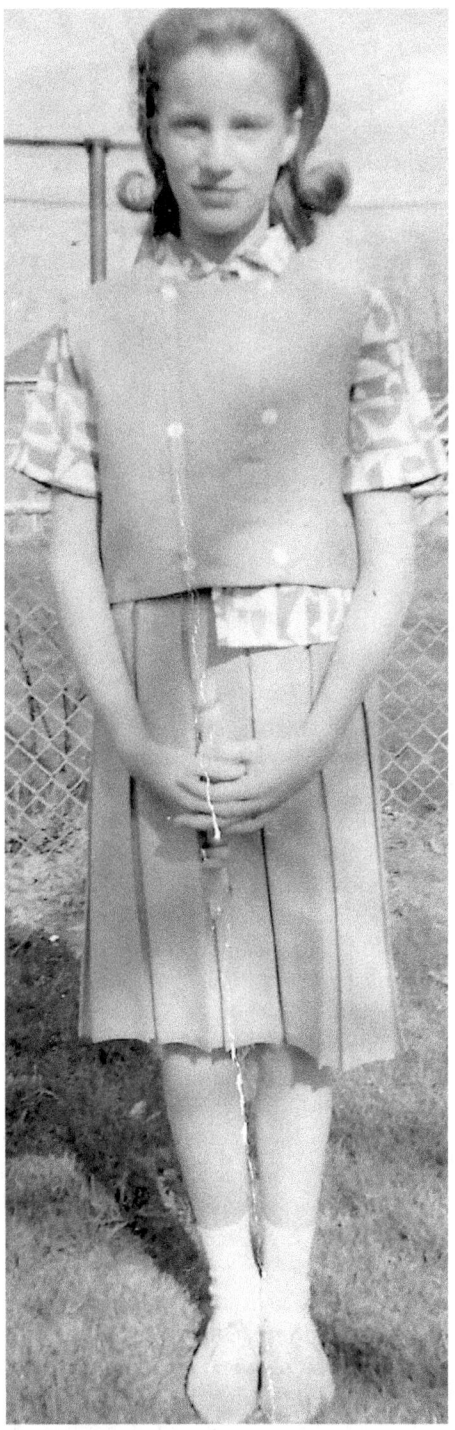

Mimi at a pensive age 12

to it by watching a movie they love or attending a play with their parents.

A short while later, the Chesterton's were on the move again, with a brief stop in Iowa. They did not stay there long, as Joan was now pregnant again. The family moved to Dayton, Ohio after Constance Chesterton was born. Mimi was overjoyed with the new addition to the family. Claudia was always extremely close to both her sisters, especially when things were going sour in Hollywood; they, in turn, worshipped Claudia and saw in her an ideal role model. Life was not kind or easy at times for the gifted Chesterton daughters. Extremely intelligent but critical, her parents pushed their three daughters toward academic achievement, not with a firm hand but with a hard thrust. All of the siblings were brilliant but grew up resentful of the unfair competition their mother brewed up, setting sister against sister in some cases. Mimi, being the oldest, felt this creeping anxiety the most, and whether subconsciously or not, began looking for a way out of an increasingly toxic family atmosphere.

Mimi did not let the shock of the latest move turn her into a shy, withdrawn young girl. Almost immediately after the family unpacked, Mimi went door-to-door in their new neighborhood, knocking and asking the surprised adults, "Do you have any children?"

Mimi had a natural ability to make and keep friends, a trait that stayed with her until the end of her life. She was also displaying her strong self-confidence by "fishing" for friends. Most children would not have had the nerve to knock on a strange door in an unfamiliar neighborhood.

Her sister Constance said, "Mimi collected stray people and stray animals. That's just the way she was." Soon the Chesterton house was an odd menagerie of unwanted pets. Mimi seemed particularly fond of hurt or damaged animals. Whether it was a dog with one eye or a deaf cat, Mimi loved them all. These were her surrogate children, a sign of her own impending maternal instincts that would blossom in her early twenties.

One of Mimi's agents in Hollywood, Mike Greenfield, described her as "fearless." She would never hesitate to try something new. In her early life, it meant finding friends. Later, as Claudia, it would have connotations with more serious consequences.

Mimi started acting in school plays in her hometown, and she came home one afternoon beaming and laughing. She gathered all her friends together, hopped up on a rock, twirled her dress, spun around and declared, "Guess who just got the lead role in the school play? Me!" All of her friends cheered and Mimi was again the center of attention.

Be aware that even though Mimi was a very outgoing and popular child, she was never a mean one. That was another of her personality traits that was consistent from childhood to the time she lived in Hollywood. Mimi would speak to anybody, regardless of his or her economic status, social standing or physical appearance. She only disapproved of bullying and rude people, and would speak up when she felt such behavior was on display. Although Claudia possessed these wonderful traits, her critics only saw what they wanted to see, the false image *Playboy*/Hollywood created. She was a sensitive soul, and she stood up for strangers and best friends equally. How many people have the moral or physical courage to do this?

Then, in 1960, Joan Chesterton took a teaching position at Earlham College in Richmond, Indiana. The family experienced the arrival of another sister for Mimi and Constance, and the family moved to yet another state. The pretty college town seemed welcoming to the Chesterton's, and they quickly adapted to a life of Midwestern peacefulness.

Constance Chesterton remembers:

> Richmond was the happiest five years for our family. We had a beautiful three-story brick house surrounded by five old sycamore trees. There was actually a shuffleboard court in the backyard. It was the kind of neighborhood where people played croquet in their front yard. From our living room, you stepped down into the library. The single wall with no bookshelves had French windows that looked into the front yard.

It was the ideal middle-class American dream neighborhood of the early 1960s. Barbecues, the sound of lawnmowers, happy families with their "2.5 children" riding bicycles around their neat, well-maintained neighborhoods, free of the anxiety that the latter half of the decade would bring. The Chestertons did not realize that beneath their shiny bourgeoisie varnish, a disaster was about to envelop everything they held dear.

The city of Richmond was almost an idealized version of the typical small American city. Earlham was one of the most progressive schools in the country, and its liberal values helped ameliorate some of Indiana's more reactionary tendencies. The city placed a great emphasis on the arts and enjoyed a diverse and solid economy. Richmond had a traditional Main Street, which appeared to have come straight from Hollywood. If a resident couldn't find what they were looking for on this boulevard, then Richmond didn't have it.

A Biography

Glen Miller Park, another favorite gathering spot for the Chestertons, was a 200-acre expanse filled with ducks, geese, a world-renowned rose garden, lakes and picnic areas. The family would make frequent outings there to enjoy the beautiful grounds, chase the waterfowl and stroll the immaculate grounds.

Mimi's high school classmates remember her vividly. One of them told me, asking that their name not be used:

> I remember seeing Mimi twice a day, once in homeroom and once in Mrs. Hoffman's Advanced Placement English class. I sat behind her, and although we were not best friends, she was always very friendly to me. She was one of the prettiest girls in school, and I was not attractive in high school by any means; but she always treated me with respect and kindness. She was also one of the brightest. She easily answered most of the questions in the Advanced Placement class.

Mary Eileen took her role as the oldest sister very seriously. She always looked after her siblings in any situation from the time they were born.

Constance told me this story as being typical of Mimi's devotion to her siblings. "All three of us were out riding our bikes one afternoon. Our youngest sister fell and tore her knee up badly. Mary Eileen looked at me and said, 'Go get Mom! Now!'" Constance said this care and sense of responsibility for her sisters would continue for the rest of Claudia's life.

Mimi made the cheerleading squad and continued to perform in school plays. She was elected to the student council. She was the epitome of the All-American girl, living in an All-American town. The family seemed to be doing fine. For once, they weren't on the move every few years. Mimi was entering a challenging time for most youth; crossing the bridge from childhood to adolescence to the teenage years can be as secure as striding across a bridge made from solid rock, or as fraught with anxiety as perambulating one made from a fraying rope. It is a delicate time in every child's mind and development. Mimi's path looked as if it would be a smooth one, a kind transition from girl to young woman. Popular, pretty, sweet natured and surrounded by a loving family, the future looked very bright for the self-assured Miss Chesterton.

She did all the things other teenagers did in Richmond. Mimi was a well-regarded baby-sitter and an excellent student. The Chestertons were a popular family in their neighborhood, and all the girls had adjusted well. Mimi had just started dating for the first time and was, of course, an ideal pupil. They enjoyed visiting relatives in Michigan and vacationing on the lakes. Summers were a time when the Chestertons savored family and friends. It was that magical time in their lives when everything aligned perfectly, and it seemed all this happiness would continue indefinitely. Those are the moments in a young woman's life where time seems to linger, summers last forever and every season is welcomed with wonder. Family pictures from this time show barbecues and the sisters splashing around in the waters of Lake Michigan.

What do Claudia's early years tell us about her future? We can detect one trait that stayed with her until the end of her life, and that was her incomparable bravery. She obviously became infatuated with performing, and decided, even as a child, that acting was what she wanted to do professionally. Claudia's strong personality formed during these years, as she became a lovely, kind and friendly young lady. It would have been easy for her to become a snob or smug, owing to her looks, intelligence and athleticism. That didn't happen to Claudia. She stayed true to herself and her values until the end.

Then, without warning, Jerry's employer, the Motor-Mower division of the Dura Corporation, went out of business. This lightning strike of bad luck hit the family in a particularly pernicious manner. After an extended time of unemployment, Mimi's father found a new job. Although the news was welcome in an economic sense, the position was not in the peaceful and familiar confines of Richmond, Indiana. The family would need to move one more time. The five years of bliss soon evaporated as if they never transpired. Pulled out of school in the middle of the year again, all three sisters had to leave friends, favorite places and familiar routines behind. None of the Chestertons felt the effects more than Mimi. The trajectory of her life while living in Indiana seemed smooth and without any potential troubles. Family, good friends, an active social life and a secure environment—everything that any of us would want for a teenage daughter—surrounded her.

A few years after the Chestertons had moved, her former classmates from Richmond High were shocked to hear that Mimi had posed for *Playboy*. One of them said:

> None of us could believe it. It seemed so completely out of character from the person we knew. We all felt she should be in college with the rest of us.

Another student at Richmond High who knew her well said:

> It was obvious from watching Mimi change in such a short amount of time that something was wrong. I noticed she was dating many older men. I'm not a psychologist, but perhaps she had daddy issues.

Chapter 2:
Evanston 1966-1970

The family's finances were in poor shape. It had taken her dad nine months before he found another position. Gerard Chesterton took a job as sales promotion manager for the Skil Power Tool Company in suburban Chicago. The effect on the Chesterton's marriage was corrosive, and made a bad situation much worse for Mimi and her sisters.

This would make the sixth state Mimi would live in before her 16th birthday. She would be the new kid in school again. The family settled in Evanston, a very wealthy suburb north of the city. The family was uprooted in the middle of the school year, and the three sisters were the outsiders once more. The combination of being taken away from friends and a steady routine and dropped into a hostile, unfamiliar environment did not bode well for Mimi.

It must have seemed to Mimi that Evanston Township High School (ETHS) had almost as many students as Richmond, Indiana had residents. Mimi's class alone had nearly 1,000 students. Most were privileged, urban, savvy and aggressive. They were also quite talented and intelligent as a group, and many would find prominent employment in the arts and journalism in years to come.

The city itself was a nice, WASP–like place to grow up, and the town placed a premium on education, the arts and entertainment. Evanston was the home of Northwestern University, one of the best private colleges in the country, known for its outstanding literature, theater and broadcasting programs. In many ways, the town was similar to Richmond, except that it dwarfed the Indiana hamlet and had one of the nation's largest cities towering over its semi-urban confines.

The family found an apartment at the southern-most part of the suburb, right on the border of Chicago. It was not the best part of town, and the Chestertons missed their single-family home back in Richmond.

On her first day in her new school, Mimi had to walk past a gym filled with older students. Joan Chesterton told Albert Williams from the *Chicago Reader* years later:

> I'll never forget that first time we had to walk into the school to register. As soon as they saw my daughter, the catcalls and whistles began. Mimi had tears in her eyes.[1]

Mary Eileen now found herself in a lonely, uncomfortable environment that was the opposite of her kind life in Richmond. The situation could not have been worse.

Her family was middle class, surrounded by wealthier families. Her parents' marriage was breaking down rapidly. As her sister Constance told me:

Evanston was a painful place for all of us, and more painful than any place we have lived since. Mimi wanted desperately to be like the people she admired and to be accepted by them. It was an unhappy transition for all of us.

Joan Chesterton wrote in one of the family's memory books about the transition:

1966 was a busy, sometimes difficult, year—everyone adjusting to a new life. Mimi enrolled as a junior at Evanston, while Connie and Julie crossed the street to attend Lincoln Grade School. Mother enrolled at Northwestern. Dad got pneumonia, and we all missed our home in Richmond.

Joan soon found a teaching position at the University of Illinois Chicago, known as the Circle Campus in those days. After a while, the family's economic situation began to improve, but the stress on the family was still palpable. Outsiders noticed it too. One of Mimi's former boyfriends remembered a lot of tension existed in the household, with Mr. Chesterton in particular high-strung to the point where it appeared he'd explode at any second.

This began a process where Mimi had to reinvent herself one more time in order to survive change. She was not a snob, so she never acted like one. She was, however, a natural at making friends, so she picked out the group of students who she thought would accept her despite the perceived inferiority of her social class. The task was made much easier because she was intelligent, athletic, outgoing and very pretty. Mary Eileen made a conscious decision to use her natural gifts to make her own path at ETHS.

However, despite the fact Mimi was kind, friendly, brimming with self-confidence and bright, some of her classmates sensed she used these traits as a veneer to shield something. One friend described her as "always friendly, but slightly distant."

Mimi, though, was not deterred by anything it seemed, and set about to carve out a niche in her new environs. Always an excellent student, she became part of the National Honor Society. She made the cheerleading squad. She also had the reputation of being one of the nicest people in the school. She was friendly toward everyone regardless of whether

Mimi in her Senior Prom dress

A Biography

Christmastime 1968

they were a jock, a shy nerd, a druggie, popular or not. Albert Williams, who was a classmate of Mimi's before going on to a distinguished writing career, said simply: "She was one of the nicest kids I knew."[2]

Mimi's sister Constance gave me a startling perspective of her:

> She was innocence personified, and in a way she kept that innocence until the day she died. She really was a cheerleader—almost everyone's idea of a perfect child, except to my parents, who kept all three of us at a competitive boil. But Mimi wasn't a rebel, even though we grew up during a period of tremendous cultural and political change. I remember I was listening to the Beatles' "A Day in the Life," with that jarring musical crescendo building toward the end. Mimi walked in and said, "That's really disturbing." I tried to explain that was the point, but she didn't get it. Another time she burst in saying, "I've just heard the most wonderful singer—Andy Williams!" This is while I was listening to Jimi Hendrix, the Doors, etc., and I was the younger sister. That's just the way she was.

As an example of what Constance was speaking of regarding their parents, and the pressure Mimi was under being the oldest, here is an excerpt of a letter written by Mimi to her parents.

> Dear Mommy and Daddy:
> I know that I love you very much but I know you couldn't say that to me without reason. I know I am a first-class pig, as Daddy said. I know I am no help around here. I am crying right now as I am writing this to you because I am sorry for all the trouble I have caused. The whole thing was all my fault …

I have redacted the rest of the letter out of respect for the privacy of the Chesterton family.

My reaction to this letter was to feel very sorry for this young lady. A parent's criticism and shaming are terrible things for a child to endure. They are emotions that are carried through to adulthood, especially when received during puberty and the teenage years. I believe we can draw a parallel from this type of incident, through the unhappy breakdown of the Chesterton marriage to some of Mimi's self-esteem problems. Not only did I feel sad for Mimi, but for the rest of the family as well. No person wins in

Mimi's first Formal (with unidentified male)

this type of situation. Although they were strict and perhaps not ideal parents, the Chestertons loved their children. In any situation where a marriage is so openly damaged, there are no winners. For this to fall on all the Chesterson shoulders, especially with three young children, is heartbreaking.

ETHS had an impressive and nationally known drama department under teacher Bill Ditton, and Mimi was drawn to it given her previous stage experience. She auditioned for the school production of *Inherit the Wind*, but not getting the role she desired, she dropped out of the show before the play had its first performance. However, she did catch the eye of the student assistant director, Todd McCarthy, now the senior movie critic for *The Hollywood Reporter*. McCarthy was a budding student filmmaker and became infatuated with the beautiful redhead. They had met when Mimi auditioned, and he was intrigued by her looks and bearings. McCarthy didn't forget Mimi, and he had an idea to shoot a film with her walking, a blank expression on her face. As she strolled, seemingly invisible to other people, Mimi then briefly interacts with them, at random. The movie was filmed at several Wilmette locales along the lake, the beachfront and Gillson Park, including its amphitheater.

The movie does give the viewer a sense of watching a schoolboy crush, which is expected considering McCarthy was enamored of Mimi, but she did not return his feelings. McCarthy titled the movie *Mimi*. He said later he was disappointed in her, because although she did exactly what he directed her to do, Mimi didn't go above and beyond the script. This sounds a bit contradictory, but perhaps the director could not articulate the nuances of the performance he was expecting from her.

Mimi, clad in a diaphanous green mini-dress, looks amazing. Whether McCarthy was disappointed or not in her performance, the film won high praise in school and was a finalist for the Kodak Teen Filmmaker awards. It was McCarthy's first movie, and he would go on to direct several more projects once he moved to Hollywood. He admitted to being a bit nonplussed, annoyed and slightly amused when Claudia said, in her first *Playboy* pictorial, that she had appeared in an "experimental movie" in high school. Her sister said that when Mimi watched the film, she couldn't stop talking about it. The spectacle of seeing herself on the screen thrilled the young woman.

Mimi (right) singing in the ETHS production of *My Sister Eileen*.

McCarthy remembered Mimi as a mature young lady, a bit remote and even shy. Considering her unfamiliarity with the school and her fellow students, this is not surprising. Mimi was also straightforward, and disdained the games her prettier classmates played when dealing with boys. They went out on a few dates, mostly to see films and plays, but the relationship was strictly platonic. McCarthy's observations that Mimi was remote and shy are interesting for several reasons. First, the possibility of an unreliable narrator is evident. Perhaps Mimi took that attitude with McCarthy to avoid giving off any possible hints that she was interested in him as a romantic figure. Then again, we know Mimi was quite extroverted, as evidenced by her love for performing either as a cheerleader or actress. Therefore, these traits that McCarthy noticed can't be taken at face value. They also run counter to what some of her classmates had to say. In all fairness, there may have been another reason, discussed later in this chapter.

Mimi threw herself into acting, appearing in several ETHS productions. Despite her beauty and flair, she remained a down-to-earth and kindhearted young lady. A classmate, Judd Parkin, recalled, "She had an inherent sweetness and friendliness. It wasn't faked or forced."

Her drama coach, Bill Ditton, echoed these comments. "She wasn't just red hair and a pretty face. She was a sweet kid, always fun to work with." All of her teachers expected great things from her in the future. One, however, took note of a flaw that would come back to hurt Mimi's career in the future. Albert Williams quoted Louise Parkin, who gave Mimi singing lessons, as saying:

> She was receptive to anything I told her, but was not, I would say, a serious student. She didn't have a lot of drive or discipline. I always had the feeling she wanted to do whatever she wanted, without doing all the necessary hard work.[3]

Interestingly, the same comments would be made about Claudia much later in her career.

Mimi's talent wasn't single-faceted. She was funny, and she could act; she also had an exceptional singing voice. Her sister remembered:

> Mimi auditioned for a community play in Evanston. Part of the audition involved singing. She walked confidently onto the stage then sat down on

the edge and began to sing. The directors were smiling, and all the kids were looking at each other in amazement. When she was done, I told her that her voice was so beautiful and she looked so confident sitting down on the edge of the stage with her legs crossed. She laughed and said she had to, because her legs were shaking so hard.

According to her classmates, around her junior year Mimi discovered boys—and men. She began dating a former ETHS student who was enrolled at a nearby college: He is now a successful author, who asked not to be identified; we will refer to him as WS. He said the following:

Well, in the time that I knew her, she was intelligent, kind and courageous, and physically lovely as well. I do think fondly back on our time together, a moment greatly magnified in importance in my own life for occurring at the same time that my father died in a car crash a week before Dr. King's assassination. My memories of her affections at that time are deep and sweet indeed. Our time [together] felt like a gift.

It is important to note that Mimi saw an individual who was in deep emotional distress and comforted him the best way she knew how. However, that was her nature: to be kind toward others. Mimi would never lose this quality. It is essential to realize that Mimi was also in emotional crises at this time. The fact that, despite her inner turmoil, she was able to feel empathy for others is most courageous. Her family stated Mimi would love taking in stray animals as pets, and that sympathy extended to humans. It would be a habit of hers that when she found a soul in need of comfort, Claudia would shelter them.

She also began to date athletes from rival high school New Trier and several other boys from her class, including Todd McCarthy, who said in an article in *Femme Fatales*, that he had a "huge crush on her." Lew Fideler, a fellow student, shared this about Mimi:

Claudia with one of her many pets (from 1967)

Around her junior year, Mimi just went boy-crazy. She was a very confident girl, and she carried herself well. Of course, she was cute and had no trouble attracting guys. I think Todd McCarthy carried a torch for her the rest of her

A Biography

life, even after we all moved to L.A. They had a few dates, but she never saw him as a romantic figure.

Despite her brewing set of internal anxieties, Mimi still impressed everyone at ETHS as one of the nicest people they knew. Fellow student Jeffrey Sweet told Albert Williams:

> As far as I can tell, she mostly made other people's lives pleasant. She always struck me as very confident of herself, but not snooty to anybody.

Claudia poses with her Senior Prom date, Gil Hoel.

Mimi Chesterton was, with the exception if her astounding beauty, a normal high school student. She went to parties at friends' homes, drank beer, went on dates to movies and joined her peers on class trips. According to WS, even though Mimi was seemingly the same sweet girl, she began to show that two of the elements were firmly in place that would carry over to her new identity. The new fascination with boys—older ones, in particular—was one. McCarthy told Ari Bass that he and the other boys in Mimi's class were devastated when they found out she was dating college guys. It didn't help their high school egos either when they discovered she was no longer a virgin, an event that occurred the summer before their senior year. It was an uncomfortable situation for Mimi. Everyone assumed since she was one of the prettiest girls in a school of over 4,000 students, she must be "easy." This perception irritated Mimi because it wasn't true, and it only made her desire to leave Evanston that much stronger.

The second, and the more insidious change, was the morphing of her love of the theater and performing into a self-consuming creature called ambition—a desperate one, according to some. It was as if Mimi wanted to show the world she had risen above self-doubt and grief to become her own person—and a movie star. She would find out 10 years later that perhaps she should have questioned her methods and motives a bit more deeply. WS recalls, "I thought of Mimi's ambitions as being unsuited to her. They were shallow, bald, cheesy, grasping and dirty for what I expected out of her." One can interpret this as being a rather cruel assessment of Mimi's future goals; however, seen through the prism of a former lover, it is understandable. The statement also shows what enormous regard he must have had for Mimi to judge her actions as being so far below his expectations.

Her prom date, Gil Hoel, told Albert Williams:

She was a nice girl. However, she was always, obviously, looking for bigger and better things. When she transferred to ETHS, she quickly latched on to what she perceived as the popular crowd. As soon as school was over, she moved on, abruptly. She broke up with me the night of the prom. She said, "This is it."[4]

This statement sounds bitter, but since it is a jilted lover's expression, one can comprehend that Mr. Hoel would not be inclined to judge Mimi fairly. He, of course, was one of the privileged members of Mimi's high school class. Not having to worry about fitting in as Claudia had to, he would have had little understanding of her motivations and actions.

What no one at Evanston Township high school knew was that Mimi was moving on, not so much from the school, but from the toxic situation with her parents' marriage. Mimi half-heartedly sent out a few college applications to schools that were less prestigious than her parents and peers expected. While her classmates were applying to Michigan, Northwestern, Stanford, Harvard and Yale, she seemed disinterested in continuing her education. Her mother was mystified and resentful at Mimi's lack of commitment to an academic path. Then, as soon as high school was finished, Mimi moved out of her parent's house. Her sister Constance remembered:

Mimi and her father pose on her graduation day.

> My parents were horrified. My mother, who was a distinguished college professor, could not believe it. She always assumed Mimi would go to college and study drama. It was inconceivable to her that her intelligent, academically gifted child would make such a decision. I remember one day when Mimi came by to get the rest of her things, I was the only one there. It was so sad. I was heartbroken.

There is some question whether Mimi actually graduated from ETHS. Her sister remembers that she was one class short, but the school allowed her to attend the commencement ceremony with the understanding she would finish the work. Most at ETHS assumed she graduated.

WS told me his perspective on Mimi's transition from the All-American girl to *Playboy* diva:

> Really, my sense of Mimi—when I, too, was a kid of 18—was that she was bright and beautiful, and maybe, from my possibly provincial perspective at that

time, a little bit too ambitious for [becoming] the "bitch goddess" of Hollywood fame. She was essentially 'running away' from her parents' home in Evanston at the time that we parted ways, that she was getting ready to pack herself off into her pursuit of showbiz success, and me going back to college being kind of happy and relieved that I didn't have to watch up close and personal her chosen descent through the various shiny demimondes that ultimately stuck to her and dragged her down. Sexy as it all seemed at the time, I didn't care much for the people who appeared to be running the store. A lot of people I respected thought she was doing wonderful things with her life. But the few messages I later got from her or her closer friends mostly made me feel sad for her.

According to WS, Mimi moved in with a local drug dealer and the two lived together for a brief time. Mimi moved out and rented an apartment on Lake Shore Drive, then began go-go dancing at a club, dating some of the older managers. She also had some modeling photographs taken and managed to land a few assignments.

WS looked back on his time with Mimi in Evanston and her evolution to Claudia Jennings in Hollywood:

She was a sweet kid, pretty face and fun mind, who brightened up a very dark few months in my life. I truly felt blessed to have met her. They called that time "the Summer of Love," and though it was hardly that sensational a season where I lived, I was thankful that she was there to help lift me out of mortal sorrow and despair—and yet glad in my heart when we parted that I wasn't drawn to go her way. Believe me, I never doubted that Mimi was an intelligent and good-hearted soul; I just thought she went for the glitz and the tinsel in a way that debased her. Like everybody who grabs for the brass ring in one way or another, Mimi's way forward was to try to get it; yet she never seemed to notice it was indeed brass and not gold—or maybe she did realize that toward the end. In some ways, though, that makes her sadder; I'd be happy to think she was getting wiser as well.

Claudia and her mother on graduation day

When looking back at this point in Mimi's life, her decisions seem to tell us that all was not right in her world. Many women of her generation did make an abrupt turn in their lifestyle, but few with Mimi's education, intelligence and talents chose this particular path.

Mimi decided her future lay in acting, and the Hull House Theater Company, one of Chicago's oldest and most prestigious drama groups, accepted her. Mimi was a woman who could have done anything she wanted to academically. She had a keen mind, an inquisitive nature and nearly unlimited intellectual capacity; yet she had caught the acting bug as a child, and her love for the theater arts never left her, as we have seen.

She appeared in a dozen productions and acquitted herself very well. Mimi was enjoying living independently, but she felt something was missing. She wasn't garnering enough praise from her performances for Hull, although the experience was good for her long-term goals. She certainly wasn't making a lot of money acting. One day, she answered an ad in the newspaper for receptionist at a well-known magazine headquartered in Chicago. She thought about it and decided some extra money working part-time would be helpful.

Alternatively, was it a calculated move on a young woman's part to escape an intolerable life and hit the jackpot? We can be sure Mimi must have heard what went on at her future employer's home. It may have seemed as if there were very little risk and much potential reward.

Her fellow students in Evanston must have shaken their heads in disbelief a few months later. Were they being arrogant, setting one standard for Mimi and another for themselves? Then again, it's possible they did have Mimi's best interests at heart. Some of them may have had a strange feeling that Mimi's adventure was not going to end well.

On September 3, 1968, Mary Eileen "Mimi" Chesterton started down a road which would lead her far away from Evanston. Considering her cultured background and interest in serious theater, it was a poor choice, and one from which Claudia would never return, physically or psychologically. However, the dark magic of American Gothic at work in Mimi's psyche convinced her to work for the single worst organization and the single worst person she could choose at this point in her life. At the time, though, it seemed like the answer to all her prayers. She would soon have money, fame, new friends and a new home—one with a kind, loving father figure to protect her. Not only that, this new opportunity would give her a chance to reinvent herself. Mimi needed what her new employer could give her, but didn't realize what it would exact in terms of emotional coin. On September 3, 1968, Mimi walked into the corporate headquarters of Playboy Enterprises and began to work for Hugh Hefner.

[1] Williams, Albert, "But She Was A Cheerleader," *Chicago Reader*, September 21, 2000
[2] *Ibid.*
[3] *Ibid.*
[4] *Ibid.*

A Biography

Chapter 3:
Hugh Hefner and *Playboy* 1969-1979

"These days even nice girls take off their clothes."
—Claudia Jennings, 1971 interview

Why Mimi posed for *Playboy* at all is the single most fundamental question to ask. It changed the course of her life like none of her other life decisions would. She had other career options, and if she was looking for a part-time job to help with expenses, there were any number of low-paying secretarial positions that were available. In addition, the odds of actually appearing in the magazine as a Playmate were not in her favor. Hundreds of women sent their photographs to Playboy Enterprises every month vying for the same distinction.

There have been answers offered that do not get to the point. The most common is that she needed the money and publicity to start her film career. Let's remember that posing for *Playboy* in the 1960s and 1970s was not as glamorous as it became in the 1980s and into the present day. Women who shed their clothes in Mimi's time were not thought of in the same terms as the self-realized, powerful females of today.

The answer is complex, and I doubt Mimi herself was conscious of all the emotional and psychological factors. Mimi's strict Catholic background brought her much grief at home. Her parents administered this discipline. The doctrines that the Church considered sins must have frightened and humiliated Mimi. She was probably taught to be ashamed of her body and to save sex for marriage, both notions she discarded before moving out of her parents' house. For Mimi, everything must have come together with her opportunity at *Playboy*. She could flaunt her body without an ounce of guilt, enjoy an active sex life, attract some publicity for her future plans and earn some cash as well. The fact that it would no doubt embarrass her parents was a bonus, even if it was subliminal and unintentional. It would seem that of all the reasons she had for posing, though, the money aspect makes the most sense.

The stipend enabled her to move to Los Angeles and begin her ambitions for a film career in earnest. While her nude modeling initially assured she could make her own decisions in life, the money guaranteed a measure of independence. The predominant reason seems to be that this was part of Claudia's plan to achieve success; at least, this is what she would tell friends and others later on in her life. *Playboy* was a means to an end. Her appearance in the magazine was only a first step to money, fame and a career in the entertainment business. After her initial appearance, Claudia was sure she would never have to pose again. It would also seem that Claudia had discovered that her sex appeal was effective in getting what she wanted. Perhaps she derived feelings of power and control from showing her body and the effect it had on men. The self-empowerment and feelings of self-esteem that posing gave her were likely powerful motivations.

In order to understand Claudia's life and career, it is necessary to understand *Playboy*'s founder, Hugh Hefner. Their lives intertwined for a decade, and it is no exaggeration to declare that if not for *Playboy*'s creator, there would have been no Claudia

Jennings. One hesitates to use the term "mentor" or "Svengali" when speaking of the relationship Hefner and Claudia developed. They began as lovers, then friends, and somewhere along the line, Claudia became convinced she owed everything to Hefner—her career, her life in Los Angeles and her stardom. Whether he convinced *her* that was the case or she convinced *herself* is an important point. It would make sense to think the more she felt grateful to *Playboy*, the less Claudia felt her success was due to her own abilities. As I spoke with her friends and read many interviews, it became apparent that one of Claudia's problems was her inability to break away from Hugh Hefner, *Playboy* and the people who frequented the Playboy Mansion. It became a fact of her personality that she gave everything to *Playboy*. She did have one notable disagreement, but other than that, Claudia always adored Hefner.

I doubt there was a male (well, perhaps some exceptions existed) in America from the mid-1950s to as recently as the turn of the century that did not fantasize about being Hugh M. Hefner—or at the very least desire his lifestyle. Who wouldn't want to live like a monarch, be surrounded by the world's most beautiful women, enjoy unlimited, consequence-free sex and oversee an enormous business empire? Sadly, as time has gone on, Mr. Hefner became more of a caricature of himself, and his business stagnated as the allure of his life has waned. The Playboy Clubs, hotels and casinos, once status symbols of a generation,

Mimi in a Bunny uniform

are now gone. Even the Playboy Mansion, the envy of all those who aspired to a taste of Hefner's domain, was recently sold for $100 million. By all accounts, instead of the opulent pleasure dome it used to be, the Mansion is badly in need of repair and smells of animal urine, and the health department cited even the infamous Grotto as having unsafe levels of bacteria.

About $185 was raised for the March of Dimes at the Mayfield High School Key Club's annual charity faculty baskeball game. Claudia looks over the spoils.

When you look at the owner of *Playboy*, it is easy to conclude that Hef was of one of the first modern "free love" advocates, continuing the mainly social and feminist traditions going back to the late 1800s. Upon further examination, he has more in common with the mid-18th-century aristocracy as far as his feelings about women were concerned. This was the period of the Hellfire Clubs. These "gentleman's clubs" were originally created for fellowship and political and religious discourse, and some even had high society ladies as members. There was no debauchery, and they were considered harmless.

However, some clubs began to alter their philosophy and adopted as their motto: "*Fais ce que tu voudres*" ("Do what thou wilt"), which sounds very much like the *Playboy* philosophy. These new clubs delighted in every sort of excess, from orgies to drinking and dining. Wives, of course, were expected to stay home with the children. Admittedly, Mr. Hefner did campaign vehemently for everything the "free love" advocates yearned for, although the proliferation of female-centered orgies and pornography wasn't quite what they had in mind.

Hugh Marston Hefner was born on April 9, 1926, to conservative Methodist parents in Chicago. His brother Keith joined the family in 1929, and they moved to the Austin district on the west side of the big city. The children grew up surrounded by culture, visiting the many museums and parks with their mother. The boys became inseparable, and Hugh developed a love of animals, at one point even contemplating a career as a veterinarian.

Hugh soon began to show some unique talents. He loved to draw cartoons and write short, fantasy-based stories. He ambitiously wrote not one but two student newspapers, which he sold to classmates for a few pennies. The teachers at Hugh's school wished he showed as much energy for his class work as he did for his cartoons and stories. He was asked repeatedly to show more dedication to his studies.

Hefner continued to give only token compliance to his instructors and began reading the works of Edgar Allen Poe, Sir Arthur Conan Doyle, and Sax Rohmer. Perhaps this is one mutual love he and Claudia shared. While Claudia's taste was not the same as Hugh's, she had a long love of reading, which caught most people off guard when thinking about the stunning young woman.

It became obvious that this highly intelligent, albeit underachieving, child was withdrawing into a sort of fantasy world—not only creating one for him, but also inventing a parallel universe in which others, too, could also participate. He formed a group called "The Shudder Club" that welcomed all who appreciated chills, horror and mystery. According to Dr. Steven Watts, author of *Mr. Playboy: Hugh Hefner and the American Dream*, the club had its own handshake, password and membership pin. He and Keith would build movie sets out of modeling clay and create different tableaus and characters. All the while, Hugh was busy writing and moved on to fully realized cartoons, composing close to 100 of them before he left high school.

If all of this sounds a bit familiar, it should. We have the image of a youth, probably wearing pajamas, being incredibly active, with a mind-boggling work ethic, obsessed with a fantasy world, isolated by choice yet creative, fashioning a club of his own vision with an eye to gather those of a like mind. Hugh Hefner was drawing the blueprint for his future dreams and an unprecedented empire.

The other factors involved in understanding Hugh Hefner's genesis were the social and religious influences of his time. He was surrounded by a Puritanical view of the human body and sex, an adherence to traditional conservative values and a tendency not to disturb the status quo. His mother and father were blessed with a more enlightened social vision, born of their true belief in Christian morality, where one treats others as one wishes to be treated. Their Midwestern Methodist beliefs were passed on to Hugh, giving him a sense of social justice with a religious grounding.

However, there were a few more family dynamics at work with Hugh Marston Hefner that help to explain his character. His mother, while strict, was also enamored of her son and paid him the bulk of the attention in the household. His father, to the contrary, was absent physically and emotionally. This created a situation where, slaved over by his mother and lacking any male authority figure in his life, Hugh began to become self-absorbed to the point where his own interests were the only things that mattered. His mother recalled that this created a situation where the young Hefner got his way in almost every situation.

Once Hugh went to high school, however, he seemed to blossom. He came out of his shell and soon became one of the most popular students. He was voted "Most Likely to Succeed," "Best Dancer" and "Most Popular Boy." He had reinvented himself with new clothes, a new "cool" personality and a natural love for everything high school students of the time desired. It was around this time that he first started referring to himself as "Hef." Hefner was especially taken with popular culture—in particular, Hollywood. They seemed to have been made for each other, one gazing and being absorbed into its fantasy world, the other created just to seduce and ritualize its willing voyeur.[1]

Hugh also began hanging the pinup drawings of George Petty and Alberto Vargas in his bedroom. These pictures showed scantily clad, glamorous women in suggestive poses, and were a feature of *Esquire* magazine.

Hefner graduated high school in 1944, and like most young men of that period, enlisted in the Army. He gained easy acceptance by his fellow soldiers by showing them his cartoons and writing songs to entertain them. Overall, the Army was a pleasant experience for young Hefner, except for one unpleasant phenomenon: For the first time in his life, he faced the ugly side of American bigotry, as he heard anti-Semitic and racist comments from his comrades. He had grown up insulated from this sort of talk in his mother's home and his liberal high school. The pure hatred Hefner experienced left an indelible impression on the young man. One of the first of many social issues *Playboy* championed was the fight for civil rights.

Hugh graduated basic training from Fort Hood and spent time at several bases awaiting assignment. Since Japan had surrendered by this time, he assumed, like most fellow soldiers, that he'd be stationed there as part of the occupying force. Instead, to his

A young Hugh Hefner in his early *Playboy* days

surprise, he found he was now a personnel clerk owing to his typing skills. Once 1946 came around, however, the Army issued a general demobilization order, and Hugh Hefner was thrust back into the civilian world.

Hefner then decided to attend the University of Illinois at Urbana, in part because a girl he was sweet on also went to school there. Hef had known Millie Williams since their high school days and corresponded with her during the war. Hugh thrived in the college atmosphere and excelled at his studies—mostly creative writing and psychology. Samson Raphaelson, a prominent playwright and screenwriter, taught one of his seminars. Among Raphaelson's many credits were *Suspicion* and *The Jazz Singer*. The two men became close, and Hefner would cite the older man as being one of his earliest political inspirations.

Intellectual pursuits were not Hefner's only activities on campus. He wrote for the student newspaper, and even took lessons and logged enough flying time to get his private pilot's license. He spent his hours happily playing board games and mahjong with his friends. Music became a major avocation, as he was an avid jazz fan and sang popular music for his fellow students, replicating the style and tone of Frankie Lane.

Another event occurred which would influence Hefner. His mother showed him the results of an intelligence test given to him as a boy. Why she chose that moment to deliver the news to Hugh is unknown; perhaps she felt the need to give her son a boost of confidence, or maybe it was just a loving gesture. The test showed her son had a genius IQ of 152, a level of intelligence obscured by his high school struggles but confirmed by Hef's college success.

The results energized Hefner and gave him a renewed sense of confidence. The test was a tangible confirmation of what he always felt inside: A vindication of self.

In 1948, Hugh and Millie decided to marry. Millie had graduated and taken a job as a schoolteacher in Lee Center, Illinois. Hef, meanwhile, still in college, had discovered a book that engulfed the country in controversy—a work seemingly written for him alone. The author felt the exact same way Hef did about a certain subject—a subject he obsessed about since he was a boy. The name of the book was *Sexual Behavior in the American Male*, and the author was Alfred Kinsey.

Hefner, finding a kindred spirit, interpreted what the book's findings meant. Sex and sexuality were the driving force behind human experience, and man's reliance on hypocrisy, superstition and religious prejudice did more harm than good. It was as if Kinsey's book was the Magna Carta of human sexual behavior, and Hefner would use it as a basis for a purer document—his Constitution to protect sexual rights. It is an amusing paradox, however, that if all the negative connotations and shame associated with sex were eliminated, then there would be no need for magazines like *Playboy*. Unfortunately, sexual research does not explain emotional upheaval and heartbreak. Not even a gifted individual like Mr. Hefner was immune to the fact that we are born—most of us, anyway—with a human component, which in many cases clings to the sex act with complex inconveniences like love and jealousy.

Shortly before Christmas 1948, on one of their dates, Millie told Hef she had an affair with one of the coaches at her school. He was shattered and ripped apart by an inner conflict. His rational side told him not to blame her, for it was nearly impossible to hold oneself up to an impossibly high moral standard. As Kinsey would argue, society should be judged guilty, not Millie. However, the emotional side of Hefner's psyche felt only pain, betrayal and anger. Hugh Hefner had to ask himself if it was going to be possible to reconcile the two views. In addition, the incident had cut him to his inner core—the romantic, super-male myth he had created—and the man known as "Hef" lay wounded and bleeding.

The incident with Millie explains much of what we've seen of Hugh Hefner. His mistrust of women, the avoidance of commitment and the seeming need to dominate all stem from that sad night. Indeed, Hef said that was the saddest period of his life.[2] It may sound like pop psychology, but Hefner's own words, and particularly his actions, would rationalize his future behavior.

With clouds professional and personal hanging over his head, Hefner graduated from the University of Illinois in 1949. He suffered through a personal malaise for a few years. Now married, he took a job he was obviously under qualified for at the Chicago Carton Company. Unimpressed by the meager wages and upset by the company's anti-Semitic and racist hiring practices, he soon resigned. A brief dabble at returning to college at Northwestern ended after one semester, and the young man found employment at a department store, where he could do creative writing and even learned art and layout work on the side. These were all skills that would serve him well in the future. Then, miraculously, it seemed Hef had found his dream job. He was hired by *Esquire* magazine, the favorite journal of his boyhood, as a copywriter. To his dismay, the job was not challenging and, when he found out the company was shutting the Chicago office and moving all its staff to New York, Hefner had a decision to make. *Esquire* offered a paltry relocation raise, but nothing else. Hef's intuition told him Chicago was the city where his destiny lay. His request denied for an additional five-dollar raise, Hef famously quit.[3]

Hefner's obsession with sex, always strong, now grew overwhelming. He graduated from making Millie watch stag films with him to having group sex with his brother and sister-in-law. His life began to revolve around sex, with social issues and individual liberties not far behind. He read the works of Ayn Rand voraciously, and decided her message of individualism meshed perfectly with his ideas of sexual liberation.

At home, however, things were increasingly dire. He and Millie had two children, but Hefner felt limited emotional attachment toward them. He began to look back

Sir Laurence Olivier lights a cigarette for Marilyn Monroe.

wistfully at his high school days when he was a prince, life was good and everything seemed possible. He decided he would start a new kind of magazine, one that had the class and excitement of the old *Esquire* combined with pictures of the most beautiful nude women he could find.

After months of hard effort, the magazine was all set to go. Hefner had borrowed $45,000 from everyone he knew, his mother included. A picture of Marilyn Monroe at a parade graced the cover and a calendar photo of her that Hefner paid $50 for was the featured nude pictorial.

The name was going to be *Stag Party*, but at the last minute, the owners of *Stag* magazine threatened an infringement suit. Hefner decided the new name would be *Playboy*, as it was evocative of the Gatsby era of wine, high living, song and women—especially women. With no time to spare, the logo was changed from a stag to a rabbit. The magazine's iconic emblem was designed in less than an hour and would become a marketing legend. Thus, in November of 1953, nearly four years after the birth of Mary Eileen "Mimi" Chesterton, *Playboy* magazine was born. It isn't difficult to see the conflicted feelings Hefner must have held toward women. His wife was not only an object of desire, but also one that represented pain and emasculation. Then, in his brilliance, Hefner turned his personal psychology—his disappointments along with his vision and business sense—into a professional Garden of Eden. His magazine, while not subjecting women to pain or violence, still made them subservient to men in their poses, their sexually aggressive language, and most importantly, showing that women wanted sex as badly as men did. There is still an aura of domination in the pictorials. Moreover, although the fact women desired sex was not a bad thing per se, it implied silently to men that women, through their suggestive poses and lingerie, were sluts.

There were no nude men in *Playboy*, a subliminal message that the sexes were not, in fact, equal. Thus, Hefner was satisfying his anguish concerning Millie's infidelities, and hitting back in a non-violent yet aggressive manner.

The second interesting trait about Hefner was his fascination with younger women, sometimes teenagers. Claudia was barely 20 when she and Hefner made love for the first time. He was 39. When an older man pursues younger women, there are generally two motivations. Mr. Hefner is the prime example of the type of individual who would possess both of them.

The first motivation would be to have what a young woman represents. A man with a 21-year-old Playmate on his arm would garner prestige, jealousy from other men, an aura of sexuality and a psychological transference of youth. A shorter explanation would be that a man feels better about himself with a young, beautiful girl on his arm or in his bed. How better to redeem one's self-esteem—and more importantly, to make his former wife or lovers jealous?

This brings us to the second motivation. When his first marriage disintegrated, perhaps it is possible Mr. Hefner had a slightly distorted view of women, particularly those who were his own age. It would be easy to understand that Hefner didn't want to revisit the anguish and drama of the unpleasant experience of his first marriage, and wanted to show his contempt for these women. Therefore, under his stewardship, the magazine sought a never-ending supply of much younger, gorgeous women, not only to be models but to be Mr. Hefner's concubines as well. He seemed to delight in flaunting the much younger women on his arm to all of America.

Hefner showed an even more fascinating dichotomy by his choice of female companionship. Although some of his girlfriends were quite intelligent and sophisticated, the majority were not. Hefner himself was highly intellectual, cultured and worldly; yet he seemed to take pleasure in associating with women who were a step down from him in class, economic level and pure intelligence. There is no doubt he could have wooed some beautiful young women, foreign and domestic, who were of equal social status. Possibly Hefner was afraid of women who were his match, because of his need to feel superior to his mate *du soir*.

There is another perplexing divergence in Mr. Hefner's behavior. You would think a man that upset by his first marriage would never enter into the same arrangement in the future. Hefner was able to make his every fantasy come to life, especially an unending amount of nubile women who wanted to have sex with him. Yet, he did marry again, twice—to Kimberly Conrad and then Crystal Harris. He also had long-term relationships with Barbi Benton, Shannon Tweed and several other Playmates, sometimes in groups of two's and three's. This would show a conflict within Mr. Hefner. His public image was that of the ultimate satyr, but privately it was apparent that Hefner was a romantic, even sentimental, figure. Constance Chesterton told me that Claudia said Hefner reminded her of a Gatsby type of figure, putting up the front of the world's greatest lover and viewing the wild revelry from a distance, only to disguise his longing for a true soul mate.

Hefner also used *Playboy* to advocate an end to the institution of marriage, or at least the traditional notions of marriage as set forth by the religious figures that guided America's morals. This made sense considering his personal sexual appetites and the constraints he felt from his own marriage. The notion of the swinging bachelor driving

Hugh Hefner holds Barbi Benson tightly, surrounded by *Playboy* Bunnies.

his sports car, wearing a fancy watch and dressed in the latest men's fashions, replaced Jack Armstrong as the All-American ideal. It was *Playboy*'s call to hedonism, secularism, consumerism and liberalism that now caught the imagination of American men. Moreover, if the average middle-class man couldn't relate to anything else Hefner was preaching, *Playboy* made it respectable to look at nudie magazines for the first time in our nation's history.

Ultimately, *Playboy* was just a glossy version of the old smut magazines of less permissive times. Hefner caught the wave of relaxed censorship to still exploit nude women, only wrapped in a pretty package of fancy lifestyles, progressive politics and New Age mumbo-jumbo. The materialism it espoused, and the sex-filled marketing of its advertisers, was palpably wrapped in liberal notions of equality and personal rights.

The women who appeared in the magazine had the same carrot-and-stick models had in years before. Money was the main motivation, and as *Playboy*'s fame grew, the opportunities for careers in entertainment, modeling and other endeavors became available. Hefner was able to wield the biggest carrot, with the stick being the danger of getting cut off from his good graces and the prospects for success he dangled in front of them.

The publisher of the world's number one men's magazine espousing sexual freedom also had difficulty in "walking the walk." In 1968, he met a beautiful, intelligent student from UCLA, Barbi Benton, while filming an episode of *Playboy After Dark*. He wooed her as if she was his high school sweetheart, even holding off on consummating the relationship for several months. However, not long after Ms. Benton and Hef were an item, he dabbled whenever and wherever he got the chance. Soon, Hefner found himself involved in a full-fledged romantic triangle when he met a Chicago Playboy Club Bunny named Karen Christy. The classic Texas blonde beauty attracted the publisher immediately, and she soon moved into the Chicago Mansion, with Barbi living in Los Angeles. Hefner traveled back and forth between the two until a photo got out to the press showing Hefner and Christy in an embrace. Benton, not a fool by any means, was infuriated, moved out of the Mansion in L.A. and promptly had a couple of affairs of her own. The whole love triangle went south from there. Hefner couldn't believe it when Christy told him she had a few affairs of her own while he was off visiting Benton. Hef exploded in anger, seemingly unable to absorb his own philosophy of sexual freedom. To many in the *Playboy* community, it showed a double standard and an unexpected flash of hypocrisy. One can make an excellent case for the troubles from Hefner's marriage controlling his psyche yet again.[4]

As a postscript to the story, Barbi Benton, like so many of Hefner's former girlfriends, remained friends with him to the end, never hesitating to speak of him in the most glowing terms possible. Of course, others did not admire the man or his empire.

Despite scandals, personal turmoil and a serious effort by the government to harass him, Hugh Hefner soon had a successful magazine on his hands. *Playboy* had become a lightning rod for many of our country's social and political issues. The magazine had impeccable writing, superior art, a look and feel unmatched in the magazine universe, and, of course, the best photography of nude women in the world.

Playboy was more than a magazine, it was a brand—exceeded only by Coca-Cola, McDonald's and Apple. Hated by the right wing and evangelicals, it was peculiar that some conservatives praised it for its more Libertarian stances. Some feminists despised it, stating that it turned back progress in women's equality. Other women praised it as liberating and empowering and point to the fact that *Playboy* employs a large number of women. Feminists must also cringe when they see the number of extremely intelligent, successful women lining up to pose for the magazine. One thing is for sure: Many male critics, in the privacy of their homes, read the magazine religiously, and if given the chance to entertain one of the women found in its pages, would kill for that opportunity.

It is certainly a testament to Hugh Hefner's intelligence and the magazine's popularity that so much social debate has been brought to America's attention by *Playboy*. The magazine tackled everything from abortion rights, race relations and marijuana legalization to easier access to birth control for women, gay rights and conservation. Most of these articles were first published in the 1950s, 1960s and 1970s, when it took great personal courage to do so.

Regardless of all the controversies the magazine was embroiled in and the growing number of books that attacked Mr. Hefner personally on a variety of fronts, there is no denying *Playboy*, and its founder, was one of the great success stories of modern America. Under Mr. Hefner's guidance, it survived, thrived and adapted to the changing world of men's entertainment. It is important in understanding Mr. Hefner and his world to remember that the top corner of *Playboy* has always read 'Entertainment for Men," so he couldn't really be accused of being a hypocrite. I suppose it comes down to how you define hypocrisy.

Cooper Hefner, Hugh's son, is the heir apparent and announced in 2016 that *Playboy* would be changing its format. Starting in March of that year, it was announced the magazine would no longer feature full frontal nudity. The magazine would now resemble

An elderly Hugh Hefner poses in the Playboy Mansion.

the *Esquires* that Hugh Hefner loved as a young man. *Playboy* as a written publication has fallen to the trends choking its readership. The sea change of online publications and free Internet pornography has forced *Playboy* into a unique challenge, and the question is whether it can survive into the next decade. Change, however, very often comes at a price. Early in 2017, less than a year after the grand experiment began, Cooper Hefner announced *Playboy* would return to its graphic roots. There would be breasts and buttocks galore, but no pubic hair, and certainly no gynecological photographs à la *Penthouse*.

Mimi Chesterton didn't care about any of this as she walked through the doors of *Playboy*'s offices for the first time. She became the head receptionist at *Playboy* after a brief time, an honor traditionally reserved for the prettiest girl in the office pool according to her friend, Bunny Patti King. She would also give tours of the corporate facilities as one of her duties.

Before too long, Pompeo Posar noticed her, *Playboy*'s principal photographer. When Posar asked Mimi to pose, she demurred, believing her breasts were not up to *Playboy* "quality." The esteemed photographer kept pressing, and finally, one night after the building was deserted, he took some pictures of her.

Over the next few months, he did some additional test shots and showed them to Hugh Hefner. They both agreed the young woman—actually a teenager—had potential, but she needed to lose a few pounds. Mimi lost the required amount of weight and went on to be the November 1969 centerfold.

The rapid transformation from Mimi Chesterton, All-American girl, to Claudia Jennings, sex symbol, caught everyone who knew her off guard. When one looks a little deeper into those months between high school and her first appearance in *Playboy*, the change was not that dramatic. Mimi, while sweet and innocent by nature, was not naïve. She had her eyes on a career in Hollywood from the beginning. Mimi, after considering all her options, felt posing for *Playboy* was the shortest path to cinematic success.

Those unfamiliar with Mimi might ask how she could be called innocent and sweet, while at the same time posing for nude photos. The answer is simple. She was able to compartmentalize her life into her professional behavior and her personal traits. Modeling, whether nude or not, is a form of acting. Mimi took advantage of the fact she was very photogenic and made enough money to launch her film career. She turned the pain and humiliation from her time in Evanston into a determined and gritty ambition. Far from being a compromise of her personal values, Mimi's *Playboy* experience proved her resolve to persevere.

A few things stand out in her first pictorial. Mimi says very directly in the article, "Modeling gets more tedious all the time," although her career with *Playboy* and other magazines are what put her on the entertainment map. She also declares herself ready for Hollywood when she says, "If you want to overcome your limitations you go to New York, but if you're satisfied with your skills then you're ready for Hollywood."[5] This was quite the statement from a 19-year-old with only high school drama productions and half a season of Hull House performances as her experience.

She was offered $5,000 to pose, but got something more. Although she was barely 19 and her employer was nearly 40, Mimi and Hugh Hefner became a couple. Looking at this in a vacuum, it was not unusual for Hugh Hefner to have sex with his models. In fact, in the days of a less enlightened corporate world in America, many young women were expected to engage in consensual—or discreetly non-consensual—sex with their bosses, co-workers or clients. In today's context, however, what went on between Mimi and Hugh Hefner is nothing less than sexual harassment. Technically, Mimi was an adult. She was free to make her own choices. The question is, was there pressure put on her by Mr. Hefner, implied or blatant—or was it a calculated move on her part? These days the bar is set much lower, as we know. Even creating an atmosphere of sexual harassment today is grounds for termination with cause.

There is nothing to suggest Mr. Hefner coerced Mimi into having sex. There is also abundant evidence to conclude Mimi had an ambitious streak, one that seems to suggest that the ends justify the means. This did not make her less kind or caring. It meant that Mimi was willing to do almost anything to leave Evanston and find success. Judging from what Hefner has said, Mimi was more than receptive to the idea of sleeping with him.

In a strange way, Hugh Hefner and Claudia were a perfect match. Perhaps that explains their unique relationship through the years. Intelligent and excellent at the art and practice of self-promotion, both Hef and Claudia had re-invented themselves in a manner designed to rebuild fragile, vulnerable egos. There is no doubt that Hefner saw something a little different in the beautiful redhead. She was intelligent, self-confident and had a great sense of humor. Looking at Hef, Mimi saw a sophisticated, highly intelligent millionaire businessman. Hef was the embodiment of her ideal man, according to the Playmate profile in her first pictorial.[6] The Playmate data sheet revealed Claudia's bent towards the magic of the written word, professing an admiration for the works of Hemmingway and other 20th-century masters. Indeed, reading was an avocation she enjoyed for the rest of her life, and one that set her apart from most of the other women who posed for the magazine.[7]

Claudia's sister Constance recalls her first reactions, and the unexpected aftermath of Mimi's decision to pose:

> When I was 14, babysitting, she called to ask me what I thought about the possibility of her doing a spread for *Playboy*. I gave her a self-righteous little speech and hung up on her. I'm sure I apologized to her in later years, and as likely as not, she would not have even remembered it. She wasn't one to hang on to resentments, at least not where family was concerned.
>
> She didn't forget her sisters, either. While living on Lake Shore Drive or staying at Hefner's mansion, she'd pick us up in a limo and take us out for the day. I remember Hefner's mansion well. Mimi would say, "I'm staying in the White Room," and we would gaze in admiration at a beautifully carved wooden wall. She would press a flower on that wall, and a door would slide open with a spiral staircase up to the White Room—at least, these are my memories, and they might have become a bit muddled over the years. I remember one time we were there, and some of the Bunnies who lived there too had defaced a photograph of one of their Bunny peers. Mimi hated bullying of any sort, and she rounded on them and said, "That is sick! And I'm telling Hef!"

Claudia was now seeing life on the other side of the tracks. She coveted the wealth and materialism that a Hollywood career could give her, but she also remained a sweet soul. Her modest background and feelings of inadequacy were being soothed by the unrealistic and irrational world of Hugh Hefner.

Life at the Mansion lived up to the public's preconceived ideas. Full of beautiful women, there was always food, drink, movies, a bowling alley, a full size pool and non-stop parties to enjoy. Sex was naturally an important part of the revelries, with Hefner often bedding down with two or three partners at a time. The house Bunnies and those from the Chicago Playboy Club were expected to provide companionship for the male guests.

Claudia got her first exposure to television while living in the Mansion. In the late 1960s and early 1970s, Hefner hosted a show called *Playboy After Dark*. Filmed in Los Angeles, it featured actors, comedians, directors, authors and other intellectually gifted folk, in addition to performances by the cream of rock and roll royalty at the time. One show might feature Lenny Bruce, Bill Cosby, Roman Polanski or Sharon Tate, with musical guests the Grateful Dead or Deep Purple. The program had the rather incongruous images of Mr. Hefner in a tuxedo, his trademark pipe in his hand, saying "groovy" and "far out" to Steppenwolf or the Sir Douglas Quintet. The audience consisted of Playmates, Bunnies and other attractive young people, all dressed in the latest fashions, sitting around the large living room where the show was filmed. One can catch a brief glimpse of Claudia dancing or sitting on an ottoman during several shows. There was also one noteworthy episode where Hefner, flanked by Claudia and Barbi Benton, introduced the guests for the evening. In another episode, Barbi and Claudia are seen standing side by side, appearing to cook something. Later in the episode, Claudia is viewed standing beside Buddy Rich as he performs a rowdy drum solo. I don't think there was ever a more surrealistic television moment than when, during Country Joe and the Fish's performance of "I-Feel-Like-I'm-Fixin'-to-Die Rag," a conga line of Bunnies and their beaus danced around the band with a gleeful enthusiasm. The programs have to be seen to be believed, no sarcasm intended.

The infamous Playboy Mansion

Mimi was more impressed with the Mansion and the lifestyle than the magazine itself. She was also looking ahead and decided the name Mary Eileen "Mimi" Chesterton was no longer adequate for the life she envisioned. The name needed to be sexier, brief enough to fit on a marquee and sophisticated. Mimi sat down with a girlfriend and picked the name Claudia at random out of a phone book. Then she asked her girlfriend if it would be all right to use her boyfriend's last name. Thus Claudia Jennings was born. The story most often heard is that Claudia changed her name to protect her family from unwanted publicity, a very sweet thought. However, this does not seem credible, since everyone in Evanston knew the minute the November issue of *Playboy* hit the stands who the centerfold was and her real name. Perhaps this seems cynical but Claudia's explanation for the name change doesn't ring true. The true justification for the name change was the same as Archibald Leach used when he became Cary Grant or when Norma Jean Baker was reborn as Marilyn Monroe. The ability to connect with the movie-going public and create a persona that is inspiring and intriguing counts for a lot in Hollywood. It is easy to believe that Mary Chesterton lacked the necessary marquee power that Claudia Jennings commanded. Claudia also felt Mimi sounded too girlish, and despite the fact she was still in her teens, a name that projected a sensual maturity was needed.

Claudia certainly didn't care about any possible controversy. In a very real way, she now had a new life and identity. Her family gradually accepted her decision to model for *Playboy*. Her mother would have rather seen her go to college and take a different path to success, but once Claudia started getting movie offers, Joan acquiesced to her daughter's choice of career. Later on, however, years after Claudia's death, she would blame *Playboy* for corrupting her child.

Mimi, now Claudia Jennings, moved into the Chicago Mansion and was given a choice room. She also received the attentions of the handsome art director for *Playboy*, Tom Staebler. He was a brilliant artist, educated at the University of Kansas before

A Biography

joining *Playboy*. Tom Staebler gave the magazine its distinctive look and style. He and Claudia dated after she and Hef were no longer seeing each other, and then became very good friends—a relationship that lasted well into the late 1970s.

Mr. Staebler remembered:

> Claudia and I became very good friends after we dated, and I got to know her family quite well. When her parents divorced, her mother moved across the street from me. Claudia wanted to use her pictorial as a launching pad for her career ... that was on her mind from the very beginning. Claudia was incredibly smart, a good friend; anytime I needed a place to stay in Los Angeles, I'd be welcome at her home. She really loved *Playboy* and she really loved Hef. I spoke with her on a regular basis. The last time was shortly before she died. She was a wonderful person, with a heart of gold.[8]

Once Claudia and *Playboy* moved to Los Angeles, she became the first among equals in the world of the Playmates. All of the girls looked up to her as a person and a role model; Claudia never acted superior to them or was mean to them. Claudia didn't act like a diva, and that certainly did no harm to her status at the magazine.

Marilyn Grabowski started her *Playboy* career in Chicago and eventually became its West Coast Editor of Photography. She said this of Claudia:

> She and I weren't good friends until we both moved to Los Angeles. Claudia stood out. She just jumped off the page, as she did in real life. Claudia had a devil-may-care attitude, and she really wanted to be a movie star. When she moved from Chicago, she hit L.A. like a storm with her larger-than-life personality. She was a little loopy at times, I'd say, and she always had some kind of drama going on with men.[9]

Claudia always had Hef's ear if she wanted, and he treated her more like a friend than an employee. The rest of the Playmates and Bunnies took notice of their special relationship, and this increased Claudia's prestige. There were limits, however, to Hefner's friendship. There was no question that if a matter ever came up where it was a choice of *Playboy*'s interests or Claudia's best interests, the magazine and Hefner would come first. The best example of this was in 1974, when Hefner wanted Claudia to do a pictorial. She declined, and Hefner used every method of persuasion he could to force her into agreeing. This is documented later in the book, but it demonstrates that Hefner, despite his paternal demeanor, could be cold-blooded if *Playboy*'s interests were in the slightest jeopardy. Most likely, an honest view of Hefner and Claudia's relationship is that they needed each other to get what they wanted. Claudia would need the money, publicity and notoriety the magazine could offer, as well as the sanctuary that the Mansion could provide. Hefner, in turn, had a beautiful, popular and recognizable sex symbol willing to appear in the magazine's pages whenever he asked.

It is common knowledge that ever since the pictures of Marilyn Monroe graced *Playboy*'s pages, Hugh Hefner was trying to find an in-house successor to the blonde goddess, one who would successfully bridge the gap between Playmate and legitimate actress, and thereby increase the circulation of his magazine and make Hefner a Hollywood insider. Jayne Mansfield was an early attempt, but she had achieved some notoriety well before she posed for *Playboy* in 1955. She appeared in the pages of the magazine several times, but many of those pictorials used previously shot photographs from her first foray. Jayne was a true talent. Aside from her amazing figure, she could act and was a first rate comedienne. Mansfield had a successful career in film, stage and television, but when the public became tired of her incessant and increasingly absurd publicity stunts, her star began to fade. By the time Mansfield was 34, she was having trouble with her career when it was tragically cut short by an automobile accident in 1967.

Stella Stevens, successful actress and a talented blonde beauty

Stella Stevens was a successful actress and a talented blonde beauty, but Hefner never put her on the pedestal reserved for the next Marilyn. She was asked to pose for the magazine and the experience was far from ideal. Stella was an interesting woman, a highly intelligent, gorgeous blonde beauty from Mississippi. She had caught the acting bug when she was a teenager in Memphis and decided to move to Los Angeles. If anyone seemed fit to be the next Marilyn Monroe, it was Stevens. She could act, was also an excellent comedienne and had classic beauty along with a Monroe-esque figure. She appeared in a few movies, where she did well, but in 1960, 20th Century Fox dropped her contract. Desperate for money and a single mother with a young son to support, Stella didn't have many choices. In a very illuminating interview, she describes her impression of what the typical modeling experience was like at *Playboy*. The magazine approached her to do a pictorial and she agreed, signing a contract for $5,000. Stella told Tony Macklin of the *Bright Lights Film Journal*, in a July 31, 2004 interview, what happened next.

What did the Playboy spread do for your career?
First of all, they lied to me when they told me they'd pay $5,000. I had been dropped from my contract at 20th Century Fox, didn't know a soul in L.A. and had a child to support.
You don't think it was a career mistake? Or do you?
Christ, yes! Because I got a job working on Li'l Abner, I called Hef up and said, "I don't want to do this." And he [Hefner] said, "Oh, no, you have a contract with us. You have to do it."

Starting your career then as opposed to today you didn't have many options, did you?
I didn't have any options at all. I was either going to make that $5,000 or starve. Then when I did it [the pictorial], they paid me half the money, and if I wanted the other half I would have to work as a hostess for *Playboy* parties. I said, "Shove it, I will not!" I truly hate that organization."[10]

This explains why, despite having a remarkable actress comparable in beauty to Marilyn Monroe and with *Playboy* experience, Hefner was never able to turn Stella Stevens into his star.

Claudia was another such "experiment." While the notoriety from her appearances in *Playboy* helped her get some movie and television roles, Claudia's career never reached the trajectory Hefner and *Playboy* needed. Claudia's career was impressive, but not the home run the magazine and its owner wanted, and above all else, Claudia was not blonde. The publisher made the conscious decision as early as 1974 to feature Claudia more frequently in the magazine; she was more valuable to *Playboy* as a pictorial than as a movie star. As it turned out, Claudia became their most popular model of the 1970s.

When her career faltered, a replacement was discovered almost immediately—the unfortunate Dorothy Stratten. This begins one of the darkest chapters in the history of Playboy Enterprises. The reason it is in the biography of Claudia is very simple. What you will read explains the mindset and the culture of Hugh Hefner and his empire in the 1970s, and the effort put behind finding that second Marilyn Monroe who would belong to *Playboy* and *Playboy* alone. The manner in which *Playboy* treated Claudia's career, and then Dorothy's quick rise to fame, couldn't be more different. The story would result in such a tragic ending that the only surprising thing is that it didn't happen more frequently to the many women who posed for the magazine.

The difference in the magazine's handling of the two women is worth investigating. Claudia was a much better actress, yet Stratten was publicized as being *Playboy*'s newest discovery—and, in fact, the next Marilyn Monroe. While Hugh Hefner pretty much abandoned Claudia's career, *Playboy* poured every effort into Ms. Stratten's future. In all fairness, Stratten was funny, smart and very sweet natured, but the two actresses were a world apart in just about every way. Stratten was a true ingénue, where Claudia was tough and street-smart. Claudia had been in the theater since she was a small child, while Dorothy was a waitress prior to becoming a Playmate, with no acting experience.

To show how obsessed *Playboy*'s founder was in making Stratten the next Marilyn Monroe, he had her hair dyed platinum blonde—Marilyn's shade. In addition, he found her a top agent and generally used the immense power of *Playboy*'s public relations department to promote her career. In an odd series of coincidences, Dorothy was the centerfold in the issue after Claudia's last *Playboy* appearance, and was then murdered almost a year to the day after Claudia's death. Dorothy was also Playmate of the Year in 1980, exactly 10 years after Claudia won the title.

It is also strange that Ms. Stratten has had a book and an extensive Pulitzer Prize-winning magazine article written about her, but Claudia's life has been virtually ignored. While there's no doubt her story is compelling, tragic and worth exploring, it makes the fact that no one has ever written much about Claudia that much stranger.

The deaths of Claudia and Dorothy Stratten were a severe blow to Hugh Hefner and the *Playboy* family. Although no one suggested Hefner was to blame for Claudia's tragic death, many people looked much harder at the founder of *Playboy* after Dorothy's murder. Her boyfriend at the time, noted director Peter Bogdanovich, wrote a book, *The Killing of the Unicorn: Dorothy Stratten 1960-1980*, accusing Hefner of sexually bullying Ms. Stratten into having intercourse. Hefner's reply to the accusation was that he hardly needed to intimidate women into having sex with him, since he always had many willing partners available. The director's allegations did not end there. Bogdanovich suggested that the entire *Playboy* philosophy was to blame, since it objectified women and thus reduced them to "things" that could be owned and treated in any manner according to the whims of their "master."[11]

Stratten's husband Paul Snider was undoubtedly an unstable, evil individual and was solely responsible for the murder. One has to wonder, though, how he felt

Hugh Hefner lost interest Claudia's career in an effort to mold Dorothy Stratten into the next Marilyn Monroe.

after seeing his wife, who he had introduced to *Playboy*, made into a star, without getting any credit or compensation from the magazine. Snider also had to listen to Dorothy repeat what Hefner said to her, such as suggesting she should drop him, and that he "was a hustler and pimp-like." He was also banned from the Mansion unless accompanied by Stratten, but that was company policy. To a sociopathic individual like Paul Snider, this was just one more insult to bear. This policy of keeping the spouses and boyfriends of Playmates isolated from them inside the Playboy Mansion was a somewhat sinister and insidious practice. Bobby Hart told me he had to wait a full year after he was seeing Claudia to get on the coveted "guest list." Inside the mansion, Hefner's wealthy friends would constantly hit on young women.

Lost in all this melodrama is a 20-year-old Dorothy Stratten, away from home for the first time and woefully unprepared for her new lifestyle. She was being pulled at by three men who wanted her, each for his own reason—one of them, Bogdanovich, was a much older man with a penchant for romancing younger women. He had wooed a 21-year-old Cybill Shepherd on the set of *The Last Picture Show* and married her shortly after the movie completed filming. Bogdanovich also raised a few eyebrows when he married Dorothy's younger sister Louise, when she was only 20, a few years after the murder of her older sister. From what her memoirs tell us, it must have been a sad, frightening and disorienting life for Ms. Stratten, despite the excitement and perks that came with being a sex symbol. Society often looks at people of great wealth, talent, beauty or any

Peter Bogdanovich with Louise Stratten

valuable virtue and considers them impervious to pain and suffering. Many forget that they are human beings and not perfect beings, especially when they are young. What happened to Dorothy was sickening, as she was literally thrown to the wolves without any defense or protection. More sickening is that we still see this happening today with young stars. Dorothy was too youthful to be put into these situations, surrounded by people who made decisions concerning her future, not for her benefit but for theirs. When Dorothy died, Hef had her buried near Marilyn in Westwood Village Memorial Cemetery as a last homage to the latest blonde deity to fail *Playboy*'s ambitions.

The sordid mess turned uglier after Bogdanovich's book came out. Hefner sued, saying the content was responsible for a stroke he suffered after reading it. Citing a fear of hospitals and his agoraphobia, Mr. Hefner had the doctors come to him at the Mansion to care for the condition. Then, at the news conference where he counter-attacked Bogdanovich, Hefner accused the director of sleeping with Dorothy's 13-year-old sister to compensate for losing Dorothy. In less than 48 hours, Nell, Dorothy's mother, sued Hefner on behalf of Louise for defamation.[12] Hefner took the suit personally, and though he blamed Bogdanovich for putting Dorothy's family up to it, he seemed to ignore the fact that a mother and an underage girl were bearing the bulk of his wrath. "The victim in this story is not some 16-year-old girl. The victim turns out to be the publisher of *Playboy*," Hefner declared at a news conference.[13] Stroke or not, this was a monstrous thing to say publicly, so callous and self-centered that it defies belief. When Dorothy's mother later withdrew the lawsuit, Hefner crowed in victory. "I knew they would never pursue the suit. The depositions have left Bogdanovich totally exposed."[14] It is unfortunate that Hefner could never put his antipathy toward Bogdanovich aside long enough to see the mother and sister of a murdered Playmate as anything more than pawns.

Dorothy's mother and sister ended up with nothing except the memory of their beautiful daughter, who traveled far from home only to be killed in the most disturbing manner possible. Bogdanovich did end up marrying Louise Hoogstraten when she was 20. However, the marriage didn't endure. The celebrated director and film critic says to this day that Dorothy was the one true love of his life.

In partial defense of Mr. Hefner, he saw Bogdanovich's book as the worst sort of betrayal, which not only took aim at the publisher personally, but at the whole *Playboy* philosophy upon which he based his professional life. Regardless, it was arguably the ugliest incident in the history of Hefner and the magazine. Today, it is a sad footnote, remembered only by grieving family members.

It should be noted that Hugh Hefner remained a beloved figure among much of Hollywood's elite and his former employees. Despite the unfortunate negative publicity that rained down upon him at times, an overwhelming number of former Playmates, friends, photographers, secretaries and others who knew him, had nothing but the sincerest affection for Hef.

Claudia and her friend Pam in Los Angeles, 1971

Claudia was certainly one of the most famous Playmates to emerge from its pages and into the entertainment world. However, when Dorothy Stratten arrived on the scene, no one mentioned what a varied career Claudia enjoyed. It was as if *no* other Playmates ever showed promise or could act before Dorothy appeared. This was unfair to Claudia, the dozens of other Playmates who had decent acting careers and to Dorothy herself. There have been better-known women from outside the world of *Playboy* who have posed, but none whose careers initially began in the magazine. If she had lived, she may have become the icon that Hef so desperately wanted to create.

The only women to come that close were the aforementioned Barbi Benton (née Klein), Stella Stevens and Shannon Tweed. Ms. Benton was a talented young woman who appeared in four different pictorials for the magazine, but was never a Playmate of the Month or Year. She had an extensive television career, much longer and varied than Claudia's. She was a guest on multiple episodes of *Fantasy Island*, as well as being a cast member on *Hee Haw*. Ms. Benton also had a successful music career, penning and singing several hits as well as playing the piano on several tracks. She appeared in a handful of motion pictures as well.

It is an interesting footnote that soon after Claudia and Hefner stopped seeing each other romantically, Barbi Benton and Hefner began a seven-year relationship. Claudia was not fazed by this turn of events, as she never wanted to be Hef's girlfriend. Claudia wanted his respect, but she wanted a career above everything else. Constance Chesterton

Claudia Jennings (arms folded to the right) stands with unidentified guests near the entrance of the Playboy Mansion.

added that Claudia did not care for the way Barbi treated Hef. Of course, it seems Ms. Benton may have had her reasons.

Ms. Tweed was a Playmate of the Year, and had a brief film career. However, her fame has come relatively recently, courtesy of her relationship with, and eventual marriage to, rock star Gene Simmons and through their popular reality television series.

There is an intersection between Ms. Benton's career and Claudia's. It speaks to the double standards in our society and the hypocrisy of television at the time. As you will read later, Claudia's biggest professional disappointment was not getting a part on *Charlie's Angels*. The reason given was that the network executives were nervous about her *Playboy* pictorials. Although *Charlie's Angels* had its share of eye candy without Claudia, the show looked prim compared with *Hee Haw*. The *Hee Haw* Honeys, as they were known—Barbi Benton, Misty Rowe, Linda Thompson, Lisa Todd and Gunilla Hutton—sent the show's ratings skyrocketing by wearing Daisy Duke shorts or miniskirts and displaying formidable amounts of cleavage. Remember, this was a show marketed to middle-class America and the Bible belt. As a side note, Misty Rowe also posed for *Playboy*, saying she wished she could have posed for the magazine every year. However, when she began working for the magazine in 1969, Claudia had no idea where *Playboy* would lead her. In many ways, it gave her what she needed. *Playboy* was her stepping-stone to the motion picture industry. She was admired at the Mansion, traits that either eluded her in Evanston or that she had to fight to attain. Her body and her sex appeal, given more merit than her intelligence and kindness, enabled her to rise rapidly in the Hollywood hierarchy, although this would reinforce self-esteem issues that would haunt her later. Claudia was now on the edge of a world she had always dreamed of entering, the land where she would lead a glamorous lifestyle, live in a mansion and meet fabulous men.

Claudia and Hugh Hefner at the 25th Anniversary Playmate Reunion

There is little question that for good or ill, the Playboy Mansion of Hugh Hefner became the home Claudia didn't have in Evanston. In the Mansion, she wasn't judged, disrespected, ignored, belittled or put under pressure. She had a surrogate father figure in Hugh Hefner, who was able to provide a lavish lifestyle, unlike her natural father. Claudia had found her sanctuary in every way imaginable. Years later, Claudia found the L.A. Mansion also had visitors who were a source of male companionship, money, influence and, as Bobby Hart would comment to writer Ari Bass, "The wrong crowd with unlimited access to large amounts of cocaine."[15]

Her relationship with *Playboy* would continue until the end of her life. Whether she would have kept posing for Hugh Hefner is not certain. Her adopted brother Keith Jennings swears that she told him her 1979 pictorial was to be her last. After all, Claudia was turning 30, and the teenager from Evanston who had used her *Playboy* experience to her benefit for 10 years had come to realize that it had turned into a double-edged sword. She hadost a few roles because of her pictorials, and no matter how many convincing performances she gave, some in Hollywood would always dismiss her as just another Playmate pretending to be an actress. There was also another pictorial shot in Greece that never appeared in the magazine, as Claudia's death occurred shortly before it was to run.

Claudia seemed to be bound to Hugh Hefner and *Playboy* for better or worse. Her first pictorial hinted (Bruce Williamson stated) that she was on her way to Los Angeles to audition for a film role. By the time her Playmate of the Year pictorial hit

Claudia with Jack Nicklaus (left) and singer Andy Williams at the San Diego Open Golf Tournament

the newsstands, Claudia used the money from her first shoot to relocate. She flew out to California, away from the cold Chicago winters and the chilling atmosphere of her parents' home. A few years later, Hugh Hefner would buy the Playboy Mansion West, near UCLA and Beverly Hills. The Chicago Mansion would be torn down eventually, and million-dollar condos soon replaced the Midwestern Xanadu, where the sign on the door once said, in Latin. "If you don't swing, then don't ring."

Hugh Marston Hefner passed away on September 27, 2017. His passing marked the end of an era in American media and culture. Hef touched many lives in a positive way, and Hollywood will not seem the same without him. The magazine is facing challenging times, and the Mansion has been sold and will now pass on to strangers. The man who dominated American entertainment for a staggering 64 years is gone.

All this was still in the future, though, as Claudia was now ready, at the age of 21, to seek her fortune in show business. In little over a year, Mimi Chesterton had gone from an unknown graduate from Evanston Township High to one of the most famous women in the world. She had a new name and a new career, yet she seemed to still hold onto her best qualities. Further glory awaited Claudia, but there was a narrow, unappealing alley of shadows between the Mansions, studios and nightclubs. Those lights drew her in, and Claudia, like a fragile butterfly, only saw the brightness and not what hid in the darkness. Los Angeles was the place that summoned Claudia to meet her destiny, a terminus appropriately referred to as the City of Angels.

Shortly before she left Chicago, Claudia took with her a picture of her sister Julie and a poem written by Constance. She would bring these with her on location whenever she was filming. They were a poignant reminder of the past that Claudia could never fully part with—the innocent Mimi Chesterton.

[1] Watts, Dr. Steven, *Mr. Playboy: Hugh Hefner and the American Dream* (Hoboken: Wiley & Sons Inc., 2009), pp.29-32
[2] *Ibid*, pp. 45-67
[3] *Ibid*, pp. 70-90
[4] *Ibid.* pp. 94-101
[5] "Acting Playmate," *Playboy* Vol. 16, No. 11, November 1969
[6] *Ibid.*
[7] *Ibid.*
[8] Bass, Ari, telephone interview with Tom Staebler, 1998
[9] Bass, Ari, telephone interview with Marilyn Grabowski, 1998
[10] Macklin, Tony, "The Ballad of Stella Stevens," *Bright Lights Film Journal*, July 31, 2004
[11] Watts, *op. cit.*, pp. 331-336
[12] *Ibid.*
[13] *Ibid.*
[14] *Ibid.*
[15] Bass, Ari, telephone interview with Bobby Hart, 1995

Chapter 4:
Fairy Tale 1970-1975

Claudia loved being in Los Angeles. It was everything she thought it would be. No more Chicago winters; the movie and television industries were at their peak; the music industry was gravitating to the West Coast; and it seemed the nation's culture was tilting toward California. There were beaches, spectacular sunsets, glamorous restaurants, exciting clubs and talented, dynamic people. Claudia even found time to start dating a bona fide television star, Michael Cole, from *The Mod Squad*. However, things were only warming up for the redheaded beauty. Claudia had auditioned for, and landed, a small part in a motion picture, *Jud*.

Jud (aka *Savage Soldier, One Too Many Mornings*) (1971)

This was Claudia's first professional film appearance after her first *Playboy* pictorial and shortly before she was named Playmate of the Year. Let's talk about the positives first. Claudia is extremely lovely, and has a brief role as a young hippie that the title character Jud meets in a coffee shop. She's gentle, sensitive and understanding of a character who is clearly disturbed. How do we know he's disturbed? After he and Claudia make love on the beach, he's still morbidly depressed. I'm positive audiences were thrilled to see Claudia nude and thrashing around, and her name and visage were used to promote the film despite the fact her screen time is limited. In a way, this embodied many of Claudia's early roles. Show her body, say a few lines (perhaps) and exit stage left. Her notoriety as Playmate of the Year, announced post-production, would secure roles and provide a strong advertising hook. These films most assuredly put the "show" in show business.

The fame from her *Playboy* pictorials had helped her secure the part. The movie and the role were nothing spectacular. If Claudia had looked closely, she would have seen two irreversible trends in her career staring back at her, typified by this film. The first was she would almost without fail have to disrobe. The second, and one Claudia never seemed able to change, was that these movies were not of the quality she desired. Her *Playboy* appearances had left a stain on her movie ambitions. The movie roles she accepted served in great part just to wipe the stain around, not remove it. Claudia was thrilled to have gotten the part, despite the fact that it wasn't exactly the sort of role she wanted. In Claudia's mind, as explained to me by her good friend cinematographer Ferd Sebastian, the work was more important than the particular film. I can't help but wonder, however, if with each film that exploited her *Playboy* image, a portion of Claudia's self-esteem peeled away.

Bobby Hart told me that Claudia's motivation for accepting a role was money. Once her career gained some traction, she would turn down a smaller part in an A-level film for a better-paying B-movie opportunity, in which she had the lead role. By the time Claudia's feelings shifted concerning her career, it was unfortunately shortly before she died.

The film's back-stories are more interesting than the film itself. Stu Phillips, a veteran B-movie composer, did the music, and later wrote the theme for the *Battlestar Galactica* television series. Bob Dylan wrote the title song ("One Too Many Mornings"), but the producer, who had mixed feelings about the final title, did not use it for the name of the film. Speaking of the title, the movie was released under several more than the ones listed above.

One of the film's extras was John "Bud" Cardos, who, if he'd spent his career in A-list films, might be considered in the same category as John Huston or Alfred Hitchcock. In some ways, he was even more versatile. Cardos was one of the original child actors in Hal Roach's **Our Gang** comedies, and had a short career as a rodeo rider. He then spent years as an animal wrangler for movie productions and was a bird handler on Alfred Hitchcock's *The Birds*. From there, Cardos worked as a stunt man, with stints as an actor in between. Cardos was a second unit director on Sam Peckinpah's classic *The Wild Bunch*, tried his hand as production manager on several films and eventually directed several of his own features. If that wasn't enough, he painted Western art in his spare time.

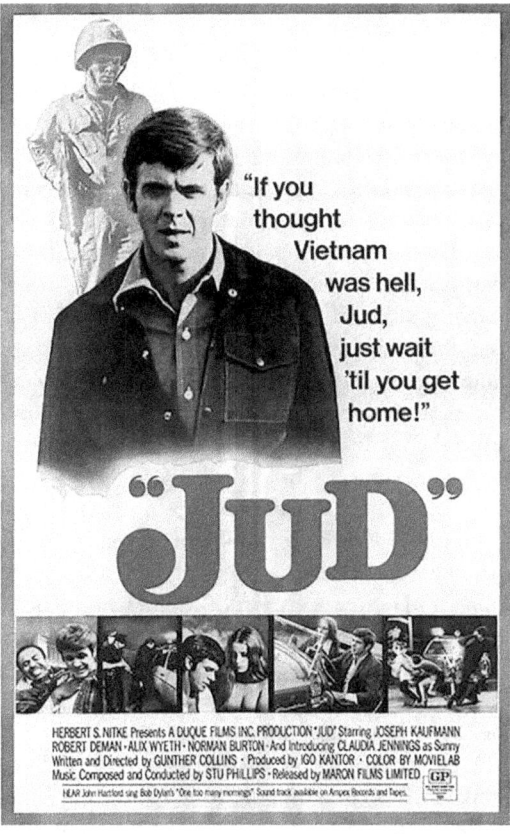

I'm not saying there is a connection, but this was director Gunther Collins' one and only film. The star of the movie, Joseph Kaufmann, had a relatively short career, but appeared in the fine Dalton Trumbo-penned anti-war film *Johnny Got His Gun*. Other than that bright moment, Joseph acted in B-movies until he disappeared from the profession.

Jud is a movie that we want to like, if not enjoy. Its premise is serious and universal, as it concerns the effect of war on our returning service members. Handled in a different manner, the film may have become a minor classic, but everything about it screams "Pay attention to this!" to the point where we can't work up much sympathy for the main character—or the film for that matter. An unfortunate state of affairs when dealing with an important and solemn topic! The production values are far from first-rate, but rather than contributing to the feeling of isolation and paranoia of our antihero, the film just looks cheap.

A young Marine, emotionally and mentally bruised, returns from Vietnam and comes back to Los Angeles, where it appears everything has changed. The people he was fighting to protect see him as a malevolent force; no one shows him respect, and in a final insult, his fiancée has made other arrangements. With nowhere to go and no other human connections, he moves into a cheap boarding house. The boarding house is chock full of stereotypical lowlifes, and once more, the grotesque nature of the inhabitants turn what could be an intelligent commentary about the disenfranchised of society into a pretty sad joke. Everyone living there is as hapless and defeated by life as Jud, but the film presents them as carnival creatures rather than human beings. The apartment building itself looks like it belongs on a military base, which does add a bit of flavor and wry commentary to the *mise-en-scène*.

Poor Jud does not fare well, I'm afraid, new friend or not. He's suffering from flashbacks as well as nightmares of massacres and other horrors of war. Most of the movie consists of meaningless encounters that barely count as action. When the movie isn't focusing on these pointless non-events, it unsuccessfully tries to convey a deep examination of Jud's character. These attempts, along with all the serious issues that *Jud* raises, are handled in such a sloppy manner that they completely drain any sincerity from the picture's narrative.

The film is brightened, albeit briefly, when Jud decides he needs a cup of coffee. He stops by the local diner and meets Sunny (Claudia), whose name is not an accident. They hit it off. She feels empathy and sympathy towards him, and is one of the first people he meets who doesn't judge him. He's attracted to her because, well, she's Claudia Jennings and one of the most beautiful women on Earth, and she treats him like a human being. In many ways, this scene shows Claudia as she was most likely away from the camera. Yes, she could play a psychopath at times, but most of her roles were complex, multi-dimensional characters. Pay particular attention to her eyes, the tilt of her head, her body language and, above all, her mouth. Enticed by the sound of the surf and the closeness of each other's bodies, Sunny and Jud meander their way to the beach. They make love in the sand and Jud begins to feel that maybe things aren't so bad after all. An amusing note about this scene: apparently it was filmed on a public beach, with the actors and crew having to scramble before the police came and busted them.

The remainder of the film doesn't go well for Jud. Sunny, being a free spirit, splits; this one dude at the boarding house keeps bugging him (it is strongly implied the man is gay) and some jack-hole goads him into a fight. Jud hops in his convertible and seemingly drives around the entire Los Angeles area, as if that is going to do him any good. Anyone living in an urban area knows that dealing with traffic and other drivers is not good therapy.

By the end of the film, we are wondering why Jud hung around an apartment building filled with people who were equally or more screwed up than he was. The filmmakers also take a serious theme and treat it as exploitation fodder. *Jud* is a dark, depressing experience, but a pointless one. As usual for most of her movies, Claudia's appearance is the one redeeming quality. Imagine an incredibly dark day filled with rain, fog and a sick gray mist. All of a sudden, a golden shaft of light penetrates the dank, dreary atmosphere. It is Claudia bringing some beauty, love, and hope into the world.

TV Guide panned the film, saying, "A trite and utterly dishonest portrayal of a returning Vietnam veteran (Kaufmann) and the adjustments he must make. When Kaufmann discovers his fiancée has left him, he moves into a boarding house peopled with 'types.' Flashback memories of the war and the suicide of a fellow house resident add to the depressing atmosphere."

Anxious to get her career going, Claudia auditioned for a role in the touring company of *The Tender Trap*. She won the part and began traveling around the West and Southwest. In Little Rock, Arkansas, at the Old West Theater, she met a fellow actress who would become her friend. Victoria Hale was a stunning young woman who was also looking toward an acting career and a life in L.A.

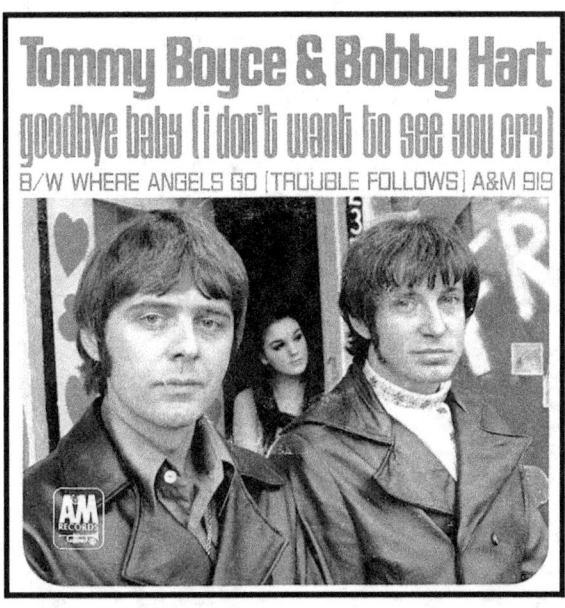

The two returned to Los Angeles after touring, when Claudia decided to invite Victoria to be one of her roommates. She had rented a three-story house on Gramercy Place and needed one more person to share the home. Another acquaintance of Claudia's, Allison Granno, personal assistant of Jess Rand—who was managing the Lettermen (the musical group, not the talk show host) and Jeff Chandler, among others—was living there as well. Claudia had moved in with her friend and noted television music director Frank Jaffe when she first arrived in Los Angeles. When Jaffe moved out, that left a spot for Victoria. The three bonded quickly, and before long were best friends.

Claudia was beginning to enjoy an active social life. She had been dating Michael Cole from television's *The Mod Squad*. The show was a major hit, and Cole was a dashing figure around Los Angeles. He was an older man with handsome dark features, and he and Claudia made a good couple. Claudia met a few other men out there, though, including Warren Beatty and Jack Haley, Jr., and soon told Cole they were through. Michael had very deep feelings for Claudia and took the news very hard. She kept Warren Beatty company for a while; she apparently really liked him, and each party saw the affair for what it was. They were a matched set, interested in having sex and fun without regret or complications. Claudia reportedly told her friend Marcia Wallace, "Every woman should experience Warren Beatty once in her life."[1]

However, Allison Granno noticed Claudia looking through her address book one day, asking questions about the individual names written in there. When Claudia asked Allison about one particular fellow, Allison said, "Oh, yeah, he's a good-looking guy; you'll like him." His name was Bobby Hart, and he had a reputation as a ladies' man. Divorced with two small children, he had left his mark on the popular music industry, with an exclamation point. He had originally wanted to be a disc jockey and moved to Los Angeles in 1958. The lean, handsome Hart soon became friends with Barry Richards, a singer-songwriter and record producer. They formed a twist band that was a fixture in Los Angeles and Las Vegas, performing for many years.

A Biography

Then, one day, Barry Richards introduced Bobby Hart to another gentleman who was to influence the rest of his life. The person was Tommy Boyce, an affable Virginian who was also multi-talented. He and Bobby started writing dozens of songs. The pair moved to New York, where they became part of the Brill Building Group of musicians and songwriters, whose ranks included the likes of Neil Sedaka, Teddy Randazzo, Don Costa, Barry Mann, Cynthia Weil and Carole King. It was there Boyce and Hart composed a huge hit for Jay and the Americans, "Come a Little Bit Closer."

In 1965, Boyce and Hart decided the grass was greener back in Los Angeles. It turned out to be an inspired and life-changing decision. The duo was soon asked to write and perform music for a Screen Gems TV faux-rock and roll band called The Monkees, with inspiration derived from the Beatles' frenetic musical comedies *A Hard Day's Night* and *Help!* Boyce and Hart penned over 30 of The Monkees' hits. In between, they found time to compose the theme for the soap opera *Days of our Lives*, which was used for over 50 years. After *The Monkees* ended, the duo kept working and penned five hits for A&M Records.

When Boyce and Hart parted ways in 1970, Bobby Hart would collaborate with Danny Janssen to write the music and lyrics for the cartoon show and band *Josie and the Pussycats*. A young singer in the group, Cheryl Stoppelmoor—only 16 at the time—would eventually become a good friend of Claudia's. She is more commonly known by her married name, Cheryl Ladd, and she became one of the stars of *Charlie's Angels*.

Bobby was left to pursuits that were more pleasurable after his split from Hart. At first, he showed only mild interest in Allison's roommate, until he finally called the house and was told Claudia wasn't home, she was shooting her Playmate of the Year pictorial. Bobby's interest was piqued, and he had to wait patiently until Claudia returned from her shoot. Shortly after her first pictorial hit the newsstands, Claudia found out she was named Playmate of the Year. The June 1970 issue featured a faux psychedelic photograph of Claudia on the front cover. The cover, while perhaps not the best in *Playboy*'s storied history, does show off Claudia's remarkable eyes and face to a decided advantage. The article catches the readers up to what had been going on in Claudia's life, and that she had been chosen for a part on a comedy album by Bill Cosby, which featured actress Susan St. James and comedian Sandy Barron. The article also discussed the tour of *The Tender Trap*, where Claudia had met Victoria Hale.[2] Claudia had an appearance on a TV special, *The Nudity Thing*, about, well, nudity in the arts. The pictorial also gave us the sad news that Claudia's Samoyed, who charmed us in her Playmate of the Month shoot, had been dog-napped. However, in the truest sense of *Playboy*'s values and the wave of consumerism that it helped create and championed, the article tells us about all the swag that came along with the title of Playmate of the Year. Looking back from our present day, some of the prizes seem a bit peculiar, but in context of the early 1970s, it must have seemed that Playboy gave Claudia everything a bright, talented, hip woman would need. There was a "Playmate pink" Capri, a Harley-Davidson Rapido motorcycle, a ski trip to Vail for two, a Schwinn bike, jewelry, a rabbit-skin ski jacket, a set of snow skis, boots and poles. But wait, there's more! She could take pictures of her trip with a new Minox camera, and write about it on her new Smith Corona Electra typewriter (some of you younger readers may want to ask an elder what a typewriter is). The article also describes the various jewelry, fashions, sunglasses and swimsuits that were prizes. Some of the more interesting prizes were referred to as items "to keep her supplied with contemporary sounds. Claudia gets a cassette recorder [find that elder, again] and [cassette] library from Capitol and an LP library from Mercury, and her career may acquire a new dimension as a result of the recording contract awarded by Monument [Records, Inc.]."[3]

If you had read that the last gift was given to most Playmates of the Year, you would have figured, cynically, that it was just a cruel joke to make it seem like a big deal. In 99.9% of the cases, you would have been correct. Remember, though, Claudia was a polished and talented vocalist. As far as we know, Claudia never took advantage of the contract for some reason. There is no doubt that if she wanted to pursue a career in music, she could have, considering she lived with Bobby Hart, who had numerous connections within the music industry for over five years.

The list of goodies aside, the article shows us a rather businesslike and sober Playmate. Claudia is duly grateful, and mentions that being in *Playboy* has earned her many fans for which she expresses her sincere thanks. She does not sound like a Playmate, for she speaks about realistic, day-to-day challenges. She states firmly (and correctly) that the film industry is changing, and that she is glad she is going to be a part of it. Claudia does tell us the film she secured a part in—originally called *One Too Many Mornings* but released as *Jud* or *The Savage Soldier*—dealt with a soldier returning from Vietnam to find the country he left does not welcome him home as a hero. She summarizes the plot articulately, and finishes by saying, "I'm glad to be associated with a film that tries to deal seriously with a serious subject."[4]

Claudia's June 1970 Playmate of the Year pictorial would be a positive turning point in her career, as far as getting movie offers. Her extraordinary beauty captured everyone's attention, of course; and her combination of talent and intelligence, combined with a down-to-earth sense of humor, made her a very hot commodity in the entertainment world. Her future endeavors could now be advertised with "Starring 1970 Playmate of the Year Claudia Jennings," not an inconsequential bit of marketing to have. The only questions, it seemed, were how far she would go and would success spoil her as it had so many others?

Claudia's friend from Evanston had an interesting story about her after she moved out of Chicago:

> I got a call from one of my old fraternity brothers, Tom Callaway. In 1969, Playmate of the Year Jo Collins visited the town and the social committee appointed Tom to be her escort. Legend has it he ended up in Ms. Collins' motel room and spent the evening. Well, he was aware I knew Claudia, and he asked me to get in touch with her. I suppose he wanted to try and make a matched set of Playmate conquests.

Mr. Callaway is an impressively talented man. He was an accomplished painter, then tried his hand at acting and eventually ended up starting an ultra-successful home decorating concern catering to the royalty of Los Angeles. When contacted Mr. Callaway shared the following story with me:

> I was a very confident young man at that time, and given Claudia's sexy reputation, I was fairly sanguine about the possibility of hooking up with her. My experience with Jo Collins, I thought, had prepared me for the encounter. She was living in New York then, so when I got a hold of Claudia, I made dinner reservations at a luxury restaurant. Well, the evening didn't quite go as planned. From the moment she sat down, Claudia looked bored to tears. It was an awkward experience, to say the least. When dinner was over, she left as soon as she could. I didn't see her again until we were both living in L.A in the late '70s and I happened to be driving down the street. I looked up, and to my surprise, there was Claudia, walking alone. She asked for a ride, and I dropped her at the address she'd given me. I thought it was a little strange at the time.

Back to Bobby Hart ... when Claudia returned from the pictorial, Bobby was finally able to get her to go out with him. He and Claudia went out to dinner and ended up spending the night together. An amusing aspect to this story is the following account from Constance Chesterton:

> Allison later told me, before Claudia's date with Bobby, that the two of them made a bet Claudia would end up sleeping with him, because he was really good-looking and very charming. Claudia said she wouldn't, but when she eventually did, she left Bobby's house early in the morning to try and sneak back into the house on Gramercy Place. The ruse didn't work and Claudia lost the bet. But she won Bobby.

As far as Bobby Hart was concerned, he had possibly met a woman with whom he could have a sustained relationship. Claudia was a great-looking gal, of course, but her personality was the real attraction. She was always up, and always full of energy. If anyone ever needed advice or help, she was never too busy to oblige.

Claudia was clearly attracted to the handsome musician; however, he was in no rush to formalize the relationship. Bobby invited her to a concert and, afterwards, Claudia told him she wasn't looking for a fling. She didn't exactly give him an ultimatum, but she made her feelings quite clear. Claudia pressed him for a commitment despite the relatively short time they had known each other. Bobby was not completely certain it was the right thing to do. Claudia was quoted as saying:

> I haven't ever lived with a guy before, but I tell you, when I make up my mind what's good for me, it probably is.[5]

Since Claudia was going away for a while, it would give Bobby some time to ponder the situation.

The girls had made friends with Chuck Barris, the producer of *The Dating Game*, through their friend and former roommate Frank Jaffe, the show's production assistant. He then arranged for Claudia to appear on *The Dating Game*. She won a trip to Greece with her "date" and was allowed to take one friend along. Claudia chose Victoria.

Off the girls went with the male winner, Phil, his friend Mike and *The Dating Game*'s chaperone. They landed in Athens and did all the essential sightseeing. Victoria stated the ladies occupied one room and the gentlemen another; when it became apparent the situation was not going to change, the guys decided to head back to the United States.

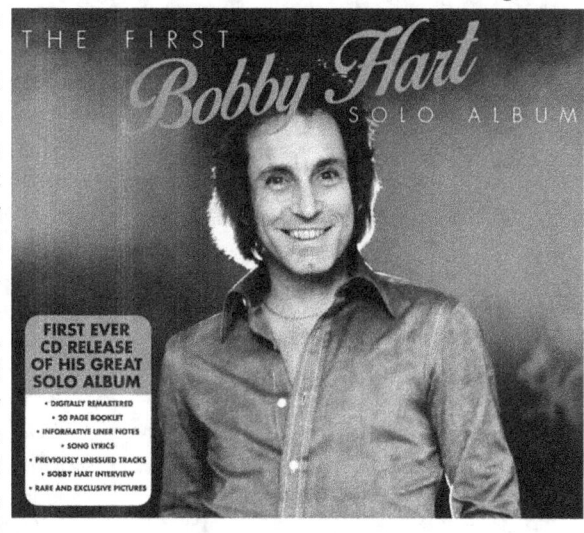

Victoria and Claudia decided, "Why waste a good trip to Europe?" and promptly flew to Rome. There, while touring the city, the girls had the good fortune to come upon the very handsome and rugged American actor Ty Hardin (first known for his starring role in Warner Bros.' cowboy TV series *Bronco*). Ty also starred in a wide variety of films from *I Married a Monster from Outer Space* to *Battle of the Bulge* and *Last Train from Gun Hill*. He befriended the young women and found them an apartment where they could stay.[6] Victoria recalls they had no money and had to keep going to the Western Union and American Express offices to get enough funds to continue their stay. The owner of the apartment, Massimo Serato, was a well-known Italian actor. He was famous (or infamous) for having an affair with actress Anna Mangnani while she was married to director Goffredo Alessandrini. Serato was delighted to have two beautiful American women stay at his flat on the *Via Vittorio Veneto*, more commonly called the *Via Veneto*. Can you imagine the impression this must have left on a young woman barely out of her teens? Claudia must have gazed out of the apartment's windows onto the opulent stores and the well-dressed men and women and imagined what it would be like to actually be a part of such a life, rather than be merely an observer. Of course, who would not have such thoughts? After a short while, Massimo made it clear that there was a *quid pro quo* involved in the arrangement.

A Biography

Claudia and Victoria were unwilling to give Mr. Serato a *quid* or a *quo*, whereupon he promptly threw them out.[7]

The girls' luck held up as they ran into a friendly *Marchese*, who gave them the keys to his flat on the Piazza di Spagna, one of the most beautiful and historic landmarks in the Eternal City. The ladies stayed in Rome a few more weeks and then returned to America. All the time Claudia was in Europe, Bobby stayed in touch, and the two began to discuss their lives, dreams, hopes and futures. He began to appreciate Claudia as a person, not just a beautiful woman. Claudia gradually became aware she was falling in love with him.

When she came back from Europe, the two of them had a long talk, and soon Claudia moved into Bobby's two-bedroom house. During this time period, Claudia won a role in the revival of the off-Broadway show, *Dark of the Moon*, and she moved to New York for six months. She was magnificent in the production, and the show had a strong cast including future television stars Earl Hindman (*Home Improvement*), Rue McClanahan (*The Golden Girls*) and Marcia Wallace (*The Bob Newhart Show*). Wallace became a lifelong friend. John Simon, the drama critic for the *New York Times* and a man considered evil incarnate by many in the acting community, said of Claudia's performance:

> She is a completely lovely girl with something sensitive, vulnerable, perhaps even haunted in her eyes and around her mouth. She makes a spotlight light up as no wattage could do it. At all times she makes you forget the dismalness of the show she is trapped in, and such a shot in the arm can set an un-fabulous invalid like our theater dancing.

Playmate Claudia Jennings strives to be an actress

By DONALD FREEMAN
Copley News Service

HOLLYWOOD — Auburn-haired, bright, full of ginger, Claudia Jennings is a fine-looking young actress who starred in the Off-Broadway production of "Dark of the Moon" last summer and won bouquets from the sternest critics.

There was this garland, for instance, from John Simon, a New York drama critic whose thorny prose usually reflects a curled lip of disdain. "When she is supposed to look beautiful, she makes a spotlight light up as no wattage could," Simon wrote about Claudia. "At all times, she makes you forget the dismalness of the play she is trapped in, and such a shot in the arm can set an unfabulous invalid like our theater dancing."

With a background that includes studies at Northwestern University's school of speech and the Goodman Theater in Chicago, Miss Jennings is of the stage and she has trouped in stock and repertory across the land. She has one of the top roles in the movie, "The Love Machine," based on Jacqueline Susann's best-seller, and soon to be released.

Television roles are starting to come her way now and she says she would like best to guest in a "Name of the Game." "They do good things on that show," she says. "They have good scripts, good people. I think it's the best right now of the television dramas."

Mostly, on television, Claudia has turned up on the talk shows, making the rounds with Johnny Carson, Dick Cavett, Merv Griffin and David Frost. In that regard, it helps matters that Miss Jennings is Playboy's 1970 Playmate of the Year. "The Playmate of the Year," she explains, "reigns from June to June. It's like a fiscal year."

MISS JENNINGS was given her title last June and shortly thereafter she was starring Off-Broadway and summoned for the first of her two appearances on the Johnny Carson Show.

She sat now, dipping into the minestrone at a Hollywood restaurant, and recalled that melancholy first session with Carson. "There I was, sandwiched between Buddy Hackett and Alan King," she said. "That was it — me and the two comics and one of them, Buddy Hackett, was sauced to the gills, which is no secret because everybody could see him. Buddy was yelling polite little things at me like, 'Got the staple in the navel, honey?'"

"My first national talk show and here I got a juiced-up comic to contend with. No way can I ever hope to match wits with professional comics so I just sat there and tried not to shrink into the chair. It was a battle of survival. Every time I'd try to answer a question, Buddy Hackett would holler some doubtful witticism.

AND THERE was the night on the David Frost Show, Claudia recalled, when she came on with Miss USA. "Big!" Claudia said. "I mean this Miss USA was big. I'd been working long hours on the play and I'd lost weight. Next to Miss USA, I looked like a waif.

"Well, David Frost makes the anouncement that 'we have two beauty title winners here tonight,' and we walk out, Miss USA and me, and we sat down.

"Whereupon David turns to Miss USA, who is all of 18 years old, and he purrs: 'We understand you pose in the nude in public.' the poor girl just stammered. David had simply assumed, looking at this voluptuous amazon, that SHE was Playmate of the Year and that I was Miss USA.

"I lifted a finger at David and corrected him. 'Wrong,' I said. 'It's me.' The audience went into hysterics."

Lowell Sun, June 12, 1971

72   Claudia Jennings

This was an incredibly perceptive observation of Claudia as a person and actress. It is easy to understand how her appeal came across better on stage. In the B-motion pictures she starred in, the quality of the cameras and film did not do Claudia Jennings justice. Her movies did not have the production values of the top vehicles she so desperately wanted. On the other hand, Claudia won universal praise for her theater appearances. Claudia made the most of her stay in New York. She dated Johnny Carson for a while when he was going through his nasty divorce.

Unfortunately, after returning from her triumphant New York stay, Claudia was hospitalized for exhaustion, which manifested itself in a series of seizures. Hart theorized that the cause was B12 vitamin shots, juiced with amphetamines, which doctors had administered to boost her energy for the grueling performance schedule. The practice was apparently common in those days. Hart said despite her reputation as an action star and a very tough cookie, she was actually quite frail.

Back in California, Victoria Hale tells of an odd incident that happened in Claudia's early days in Hollywood.

> In those times, just about everyone went to psychics or palm readers. It was the thing to do. We went to a psychic and she did Claudia's reading. The woman told her that she saw a horrific car crash in her future before she would turn thirty.

Years later, Claudia would seek out other spiritualists. She told friends and family that none of the palm readers, tarot card readers and the like could tell her anything about her life past age thirty.

These stories add a rather eerie backdrop to Claudia's story. If you look at her life as a Shakespearian tragedy, which it arguably was, this certainly fits perfectly as a harbinger of bad things to come. Think of the three witches in *Macbeth* who predict his end. The circumstances of Claudia's death get even more bizarre as we much later make our way to the very morning her life ended.

Around this time, it began to dawn on Claudia that her *Playboy* notoriety would not bring her instant success. In the next few years, she would win roles that capitalized on her Playmate of the Year notoriety, and in some cases, display her considerable acting skills. Everyone connected with the productions unanimously agreed that Claudia was completely professional, down to earth and a lot of fun to work with.

There were several movies that I call Claudia's "popcorn films"—if you went to the lobby for popcorn, you'd miss her appearance. The following is a great example.

The Love Machine (1971)

One of the first boyfriends Claudia had in Hollywood was Jack Haley, Jr., son of the beloved "Tin Man" from *The Wizard of Oz*. After dating her briefly, Haley offered her a small part in the film adaptation of Jacqueline Susann's *Roman a clef*, *The Love Machine*. Haley told Ari Bass:

> Claudia had been a personal friend of mine. So I was doing this picture with a lot of beautiful girls in it, and I said, Claudia, let's do it. You know, Claudia

was a real live wire; she was great fun to be around. When she did *The Love Machine*, it was a lark for her ... It was not a major career move ...

The film wasn't exactly a major career move for anyone involved in the project. Despite the Burt Bacharach-Hal David tune sung by Dionne Warwick, "He's Moving On," *The Love Machine* is a perplexing semi-bomb, veering from soap opera to comedy and finally outright embarrassment. Looked at as a comedy, it's a campy delight, except for a Susann-specialty suicide and a scene where the lead character beats the hell out of a prostitute. These scenes twist the movie into a turgid melodrama and remove any sense of light-heartedness. There's a lot of gay bashing and homophobia, but this was the early 1970s, so it's fortunate that a gay character even ended up in the film.

The plot centers around an irresistible TV newscaster, Robin Stone (John Phillip Law), who rises to the head of the network and weaves a spell around every woman he meets, eventually getting the wife (Dyan Cannon) of the network chief (Robert Ryan) to fall for him.

Apparently, the actor slated to play Stone suffered a severe injury in an automobile accident shortly before production was to begin, with Law cast as a replacement, and his performance brings many things to mind—mainly inanimate objects. His emotional range in the film varies from vacant to somnambulistic. Some critics described his performance as being identical to his character's name, but that's too easy. He's more like a wax figure: remarkably lifelike, but incapable of living.

Robin cheats on his girlfriend, Amanda, with Claudia, who shows up about 24 minutes into the film. Darlene (Claudia) asks for something to eat and Robin directs her to the fridge. We do get to see her naturally glorious red hair and hear her precarious Southern accent (why did so many directors insist on Claudia playing Southern girls, I wonder?). I've seen more revealing HAZMAT suits than the bathrobe our girl is wearing in this scene, so I'd have to say Claudia's presence is pretty much wasted in the film.

However, if you want to sit through the rest of this cinematic gem, there are some highlights. The fashions, men's and women's are a hoot. Dyan Cannon, to show you what a beautiful woman she is, manages to wear even the most ridiculous-looking outfit with class. Comedian Shecky Greene manages to be unfunny, except for his clothes, which take on a life of their own. The young starlet who plays the model Amanda, Jodi Wexler, although not a great actress, had a certain look and aura about her which seemed to indicate some success for the future. For reasons unknown, she never made another film after *The Love Machine*.

The absolute best thing about the movie is the protracted ending—and no, I'm not speaking of the credits. There is a huge "bitch" brawl, which pits Dyan Cannon versus

Robin, gay photographer Nelson (David Hemmings) and Nelson's big gay lover. It degenerates into a food fight, with Ms. Cannon and Hemmings spooning jiggly stuff off platters and chafing dishes into each other's hair.

This film must have an all-time list of cameo appearances: Jacqueline Susann herself; the voice of Don Rickles; the first twin Playmates of the Month, Mary and Madeleine Collinson; Liv Lindeland, another Playmate of the Year and the first that revealed pubic hair in her pictorial; and lovely actress and model Gayle Hunnicutt. Ms. Hunnicutt was married to David Hemmings at the time, which explains her presence. Pointedly, Jack Haley, Jr. didn't make any more regular features. He concentrated on directing and producing documentaries and television shows, mostly about the entertainment industry, and was very successful. Evidently, John Phillip Law ended up having a good experience on the film after all. He gave each of the female stars an ankh medallion, the symbol of the film. There is a striking pose of Claudia wearing hers here in the book.

Claudia wears the Ankh pendant given her by the star of *The Love Machine*, Jan-Michael Vincent.

Roger Greenspun of the *New York Times* wrote on August 6, 1971:

> About *The Love Machine*, which opened yesterday at the Loew's State 2 and Orpheum Theaters: I'm not sure how to put it, but the book is better. Anyone who has stumbled through *Valley of the Dolls* and even beyond, hoping for yet another camp masterpiece in the tradition of, say, *Youngblood Hawke*, will know what I mean. And he may go right on stumbling. For although *The Love Machine* has enough dumb lines to qualify as a veritable anthology of unintentional humor, it hasn't the energy or the wit or, finally, the commitment to its own absurdities to provide the exhilarating sense of life that is the real appeal of the good-bad movie.

These modest successes did not deter Claudia from playing the part of a successful, intelligent, savvy, self-assured Hollywood sex goddess. She was getting used to the Hollywood lifestyle and feeling more comfortable as Claudia Jennings. The good times and toys that came with the world she had entered felt natural as they became more and more familiar to her.

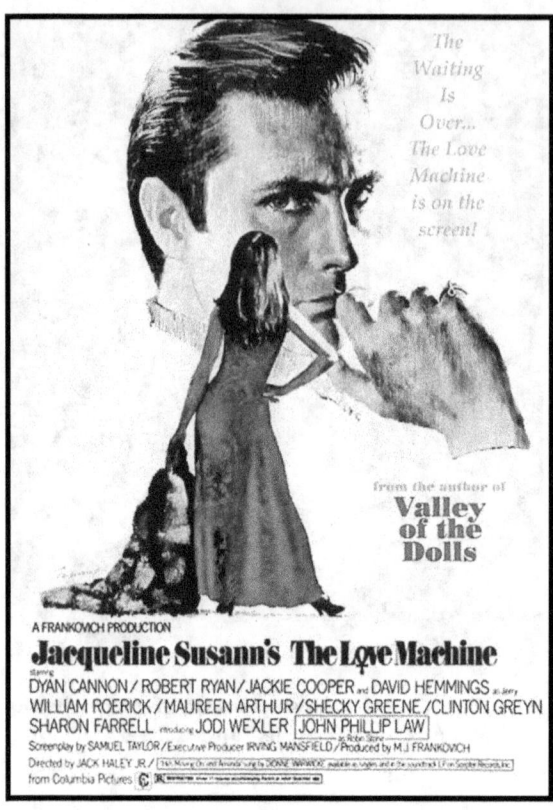

She felt confident enough to give an interview to the magazine *New Woman* in 1971. She declared that her work with *Playboy* was a necessary compromise in order to reach her ambitions. She said confidently that she was in "control" of her own destiny. She further explained that any notion that she was a "sex goddess" was a calculated move, and that she would never do anything like it again in her career. It is difficult to determine if this was a sincere statement on Claudia's part. Claudia would not only continue to do pictorials for *Playboy*, she would quite willingly shed her clothes in one film after another. Rather than hold Hugh Hefner and his empire at arm's length, she embraced them willingly.

As for her relationship with Hart, she stated: "He is totally sympathetic to everything I feel. We're completely committed to each other." She further posed herself as the ultimate feminist role model by saying that the couple had no plans of ever marrying:

> I wish I could find one good reason for marrying, but so far, I've only found reasons for not marrying. That document isn't going to make your relationship work, if it isn't a good one, so what's the point? Even if I were going to have children I wouldn't marry. Naturally I'd want to rear them with my man helping me, but a piece of paper won't keep him with me if he doesn't want to stay. The children wouldn't suffer from having unmarried parents because I wouldn't live in a community that would hurt them for it. I was reared a Catholic in the Midwest and I think I was taught a lot of harmful things. I wish I could believe in life after death, though, because it's such a nice thought. Reward for living a good life is so fair. I'd like to think its true, but I'm afraid I'm more of a realist than that.[8]

How Claudia truly felt was far more complex. According to Barry Richards and others, Claudia did want a family and did want to get married. She had seen the ugly side of marriage firsthand in her parents' declining relationship. This didn't prevent her from wanting to start a family of her own. Bobby Hart was older and had been through a divorce. He already had two children. His reluctance was quite easy to understand.

The differing view on marriage and children was the first micro-fracture in Bobby and Claudia's relationship.

Claudia soon introduced Bobby to her *Playboy* family. It took almost a year for Bobby to get on the notoriously difficult-to-crack guest list. Finally, invited to the Mansion one day, he met Hugh Hefner, and during one short game of Monopoly, divined much about the true nature of *Playboy*'s founder.

The story is in the book *Psychedelic Bubble Gum* by Bobby Hart with Glen Ballantyne:

> One morning after we had been together for a few months Claudia invited me up to the Playboy Mansion West to meet Hugh Hefner. Apparently it was a big deal to get a boyfriend on the guest list but she said, "We've been together long enough now to be seen as a couple and Hef says he's looking forward to meeting you."
>
> As evening shadows lengthened, Hef proposed a game of Monopoly and we settled around a table in one of the well-appointed sitting rooms of the Gothic structure. I was soon to find out that Mr. Hefner took his Monopoly very seriously. I had never prided myself as being an aggressive competitor when it came to board games. It seemed to me that the object of these contests was having fun. Within 10 minutes of realizing that I was on trial in some bizarre court of social acceptance, I had already failed my evaluation. On the way home, Claudia gave me a subtle lecture about staying more focused when I was around Hefner. "Hef has a genius IQ and he uses games like Monopoly as a method of sizing up new acquaintances, and it's easy to lose his respect if you don't stay on your toes."
>
> Mentally I was toying with my rebuttal, "Hugh Hefner might have to reawaken my respect, if I ever see him again." We never became close friends.[9]

Although Bobby stressed Hefner was always a gentleman and kept him on the guest list, it's apparent what dynamic was at work in this incident. Hef was staking out his territory as the alpha male, using backgammon, Monopoly and other board games in lieu of dueling. Moreover, the idea that a host would force a guest to "stay on their toes" seems to be the antithesis of a welcoming gesture. Bobby Hart, being a spiritual man, was largely immune to Hefner's provocation. Of course, there was an unspoken and perhaps even unconscious tension between all, considering that Claudia and Hefner had a brief intimate relationship.

The Rise of the Exploitation Film

Claudia made a name for herself by starring in what were called in her time B-films and drive-in movies. For the last 30 years, the term "exploitation film" has usurped the anachronistic descriptions of Claudia's time, the first reason being the rise of independent filmmakers and the second the demise of drive-in theaters.

Exploitation, as it pertains to cinema, by its definition means to use curiosity, a political point of view, sex, a particular fad, violence or anything lurid to target a particular audience as a means to make a profit. Filmmakers, especially the low-budget ones, will often use what they perceive to be the audience's worst instincts and then pander to

them. These movies manipulate the viewer psychologically to fulfill their desires and fantasies.

This subgenre has grown many branches over the years, to the point that several can coexist within a single film. For instance, a sexploitation film may also be a carsploitation film, a hicksploitation film, a slasher film or a blaxploitation film. What makes the exploitation film different from an A-list film with similar traits is the amount of analysis, sensitivity and exposition given to the subject at hand.

The perfect contrast-and-compare examples for modern audiences are the films *The Virgin Spring* (1960) and *The Last House on the Left* (1972). In director Ingmar Bergman's hands, *The Virgin Spring*, based on a 14th-century Swedish poem, is not only beautifully photographed and acted, it asks serious questions about religion, justice, guilt and whether human beings can truly cope with tragedy and loss.

The Last House on the Left's director, Wes Craven, admitted his inspiration was Bergman's film. Despite being a well-made movie, Craven's project turns into an exploitation nightmare full of rape, several graphic murders and an overall atmosphere of sleaze. It doesn't hurt that David A. Hess' portrayal of one of the murderers is authentically scary, and the lines between film and documentary blur when he is on camera. Where Bergman's film emphasized the philosophical and religious themes inherent in his story, Craven made sexual violence and gore paramount to his film. There is still an examination of man's nature and our race's penchant for violence, but it is subtle compared to the exploitive aspects of *The Last House on the Left*.

One other shining (no pun intended, honest) example would be *A Clockwork Orange* by Stanley Kubrick. A brilliant film, made from a superb novel, it still stands as a masterpiece after almost 50 years. If we took Kubrick's art, majestic score and budget away from the film and replaced Malcolm McDowell and the rest of the august cast with lesser actors, what would remain? It would have been only one of 100s of movies made in the 1970s with violence, rape, nudity and man's savagery as their compelling elements. Even with Kubrick's superior vision and storytelling abilities, many critics and audiences reacted with horror at what they saw on the screen. Remember, too, that Kubrick himself was shocked and sickened by the copycat crimes that followed. The critics' and public's main complaint was that *A Clockwork Orange* painted too grim a picture of our society's future, when the real cause of the upset was its accurate portrayal of our present. Kubrick requested and Warner Bros. pulled the film from U.K. distribution in 1973, one year after its release. He and his family had received death threats and dealt with angry demonstrators outside his home. Filmgoers in Britain would not be able to view the film for another 30 years.

Some directors of the most extreme exploitation films didn't have to expend the effort to restrict their viewing. To this day, there are some films made in the 1970s that remain banned in certain countries. It's odd that *The Texas Chain Saw Massacre* was banned in almost as many countries as the notorious *Cannibal Holocaust*, considering the latter has an abundance of gore, rape, cannibalism and the filming of animals actually being tortured and killed.[10] *The Texas Chain Saw Massacre*, although psychologically horrifying and full of violence, has less gore than an average episode of *The Real Housewives of Beverly Hills.*

Claudia entered the movie industry just as the exploitation film was gaining traction. Herschell Gordon Lewis had broken one of the first taboos with his extreme gore films (in gaudy color) of the early 1960s. As the decade moved forward, films became even more violent and filled with nudity. Rape and violence towards women became a staple of the film industry. Claudia came along at a perfect time to be a trendsetter, and as such, many modern actresses owe her a debt of thanks. She was one of the first female action leads in the movie business, and she got to kick ass instead of having hers pummeled. She was the most popular action star as well, surpassing a host of exploitation actresses such as Pam Grier, Roberta Collins, Dyanne Thorne, Sybil Danning and Cheri Caffaro as the undisputed queen of the exploitation film. These women were fine exploitation stars, but their performances, unlike Claudia's, tended to be self-conscious and bordered on self-parody at times.

Of course, one cannot discuss the genre of exploitation without mentioning its undisputed master, Roger Corman. Although many of his films were not exploitation vehicles, his production company, New World Pictures, gave the movie theaters of the world more spectacles than they could handle. Mr. Corman was a pioneer in many areas. He was renowned for discovering new talent, admired for the profitability and efficiency of his movie-making technique, and most important to this book, respected for his vision of creating a new paragon of actress.

In the book *Attack of the B Queens*, Justine Elias writes of Claudia:

> She made only a handful of films before her death in a car accident at the age of 29, but for a few years Claudia Jennings reigned as a drive-in goddess, as roguish and believably athletic as a young Burt Reynolds.[11]

The comparison is spot on, although Claudia had to reveal more of her body than Mr. Reynolds was ever required. Reynolds did reveal his frame in *Playgirl* and a few other publications, but the nudity wasn't as graphic as Claudia's pictorials (disappointing, I am sure, to his female admirers). The point being, Roger Corman saw the potential to make Claudia a new variety of star and succeeded beyond reasonable expectations.

As sex and violence in the B-movie universe became more widely accepted, the level of such activities evolved as well. The public saw an outpouring (literally) of cannibal and zombie films, with the undead or Amazonian tribes ripping intestines from the bodies of their still-living victims. As the atrocities of these films increased, the audiences required a bigger "high" to meet their needs. The original *Night of the Living Dead*, although still effective and well made, is less violent and gruesome than a handful of today's television programs, not to mention the underground culture of sado-porn represented by features like *A Serbian Film* or *August Underground*. Many people think the torture porn films of Eli Roth and others are a recent trend; actually, the Japanese Pinky Violence films of the 1970s, which were never exported to Western audiences until recently, were savage and full of sexual violence. The sophistication of special effects continues to gain momentum. The brilliance of Tom Savini is now being taken to a new level by a new wave of special effects artists. Masters such as Rob Bottin, Rick Baker and Giannetto De Rossi, along with directors such as Takashi Miike, Tom Six and Olaf Ittenbach, have been surpassed by a new wave of SFX artists who continue to delight and disgust audiences.

I believe it's important to pay homage to the great ancestor of the exploitation film. Man has always enjoyed watching theater or reading about scary or horrifying events. Shakespeare's plays were full of violence of every sort. In the middle ages, corpses and human body parts were used as theatrical props. However, in 1897, a new level of brutality was reached when *Le Théâtre du Grand Guignol* opened in Paris.

Translated as "The Big Puppet Show," the theater's traditions did in fact begin with puppet shows created in late 18th-century France. The character Guignol was a puppet that appealed to adults and children, much like the cartoons of modern America. Inserted into the slapstick was a fair amount of wit and sarcasm. The original audiences were the *canuts*, or silk weavers and their families, which was the occupation of Guignol's creator Laurent Mourguet.

When *Le Théâtre du Grand Guignol* opened, the concept of the puppet was expanded to let the audience know this would be a live performance with "flesh and blood" puppets. Dispensing with the classic theatrical narrative of Shakespeare and other writers, where violence and depravity served to give meaning to the plot, the plays of the *Grand Guignol* were an excuse to raise the illusion of torture and murder to the most realistic degree possible. Instead of the mild violence of the "Punch and Judy" puppet shows, the Theatre's spectacles featured full on mutilations, rapes and barbarity upon living human beings. The plays of the *Grand Guignol* displayed a different psychology from the puppet shows. The colorful characters made from cloth bashing each other with little clubs were closer to irony and humor than true violence. However, the Theatre showed something the audience couldn't dismiss, a live actor, being murdered or savaged, in a realistic manner.

The source material for the earliest plays were drawn from such authors as Guy de Maupassant, but more frequently from a young author named

André de Lorde. His stories were extremely gory, and included just about any depravity the human mind could think of. The plays of de Lorde celebrated the most extreme abuses of human behavior, that one wonders how much the Marquis de Sade influenced him. The police were not pleased with the subject matter and severely censored the stage productions; however, the restrictions relaxed and soon any perversion, horror and immoral act that one could dream of were acted out on a live stage. The Theatre was notorious for presenting the first prostitute character on the French stage. However, the most important contribution the Theatre made was its concept and the new tradition it started. Here was a form of horror that didn't draw its traditions from the European Gothic tradition. The Elizabethan and Jacobean plays gave some inspiration, but this heritage of horror came from the everyday lives in the Parisian street. Whatever the fear was—disease, murder, mutilation, rape or revenge—the *Grand Guignol* gave its audiences the chance to experience it vicariously.

The *Grand Guignol* exposed two nerves in its audiences that were quite remarkable. The plays were primarily about murder, revenge, rape, mutilation and other similar activities; yet, the audiences were far from repelled. Quite the opposite—many became sexually aroused and made love during the performances, in special enclosed seating areas set aside for the amorous. This phenomenon showed that the *Grand Guignol* was indeed a child of Sadean philosophy and formed a direct link between the perverse and sexual fantasy. Those who weren't spurred to spontaneous sexual behavior were thrilled at the bloodletting and packed the house each night. There was a small minority, because the effects were so far ahead of their time, which fainted or vomited during performances. The *Grand Guignol* predicted the rise of the exploitation film, with its unsavory themes, realistic gore and delirious celebration of torture, murder and sexual violence. There was also a theme of disorientation and the altering of consciousness from insanity, panic, hypnosis and drugs. Many of its plays had themes of total body destruction and disease, precursors to the films of David Cronenberg. The *Grand Guignol* plays also inextricably linked sex with horror in its audiences' psyches, which is a key to the popularity of the exploitation film. Somehow, the Theatre was able to secure that link between violence and sex and make it seem acceptable. Just as in exploitation movies, the plays of the *Grand Guignol* emphasized gory effects and terror over the narrative. The only reason the film industry took so long to break many of these barriers was restrictive censorship laws, which still continue to plague it today. The Theatre only showed a glimpse of how powerful the motion picture would be as a tool linking fantasy, desire and dread.

A film that gives a fairly good representation of what the *Grand Guignol* must have been like is a misogynistic gem called *Blood Sucking Freaks* (aka *The Incredible Torture Show* [1976]). Its excesses are too numerous to list, but suffice it to say the movie would make the Marquis de Sade blush. The film takes place in a theater where people are tortured and murdered on stage in front of an appreciative audience. It is a good example of an exploitation film that is also a cult classic. Of course not all cult films are exploitation movies, such as those by the Coen Brothers, and by the same token, not all exploitation films are cult classics.

It is interesting to note that most films of the exploitation genre to survive are the ones dealing with sex and horror. Carsploitation has all but vanished from the screens with the exception of the *Fast & Furious* franchise, and hicksploitation, unless combined with a generous dose of sex and horror, has faded away as well. However, the B-movies brought something to worldwide cinema that seems to have attached itself to the cerebral cord of both filmmaker and the audience.

Judging by what I have watched recently, exploitation films in general are getting more and more extreme. The trend seems to be to repeat what others have done, add more CGI effects and add jump scares by the truckload, as well as more sex, violence or both. Unfortunately, this is done more often than not to make up for the particular film's shortcomings. If the directors and writers could get more creative and put some thought into their projects, the trend would not be so unsettling.

There is no lack of talent, indicated by the number of well-made films in the past 20 years. However, the narratives, logic and intelligence of these movies have been sacrificed for an excessive amount of special effects, weak scripting and clichéd endings. There have been some truly brilliant independent films made in the past few years, some every bit as artistic and well made as the best of the past. However, the amount of remakes, reboots and re-imaginings of past films, not to mention the bane, with few exceptions, of sequels *ad nauseam* has not given us better and more original movies.

The *Grand Guignol* finally closed its doors in 1962. The shows weren't less exciting, but the audience's tastes were changing. World War II was more horrible than anything that could be replicated on stage. It is thus quite astonishing that in only a few years the movie screen would show more graphic horror than ever before, ushering in the age of the exploitation film.

All in all, I am comforted by the fact Claudia never ventured into the darker fringes of exploitation cinema.

The Stepmother (1972)

The year 1972 marked the busiest period in Claudia's professional life. She would barely have time to catch her breath between films and television appearances. Perhaps she should have thought twice about appearing in this murky potboiler about sex and murder, which takes place in Mexico. The filmmaking is almost as inept as *Jud*, the plot is barely coherent and the acting is cheesier than Olive Garden lasagna.

Whatever her reason for accepting the role, Claudia does her best and manages to stand out, a difficult task in a cast of veteran actors. We get to see her dance a little and speak a few lines of dialogue, and of course, she is heart-stopping beautiful. She has a full frontal nude scene that defines the word *gratuitous*. Of course, there are some other lovely women in the film, which is good because the producers had to give the audience a reason not to walk out. Sadly, Claudia's screen time is limited, but on second thought, maybe that's not a bad thing.

There is some talent in the cast, but it's a damning observation when Larry Linville from television's *M*A*S*H*, who plays architect Dick Hill, acts the pants off the rest of the gang. Alejandro Rey (most famous for his role in *The Flying Nun*) plays the main character, Frank Delgado. I'm sure there were evenings when, while filming, he was praying for Sally Field to fly him away. He is jazzed up in this film to the point where you imagine the dude is drinking way too much coffee, or he's totally pissed off at his agent. Katherine Justice, who plays Delgado's unfaithful wife Margo, was a regular on *Falcon Crest*, *The Guiding Light* and about 50 other television series. Veteran actor John Anderson, who appeared in *Psycho*, as well as *MacGyver* and *Dallas*, plays overzealous police detective

Darnezi, who is sort of an Inspector Javert to Delgado's Valjean.

Marlene Schmidt plays Hill's smoking hot wife Sonya, which was fitting considering she was a staple in many 1970s sexploitation films. Duncan McCloud of *Beneath the Valley of the Dolls* fame plays the Chief Inspector, and Rudy Herrera, Jr. plays Steve Delgado, the stepson. Claudia plays Rita, a pot-smoking hippie porn actress. Rounding out the cast is David Garfield, who plays Goof (seriously), a porn producer married to Rita. Garfield was the son of the late great actor John Garfield, and had a brief career as an actor and film editor. After watching his scenes, you'll understand why he never attained the same status his father did in Hollywood.

The movie sounds like it should have been a lot of fun; however, watching it is the mental equivalent of swimming through mud. Although the acting is decent, the directing and cinematography fall short. The camera work is uneven, with some excellent technique ruined by far too many soft-focus shots—the kind that make you think you've developed instant cataracts. There are jarring freeze frames and pretentious slow motion shots, none of them effective. There is also an arty attempt at a reappearing/disappearing shot of the detective that is supposed to show how whack Frank is becoming. The lighting is dim where it should be brighter and garish when it should be muted. There is enough nudity in the film to tease, but not enough sex to make it into genuine exploitation territory. The pace is tedious, hopping from the police station to the unfinished beach house. *The Stepmother* gives one the impression of a mediocre made-for-TV movie, with a splash of nude female flesh. Hey, otherwise, the look of the movie is perfect!

Frank Delgado is a successful but super-stressed and insanely jealous architect. He has a lovely home and a hot wife, Margo, so you'd imagine his outlook on life would be a bit rosier. Well, Frank comes home from a trip to find Margo canoodling with his latest client, Alan Richmond (Mike Kulcsar)—one whose deal is worth *mucho dinero*. I did mention Frank was insanely jealous, didn't I? Well, he waits for the man outside and throttles him until the dude's dead as disco.

Frank gets the corpse to the beach to bury it, which to me is counter-intuitive. On the one hand, waves and water can be unpredictable. They wash sand away under certain ideal circumstances. Second, what do people like to do at the beach? Dig!

Anyway, Frank has his mojo working, because at that instant, a young Mexican kills his woman and leaves her corpse close to Frank's stiff. The film drifts dangerously into racist territory as the Mexican, who is lower class to boot, is framed for the killings. Did I mention Margo, Frank's second wife, is a *gringa*?

Even though Frank is still nervous and pissed off, Margo invites some friends of theirs over for the weekend. The group consists of Dick and Sonya Hill, Frank's business partner and his wife, and pornographic film producer Goof with his wife Rita. They drive to the home of the murdered man, a lovely beach house, which doesn't help Frank's rapidly eroding mental state. Frank runs around looking like he's got a hand grenade with the pin pulled lodged up his keester, nor does it help when he sees slow-motion shots of the dead guy running to him on the beach á la Bo Derek. Despite the fact he is continually screaming, Frank is even more crazed because no one seems to notice or care.

The police show up once Alan's body is found and interview all of Frank's friends who were around at the time of the murder. At one point, the Inspector asks Rita where she was around the time of the crime, and Claudia replies, speaking one of the best lines of the film: "Stoned … ripped."

There is a ludicrous scene where everyone is dancing and screaming in the surf that makes one wonder whether the cast knew the cameras were rolling. Oh, and Frank wears a suit to the beach—not a bathing suit, but a business suit.

Meanwhile, the police are turning up the heat on Frank despite having a perp behind bars—like that's really going to help his already super-heated mental state. He and Dick are up on the roof one night and quarrel. Before you know it, his partner (I guess ex-partner is more accurate) falls to his death after being shoved by Frank. Later on, during a cozy little lunch, the merry widow, Sonya, tells Frank, not so subtly, "I miss Dick." Well, hello!

Frank needs to go off on a business trip, but before he leaves, who should show up, but his son from his first marriage, Steve. So, this is where the "stepmother" stuff comes in. In no time, Margo has Steve smoking pot and making out. Soon, it gets a bit more serious. The movie cuts to Frank in Acapulco, where who shows up in his hotel for a little "room-servicing" … Sonya? The plot thickens.

The Stepmother can be looked at two ways. If you are expecting a 1970s sleaze-fest with a convoluted plot, mediocre artisanship, inane dialogue and a fair amount of female flesh, you won't be disappointed. If you set the bar higher than that, only Claudia's appearance will make viewing this worthwhile. What ties this cosmic joke all together is an equally cosmic punch line. This film was nominated for a Best Original Song Oscar for "Strange Are the Ways of Love." Strange indeed! Of course, it didn't win.

The director of this masterpiece was Howard "Hikmet" Avedis, the husband of Marlene Schmidt. Avedis is actually a well-educated man, having a Master's from the USC film school and a B.A. in English Literature. He had a decent career in horror and exploitation films, such as the notorious *The Teacher*.

Once Claudia was able to catch her breath, she and Bobby felt secure enough with each other to seek out more suitable living quarters. After temporarily moving to a larger house on Pyramid Drive in the Hollywood Hills, the couple moved out of their increasingly cramped quarters when Claudia found a beautiful dream home not too far from their old one. In 1972 they bought the former home of Broadway and film legend Gower Champion, an impressive estate perched on a hill on Woodrow Wilson Drive, despite the fact Claudia had a busy schedule of movies coming up. Bobby noted the property had expansive lawns and peaceful gardens, and was dotted by lovely fruit trees. "I'll always have Claudia to thank for finding the house on Woodrow Wilson. We moved in on Memorial Day of 1972. She had fun decorating it in her own personal style."

The couple eventually got some time to themselves. They decided to introduce each other to their respective families; they went to Ohio for Bobby's family reunion, then on to Chicago to see some of Claudia's family and friends. Finally, they were off to Michigan, where Mimi Chesterton had spent so many summers as a girl, to celebrate Claudia's family reunion.

Claudia's next film would enable her and Bobby to work with each other. In years to come, the time spent apart would seriously affect their relationship; thus, the chance to work together on her films was a welcome opportunity.

Unholy Rollers (aka *Leader of the Pack*) (1972)

This was Claudia's first film for Roger Corman, and the first where she got top billing. The film critics vilified the film and Claudia. One critic cruelly noted that Claudia should be arrested for impersonating an actress. In most video review tomes, it rates one star or less, a "turkey" in one noted reviewer's system. Not all critics were harsh, and some praised the film and Claudia's performance. As Claudia's breakthrough film, *Unholy Rollers* established the character she would be identified with until her death. Beautiful, fearless and ruthless, Karen Walker epitomized the Hollywood Bitch Goddess that many thought represented Claudia's true nature. Corman, however, saw something special in the young actress and would choose her to star in three more films.

The film is noteworthy because it marked Claudia's debut as a major actress. She would show her ability to carry a movie on her back and show a wide range of emotions. The film also established Claudia as an actress who could do her own stunts and would try anything in front of a camera. She endured a lot of bumps and bruises during the filming, but she never once complained. There are more details about this film and the others she made with New World Pictures in the interview with Roger Corman that comes in my review of *Deathsport*.

Claudia stars as a new type of female anti-hero in *Unholy Rollers*.

That the film was on the receiving end of so much abuse is too bad, because this is an admittedly flawed but brilliant feminist/anarchist movie, and Claudia's performance is excellent, especially when you consider she was only 23 at the time. Her movements when she has no dialogue show her strong stage background, and her facial expressions are spot on. The film is also a satire of entertainment in America, with darts thrown at the commercialism of our society for good measure. However, the film also shows in unflinching detail the cruel, casual sexual and physical abuse of women rampant in society. Claudia gives a brave and realistic performance as Karen Walker, the protagonist who doesn't take shit from anyone.

One can also view the film as the struggle of an individual against society's pressure to conform. Everyone in the movie, her boss, her teammates and even her friends, keeps telling Claudia to "stick to the game plan." Perhaps this is where Claudia and her character Karen Walker are similar. Claudia did things her own way, even if that meant sacrificing the opportunity to access better roles.

Several interesting aspects to the production of *Unholy Rollers* should be mentioned. Claudia was a good athlete, but Bobby Hart said that once she earned the part, she went out and practiced roller-skating almost every day. She did have to audition for the role, as Corman didn't have her in mind specifically for the part. Many professional roller derby skaters were hired for the cast and really let the young starlet have it during filming, cutting her no slack for being a movie star.

Claudia's boyfriend, Bobby Hart, was the musical director. Louie and the Rockets, a band managed by Tommy Boyce's old manager Jay Gigander, performed the soundtrack's raucous 1950s-style rock music. Bobby Hart paid for the recording studio time and co-writes an original song, "Stay Away From Karen," with Danny Janssen. Hart recalls the entire budget for the movie's soundtrack was $1,000. The only way to meet the figure was to call in a few debts. Bobby asked an old friend who had the rights to several songs in his catalogue to lend them for the film. He recalled, despite his efforts on behalf of the production, that he never received a copy of the finished film.

Unholy Rollers rates high on the exploitation-meter, no doubt. There is simulated sex and a lot of nudity, plus more than a few scenes of Claudia getting the crap beat out of her. There is no gore or messy violence, but some sleazy sexual harassment scenes raise the level of the gross-o-meter.

Some cast notes: Alan Vint, who plays the boyfriend of Claudia's roommate, was the brother of Jesse Vint, a noted Corman veteran. Jesse and Claudia would become lovers on the set of *Deathsport* and carried on a brief affair.

The film opens with Karen Walker (Claudia) working in a cat food factory, chatting with her friend Consuelo (Roxanna Bonilla). Her supervisor walks up to her angrily, asking why she went over his head to ask for a raise. During this conversation, he's continually groping Karen, who pushes him away. He tells Karen to come to his office to discuss the "raise," and grabs a handful of her ass as he walks away. Karen has had it up to here with all this crap and cat food, and pulls a classic Lucy maneuver à la the "efficiency expert" episode. She flips the can-filling line speed to "way too fast," and the unsealed cans start whizzing off the end of the conveyor track like Frisbees, dumping a pile of unappetizing goo all over the factory floor.

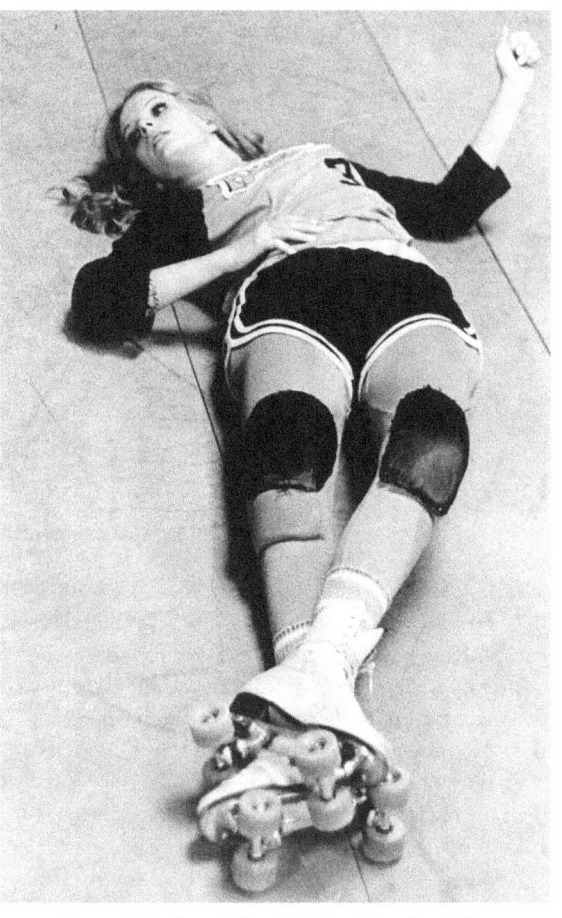

Karen Walker (Claudia Jennings) chills.

Now unemployed, Karen comes home to her stripper roommate Donna (Candice Roman) and her car thief boyfriend Greg (Alan Vint), doing the nasty, explicitly and with a lot of enthusiasm. They sit down and Karen tells them she's out of work. Then she and Donna, in one of the best scenes in the movie, go grocery shopping. After loading up their basket full of goodies, they go to the first available open checkout line. However, the clerk puts the little chain across the aisle and tells them she's now on break. The ladies are justifiably miffed, and when a supervisor comes over to see what the ruckus is, all hell breaks loose. The supervisor tells Donna and Karen that it's time for the clerk's break and they should move to the next available aisle. This doesn't sit well with Karen, who spies an impossibly huge display of canned goods, which she proceeds to destroy. In the commotion, the girls and the groceries escape.

Karen (center) in The Avengers' locker room

This scene is also significant for bringing together some of the larger themes of the film. The images of objects and people falling is a constant one, starting with the cat food cans in the beginning, the roller derby skaters crashing onto the rink and the last scene where Karen is knocked to the pavement. I believe one can interpret this as the need for the individual to rise when oppressed, and at the same time, bring down the system by resorting to pure anarchy. There is also the political message. The ruling class does not only oppress individuals; the proletariat often suppresses the proletariat (i.e., the checkout clerk) to the benefit of neither. Of course, it follows logically that the ruling class, for its own benefit, sets individuals in opposition against one other.

When viewed as class struggle, many of Claudia and Roger Corman's films are quite subversive. The dynamic frequently sets the proletariat hero against law enforcement (usually corrupt), aided by other proletarians bent on the destruction of the hero. This formula was used in *Moonshine County Express* and *The Great Texas Dynamite Chase*. The Sebastians also made Claudia's character in *'Gator Bait* one of the greatest subversive heroes of all screen history. The sub-proletariat individualist and non-conformist Desiree battles corrupt law officers and a murderous rapist appears to be bent on her destruction. This political nuance makes viewing these films more enjoyable and shows the filmmaker's fundamental understanding of such a theory.

Karen sees that the local roller derby team, the Los Angeles Avengers, is holding try-outs. Attracted by the money and promise of quick fame (does that resonate with you as far as Claudia's own story goes?), she does well and makes the team. The team's manager explains the basics of the game to Claudia: "hitting, kicking, fighting and jamming." He also points out the rules for success: to incite the fans and to be seen on television. The most important rule, however, is: "Always go with the game plan." It has an Orwellian *1984*-ish scent to it that grows stronger throughout the movie.

The next scene is a creepy one where Karen has her physical examination. The doctor's office is properly dingy and dark, accentuated by an ice-filled glass on the examination table. The look on Claudia's face when she sniffs the glass is priceless and very convincing. After Karen disrobes, the doctor starts to feel her up and Karen protests, "Hey, where are your instruments?"

Doctor: Young woman, the human hand is the most efficient instrument ever devised.

Karen: Are you a real doctor?

Doctor: I pursued my studies at not one but *three* medical schools.

Just as the doctor is about to get serious, they are interrupted by the team's star, Mickey (Betty Anne Rees), looking strung out and asking for some more pills. Karen takes the opportunity to put her clothes back on and split after asking if she is healthy enough to play.

In Karen's first game, she makes a good first impression by showing up the other team and drawing attention to herself. This

delights the owner, Mr. Stern, who wants Karen to replace Mickey as the team's star. Stern also likes her "showmanship," which, he keeps telling his hapless son-in-law, is the secret of success in roller derby.

The editing and action sequences of the actual contest are flawless. The camera catches every kick, elbow and fall as if it were a ballet on roller skates. The stunt scenes are seamlessly woven into the action, so it's impossible to tell where the actor ends and the double begins. The cuts between the infield, the fans and the skaters on the track all morph into a rhythmic display of cinematography and editing.

In the locker room after the game, Karen is hazed by the other skaters, who tell her, "You got a uniform, but you ain't part of the team." Of course, their biggest quarrel with Karen is that: "She didn't follow the game plan." Karen is defiant, but agrees to go with the rest of the team to their favorite bar. It becomes apparent after a short while the rest of the team isn't there to make nice with Karen unless she changes her attitude. Not bloody likely! Mickey, who is not only the star but the alpha dyke as well, approaches her. When Karen rebuffs her advances, the team grabs Karen and holds her down spread-eagle on a pool table. They proceed to strip and humiliate her, but Karen bounces up naked and calls everyone a bunch of bad names.

One of the male skaters, Nick (Jay Varela), comforts her, gets her clothes back and offers her a ride home on his motorcycle. They hop on and Karen notices Nick has a gun holstered on his bike. She proceeds to grab it, and for some reason, starts shooting at every landmark and building in L.A., including a Randy's Donuts. You'd think she'd attract a lot of police with that stunt. I suppose that's just par for the course in L.A. The pair decides to go to the rink and get some extra practice time in. Karen proceeds to

beat the living crap out of Nick on each circuit, leaving him to wonder what kind of nut he just picked up. It turns out to be part of Karen's mating ritual, as she soon begins a sexy striptease on roller skates, leaving a trail of garments for Nick to follow. The photography during this sequence is particularly good, as the camera's movements and the faces of the skaters build up to an erotic climax—literally. The last shot inside the arena is Nick and Karen in a naked embrace on the infield with their skates on. Hey, it could happen!

The next morning Donna and Greg pick up Nick and Karen from the arena. They spend the day in blissful pursuit of good ol' American activities—ping-pong, miniature golf and ... tattoos. However, Karen is the only one up for ink, and gets a skate with wings and "Avengers" needled on her forearm. I thought Claudia's facial expressions as she gets the tat extraordinary, as in a few seconds she goes from pain and defiance to bewilderment and sadness.

The team travels by bus to San Diego to meet their hated rivals, the San Diego Demons. I guess it's their *only* rival, since that's the only other squad they square off against. During the ride, Nick introduces his wife Tina to Karen, who's only a little sarcastic in the exchange of pleasantries.

Eventually, Karen supplants Mickey as team star. She starts endorsing products on television, buys a nice house and goes car shopping with her friend from the cat food factory, Consuelo, who insists that the automobile must have: "Chrome ... Lots of chrome."

This descent into commercialism and consumerism puts off her friends Greg and Donna. Despite Karen's efforts to convince them otherwise, they move to Oregon to open a striptease auto repair shop. Yes, you read that correctly. The fact that Karen has now embraced materialism shows that she has forgotten her days as the proletarian hero. She has now set up a conflict where two mutually exclusive desires exist. Karen can't be the rebel and the wealthy symbol of the ruling class simultaneously.

Nick takes Karen to a shooting range to teach her how to handle a firearm safely. He goes through all the proper procedures (well, it would be nice if they were wearing ear protection, but this is the movies), then hands the gun to Karen, who proceeds to out-shoot him. She then points the gun at his nose and taunts him about his wife. Of course, this makes both of them horny as hell, etc.

Eventually, Karen starts running out of friends. The owner is sick of her ad libs (instead of following the game plan), her teammates hate her because she's a selfish showoff and even Nick is getting tired of her antics. Of course, none of this phases Karen, who couldn't give a rat's ass what anyone else thinks.

One night it *does* bother Karen when Mickey and one of the hated Demons gang sneak up on her and literally kick the stuffing out of the poor lass, while she is pinned against the rail. Mickey is fired and joins the Demons, which makes Karen the undisputed number one star.

After the game, Nick feels Karen is threatening his manhood, and when Karen suggests he doesn't have any, he gives her a vicious slap to the face. Karen, true to her nature, simply says, "You even hit like a girl," and right-

Claudia rests on set during filming.

fully kicks him in the family jewels. This is a very ugly scene in a movie that's full of them, and though this exchange is beautifully acted, it is repulsive.

At the next derby, with Mickey skating for the Demons, things get heated and it seems mayhem will break out at any second. The crowd is frothing at its collective mouth, and the teams are getting down and dirty on the track. At one juncture, Mickey and Karen get tangled up, and a one-on-one match race is declared. The two ladies take their positions, and Karen immediately starts whaling on Mickey, who goes over the railing and gets knocked out cold. This does not improve the mood of the crowd or the teams, and Stern decides he needs to bring another skater—Beverly (Charlene Jones)—up to the Avengers to take over for Karen when the time comes that she will inevitably crack.

Afterward, the rest of the Avengers ambush Karen, rip the antenna off her new car, give it a good long scratch with a switchblade and proceed to beat the daylights out of her. Karen reacts as every other person would. She hops in her car and proceeds to mow down trash cans, hobo fires, stacks of oilcans and everything else that is piled high. Of course, none of this attracts any attention from the local police. They were probably still looking for the crazy lady on the motorcycle firing a gun at a giant donut.

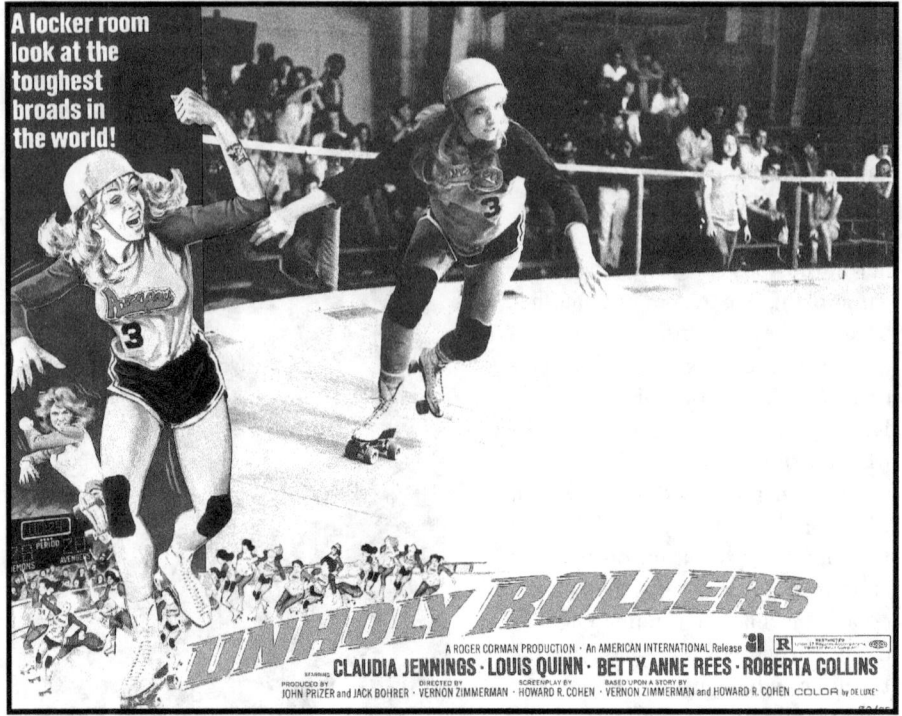

Before the next match, Stark barges in on a topless Karen and gives her an ultimatum: Either "follow the game plan" or get fired. Karen is not impressed and tells him to knock the next time he enters a room. Touché! Things do not improve for our girl on the track, unfortunately. As she prepares to jam around, Beverly steals her helmet and becomes the de facto new number-one star. Karen starts to skate faster and faster when suddenly she goes berserk, as in an all-time roller derby wobbly. She not only beats up all the players on the other team, but her own as well. She dumps over the benches in the infield, smacking around anyone who comes within elbow-shot. Then, in a spectacular inspiration, she skates outside the arena and starts whaling on patrons, pedestrians and anyone who gets in her way. Karen, definitely not going by the game plan, skates into the street and starts taking on automobiles. Yes, you read it correctly: She starts beating up cars. Unfortunately, one of the vehicles doesn't see her until the last moment and smacks into her. We wait with bated breath to see if it's the end of Karen; then, in an ambiguous ending, she rises to her feet—uh, I mean, *skates*—and lifts her tattooed forearm in a gesture of defiance. The End.

Of course, the audience wants to believe Karen is not seriously hurt—just a flesh wound and all that. That's not really the point, though, because the fact that she stood up and was unrepentant means more than if she eventually died. Karen gives us the ultimate reaction of the individual—and, specifically, a woman—to a world where the rules are set in opposition to her pursuit of happiness.

Overall, *Unholy Rollers* is an outstanding B-movie. It has all the female nudity, foul language, and roller derby sequences one could possibly ask for. I frankly thought it superior to *Kansas City Bomber*, which only had its much bigger budget and Raquel

Welch's much bigger hair to recommend it. (Oh, and a very young Jodie Foster, too.) Considering its budget, *Unholy Rollers* delivers what it promises, and as noted, makes some pithy commentary on American society. Many reviewers have stated that Claudia's character has no redeeming qualities and is a badass. To me, she is the only one in the film besides her roommate and best friend who is honest and has logical reasons for her behavior. She suffers sexual harassment at every turn, and the one man she thinks she can trust turns out to be married. You'd be pissed, too. Her generous side is shown when she tries to give the mother who rejected her some money (an excellent cameo by veteran Kathleen Freeman). She also gives money to her roommate's boyfriend when the pair moves to Oregon.

Claudia's character is not bad; she is strong and confident, and therein lies the difference. She was born into a marginalized section of society; therefore, she knows no other way to behave. It is a great performance, probably the best of the early portion of her career. Claudia, showing a good range of emotion, is funny, sexy, skillful in the skating sequences and quite believable when she goes off her nutter.

Martin Scorcese, one of Roger Corman's earliest discoveries, supervised the first rate editing. The picture overall is superior to *Rollerball* and *The Kansas City Bombers* despite having a miniscule budget. *Unholy Rollers* is not weighed down by fluff and instead opts for brutal realism that sets it above the other two star-filled lavish productions.

An added bit of trivia for *Beverly Hills 90210* fans; Joe Tata who plays Marshall in the film, would later figure prominently in the Season Six Episode 17 called "Fade In, Fade Out." Much of the show takes place at a film festival honoring Roger Corman and scenes from *Unholy Rollers* are shown, where Joe and Claudia can be seen.

Scott Von Doviak asked, in his excellent work *Hick Flicks*: "By now you may be wondering if there is not one woman in all of hicksploitation who transcends the status of mere sex objects."[12] His answer, of course, was Claudia Jennings, citing her beauty and toughness. I do disagree with his conclusion that, "Her cinematic legacy is a minor one, but in the realm of the hick flick she still reigns."[13]

Claudia was just getting started, and one can see her improvement from film to film. Going back to the theme of consumerism I noted, there is a constant barrage of commercials spoken by the arena announcers during each match. It is worth your time to listen to them, as many are hysterically funny. To show their appreciation and friendship, the roller derby professionals in the film gave Claudia a bronzed skate, used in the movie. She remained friendly with many of them for the rest of her life.

Her fellow Chicagoan, film critic Roger Ebert, praised her work in *Unholy Rollers* noting she "gave the most vicious female performance in a long time."

The *Los Angeles Times* had a slightly different interpretation of Claudia's performance.

Karen learns how to use firearms.

This rollette is no tart with a heart and a disappointing, sentimental love affair and a broken home to remind us there are reasons for her hard exterior. No, indeed; Karen is a slut through and through, and as such, she rings real.[14]

Karen shows off her ink.

The *Times* review, while congratulating Claudia on her interpretation of the character, doesn't expand on the reasons for her fierceness; that she's been sexually harassed, rejected by her mother and surrounded by dishonest people who would brutalize her even further if she allowed them. I wonder if anyone has ever done a study on how male film critics see strong female characters, as opposed to female film critics.

Variety gave a more balanced review, saying:

Unholy Rollers is another gander into the rough, tough world of the femme roller derby, a follow-up to Metro's *Kansas City Bomber* on the same subject. Same type of violence and near-mayhem highlight this story of the rise and fall of a skating star. While the script by Howard R. Cohen concentrates more on the violence of the track than a straight story line, there's sufficient propelling narrative to keep audiences amply rewarded. The yarn focuses on Claudia Jennings, who leaves her factory job to win a place on a roller team and almost immediately becomes its star through her departure from the routinely planned phony action of opponents on the track and instead plays it for real. Jennings does yeoman service with the role which necessitates her taking plenty of lumps.

It is difficult to judge which one of Claudia's performances was her best. *Unholy Rollers* is a superior film, with directing, acting and cinematography that belie its humble origins as a B-movie; however, more than any other of her films, this was Claudia's movie. Although she would give fine performances in some later projects such as *The Great Texas Dynamite Chase*, *Unholy Rollers* comes closest to showing Claudia was a legitimate A-list leading lady.

Maternal Instincts

With a short break between films, Bobby and Claudia's home life soon became idyllic. The home, with its sweeping yard and fruit trees, was a dream, and friends constantly surrounded them. When Bobby's son, living with his ex-wife in Arizona, was having problems in school, he moved in with the couple. Claudia was enthusiastic from the start. She missed her sisters terribly and this was a way to mitigate that emptiness. There were soon children, animals and friends hanging out at all times. Claudia was perfect for Bobby, Jr. and was devoted to him. It showed a side of her character that no one who knew her in Hollywood realized existed.

Eventually, another young man became a frequent visitor to the household. Barry Richards' son Paige, who had been living with his mother in New York, moved west to be with his father. He shared his memories of Claudia with me:

> She was a second mom to me in every sense of the word. I remember her being so full of life and happiness. She went to all my basketball games like any mom would do. We would go on trips to the zoo and all sorts of fun activities. I even remember she and Bobby took me to the Playboy Mansion once.
>
> I remember that one birthday she got me a Miami Dolphins cake, which meant a lot to a young boy. She went all out to treat me like her own son. We would have "right and wrong" talks all the time and she was very nurturing. She took her role as my mom seriously. Claudia did that with all the kids around Bobby's house. If they ever had to leave me alone with Bobby's sons, who were a bit older than I was, she'd tell them to treat me nicely.
>
> There are so many things about those years I'll never forget. Claudia was always so upbeat, all the time. And she had her favorite cat, Luther, which was deaf. Although we were children, we were treated like mini-adults. After all, there were half-naked Playmates and women running around, and a constant flow of movie stars and other celebrities at the house.
>
> One of my most enduring recollections of her was of the first Christmas I spent out West. Claudia was sitting there in her green velour bathrobe, showing me how to string popcorn and cranberry garlands. All of a sudden, my dad, who was sitting in a rocking chair, went back too far, and rocked himself backwards into the Christmas tree. She started laughing and there was something about her laugh. It was truly infectious. You couldn't help but laugh with her.
>
> I still remember so much about her, even though it's been over 30 years since she passed. I can hear her voice in my memory. I become very emotional thinking about Claudia again, because she adored me and I loved her.[15]

One day Claudia noticed another boy, who was spending the night with Bobby, Jr. The young man's name was Keith Glass and he was Barry Richard's nephew. Keith Glass, now Keith Jennings, spoke of his friendship with Claudia:

> She asked Bobby, Jr. and me if we were hungry and Claudia said she'd make us something to eat. Claudia heated up some green beans and made macaroni and cheese. After she served us, she was holding the pot of macaroni and cheese and just saying to herself, "I'm not hungry at all, I really don't want anything," all the while taking forkful after forkful and eating it. She kept repeating, "I'm not going to eat any of this," until she finished what was in the pot. It was so funny and so was Claudia. During this time, Claudia was asking me questions about where I lived and things about my family, just a little bit at first. Then

Keith Jennings (née Glass) with Claudia and Bobby Hart

Claudia went off and did a few things about the house, did the dishes, etc., while Bobby, Jr. and I watched TV and talked.

As it got close to bedtime, Claudia got us set up in the den, where there was a sofa bed for Bobby, Jr. and I had my sleeping bag on the floor. She tucked Bobby, Jr. in, kissed him goodnight, then sat with me on the floor, and we chatted for a few hours about everything. She interjected some things about her life and her problems being raised in such a strict home. We each poured our hearts out to each other and ended up in tears, and then Claudia reached over and we hugged each other for what seemed liked years but probably was only 10 minutes. I mean, here I was, a little kid, and had only just met her, yet I was telling her how unloved I felt, how I was bullied at home and at school and how lonely I felt. Claudia clearly knew I needed someone or something. The fact she was so open about her own life with someone she barely knew was a gift I will keep with me the rest of my life.

Then she turned to me and said, "You know, from what you said, you don't seem to have a mother or family except for your Uncle Barry, and I don't have a brother, so I am going to be your sister. I am going to adopt you as that. You now have a family, and if you ever need me, you just call me and I'll be there for you.' I was beaming with joy, and then she tucked me in and kissed me.

Keith Glass officially changed his name to Jennings later on. He asked Claudia first, and her reply was, "Of course. Why not? I got my name out of a phone book!"

Then, after Claudia's death, with the approval of Bobby, his uncle and Maureen McCormick, Keith Glass legally became Keith Jennings.

Many people mistakenly refer to Keith Jennings as a "fan" or a "groupie." He was a fan, although definitely not a groupie, but he was also as devoted to Claudia as any family member would be. His Uncle Barry, after all, was a best friend with both Claudia and Bobby Hart.

Keith recalled another incident that was not as cheerful, but one that Claudia turned around with her unique sense of humor.

My family lived a pretty long way from Laurel Canyon. I lived in Thousand Oaks. One day a fight started with one of my brothers at our home, which happened often, way too often for my good. I ran to my Mother for protection, standing behind her, and my brother kept throwing punches. I was begging my mother to tell him to stop. She just laughed, saying, "He is not going to hurt you and you guys knock it off" (or something to that effect), and at that moment he struck me. Now I was standing behind my mother in the hallway of our house, up against a wall, and the force of his punch made my head hit the wall and he broke my nose and knocked out one of my front teeth, and the other bent up to the top of my mouth, and six other teeth moved around and were displaced. I remember falling in slow motion, holding my mouth as I hit the floor. My mother begins yelling at me, "don't bleed on the rug," and things went downhill from there. I was rushed to the hospital where they sewed my teeth back in.

Later for my 18th birthday, when I desperately wanted and needed my nose fixed, Claudia called around town to help find me the best plastic surgeon. She had me call her doctor, Richard Grossman, who treated Claudia for her ribs during an accident on *Great Texas Dynamite*. Dr. Grossman found me a local plastic surgeon in my area, and Claudia loved how I looked after the surgery, and we were both so happy I had it done. A week after I got beat up, I ran to a phone booth and called Claudia. I was crying when I told her what happened. She was really pissed off and told me to carry a baseball bat when I was home.

Claudia then said if she had to drive all the way out to Bum-Fuck, Egypt to get me, that she would, and that she would have a few choice words for my mom! She also gave me her answering service's direct line, and every time I

A publicity head shot of Claudia

called her, whether she was on a movie set or anywhere, she always took my call. She was never too busy to speak with me. That's just one of the reasons why I loved her. [16]

According to her sister Constance, Claudia was enamored of children in general and large families in particular. One of her friends came from a household of 12 children. Apparently, Claudia was in awe of this, and was fascinated to hear they had to dine in shifts since their table wasn't large enough to accommodate everyone at one sitting.

Claudia's love of animals was another unique facet of her personality. Unable to keep more than one or two at a time in Chicago, she soon had a menagerie in the Woodrow Wilson home. A pleasant quirk that she had was naming her pets after foods. For instance she had a dog (who was afraid of everyone except Claudia) called Bananas. There was also a rather large fluffy cat named Popcorn.

It seemed like every day was a grand occasion at the house on Woodrow Wilson. The holidays were particularly festive and Claudia celebrated them with as much gaiety and with as many friends as she could. It was her way of recapturing the happier times with her family. Christmas and Thanksgiving were always special events; however, the house served many purposes. It became a regular pool party for all of Claudia's Playmate friends. It was also a sort of sanctuary for Bobby and his friends to meditate and study. For the children it was a place of adventure, with fruit trees they could pick from and two wonderful parent figures.

Barry Richards' memories of those days are as follows:

Bobby had a big swimming pool at the house, and some of Claudia's friends would come over and sunbathe. Since they were mostly models, actresses and Playmates, they weren't shy about shedding their swimsuits. I have to say I enjoyed spending time over there.

Claudia was always so much fun and great with both of Bobby's boys, Bobby, Jr. and Bret, and my son Paige. We'd go out to Arizona to Oak Creek Canyon, where Bobby's family had a cabin, and just have a great time.

The house was a sanctuary for Claudia. We always had tons of visitors. That's what people did in Hollywood; they threw parties. Our neighbors were Harrison Ford, Anthony Perkins, Sally Kellerman and Sissy Spacek.

One year Bobby and I decided to set up a Christmas tree lot for fun, when a friend of mine got a whole shipment of trees. The deal had fallen through, and I ended up with them. Since we had money invested in the trees, it was in our best interest to try to sell them. Well, I had to set up a small shack. I'd stay there overnight—a beautiful girlfriend of mine would come over with a takeout meal from a fancy restaurant with a candle and share my sleeping bag. Well, Claudia was our best salesperson, hands down. One night, we decided to throw her a surprise birthday party. After we were done at the Christmas tree lot, we came home. When we walked through the door, about 40 people screamed "Happy birthday!" as loud as they could. Poor Claudia almost fainted. It really took a while to get her composed enough to enjoy the party.

Bobby and Claudia visited me once, when I was in London. I was living in Cornwall Gardens sharing a Tudor house in central London. I was working on a solo album with George Martin, the man who produced The Beatles, in his studio. Harry Nilsson and Paul McCartney were recording right next to us.

We met so many great people. One night we were invited to a dinner party given by Maurice Gibb and his wife at the time, Lulu. I remember the look on Claudia's face just looking around at all these celebrities in this amazing house.

Bobby and Claudia would have arguments, like every couple. I always knew when they were having a tiff because I was their best friend. I would have to mediate. I'd be in the kitchen with Claudia and she'd say, "Tell Mr. Hart this or that," you know? So I'd tell Bobby what Claudia had said and he'd say, "Well, tell Miss Jennings this." I'd have to do the same thing with Boyce and Hart when we'd be in a car and they were fighting. Tommy would say to me, "Tell Mr. Hart I'm not ready to forgive him," or something like that. Then Bobby would respond, "Well, tell Mr. Boyce that's fine with me." It was kind of cute, and everyone always made up at the end.

I think the things I remember most about Claudia were all the little qualities she had that made you cherish her. I'd give her back rubs or foot rubs and press firmly until she squealed. I introduced her to California avocado sandwiches. Sometimes we'd all curl up on the couch and watch television; everything seemed so normal and natural. She was very easygoing, too. I'd say, "Claudia, you're such a dumb redhead" if she messed up, and she would laugh in a goofy way that would make us all crack up. She had the most infectious laughter and was so much fun to be around.[17]

Claudia's sister Constance remembers those years in this manner:

When Claudia moved to California, she met the love of her life, Bobby Hart. They lived together in a beautiful house in the Hollywood Hills. Bobby was one of the warmest, kindest, most balanced people I have ever met. He meditated every day and stood quietly but serenely apart from the drug-crazed party atmosphere that L.A. was in the early 1970s. Claudia always told us to be quiet when Bobby was meditating. I remember trying to plunk out one of his songs on his piano, and he came up behind me to help me with the chords.

One last thing I want to say about her beauty. Even the most beautiful photographs she ever had taken do not truly show how incredibly beautiful she was, especially while in her 20s. She had the kind of beauty that stopped conversations. If we walked into a restaurant, within 30 seconds of her arrival the entire restaurant would go dead silent. Over and over this happened. She was always beautifully dressed, but it wasn't that. She had the kind of beauty in real life that startled people into silence. Maybe it was the way she carried herself, or some unusual aspect of her beauty like her strawberry blond hair and green eyes, but sometimes even I, who had grown up with her, could not believe how beautiful she was. I saw this beauty without envy, because I knew it burdened her sometimes. I was happy to bask in some of her glow."

Claudia gave a curious newspaper interview to the *Tucson Daily Citizen* in 1971. The title was "Playboy's Playmate Chooses Carpentry Over Hectic Life of Model, Actress."

The interview is a little bizarre, and as was typical for her interviews in those times, she comes off as being a bit strange. She also adopts the air of a Hollywood princess a touch too easily. The article opens with the information that although Claudia is famous for her nude modeling, she has just returned from London from a shopping spree for clothes. The interviewer notes the irony, and Claudia then talks about her *Playboy* photo sessions.

> Most of my friends don't even think they look like me. People look different when they're nude. It was a lot of fun having them taken, and I certainly enjoyed the $5,000. It was the quickest money I've ever made.

She then goes on to discuss the public's reaction to her pictorials.

> I was expecting a lot of dirty letters asking me to go to Spain, but I was surprised. They were all very nice.

When asked about her trip to London and her infamous shopping spree:

> London is a fantastic place to shop. I bought about 800 dresses in Biba, the Quorum and the other boutiques.

Claudia then offers some information about her private life. "Claudia, whose mother teaches at the University of Illinois, describes herself as a closet Lib. 'I'm becoming more radical all the time.'"

The article continues by mentioning that Claudia and Bobby Hart were living together in Hollywood Hills.

> I'm not too interested in getting married. Nobody has given me a good reason yet. I wouldn't flirt from one man to another, and I wouldn't mind having a child. A child understands more than people think.

The article then states Claudia is a good cook, but the thought that women are born to cook makes her a little rebellious. On the whole, she prefers carpentry. For their (Claudia and Bobby's) home, she has just finished a Japanese-style table and five chairs. Then the piece meanders a bit, explaining that the ankh symbol pendant around her neck was a gift from her co-star in *The Love Machine*, John Phillip Law.

Her parting words: "I live such a normal life," complains Claudia. "I travel all the time and I'm tired of planes and airports."

The author of the article concludes with, "Her idea of Heaven would be to settle down and not get married."[17]

It is difficult to determine whether the writer or Claudia set the tone for the article. It seems disjointed, hopping from subject to subject with no natural order or reason. A few things do stand out, such as the emphasis on having a child. It seems as if the mention of her carpentry pursuits was to demonstrate that Claudia wasn't your typical female domestic partner, but her exaggerated shopping spree was needed to confirm a stereotypical Hollywood femininity. It would not be the last of her interviews that would be puzzling. At times it seems to encourage readers to see the worst aspects of a Hollywood actress, while at other times she comes off as being earnest and down-to-earth. One supposes that when an actress gives any type of interview, the main purpose is publicity.

Although Claudia loved shopping for herself, she was generous to her family and friends as well. Her sister Constance told me:

> She gave the most beautiful gifts. For one of my first apartments she bought me a beautiful comforter; another time, a blue leather cosmetics case. I have never owned its equal.

Claudia's habit of giving was echoed by many of her friends that I interviewed. Claudia also attracted as many friends as she could, another childhood trait.

One of these friends, Sally Kirkland, recalled:

> Every woman Claudia met became like a sister to her. And that meant for life. She would do anything for her friends. She knew everyone and everyone knew her.

One of these friends was Claudia and Bobby's next-door neighbor, Simone

Claudia on a modeling assignment in Greece

Boisseree. Simone is a fascinating woman. She was a flight attendant and a renowned stuntwoman, and eventually started her own company making bedding for private jets. She and Claudia hit it off instantly and would remain close until Claudia's death:

> Claudia had a heart of gold. She was just the nicest, sweetest person you could ever meet. And, God, she was beautiful! She was one of the few women who were more beautiful without makeup than when she was all dolled up. If you ever needed help with anything, Claudia would be there for you. She would literally give you the clothes off her back. She was much more talented than people gave her credit for, also. She was always so kind to everyone. I never once heard her say a bad word about anyone. She was also very intelligent. Much smarter than I was, I can tell you.
>
> I loved going over to their house for parties or holidays, or just to hang out. They looked like a perfect married couple. Bobby and Claudia seemed to be made for each other. Bobby was just so sweet to her. He was a nice man in every sense of the word.[18]

Claudia would always be the first one to offer advice and to help her friends if they had doubts and questions. Victoria Hale remembers one discussion she had with Claudia that was very telling. They were discussing their careers, and Claudia asked, "Don't you have a road map, honey?" Victoria was a bit perplexed. Claudia explained: "A plan in your head of how your career is going to go."

A part of Claudia's plan was to be accepted into Hugh Hefner's world of *Playboy*. He had moved part of his empire to Los Angeles, and it instantly became the place for celebrities to gather. However, this was one time where the genius of exposing female flesh failed. He was never accepted as part of the Hollywood elite. They ate his food, drank his alcohol and had sex with his models; however, he had no credibility in the film industry, which he had sought since Marilyn Monroe's pictures graced *Playboy*'s pages. Claudia thought, like hundreds of women who have posed, that *Playboy* would be her ticket to stardom, so she and Hef became friends. Marilyn Grabowski, *Playboy*'s West Coast Director of Photography, and Claudia would become like sisters. Many young centerfolds would befriend her and look up to Claudia for guidance.

Susan Miller, a stunning blonde centerfold in the early 1970s and now a successful massage therapist, told this story:

> I was at the Mansion and about as intimidated and lonely as I could be. Then I saw Claudia standing by herself, looking so confident and oh so beautiful. I went up to her and asked her if it was true that in order to become Playmate of the Year, a girl had to sleep with Hugh Hefner. She looked at me with that wry smile that only Claudia had, and said, "Honey, if it were only that easy." From then on, she became my best friend in L.A.

Susan had another story that seemed a typical, frivolous Playmate adventure, but it would be an ominous sign of things to come.

Claudia and I were in Chicago when she was invited by Stan Herman to spend a weekend in the Hamptons at the house of a friend of his. Now, Stan was a big real estate tycoon in Beverly Hills, and was a frequent guest at the Mansion. He was also a partner with Hef in a private club they owned called *Pips*, where everyone used to go to play backgammon and party. Stan had his eye on Claudia for a long time. She agreed to go, but only if I could go as well. As it turned out, one of the Jet Bunnies from Hef's private plane also came with us. Well, we flew to New York, and this huge limousine picked us up and took us to a beautiful house in the Hamptons. Stan put me and the other girl in one room and put Claudia by herself in another. Well, Claudia came to me, saying she didn't want to sleep with him and what should she do? So I gave her a sleeping pill and we all had a little to drink, and pretty much kept it up until Claudia fell sound asleep. Stan was pretty mad.[19]

This was not the beginning of Stan Herman's pursuit of Claudia. Herman was also a regular at the Mansion, where he would sometimes try to pick up Claudia, even when Bobby was with her.

Susan and Claudia even found time to play a practical joke on the very charming and quintessential nice guy, Tommy Boyce. Bobby Hart had graciously gone out to help Susan pick out a stereo system. When they got back, Susan and Claudia told Tommy they were going to take him out shopping, just to do something nice for him. The ladies took him to one of the more exclusive stores on Melrose, Fred Segal. There they picked out the most expensive suits and boots they could find for him. What Tommy didn't know, of course, was that Claudia had lifted his wallet and taken one of his credit cards out. When they were done shopping, Claudia proudly paid and Tommy had a new wardrobe. Once they were back at the house, Susan and Claudia told Tommy the truth. In keeping with his nature, Tommy Boyce took the prank graciously. Besides, no one ever got mad at Claudia—and if they did, it didn't last long.

Another striking professional agency photo of Claudia

Susan remembered another story that showed how talented Claudia was. They drove up to San Francisco, where Claudia was playing the role of Rusty, Lenny Bruce's wife, in the play *Lenny*. One evening, the real Mrs. Bruce, Honey, was in the theater.

A Biography

She came up to Claudia after the production and hugged her, saying, "I'm so glad it was you!" This showed once more that Claudia was capable of delivering a superior performance on stage. In a stage production, unlike in a B-movie, there is sufficient time to rehearse and practice the nuances necessary for a convincing realization. On a tight shooting schedule, there is often time for only one take; therefore, a performance in a drive-in feature is incapable of attaining a more sophisticated level of performance.

As a footnote showing how sensitive and sweet Claudia was, one of her fellow actor's 13-year-old son joined the cast for dinner after a performance. He was obviously quite taken with Claudia, and after dinner she gave him an autographed picture that said to marry her when he grew up. It was this sort of kind, personal gesture that couldn't be forced; it was just who Claudia was.

Susan also said something quite funny happened while up there. They were supposed to spend a few days at Neil Young's ranch. They came driving up to the entrance, and David Crosby was home. He evidently hadn't been told visitors were coming, and promptly ran them off the property. I'm sure Neil Young and the rest of the guests were not pleased with their band mate when they heard.

Paradoxically, as time went on, the more glamorous Bobby and Claudia's lifestyle became, the less satisfying it was for Bobby. As attracted as they were to each other, and the wonderful qualities each possessed, Bobby's introspective nature and Claudia's love of the limelight began to grate against each other. In the book *Psychedelic Bubble Gum: Boyce & Hart, The Monkees, and Turning Mayhem Into Miracles*, by Bobby Hart and Glenn Ballantyne, Bobby explained:

> Being part of the show with Claudia on my arm as we frequented the Hollywood scene had been fun for me in the beginning. We were photographed dressed to the nines as we walked movie premier red carpets. It made me feel like somebody special, and I could see in Claudia's eyes that all the attention was having a similar effect on her.
>
> But soon, even my inflated ego was able to recognize that the novelty had begun to wear off … It hadn't taken long for the inferno of this public life pressure cooker to begin to overheat our personal nervous systems.[20]

Despite her public proclamations to the contrary, Claudia had decided that she truly wanted to marry Bobby and have children. She saw it as a natural progression of their relationship. Bobby, who had been married and already had two grown boys, was not enthusiastic and told Claudia he loved her but he couldn't commit to marriage or more children.

For the duration of their relationship, Claudia continued to press Bobby for marriage and children. This left Bobby perplexed, since Claudia had said in interviews that she considered marriage an outdated institution. This disagreement was the first fracture in their love affair. As time and Claudia's most intense stretch of work began, it kept the two apart for greater and greater periods, adding additional stress to their lives.

Sisters of Death (1973)

It is not a favorable sign in the movie business when a film made in 1973 isn't released until 1976. It's a shame, because *Sisters of Death* had the potential to be a creepy little thriller. I am going to make a little confession. The first time I watched the film, my impression was Claudia had made an error appearing in this questionable spool of celluloid. However, after repeated viewings, it's still pretty dumb—but not half bad.

Claudia was the first one cast in 1973's *Sisters of Death* because as her director, Joseph Mazzuca said, "We needed a name. Claudia's *Playboy* reputation gave us that." Unfortunately, despite a decent cast with five lovely actresses amongst it, the movie lacks pace and continuity and the end is convoluted and just not believable. I guess you can't have everything, eh?

Claudia did not want to disrobe for the part, and Mazzuca wanted a PG rating, so she was filmed with her back to the camera in one scene undoing her bra. The shoot was in nearby Santa Barbara, making it possible for Claudia to travel home and see Bobby on weekends, which was a bonus. She accepted that it was a substandard film even for the usual low-budget market, so she took it as an opportunity to practice her art and make some money.

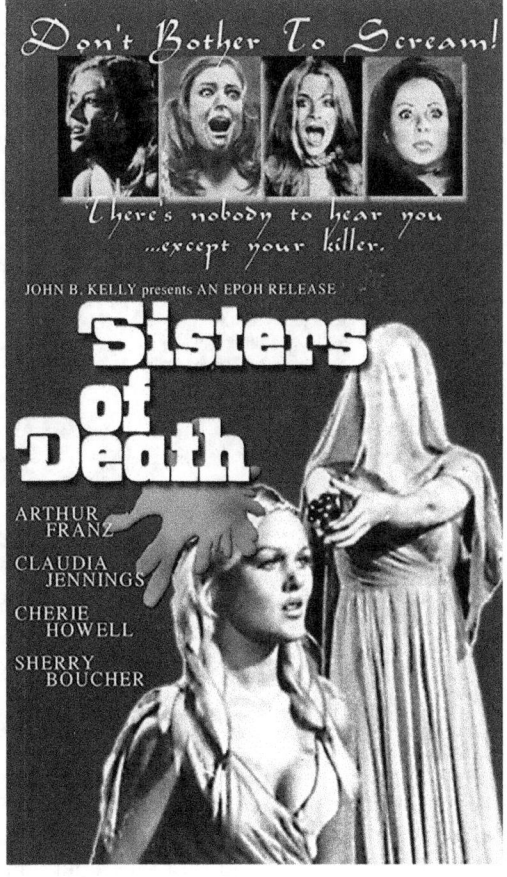

Mazzuca remembered:

> Claudia was good to work with ... open and willing to do anything. We shot the film in two weeks with no stunt doubles. She was always cooperative, fun to work with and didn't mind working the long days. During the undressing scene I could see the relief on her face when I told her she wouldn't have to appear nude.

Similar in premise to *The Single Girls*, the story concerns a group of women trapped in a spooky mansion while being murdered, one by one. The beginning of the film shows promise, as we witness an initiation ceremony of a secret female sorority, although why it's secret and why we should care is never made apparent. The color, music and lighting are remarkable, very reminiscent of the Corman classic *The Masque of the Red Death*. The sisters are draped in diaphanous blue gowns with gossamer blue hoods, while the two initiates, Judy (Claudia) and Liz (Elizabeth Bergen), kneel in front of the others. One of the sisters chants in a monotone, asking if Judy is ready for the final challenge, and Claudia answers yes. The high priestess or whoever, puts a bullet into a two-barreled pistol, clicks it closed and cocks the evil-looking mother. She places it next to Claudia's

head and pulls the trigger. The scene does build considerable tension, so when Liz is asked if she's ready, the audience assumes she's a shoo-in. The grand high muckety-mucktress loads, clicks, cocks and fires. Whoa—somebody screwed up big time. Poor Elizabeth's head is not repairable, and the rest of the sisters are screaming their asses off. A shame, because Liz was really pretty. A good beginning for the film, but unfortunately, that's the peak.

A few fun continuity screw-ups appear in the opening. At the beginning of the ceremony, the two pledges are kneeling on a red platform. A few minutes later, in close-up, the number of platforms has grown to three.

We move ahead seven years, where we see what's happened to the remaining sisters. They've all received anonymous letters inviting them to the Sisters' seventh-year reunion. There is a wad of cash in each, promising them the time of their lives. They are instructed to meet in Paso Robles, which would be a good reason to go—I mean, check out some wineries, etc.

Judy is a successful model, trying to get the governor's son to make her an honest woman. Sylvia (Chéri Howell) is not doing as well. She's a drunk and a whore—hey, not my words; she tells the others that. Penny (Roxanne Albee) is a flower child, and one that gets on your nerves real, real fast. She and her old man have a nonsensical conversation about the good being good, but maybe there is no good, so it's best not to seek good where there is no good. I could swear I was listening to a song by Donovan. Well, the dude puts his sacred necklace on Penny, saying it will protect her and she'll be all right. Obviously they don't watch many horror movies on the commune.

Diane (Sherry Boucher) is a smoking hot chick whose shorts are barely legal. She's hitchhiking to the rendezvous point and a kindly old Mexican pervert picks her up in a dusty farm truck. After a few minutes of him pawing various parts of her body, she plucks a Bible out of her backpack and starts reading, which stops the groping at once. Francie (Sherry Alberoni) is driving like a speed demon trying to get to the rendezvous in time. She's perky as a busload of cheerleaders, 40 pounds of coffee, and a dozen daytime television talk show hosts.

Waiting at the hotel where they all are supposed to meet are a couple of ne'er-do-wells, Joe (Joe Tata) and Mark (Paul Carr). The girls finally show up, and it seems every other word in their conversation is "Hi." Well, it *has* been seven years since they've seen each other. The boys introduce themselves to the girls and convince them they're not perverts by handing them a letter from their host and off everyone goes on the grand adventure. The vehicle is one of the strangest ever seen in motion picture history. A combination of the Griswold's station wagon and the Munster-mobile, the windows are covered in tattered bed sheets for some bizarre reason.

After what seems hours, poor Penny, who is already uptight, starts to freak and asks Mark where the heck the place is and why the heck they're not there yet. Of course, this gets the other ladies worked up, and I'm sure Mark and Joe are wondering why they took the job. The answer is $500 worth of reasons.

Fortunately, they find the place—a large mansion which resembles a cross between a Motel 6, a haunted house and a concentration camp—since it has the various virtues and drawbacks of each. The gang drives through an electric fence, but that is soon forgotten when they pull up in front of a beautiful pool with a banner proclaiming: "Welcome Sisters." There's also a full bar and buffet laid out. As everyone toasts and noshes, a creepy guy, Mr. Clybourn (Arthur Franz), watches, unseen.

The girls decide to explore the house and go swimming, which makes poor Joe hotter than Georgia asphalt. He and Paul leave, but after a few minutes of ridiculous conversation, Joe convinces his partner they should sneak back in. Unfortunately, the mystery man has closed the electric fence by remote control, so our two stooges have to climb over to crash the party. The girls aren't upset at all by the appearance of two guys they barely know, so everyone gets drunk and passes out.

Here's where the movie probably miscalculated its audience. The film wasn't sleazy enough for a true exploitation film. It also didn't have enough tension and energy for a suspense thriller. So maybe there should have been some knockin' boots, or some gory killings. But alas, we're left with a glorified TV movie of the week, with just Claudia to enthrall us.

The next morning, Mark and Joe go to leave, but they find that the electric fence is turned on. The girls also wake up to find a picture of Elizabeth in each of their rooms. They all sit down and agree something isn't right. A little later on, Judy and Mark are walking around the house when Mr. Clybourn confronts them. He tells them he invited them here to take revenge on the girl who murdered his daughter. Judy tells him it was an accident, but Clybourn says he has proof it wasn't. One of the girls evidently witnessed the killer putting a live bullet next to the pistol used in the ceremony. When Mark tries to reason with him, Clybourn pulls out a pistol and tries to ventilate Mark's melon. A bust of Queen Nefertiti catches the bullet instead, and everyone runs away like it's a Monty Python sketch.

You know, this movie's a weird thing. For a thriller, almost nothing happens, contrary to what you'd expect. We see a tarantula crawling over Sylvia's tummy, which Mark swats off and crushes. This is the best special effect in the movie by the way, because crushed spiders have lots of goo. Mostly, however, we see nutty old Clybourn making bullets and the girls and guys talking.

Finally, everyone is starting to lose it a bit. Mark tells everyone to stay together, so Penny goes off to say her mantras, clutching the sacred bead strand that her spaced-out old man gave her for protection. Faster than you can say "Hare Krishna," she is garroted by an unseen person using her own necklace. Talk about a buzz kill! Judy finds her body and bellows a very realistic, bloodcurdling scream.

Well, everyone is freaking big-time now. Mark decides to find something to dig with to tunnel beneath the fence. Joe just happens to find the electrical box, and starts digging away to open it. Judy helps Mark, Francie takes a shower and Sylvia twists her ankle and then disappears.

Just when you thought things would get better, everything turns to shite. Mark discovers a wall below the fence, so that option is screwed. Worse, when it looks like Joe is going to be able to cut the power to the fence, a ferocious Cujo-sized German Shepherd comes out of nowhere and attacks him. Question number one: I know it was a big house, but canines have great hearing, and insane animals generally don't shut up for that long. So why didn't we hear this monster before now?

Question number two: I love dogs as much as anyone, but if a mutt came after me snapping at my you-know-whats, I'm sorry, but I'm going to kick the ever-loving snot out of it. Now, I know Joe was fatigued and probably not thinking straight, but why, instead of defending himself, did he turn and run directly into the electric fence, turning into a giant waffle in the process?

Well, the fortunes of the dwindling group don't improve when Francie is found in the shower with a large pair of shears in her back. Diane suffers an equally unpleasant fate, and when Paul leaves Judy alone, Clybourn conks her on the noggin and starts stripping her. This is a little more serious than staying up until the wee hours and making bullets.

When Judy wakes up, she is in dressed in the Sisters' blue gown and tied to a chair, with crazy Mr. Clybourn playing the flute and another veiled sister standing next to some large object that's draped in canvas. Clybourn flashes back to he and Elizabeth winning flute contest after flute contest back in the good old days. Everyone is in the attic except Mark, who is frantically running around looking for Judy. Clybourn explains that the whole thing was a set-up. There was no witness. He and his mystery helper were trying to flush out the guilty Sister. It turns out to be Sylvia, because she's felt guilty all these years about Liz's death, and that's what turned her into a drunk and a whore. Sylvia also slips a noose over Judy's head to make sure she ain't going anywhere.

Crazy Clybourn then unveils his surprise: an honest-to-God Gatling gun, with bullets, real and blank, made by none other than the dude himself. Judy starts screaming her ass off, which alerts Mark to her location. Of course, that pesky pooch shows up ready for Alpo time, planning on using Mark for his chow.

Mark wins one for the human race just as Clybourn starts firing. By this time, he's off his nut, and what Judy says next would definitely send him running to Dr. Phil. She explains—quite calmly given the situation—that Elizabeth told her that she wanted to get away from her dear old dad, and begged Judy to put a live bullet in the gun at the sorority initiation. Everyone freaks out at this point, with Judy and Mark just wanting to blow this pop stand. Judy grabs the kook's pistol, Clybourn ventilates Sylvia by accident, and we can tell we're headed towards a wow finish.

Mark has found a can of gas that he hurls against the fence, blowing a hole in it. Clybourn, trying to shoot at them from the attic, gets it right in the chest with a spectacular trick shot by Judy. She nails the old bastard from about 100 yards away, shooting upwards, holding the pistol with one hand. Could happen.

The couple approaches the car, and Mark says, "We made it." Judy points the gun at him, thinking there are too many loose ends, and says, "No, *I* made it." *Finis*.

Which really sucks for Mark, because he probably figured Judy would be pretty grateful; maybe she'd even dump the governor's son for him. But no, he went through that entire ordeal just to end up as dead as the others did.

This film seemed totally worthless at first viewing, but improved the second time around. The music is quite effective; the interior scenes are well photographed, for the most part. The exterior scenes, on the other hand, seem disconnected from the rest of the movie, from unbalanced open space frames to the boom being visible for most of one particular sequence. If you want to make a film that will be considered amateurish, you've found the right formula.

The acting is uneven, despite the strength of the cast. Arthur Franz had an illustrious career on television and was featured in *The Caine Mutiny* and *Invaders from Mars*. Cheri Howell was an accomplished B-movie actress and Sherry Boucher, while not having the extensive career of Claudia, ended up marrying actor George Peppard. She also produced a number of TV shows in her time.

Paul Carr and Joe Tata, best known for their respective appearances in two of television's most beloved soap operas—Carr in *The Young and the Restless*, and Tata in *Beverly Hills 90210*—had fine careers. Sherry Alberoni was a Mouseketeer, then had a limited career in film, but found her niche in voice-overs for cartoon work. Roxanne Albee had a brief career, appearing in several un-credited episodes of *The Monkees* and a handful of movies—usually as a beautiful girl in a walk-on role.

Claudia was happy with her performance in *Sisters of Death*. She was by far the strongest performer in the cast, carrying every scene with ease. She goes from confident to fearful, terrified and mercenary without difficulty. Claudia once again shows her natural skills, as when she has to comfort Penny; she puts a protective arm around her and clutches her hand. She has no difficulty hitting her marks or knowing where the camera is going to be in a given scene. I imagine this was a product of her extensive stage training.

When interviewed by James M. Tate of *Cult Film Freak* in 2004, Sherry Alberoni was asked what it was like to work with Claudia. Her answer reflects the universal feelings her friends and fellow actors had for Claudia:

> Oh, I loved Claudia! There was no Internet back then, so it wasn't too easy to learn everything about everybody with the push of a button ... but I had heard through the grapevine that she had been in *Playboy*, so I don't know what I expected of her, but I know I didn't think she would be as nice and down-to-earth as she was. She wasn't as glamorous as I figured she'd be; she was very pretty but didn't live in her make-up.
>
> She was a lot of fun, had an infectious laugh and was truly a sweet girl. I was shocked and extremely saddened when I heard on the news that she had gotten killed in a car crash. If I recall, she was dating Tommy Boyce—or was it Bobby Hart?—and it was all so sad to me because I knew and really liked her.

Director Joseph Mazzuca did the best he could, I suppose. However, if you're going to do an exploitation film right, you'd better work something a bit more lurid into the proceedings. By the same logic, if you want to make a PG-rated thriller, you'd best inject some superior thrills, lighting, atmosphere and a clever plot. If the rest of *Sisters*

of *Death* was as good as the first five minutes, we might have seen a minor classic. As it happened, no distributor would touch it, and the film wasn't released until 1977.

As another gesture indicative of Claudia's sweet personality, at the end of the filming she presented Mazzuca with a gift. During the shoot, the heel on one of Claudia's shoes kept breaking, and filming had to be suspended each time to get her a new pair. Claudia jokingly called the director "Shoeless Joe" and presented him with a bronzed broken shoe as a memento of the experience. Although Mazzuca thought the sentiment was lovely, he was confused by the name "Shoeless Joe," evidently not being a baseball fan ("Shoeless" Joe Jackson) nor a Broadway show fan ("Shoeless Joe from Hannibal, MO" from *Damn Yankees*).

Group Marriage (1973)

If Claudia had appeared in the beginning of this film instead of halfway through, it might have been her greatest role. It certainly was one of her best performances, leaving me to wonder what critics could have found so awful to savage her acting. She does a beautifully measured job here—and remember, Claudia was only 24 when it was filmed. Despite being one of the youngest members of the cast, she seems far more mature than the rest of the actors, although some of the characters were obviously meant to be idiots.

Directed and co-written by Roger Corman protégé Stephanie Rothman, *Group Marriage* is a remarkable bit of cinema. Ahead of its time in exploiting true feminism, it also championed gay marriage, had a male character that was the equivalent of a dumb blond, showed a whole pumpkin truck of nude male ass and featured a non-stereotypical Asian and an African-American in its cast.

The film is also hysterically funny, with the screenplay showing influences from S.J. Perelman and the screwball comedies of the 1930s and 1940s. It is a beautiful movie to watch, especially the beach scenes, which can be breathtaking. In general, the outdoor scenes seem like they are from another movie, whereas the cheap-looking indoor sets are limp, lifeless and turn the film from an A to a B.

The music is used in an odd way, with each character and scene having its own theme song. John Sebastian of *The Lovin' Spoonful* wrote and performed the title song, a jivey little folk-rock number. Then, at times, some lovely harpsichord music plays, supplanted by a jazz flute trio, then a thoughtful piano solo, and back again to the harpsichord … well, you get it.

Former Playmate of the Year Victoria Vetri, who posed for *Playboy* under the name of Angela Dorian, plays Jan, and is the star along with Solomon Sturges as Sander. Vetri had a promising career, appearing in dozens of movies and television programs. She was a serious actress and barely missed out on roles in *Lolita* and *West Side Story*. But she is best remembered for starring in Hammer's *When Dinosaurs Ruled the Earth*. In a tragic and bizarre twist of fate, she was later sentenced to prison for the attempted murder of her husband.

As the story opens, Chris (Aimeé Eccles) is a lovely young Asian-American lady who is a decent mechanic and works at a car rental agency with her friend Judy (Jayne Kennedy). After a beautifully written

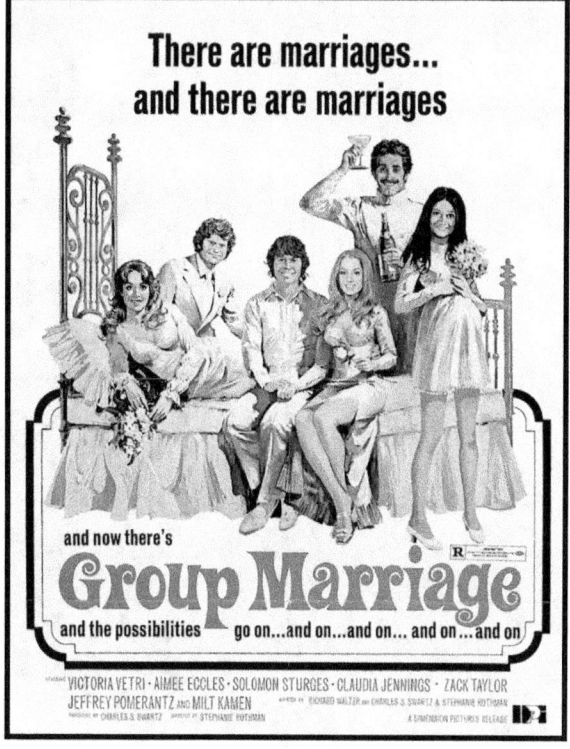

"question game" routine with a frazzled customer, Judy and Chris talk about Sander, Chris's useless boyfriend, who owns a bumper sticker company. One of his more mainstream stickers reads, "Santa Claus is a Faggot." I must give warning here that although the film gets props for being progressive, there are a fair amount of anti-gay slurs and misogynistic colloquialisms as well.

Well, it turns out Sander's car won't start, so Chris has to pick him up. It just so happens there's a handsome parole officer, Dennis—also without a vehicle—thumbing a hitch. Chris picks him up and drives over to Sander's, who ain't happy his beautiful girlfriend has picked up a stranger and is looking him over like he's a big 1970s-moustache-wearing hot dog. Dennis accidently gets one in the yarbles, and Chris, feeling badly, invites him to dinner, much to Sander's disgust.

As Dennis lies on the couch, the full measure of Sander's contempt starts to dribble out at Chris. At one point Sander asks Dennis if he likes spaghetti, after Chris offers to make dinner. "Good. You can have the whole can," he snorts.

The dialogue is very tongue-in-cheek, and could easily have ventured into *Who's Afraid of Virginia Woolf?* territory if the humor wasn't kept in the forefront. So before you know it, after Sander falls asleep, Chris hops up like a bunny, hightails it to Dennis' room, and they make beautiful music together.

The next morning, Sander doesn't take it well, as Chris asks him, "Why does everyone think you only have to like one person?" However, Dennis offers to take Sander and Chris out and meet his woman, Jan, to cheer him up. Sander whines she's probably ugly and pisses and moans all day.

A Biography

A publicity photo of the female cast of *Group Marriage*: Angela Dorian (aka Victoria Vetri), front; Claudia Jennings, left; Aimeé Eccles, center rear; Jayne Kennedy, right

That night Sander meets Jan, and wowie-wow-wow-wow. Just your average Playmate of the Year dressed up for an Oscar ceremony. It's obvious from the moment they meet, Sander has but one thing on his mind.

However, when they get back home from dinner, they all crawl into bed and Chris starts having pangs of jealousy. She sabotages the partner swap by staying up and watching television until the test pattern comes on. During the late-night broadcast, there is a reference made to the film *Attack of the 50 Foot Woman*, by the way. At one point Sander begs her to turn off the TV, saying, "Dennis is asleep, and if I try to make love to Jan, it will be necrophilia."

Eventually, the two couples stake out two separate but equal bedrooms, and the house is filled with the sound of sex and 1970s music. Noticing that her new home is a dump, Jan goes out shopping to spruce things up. The couple next door, a very awkwardly portrayed gay couple, makes silly comments about the shenanigans. There is one scene where they try to make dinner for everyone; it is so ill conceived and poorly executed that one wonders what Rothman was thinking.

On the other hand, there are scenes that are shot with such incredible finesse and style that they astound you. The scene where Jan goes shopping is as fine a piece of moviemaking as you will ever see. You are transported from a sloppy house in California to a market in Paris. There are a few frames where Jan reacts to a clerk that are so honest and compelling that her face becomes a work of art momentarily.

Later on, the group heads to the beach. In another exquisitely shot scene, the beach, water, sunset and rocks all become one. You will not find a better-photographed sequence in a B-movie. The shot gets better as Jan walks along the beach and rocks, deep in thought, when she sees a man on the beach off in the distance. They have a chat and it's not really "small talk," since we slowly realize the man, an off-duty lifeguard, is in the buff.

Well, his car won't start either, so Chris hoists herself on top of his engine with her long hair dangling down (not a good idea for all you automobile self-repair enthusiasts out there—belts, fans and fan blades). She asks him about his distributor cap and he tells her he doesn't know what that is. Okay, so he's good looking, but not a rocket scientist—cue the feminist irony here.

As the gay couple watches the group come back from the beach, one of them asks the other, "What do you call two women and three men?"

"A full house?"

Phil tells the group he has nowhere to go, since his wife is divorcing him. The group invites him to stay until he can find a place to live, but the guys have a better idea. They'll find Phil his own companion. The next day, Sander, Phil and Dennis are jogging when Elaine (Claudia) comes bouncing by. Entranced by her beauty and flaming red hair, they ask her to join the group. We get some nice shots of Claudia jogging from the foreground and background, as Phil runs alongside her trying to convince a stranger to move in with five other people. Could happen.

Elaine comes by to check out the scene and tells them she's interested. She also tells Phil she wants to see him in her office the following morning. Just then, the doorbell rings and a procession of perverts arrive to audition for the sixth addition. It seems Phil forgot he put an advertisement in the local underground newspaper for another female—only the newspaper put "male" by mistake. What could have been an opportunity for some perverse fun unfortunately fizzles.

The next morning, Phil goes to see Elaine in her gleaming law office. She hands him a subpoena, and he realizes that Elaine is his wife's lawyer. Oh, snap! The two then get into an unfriendly discussion, where Phil's chauvinistic side brings out Elaine's, and, well, here's some of the dialogue:

> Phil: At least she wasn't a mouth. She knew when to shut up and put out!
> Elaine: Then she sounds like your ideal woman: A dumb cunt!

There is not a lick of humor in this exchange, as Claudia does a wonderful job looking and acting pissed off. I think it's one of her prouder moments, as she's at first apologetic, then sympathetic and finally at her angry best. This was another scene where Claudia was not a mannequin. When she stands up from her desk to strike back at the Neanderthal (albeit a cute one), she is hitting her marks and camera cues perfectly.

After the fireworks and unexpected vulgarity, we see poor Phil wandering the city to some pathetic music, wondering what to do with his pathetic life. As the five friends sit around that evening, the doorbell rings and Elaine shows up with the hots for Phil; we're treated to a ringside view of their "honeymoon night." Of all the relationships in the film, Phil and Elaine make the least sense. Dennis and Sander show some wit and some intelligence, whereas Phil needs to think seriously about involuntary actions like breathing. I guess opposites attract.

It doesn't take long for reality to sink in for our happy couples. A TV news station picked up on the story from the underground newspaper, and they soon make sure every redneck bigot and Nixon supporter is out to get them. In short order Dennis gets fired; the gang starts getting obscene phone calls constantly; Sander forgets to pay the power bill on a morning where everyone's nerves are at a breaking point; the house is vandalized and firebombed, including their vehicle, sort of bringing the film into *Easy Rider* territory; and then Chris really shits the bed by announcing she's pregnant, which sends Jan into a tizzy since "she don't know nothin' about taking care of no babies." The guys are useless, since none of them are sure who the father is.

Well, my friends, what a frigging mess we have here. But it gets worse, sort of! As Phil reports to work, he finds Jan has been shagging one of his fellow lifeguards. Sander is crestfallen, but as Jan honestly explains, their whole arrangement was based on freedom, and she doesn't feel that anymore. Here's where the hypocrisy of the group's arrangement lies. Even though there are six (well, now five, since Jan splits), they live just like married couples, sharing space and a common kitchen but not bed partners or even experimenting with some interesting combinations. They might as well be a bunch of freshmen in an upscale dorm.

They all decide to get married anyway—despite the fact, as Elaine assures them, they will be arrested, since marriage is legally defined as between one man and one woman. But Elaine vows to take the battle to the Supreme Court if necessary. In this way, the film predicts the controversy surrounding gay marriage, which continues to the present day.

The day of the wedding arrives and it looks like something out of *A Clockwork Orange* or *Tommy*—very bizarre to say the least, from the decorations to the garb of the guests. The third bride turns out to be Chris' friend Judy (Jayne Kennedy), and the ladies look fabulous while the men look like they spent the prior evening raiding the closets of Barry Manilow and Maurice Gibb. Jan is there to support her friends, and the gay couple is there to get married, along with everyone else.

As the happy couples finish the reception, they depart under a shower of flowers and rice into the waiting arms of California's finest. Chris picks that moment to go into labor, but first fixes the stalled police car in which she's riding. Off everyone goes, as John Sebastian comes back on the soundtrack with love triumphing over all. We hope.

Stephanie Rothman was a gifted director, but quit the business because she was tired of all the bullshit she had to go through. She made some fine films before letting go, such as *The Velvet Vampire* and *The Working Girls*, but was frustrated by having to direct strictly exploitation efforts. Heavily influenced by French directors Georges Franju and Jean Cocteau, one can imagine the sort of work she could have composed if given the freedom, the budgets and the support she deserved.

Rothman does a fine job here by switching audience expectations regarding the traditional roles of men and women. The women are all competent, intelligent and do guy stuff better than guys, i.e., work on cars, etc. The guys are cute but really dumb and clueless. In my opinion, Jan is the only one who makes choices that are in her best interest and stays true to her character.

Rothman enjoyed working with Claudia, but both were swimming against the same tide. The director wanted to move away from the exploitation genre, while Claudia would never get her chance. *Group Marriage*, overall, was a step up from her previous film, but not much. Claudia got to show a lot of skin in this uneven comedy that attempted to advocate a lot of worthwhile ideals, with the exception that it has a lot of anti-gay slurs and stereotypes. Of course, the ending helps compensate for the virulent homophobic language earlier in the movie. The film has the rare distinction of having cast two Playmates of the Year: Claudia and Victoria Vetri. Rothman made sure that the movie didn't take itself too seriously. There are also three very beautiful women copulating with three attractive men in various combinations. Unfortunately for Claudia, doing this picture probably undid much of the good her appearance in *Unholy Rollers* had created.

The Single Girls (aka *Bloody Friday*) (1974)

Claudia's first of two collaborations with the husband-and-wife team of Ferd and Beverly Sebastian was a solid B-effort called *The Single Girls*. The film, a 1970s variation of Agatha Christie's classic *And Then There Were None* with a bit of sardonic humor thrown in, concerns an island full of five men and five women who are there for a sex-focused sensitivity training class.

When researching this book, I had the pleasure of speaking with the Sebastians several times about their friendship with Claudia. They treated her as a daughter and loved her dearly. They shared many things about their films and Claudia with me, and most of the interview can be read in the synopsis of *'Gator Bait.*

Filmed in only five days with a budget of $35,000, *The Single Girls*' cost belies the quality of the film. Ferd was the cinematographer on land, and his son shot the underwater sequences. The photography is superb overall, with just a few night scenes a little too murky to make out the action. But the colors of the Pacific and the bright flowers in a scene shot inside a greenhouse all come alive in Mr. Sebastian's capable hands. The location was Paradise Cove, a private beach west of Malibu, and included the caves, woods and greenhouse that appear in the movie. The other location was an upscale resort hotel, the Westlake Inn, where the crew also had dinner. Ferd told me the crew had lunch on the beach each day. All the interior shots took place in the hotel. The seaplane seen in the opening of the film was a real plane that took tourists to Catalina Island. This was an ideal location for the Sebastians, considering all the locales for the movie were less than 15 minutes from their home. He told me it was "the simplest, easiest shoot there ever was." *Time* magazine even did a feature on the Sebastians, calling them the "Ma and Pa Kettle of the Movie Business."

Here is a brief part of my interview with the Sebastians concerning the film and Claudia.

Eric: Where and when did you first meet Ms. Jennings?
Ferd: At the casting call for *The Single Girls*.
Eric: What was the main reason you cast her in that movie?
Ferd: She was perfect for *The Single Girls*. She was a talented actress and I could not ask for a better one. But she was more than that. She gave 100 percent of herself before the camera and behind it.
Eric: Had you seen any of her other work before you hired her for *The Single Girls*?
Ferd: I never saw any of the other work she had done.
Eric: How did your friendship with Claudia begin?
Ferd: During the filming of *The Single Girls*, Beverly and I both started liking Claudia very much. She was easy to work with and filmed wonderfully.

Ferd and Beverly put together an impressive film with a good cast. Of course, the title (and only) song on the soundtrack is "Ms. America," sung by Bobby Hart and written by Hart and Danny Janssen. I happen to feel it was very sweet to have the powers that be let Bobby do the music, and it must have made Claudia happy. Along with *Unholy Rollers* and *Truck Stop Women*, Claudia always tried to have Bobby involved with her films as a way of including him in her professional life.

Even though *The Single Girls* is a B-movie, the cast has some decent star power. Besides Claudia, Greg Mullavey plays George. He was widely known for the spoof evening soap opera *Mary Hartman, Mary Hartman*, which introduced Billy Crystal to America. He was also married to *Petticoat Junction*'s Meredith MacRae for many years. Albert Popwell, who plays Morris, was a prolific actor and one of Clint Eastwood's favorites. He appeared in four of the *Dirty Harry* films, including the iconic scene where he lies prostrate and wounded, Eastwood standing over him asking, "Do you feel lucky, punk!!!" Popwell was also the star of two blaxploitation classics, *Cleopatra Jones* and *Cleopatra Jones and the Casino of Gold*.

Victor Izay plays the kindhearted Andrew, and was a B-movie veteran of films such as *Billy Jack* and *Blood Orgy of the She-Devils*, and then he went on to a stellar television and movie career. You can see him in *The Waltons* as Dr. Vance, or in *Wild Hogs* and *Employee of the Month*. Chéri Howell, who plays the seductively trampy Shannon, appeared alongside Claudia in *Sisters of Death*; then, in an abrupt career change, she became a dentist. The beautiful and talented Robyn Hilton plays Denise, a breathless

Allison (Claudia) participates in "The Blind Walk," to increase trust among the group.

blonde Hollywood bimbo, to perfection. Her most memorable role came as Governor William J. Le Petomane's secretary, Miss Stein, in Mel Brooks' *Blazing Saddles*.

Jean Marie Ingels as nice Jewish girl Phyllis was another veteran television actress who added professionalism to the production. One other cast member with an interesting back-story was Merci Rooney. A former Playmate of the Month as Merci Montello, she married Mickey Rooney, Jr. after they met at the Los Angeles Playboy Club. Mrs. Rooney plays the doomed Cathy, and after this film, her acting career never gained any traction. She retreated from the limelight and never worked in any major productions again.

The movie opens with the title song "Ms. America," then segues to some funky 1970s guitar jams as we view a scuba diver gliding through the Pacific. Then a seaplane lands, and a group of men and women disembark onto the dock. The scuba diver is cleaning his equipment when a very hot passenger, Cathy (Rooney), stops and checks him out. The diver cleverly asks her, "Have you ever been down?" and she replies, "Hasn't everyone?" They enjoy an underwater frolic and later we see Cathy walking to the hotel through the woods with a big towel wrapped around her head. The camera then follows the eyes of a stalker armed with a spear gun. By the time Cathy sees the assailant and reacts, it's much too late. Skewered by the spear, she becomes a human martini olive. The killer covers her lightly with brush and branches, yet leaves her arm grotesquely pointing outwards, uncovered.

Back at the hotel, Dr. Stevens informs the group from the seaplane that they are there for sensitivity training, which will involve sexual encounter sessions. He goes around the group and asks each individual to tell a little bit about him or herself. Allison (Claudia)

Allison takes a shower in *The Single Girls*

volunteers that she's just broken off an engagement, and that she gets so mad at men she wants to kill sometimes. Did I mention Allison is a nurse? So immediately she's on the suspect list. George (Mullavey) is an emotionally repressed, glasses-wearing stutterer, so *he's* obviously a suspect. Pretty soon the nice little group chat breaks down into a *One Flew Over the Cuckoo's Nest*-type chaos, which is intentionally hilarious. All that's missing is someone screaming, "Nurse Ratched, I want my cigarettes!"

Dr. Stevens decides a new exercise is in order, so he tells the group they will be "milling" for a while. They are to mingle in the dark and lose their own identities by merging them with the group's identity. Oh, yes—they are encouraged to remove their clothing as well. It kind of sounds like the parties we used to have in seventh grade, except the women in the film are all spectacular.

I guess Dr. Stevens didn't fully explain the rules of milling completely, because about three minutes into the exercise, someone screams and pretty much puts the kibosh on the mood. It turns out one of the guests tried to make a blue plate special of Denise's (Hilton's) left breast. The perp used his teeth to sample the goods, which freaks the gang out.

Later that night, as everyone relaxes in the cocktail lounge, we see so many psychodramas played out (much to our amusement) that it looks like modern reality TV. Shannon (Howell) wedges herself in between every couple, trying to vamp on the guys. Andrew (Izay) and Phyllis (Engels) develop an attraction to each other. Lola (Joan Prather) and Blue (Jason Ledger) make plans for her deflowering, and Claudia and Morris chat each other up at the bar. George sits next to the couple, looking suspicious and creepy. All of this goes on under the watchful eyes of Dr. Stevens and his Goth assistant, a sweet-looking brunette in a white dress who says nothing during the film.

Well, wouldn't you know it—just when everyone's having a great time, who should barge in out of nowhere but Allison's ex-fiancé, Bud (Ed Blessington). He doesn't waste any time demonstrating why he's the number one asshole in the county by making racist comments towards Morris and Allison, and then assaulting her physically and verbally. Well, he just rose to the top of the suspect-o-meter, thank you very much.

By the way, there's also lots of cowbell on the soundtrack; and as everyone knows, the only cure is more cowbell. Speaking of the soundtrack, the ominous music (i.e., the killer's lurking) is very effective.

The doctor, sensing the buzz-kill, brings a belly dancer out to perform. This proves to be a real crowd-pleaser, as everyone gets up to dance. Allison grabs the awkward George and they boogie on down. We get to see Claudia dance for a while, which is a treat, as it has happened far too infrequently on screen. Shannon then tries to seduce Allison's jerk ex-fiancé while the gang is dancing.

After the dance, Andrew and Phyllis go back to her hotel room to consummate their relationship, but a snagged zipper on her dress douses the flames of passion. Then Phyllis hears a noise, and its cold shower time for poor Andrew. Later, as all the girls prepare for bed, they see a murky figure outside their room, making them a tad uncomfortable.

The next morning, Allison takes one of the motorized rafts over to the cool-looking caves, further down the coastline from the hotel. The ocean scenes are beautiful, and Ferd Sebastian takes full advantage of the rock formations and natural scenery to give a very lush feel to the shots. As Allison glides along, Bud catches up with her in another raft; she agrees to let him accompany her to the caves. After exploring the caves and being chased out by some nasty bats, the couple has a sincere discussion on the beach. When it looks like they might reconcile, Bud shows his true Neanderthal controlling misogynist self, and Allison asks him to split. As Allison is sunbathing topless, ominous bad-guy music plays, and George about scares the you know what out of her. So George has just added to his possible killer cred, courtesy of this scene.

Later on, back at the hotel, Dr. Stevens has another exercise for the group: The Blind Walk. The men and women pair up, and one is blindfolded, while the other guides them with a palm frond. The doctor explains the purpose of the exercise is to build trust with their partners, but we know what it's really for.

Quickly, a still-seething Bud confronts George and Allison and delivers the unquestionably ugliest line in the film: "What is it? Ball the handicapped day?" Then, in a victory for nerdy, four-eyed, emotionally stunted individuals everywhere, George beats the hell out of Bud pretty much without raising his pulse. Awesome scene, by all accounts.

Andrew has led Phyllis off the trail into woods for a little loving. They walk deeper into the shrubbery, oblivious to the human shish-kabob inches from their feet, when the palm frond momentarily drops from Andrew's hand. It is picked up and handed to Phyllis, who becomes alarmed when Andrew doesn't reply to her. She removes her blindfold, sees the killer, nearly trips over Andrew's body and is chased into a greenhouse. Talk about a bad evening.

However, the next sequence is the *tour de force* of the production. From the moment Phyllis enters the building, the camera angles build tension dramatically, while the vivid colors of the greenhouse give the scene a lurid, nightmarish intensity. I imagine if we could have filmed one of Gauguin's dreams, it might have looked something like this. Phyllis is eventually cornered, and the killer puts divots into the poor girl's face, furrowing her with a three-pronged garden fork. To the Sebastians' credit, the gore shots are mild, with most of the damage done off screen.

The evening has only begun as the camera cuts to the girls' room, where an unseen figure is cutting up Allison's dresses, undies and other clothing with a large pair of scissors. Bud and Allison, who have reconciled yet again, walk into the room and discover the mess. Bud goes to get help and unwisely tells Allison to lock the door, since the mysterious clothes shredder is still hiding in the closet. Allison takes a shower, and the audience gets to see what it came for. After some tense cat-and-mouse scenes, the unseen figure departs, and Allison is safe.

Not so for Lola and Blue. As Lola is living out her fantasy of having her virginity taken, she walks alone in the woods when Blue grabs her. He ties her hands behind her back and proceeds to remove her white dress. The sequence is quite erotic and effectively shot. So it's a real bummer when the killer gives Blue the *coup de grace* with a big old axe and then dispatches the lovely Lola.

The next day, everyone realizes something is amiss. I don't know, maybe it's because a whole lot of folks ain't around any more? One of the girls finally notices Cathy is missing—duh! Allison and Shannon go off to the caves to search for Lola and Phyllis, while Denise and Morris frolic on the beach. Yes, they run around while half the hotel has vanished; however, they are thrust back into reality when a severely injured and partially concealed Andrew grabs Morris' hand. George comes running over and reveals himself to be an undercover policeman, who has been chasing a serial killer for six months. Told that Allison and Shannon have gone to the caves, George takes off in hot pursuit.

The ladies are hunting through the creepy caves when they discover Lola's body. Allison lets out a yell, but Shannon is curiously unperturbed. She explains that all the men belong to her, so naturally, the ends justify the means. When Allison asks why she had to kill everyone, Shannon explains simply, "Because it makes me feel good." Well, I guess everyone needs a hobby, but it doesn't comfort Allison when Shannon whips out a BEK (big effin' knife) and tries to kill her. With her arm suffering a GBI (grievous bodily injury) from a knife wound, Allison bolts to the beach, with crazy Shannon running after her in a blood frenzy. Fortunately, George shows up and neutralizes the deranged Shannon before she can inflict more damage.

The movie ends with a shot of a playful George and Allison walking along the beach, holding hands and making all kinds of plans. Seriously, the scene, filmed at sunset, is quite beautiful, and if the right music were playing, you'd think it looked every bit as good as the opening of *Grease*.

The Single Girls holds up very well when viewed today. It is an example of low-budget filmmaking done right—a responsible exploitation film, as it were. The female nudity is there as a prerequisite to be competitive in the 1970s market, and because the violence is subtle compared to its contemporaries, the movie is not as creepy as most slasher films. Smooth direction, competent acting, excellent photography, killer locations and some gorgeous females all set this film apart from some of the trash the decade produced.

Unfortunately, Claudia would star in some truly dreadful projects in her time, but this film is not one of them. She gives yet again a mature, balanced performance. I believe my favorite scene is non-verbal, where she reacts to another character by giving her trademark half-smirk. The gesture is so human, natural and so Claudia as to be priceless. If you examine the great actresses of our generation, the skills that set them apart are their eyes and general facial mannerisms. Sophia Loren comes to mind, as witnessed by her performance in *Arabesque*. The same nuances can be seen in the films of Marilyn Monroe, Jane Fonda, Myrna Loy and dozens of others. Claudia had not matured as an actress at this point, nor was the material and money there to support her ambitions. However, all the pieces were in place for her to succeed when higher quality work was offered her.

The Single Girls, made in 1973, marked another turning point in Claudia's life and career. She began a lifelong friendship with the husband-and-wife team of Beverly and Ferd Sebastian. This incredible duo was a two-person studio. Beverly would write and direct; Ferd would do all the cinematography. Usually, anything that needed doing on the set became their tasks. This also marked a point in Claudia's career where she became firmly entrenched in the world of the B-movie.

40 Carats (1973)

Next, Claudia was cast in her second big studio production, a feature directed by Milton Katselas, adapted from the ultra-successful Broadway show. The film had an all-star cast and a truly fine screenplay. It's easy to overlook this film; it has many faults, including some scenes that translate uncomfortably from their stage roots and an embarrassing dance sequence. However, the acting is quite superb across the board, especially Ann (Liv Ullmann) and Peter (Edward Albert) as the May/December lovers. Gene Kelly and Deborah Raffin as Ann's ex-husband and daughter, respectively, contribute creditable work as well.

When Claudia got this role, it probably seemed as if she had made a breakthrough into respectable cinema. Director Milton Katselas recognized one of Claudia's prime character traits: the need to please. "She would ask me after a scene if she did it all right, several times. She needed reassurance." Veteran actors and a big budget surrounded

Peter (Edward Albert) introduces his new girlfriend (Liv Ullmann) to his ex (Claudia).

Claudia, and great things were expected of the movie. The pressure on cast and crew must have been intense.

The film's central message, which tends to get lost in all the shenanigans, is that life is neither a spectator sport nor a sure thing. There is a leap of faith involved in all we do as human beings, especially when falling in love. All things being equal, the odds of finding happiness is illogical, so why not go with the heart? The screenplay and acting convey this eloquently and without too much melodrama.

In a way, it was a perfect vehicle for Claudia. The characters are impulsive, just as she was, and there are an awful lot of May/December relationships in the movie, which were also prevalent in Claudia's life.

I hope I haven't gotten you too excited, because Claudia doesn't have a lot of screen time. She is glimpsed briefly early in the film during a party sequence. Then at 1:19:00, Peter brings Ann, now his fiancée, to meet his friends, basically a bunch of wealthy spoiled trust fund brats. Gabriella (Claudia), one of Peter's girlfriends, saunters up in a nearly see-through outfit and flirts heavily with him, ultimately giving him a big sloppy one. As she slinks away, she looks Ann up and down and shrugs in a spiteful, malicious manner—or a bitchy one. Whatever it is, it ain't nice.

To show you how the Hollywood publicity machine works, Claudia's publicist had this article placed in the *Los Angeles Times*:

> Claudia Jennings has been signed for the key role of Gabriella in *40 Carats*, the Frankovich Production for Columbia Pictures starring Liv Ullmann, Gene Kelly, Edward Albert and Binnie Barnes. Based on the Broadway and international stage hit, *40 Carats* is being directed by Milton Katselas from a screenplay by Leonard Gershe. Mike Frankovich is producing.[21]

I guess it all depends on how you interpret "key role." Claudia did a fine job in her limited role, but her appearance in *40 Carats* didn't open the door to more A-list pictures—at least none in which she'd be offered a major part.

The film is another "don't get up and take a bathroom break" film for Claudia-watching.

'Gator Bait (1974)

Written by Beverly Sebastian specifically for Claudia and filmed in only 10 days, *'Gator Bait* stands out among the rape and revenge films of the 1970s. Mentally exhausted from appearing in so many films in a short amount of time, Claudia asked Beverly to write her a screenplay with as little dialogue as possible.

There are many ways to view an actor's performance in a particular film. Take Boris Karloff's work in *Frankenstein*. He has almost no dialogue in the film, yet his performance is as complex as any in cinema history. How many actors could convey innocence, wonder, anger and lust with facial expressions, gestures and a few grunts? This is what Claudia accomplishes in *'Gator Bait*. It is not a perfect film, and Claudia does not give a perfect performance, but it is a thoughtful film and is much more than the sum of its parts.

The movie was shot on location in a real swamp in Texas. The alligators and snakes you see are very real. Ferd Sebastian said the snakes were kept in the shower stalls of the hotel where the crew stayed. One afternoon, a housekeeper almost suffered a heart attack when she opened the curtain and saw a dozen snakes wiggling around. The Screen Actors Guild also mandated separate bathrooms for males and females on the set. Ferd sensibly told the crew that the large tree on the left was for women and the large tree to right was for men.

The first impression the movie makes is the manner in which the swamp becomes a living character. Using only a single handheld camera, Ferd brings the bayou to life, much like the desert in *Inferno* or the hellish Mexican terrain in *The Treasure of the Sierra Madre*. The haunting strains of the title song "Desiree" plays and we glimpse the water, trees and undergrowth of the swamp.

Desiree (Claudia) sets a trap for the Brackens.

Desiree (Claudia) is a Cajun poacher, which is illegal, but she has an uneasy truce with the Sheriff (Bill Thurman). That is until one day the Sheriff's idiot son Billy Boy (Clyde Ventura) and his equally idiotic friend Ben Bracken (Ben Sebastian), while driving the Sheriff's new boat, catch Desiree red-handed hauling in alligators. The boys talk excitedly about raping her before they arrest her. After a short chase, they have her cornered, and it looks like we'll get to see Claudia naked for sure. Her outfit is a little skimpy to begin with; just a worn denim vest and matching hot pants. Well, Desiree ain't that easy, and with a so-so rebel yell ("Yee-haw!"), she tosses a bag of live snakes into the boys' boat. In a scene of pure country comedy, Billy Boy tries to kill the snakes by shooting them even though they're squiggling around on the bottom of the boat. In all the commotion, not only does Desiree escape, but also Billy Boy manages to blow his friend's head off. *And sink the boat.*

Leroy Bracken (Douglas Dirkson) grabs Julie (Janit Baldwin).

The beauty and intelligence of this scene, and what so many of the hicksploitation and exploitation films of the 1970s lacked, is a reversal of identification. The mostly male audience of the time couldn't wait to see Claudia naked and writh-

A Biography

Claudia's iconic *'Gator Bait* pose

ing under the assault of these two slobbering goons. Filmmakers typically tried to give the audience what they thought they wanted through nudity, violence and the degradation of the female.

However, in this single scene, *'Gator Bait* turns that audience identification around. Indeed, this was to be Claudia's signature in many of her remaining films. She almost perfected it in *Unholy Rollers* as Karen Walker, but here she creates the concept that women are not only as an equal to man, but a threat to men as well. The men are reduced to buffoons and weaklings, which makes the audience reluctant to embrace them psychologically. Not only that, but Desiree never gives a hint that she needs or wants the company of a man. Billy Boy makes his way back to his pappy the Sheriff, who's more pissed off about his new boat than the Bracken kid. Billy also tells a small fib, one that will drive the film's narrative to its end. The Sheriff is told Desiree shot Ben. Now poaching is one thing, but murder is quite a different matter. The Sheriff reluctantly goes to see the Bracken family to tell them the grim news. How shall I describe the Brackens? If the mountain men from *Deliverance* mated with the family from *The Texas Chain Saw Massacre*, they would probably look and act like the Brackens.

When we see their lovely homestead, decorated in early Victorian filth, a pretty albeit muddy young woman is hanging up laundry to dry. She is suddenly attacked while another man just watches. Along comes T.J. Bracken (Sam Gilman), the patriarch of this degenerate tribe, who proceeds to bullwhip the snot out of the man while yelling, "Pete Bracken! I oughta kill you, ya horny bastard! That there's your sister! What the hell you tryn'a do? Get her knocked up with some dimwit kid, turn out like you? Huh?" Well, you can see that the family needs some counseling.

Predictably, the old man doesn't take the news of his son's demise very well. We find out there is no love lost between Desiree's family and the Brackens, going way back. In fact, Leroy Bracken, the most disturbed of the bunch, kind of limps around, the result of Desiree making him a capon after he tried to rape her. T.J. decides they're going to mount an expedition into the swamp to retrieve Ben's body and kill Desiree. The Sheriff protests, but it's clear who's calling the shots in this neck of the swamp.

There are some excellent scenes of Desiree and her family interacting while the mutants are gathering their forces. She has a younger brother, Big T (Tracy Sebastian), and a post-adolescent sister Julie (Janit Baldwin). Big T is mute, and the way he and Claudia interact is handled much more sensitively than you'd expect from an exploitation film. Claudia does a fine job conveying her concern and leadership as a surrogate mother to the children. She leaves them to go off to trap, and we just can feel that something bad is going to happen.

The audience doesn't have to wait long, as TJ and the gang show up and start raising hell. Pete and Billy Boy drag Julie inside the family's cabin and start to rape her. Leroy tries to cut in line, eliciting a string of insults from the other two about his manhood. Enraged, Leroy sticks his shotgun between the hapless girl's legs and fires. He sadistically asks, "Am I man enough now?"

Well, the movie is on firm exploitation ground now, and things are only going to get worse. The rabble sets fire to Desiree's cabin, and Big T manages to escape and find his sister. As expected, when Desiree comes home and sees what the men have done to Julie, she declares all-out war on them. Claudia exhibits a very nuanced bit of acting here. She initially lets out a cry of grief at the sight of her sister's lifeless body, one that is convincing and heartbreaking; however, Desiree quickly and correctly decides that she has no time to mourn at the moment. She knows the Brackens are coming to kill her and her brother, so she reacts accordingly.

Soon the men are in a three-way battle, their nerves frayed and they start fighting among themselves; Desiree is like a vengeful ghost killing them one by one, and as they are lured deeper into the swamp, the swamp becomes a third enemy.

Claudia shows off her physical skills nicely, perching on a tree branch, hopping silently through the bayou and, in a spectacular *tour de force*, driving a speedboat with her foot while blasting away with a shotgun. I might add, for a woman who's lived in the bogs all her life, her hair and make-up are perfect.

By the way, the Brackens never refer to her as a Cajun, but as "coon-ass" and her family as "coonies." Speaking of that, many critics raked Claudia over the coals for her accent in this film. I'll be the first to admit, at times it sounds like a combination of Tonto, a caveman and Frankenstein. Seriously, though, how many of you have ever met a Cajun from deep in the bayou? One thing is for sure, the audiences in the Deep South loved the movie, and Claudia's accent didn't bother them one bit.

As the movie ends, we see the Sheriff and T.J. Bracken get into a celebrity death match that, for my money, is one of the most realistic fight scenes in cinema. The crazed mutant who must now hunt for Desiree alone also murders the sheriff. Pap Bracken is left weaponless and lost in the middle of the swamp. When Desiree and Big T confront him, he reveals some filial connections between himself and Desiree, which you think would break down a few barriers. Hell no! She and Big T leave the rat to the swamp, with no hope of survival, and they walk away.

Sam Gilman (T.J.) was a fine veteran actor who appeared in about 100 television roles and the films *The Missouri Breaks*, *One-Eyed Jacks* and *Every Which Way But Loose*. Bill Thurman (Sheriff Thomas) was another actor who distinguished himself on the small screen, as well as major releases, appearing in movies such as *Close Encounters of the Third Kind*, *The Last Picture Show* and *Silverado*.

'Gator Bait was a departure for Claudia in many ways. She didn't have to use her body as a lure for the film, and although she was scantily clad, there were no sex scenes in the movie. The lack of dialogue meant she had to use her non-verbal acting skills, and in doing so, she did herself proud.

The movie stands out among many of its contemporaries in being a more restrained, yet no less powerful, statement on rape and revenge. The death of Julie is no less harrowing, but it is handled with more subtlety and respect than in films such as *I Spit on Your Grave* and *The Last House on the Left*. 'Gator Bait has almost no gratuitous nudity and the violence is nowhere near the orgiastic extremes of other similar genre movies.

Girls, Guns and Ghouls gave the film a positive review and noted Claudia's efforts in the film:

> Sweet Lord a-Mighty, I've become a Claudia Jennings fan. I've known for years about the Queen of Seventies drive-in, but only recently has my thirst for all types of eccentric cinema become so all-consuming that I'm seeking out names from every recess in my mind. So here we go with Claudia heading up a fantastic backwoods-redneck swamp drama. I've seen this film cop a lot of

negative reviews by folks out there, and I just can't understand why ... I truly feel it's a little gem of drive-in exploitation that holds up in all areas.

I'm so sorry Claudia Jennings died so young (about 29, I think, in a car accident), because she really did have a screen presence and after this, my first viewing of a Claudia film, I've watched *The Great Texas Dynamite Chase*—and that's just as compelling in many different ways. More Claudia movies will be watched!

Of course, when Desiree returns with Big T, they discover the death of their sister and revenge is in the offing. Now an avenging fury, Desiree is shown to be a capable hunter at the start of the film; now we really see her survival and battle skills. The pathetic villains are picked off one by one as Desiree turns the Everglades against them. This film was somewhat of a revelation for me. I just loved the bayou setting, the sweaty villains, the boat action, the banjo music and the "Desiree" theme song that we hear at certain points. Let's face it, though; this is all about Claudia. She just looks fantastic in her cut-offs and vest, looking wilder and more untamed each scene we witness. The picture on the VHS box is the greatest picture of any woman ever taken. There, I said it. She really is a force of nature; the men don't stand a chance against her in her swamp. Claudia doesn't get to say much, but when she does speak, her semi-English utterances carry more than enough weight.

Don't believe all you hear or read; this is a most enjoyable film, and while it's no *Deliverance*, keep an open mind and you'll enjoy your time in Desiree country. I don't know how easy it is to get a hold of it from your local video library, but it's well worth the effort to track down. Now, If only I could get that song out of my head.

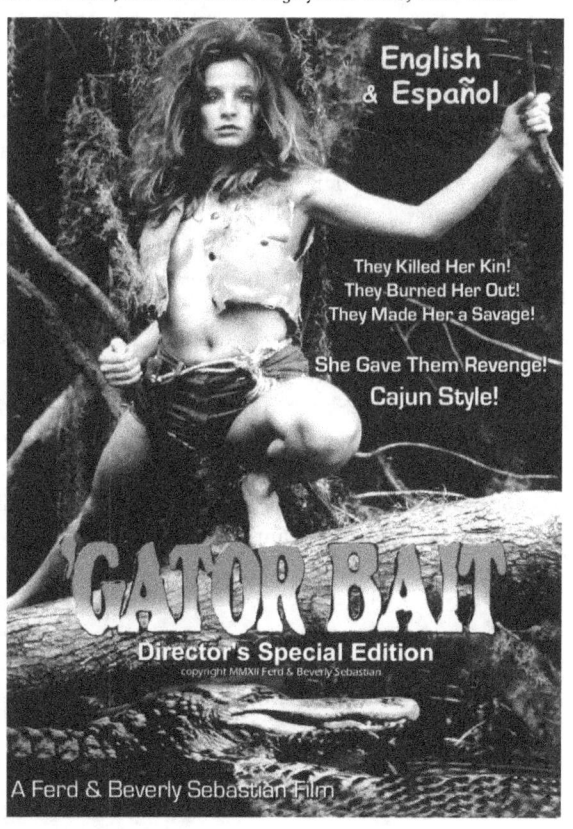

'Gator Bait was a tour de force for Beverly and Ferd Sebastian, and in an odd way an opportunity for Claudia to show some real acting chops. Unable to rely on nudity or dialogue, she still commands the audience's attention in every scene.

The Sebastians had some incredible memories of Claudia and the making of *'Gator Bait*.

Eric: Claudia always talked about making it into A-

A Biography

movies, and yet she loved doing films like *'Gator Bait*. Do you think her appearances in *Playboy* hurt her career?

Beverly and Ferd: As an actress in B-movies, it helped her. We handled *'Gator Bait* like an A-movie release. We hired a plane and went to two or three theaters a day when it opened in Louisiana. The difference was, our movies were in drive-ins. When we came into a theater, the concession stand was packed. Claudia would sit on the counter, sign pictures and talk with them until we had to catch the plane. I will guarantee you that if we had brought Liz Taylor in, we would not have had the crowds we did. Some theaters had 5-mile long lines out on the highway waiting for the second show, as the first show was packed with walk-ins sitting on the ground. Highway patrols were normal at the openings. So *Playboy* did not hurt our business. Did Claudia think *Playboy* was a positive or a negative? She had learned a great lesson in life. Never look back.

Eric: What is your best memory of Claudia?

Beverly and Ferd: The picture below is my best memory of Claudia. A barefoot girl in the swamp, waiting for the next scene. Claudia cannot look bad even when she is resting. *'Gator Bait* is my all-time memory book of Claudia, from riding down to the swamp from L.A. with her and our young son Tracy, who would be playing her younger brother [in the film], as they worked out the sign language between them for his part. He was to portray a mute in the movie, acting in scenes in the movies where she stood in her boat at high speed, steering with her foot and shooting a 12-gauge at her attackers ... Pulling an 8-foot 'gator that she had trapped into her boat ... Seeing her sister murdered where she gave a cry that showed so much pain it will still bring a tear 25 years later ... Seeing her play with her little brother as they chase an armadillo around the crew and actors after work. The actors, being Hollywood health nuts, said they could not stand southern-fried cooking anymore, and they went on strike! So I said, fine, you all take turns cooking. They liked that. So one night we would have steaks, one night broiled chicken and one night sandwiches. But then it came Claudia's turn. She was not working that day, so she spent the whole day preparing food for the crew. So when we came back from the swamp, she had the table prepared. On each plate she put a whole strawberry pie. She said that was the only thing she made good. That *wasn't* the only thing she made good! She made our lives better. To really see the Claudia that we knew, you have to see *'Gator Bait*. For that period of time she *was* Desiree, because Desiree was the real Claudia Jennings—bold, human, kind, unafraid and beautiful in spirit and in body.

Willy & Scratch (1974)

1974's *Willy & Scratch* was written, edited, directed and produced by Robert J. Emery. Mr. Emery started as a director of exploitation films, but moved into mainstream productions, and is also a popular author. He graciously shared his memories about the film and about Claudia.

A friend of mine, a make-up man by the name of John Mocsary, told me of an old Western town attraction in Venice, Florida, of all places. The attraction had fallen on hard times and was closing to the public permanently. I visited this amazingly authentic Western set and was so taken by it that I quickly wrote a screenplay that could be shot entirely on that location, and I put some financing together. The budget was low and the shooting schedule tight, although I do not remember the specifics of either since it was so many years ago (early 1970s). I do remember it was a very stressful shoot because of the lack of money, the short shooting schedule and a very small production crew. Although the film received some domestic and foreign distribution (very little), it was not a very good production and I am sorry to say it never made its money back. I have no idea whatever became of the film in the years that followed, nor do I have a copy or even any stills from it.

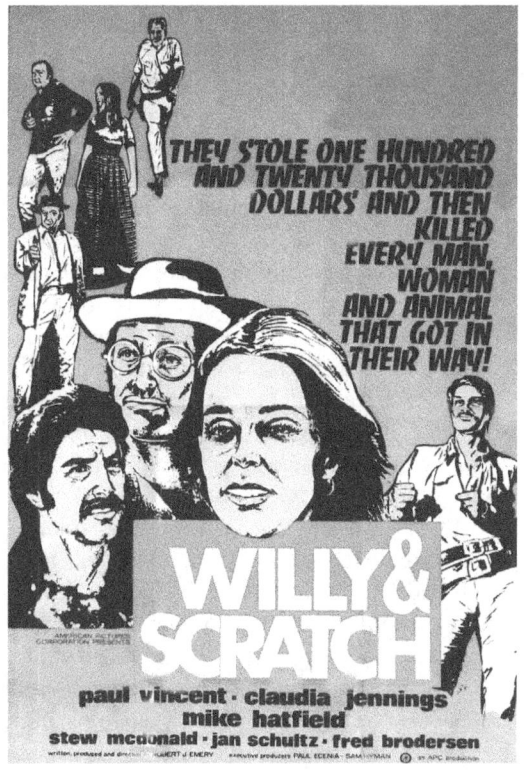

When casting the role of the young wife who enters the deserted town with her husband and two other men (they are outlaws on the run), I immediately thought of Claudia Jennings. Like many, I was aware of her classy involvement with *Playboy*, but I had also seen a couple of her films and I thought she could handle the role. I decided to make her an offer, and to my delight, she accepted. Her character's name in the film was Jennifer.

There is one amusing story concerning Claudia when she first arrived on the Venice, Florida location ... the entire film was shot on that Western set, except for some scenes that were shot later in Brooksville, Florida that did not involve Claudia. Anyway, it was my hope that we could take advantage of Claudia's natural beauty and her *Playboy* fame. I decided that it would be good for the film if she did not wear a bra. However, I was hesitant to ask. The first time I met with Claudia was just after she checked into her hotel room. We sat and chatted while she ate two baked potatoes sent up by room service (she said eating baked potatoes was how she controlled her weight). At one point, while we were talking, she became aware that I was nervous about asking her something. Finally, I worked up enough courage to ask if she would mind not wearing a bra in the film, because the wardrobe we had chosen would accentuate her breasts if she went bra-less. She laughed and said, "Is that what you're nervous about? Well, don't give it a second thought; we'll just let these little beauties hang loose." The first day on the set, Claudia called me over, and with a smile said, "Let's put you at ease. Give me your right hand." I gave her my hand and she cupped it over her right breast and laughed. "Now that's out of the way, let's get this production going."

The lady had a wonderful sense of humor and kept everyone at ease.

Claudia was very precise about her acting, in that she wanted to know exactly what a scene was about and how I intended to shoot it so that she would be prepared. I appreciated that, and encouraged her to feel free to give me any input and ideas that she had. Most of the time all she wanted was specifics about character motivation and camera angles.

Her leading man was a New York actor, Paul Vincent. He played the good guy, Willy, who along with his partner, Scratch (Michael Hatfield), came across Claudia, her husband (the late Paul Ecenia) and his two sidekicks while they all were hiding in this old abandoned town. After Willy and Scratch kill Claudia's abusive husband and his men, he and Claudia's character get friendly, which leads to a love (sex) scene. The scene was to be shot with both actors totally nude, but it was shot in such a way that the film would receive no more than an R rating. I—being the young prude that I was back then—was nervous about my leading actors being nude, especially since I wanted Paul Vincent to be directly on top of a very nude and fetching Claudia Jennings. Claudia and Paul, on the other hand, were pros, and stripped down like it was nothing special. They pretended to make love—very passionate love—on the floor of the saloon. With the camera mounted on the floor, we shot through strategically placed legs of chairs that blocked strategic parts of their bodies. We got our R rating.

I never saw Claudia again after the film was completed. However, we did keep in touch via phone for a long time after, since we had become friends. It was difficult not to be Claudia's friend, because she was warm and open to everyone—a very easy person to be around.

Like everyone who knew this lovely lady, I was devastated when I heard of her untimely death.[22]

Truck Stop Women (1974)

This film was typical of the drive-in features Claudia appeared in during the early 1970s. With an emphasis on displaying her charms and portraying her as a sadistic criminal, *Truck Stop Women* demonstrated what audiences would identify as the quintessential Claudia Jennings character. This was no working-class, feminist hero like Karen Walker from *Unholy Rollers*, or the noble, avenging savage Desiree from *'Gator Bait*. In this film, Claudia commits about every original sin, and violates a few new ones. She could easily be considered one of the screen's best villains, a living nightmare having no feelings for fellow human beings—perhaps the sexiest sociopath of all time.

Despite the jovial truck-driving soundtrack, sung by Claudia's then-boyfriend Bobby Hart, the plethora of R-rated nudity and the adequate car/truck chases, the movie has a level of violence and a sense of depravity that exceeds any of Claudia's other films. Once again, it was nice that the producers used Bobby's music so the two could spend some time in each other's worlds.

However, rompin', stompin' music can't disguise the joy the perpetrators show while dispensing the mayhem. The first scene is a gory assassination of a mobster by a rival and his henchman, who shoot the man and his girlfriend in a tub. Their bullet-riddled bodies bobbing in the bright red tide seems like something out of a Mario Bava or Dario Argento film.

After the murders, Mr. Smith, (John Martino, the unfortunate Paulie Gatto from *The Godfather*—"Leave the gun ... take the cannoli") and his henchman Rusty (Speed Sterns) visit their boss on the West Coast.

The scene switches to Cali, where Mr. Big (Nicky Blair), the head of the West Coast mob, is telling Mr. Smith and Rusty that he wants a woman named Anna out of the picture, in order to profit from her hijacking/whoring enterprise that made New Mexico so famous. Mr. Big gives Smith his very own truck stop as a base of operation, and as a way of financing it, Smith has his permission to rip off East Coast mob money headed that way. Mr. Smith assures the boss he can take care of it by saying, "Fa-get-about-it." By the way, you may wish to keep track of how many times Mr. Smith utters this phrase.

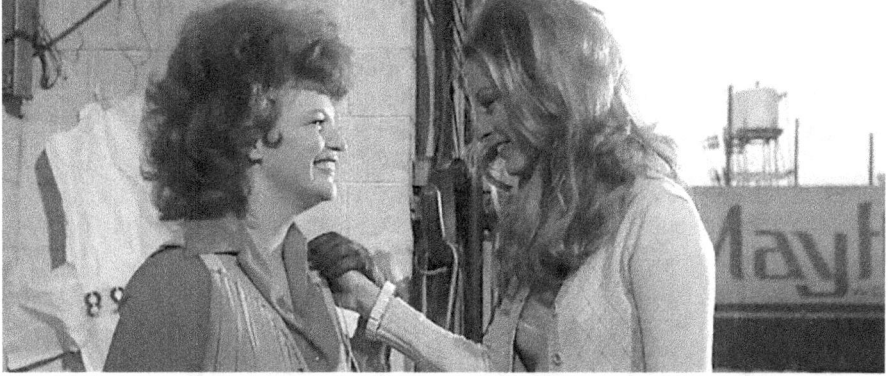

Lieux Dressler (mother) and Claudia (daughter)

Claudia Jennings as Rose, in *Truck Stop Women*

All in all, *Truck Stop Women* is a well-crafted gem of exploitation. The action flows well, the holes in the plot are small and the acting is far above most efforts of the exploitation genre. Superb direction and a marvelous cast make this an enjoyable viewing experience. Add the copious amount of nudity and violence and we have a movie that has something for everybody.

The scene cuts to the backsides of two lovely ladies: Claudia and her friend Tina (Jennifer Burton), standing by a disabled car, somewhere in Bumfudge, New Mexico. When I tell you it's shocking that cars, trucks, RVs and about a 100 police vehicles lining both sides of the highway hadn't stopped already, I'm not kidding. Claudia's legs seem to go on for days, accented by her black go-go boots and gold hot pants.

Along comes a well-meaning trucker, who seems nice and probably would be again just as soon as he gets out of the hospital—because this is the scene, as the ill-fated Good Samaritan looks at their engine, where Rose (Claudia) massages his head with a mean ol' monkey wrench, then slams the hood down on this fool just for good measure. The look on Claudia's face as she commits this atrocity is quite extraordinary—a combination of savagery, sexual thrills and joy. Our happy gals hop into the truck and peel down the lonesome New Mexico interstate, inexplicably singing "Red River Valley" while the movie's theme song fades in and out. The ladies spot a hitchhiker, a handsome young man, and flip a coin for him. Tina wins, and as soon as our cowboy climbs in, Tina is dragging him to the back and tumblin' his tumbleweeds. Then, just as quickly as he came, the cowboy is gone, getting thrown out of the truck by the girls, who enjoy a good giggle. Oh, I'm being rude—our T&A scoreboard thus far are two in the bathtub scene, four courtesy of Mr. Big's girlfriends and one-half for Tina while riding the cowhand (and it's still early.)

Rose and Tina are prostitutes, as well as armed robbers, who work for Anna (Lieux Dressler), a kindly lady who runs a crappy, nasty truck stop and cathouse. She also happens to be Rose's mama! It's just a guess, but I'm thinking there's some therapy long overdue in this mother-daughter relationship.

The set design of the truck stop is excellent. Anna's office looks like a cluttered-up dump, but it does have a camera in each room where she can spy on the courtesans and their customers. The whores are trained to coax information out of the johns in order to provide fresh business for Anna's hijacking side gig. The sleazy hotel rooms where the hookers ply their trade are designed so well that you can almost smell the

In the climax of *Truck Stop Women*, Rose, Rusty and Mr. Smith prepare to double cross Anna.

sweat and cheap cologne. The girls also take care of the kinky Sheriff, to guarantee his dutiful protection of Anna's rackets.

Rose, even though she pulled off a major score, is grumpy and rude when she returns home. The cook at the truck stop's diner serves her a plate of food; Rose takes a brief look at it, picks it up, and smashes it down on the counter, screaming, "You wouldn't serve Jacqueline Onassis chicken fried steak, would you?"

While everyone muses what fortunate insect crawled up Rose's rump, we meet the rest of Anna's crew: Winter (Len Lesser), Curly (Dennis Fimple) and Mac (Gene Drew), a collection of grease monkeys who are very loyal to Anna. You may recognize Dennis Fimple as the gentleman who played Uncle Hugo in *House of 1000 Corpses*. Len Lesser, of course, played the lovable Uncle Leo on *Seinfeld*, in addition to his long career in feature films such as *The Outlaw Josey Wales*.

The lighting and set design really work in *Truck Stop Women*. The garage and truck bay have a gritty realism, while every light is lurid and makes each scene appear perfect. Lester's camera angles give the film a sleazy, hard-edged look.

While Rose is sulking, who should walk in but Mr. Smith and Rusty? When Smith's charms don't work on Anna, he turns to Rose. Claudia, seeing an opportunity, decides to throw her lot in with the bad guys. She quickly hops in Smith's car and takes off with the two gangsters. The scene eventually shifts to Smith's bed, where Rose sexily tells him, "Now I'm gonna show you the only good tricks my mama ever showed me." The camera follows Rose's face down Smith's belly until it cuts away to show the voyeuristic Rusty watching them while eating his ever-present candy bar in a particularly repulsive manner.

The segment is very effective, as it simultaneously shows Rose's demoralization and her ability to use sex as a strategic weapon. Claudia plays the scene well, as its success depends on her ability to manipulate men as seen earlier in the film. She is more than convincing. Back at Anna's, a former partner in crime and lover, Seago (Paul Carr), shows up to tell Anna about the money coming in from the New York mob. Then, I suppose, in order to pad the running time, we are treated to a short video mixing naked women, trucks roaring down the highway and lots of Bobby Hart's singing. I found

A Biography

Rose and Mac (Gene Drew) discuss business.

the little intermission jarring and disruptive, but it does raise the T&A count past any measurable level.

Maybe I'm just too conservative, but the film was paced well, and built up solid tension, so why stop the momentum? It would be like Alfred Hitchcock inserting a laundry detergent commercial after the shower scene in *Psycho*.

Getting back to the movie, Anna finds out that Rose is working for Smith now, and that pisses her off to no end. She rushes over to his truck stop, where she finds Rose shooting pool clad only in a bikini with some of the other courtesans. When Rose won't go peacefully, Anna promptly wallops her, throws her over shoulder and storms out. Then we get to see a lot more T&A, but some of it belongs to Uschi Digard, a former Russ Meyer protégé, so it is more than all right. Concurrently, we see one of Anna's men crushed to death when an unseen villain with a strange ring drops a truck on him. Curly and Mac, after discovering the murder, find Winter hung by his own chains. Things look bad for Anna's operation. Rose, now sporting a shiner, has been busy too, going back over to Smith's side. However, even she is revolted when Rusty murders a driver while hijacking his truck. Later, as Seago is massaging Anna's shoulders, we see he is wearing the ring the killer had on the night her men were murdered. Anna figures out Seago is just trying to rip her off, too. The plot thickens, or perhaps it's just congealing.

The next day, Anna takes off to hijack the money truck, with Rose, Mac and Curly in tow. They find the cattle rig with the goods in it and put fake markings on the side. They grab the money and leave the empty containers for Seago to find. The rest of the crew depart while Anna waits for Seago's ambush. There is a well-shot truck/car chase with good stunt work and fine editing in this part of the film, as we watch Seago and a henchman in hot pursuit. Seago crawls his way into the cabin and pulls a gun on her, forcing her to pull over. Seago, his gunsel and Anna go into the cattle wagon to search for the money. Just as the minion finds the empty cash boxes, Anna distracts Seago with a kick in the nuts and grabs his gun. As she climbs out of the truck, she starts shooting to panic the bovine passengers. Here is where we see the sadism that runs in the family, as Anna shows an almost orgiastic delight in killing the two men. Besides, it really is a clever and quite nasty way to finish someone off. Imagine all those sharp hooves, half-ton bodies and hundreds of pounds of manure, surrounding and crushing you to death. Well, Seago had it coming. He also left a present for Anna: two machine guns in his car.

Rose appears in a seductive mood

It was Mac's job to take Rose home, but she makes him stop at an incredibly authentic-looking sleazy hotel so she can take a shower. In a great scene, Mac eats a piece of KFC while Rose is trying to get him to reveal the rendezvous point where Anna will be splitting up the money. As Claudia slowly opens her towel, revealing her spectacular frame, Mac's willpower caves in, and as she climbs on top of him, we hear him saying, "Jesus, Rose!"

The next day, the scene is set for a good old-fashioned shoot out. Set in an old ghost town, it begins with Rose and Smith thinking they have the jump on Anna, while Anna has set them up for an ambush. The mob goons are in three cars, led by Smith and Rose. Anna lets their car pass, then blocks the road with a truck and lets her machine-gun-armed whores massacre the hoods. That leaves Rusty, Rose and Mr. Fa-get-about-it facing off against Anna, Curly and Mac. Smith then puts a gun to Rose's head, figuring maternal instinct will win out. He's right, as the truck stop gang drops its guns. As soon as they do, Rose gives them a devilish smile, showing them she's sold them out yet again.

As they head to where the money is hidden, Tina drives a tractor through the building, mowing over Smith and Rusty. A gleeful Anna turns to Rose and tells her she knew she could count on her. Well, not so fast there, my friends! Rose picks up a gun and says, "Now it's all mine, mama," and fires one off at the old bird. Mac, however, proves Jack Daniel's is thicker than blood, and puts not one but two rifle shots in Rose's back. I guess Rose overestimated her powers of seduction. The film ends with Anna, genuinely anguished, having won the day, but she lost her only daughter and the few dreams she had left.

There is a lot of poignancy in the scenes where Anna talks about Rose. At one point she's looking at a picture of Rose as a young girl (no doubt, a borrowed one of Claudia from her youth) and wonders what happened. It might be a case of art imitating life, because as far as we know, Claudia's mother Mrs. Chesterton was at peace with her daughter's career decision. However, one can imagine that she must have glanced at Mimi's childhood photos from time to time, wondering about things that might have been.

A Biography

Claudia and Bobby Hart, 1972

Truck Stop Women is an odd film, because if it had been treated as a straight exploitation film, the movie would have been too oppressive, dingy and depressing to watch. The bloody assassination at the film's beginning is accompanied by Bobby Hart, Danny Janssen and Jimmie Haskell's bouncy country swing music. Although somewhat incongruous, it lessens the horror of the scene.

The prostitutes in the movie seem to be a jolly, contented bunch, most of them as horny as their clients. They don't act degraded or exploited.

I think the movie also has a subtle racist and nativist point of view. Cleansing the influence of foreign and unwanted elements—i.e., the New York and West Coast mobs—is a priority, and as such they are considered to be invaders, along with those who are their allies as in the case of Rose. The purity of the West must be maintained, even if they hijack trucks and run brothels. Of course, there are no Native Americans or any other non-Caucasians in the film, which you have to admit is mighty unusual for New Mexico.

The pervasive air of sadism that permeates the film is quite unique for this type of drive-in fare, as well. When people are killed, the film lingers on the victim's terror, the perpetrator's joy or both. It doesn't quite reach the level of Peckinpah's blood-and-guts operas or the brutal zombie flicks of the time, but there are enough individual scenes to let the audience realize they're not watching *The Love Bug*.

After the original cut, the producers asked for more nudity; hence, some of Claudia's scenes were shot post-production and the additional pictures during the "intermission" were added.

I loved this movie from beginning to end. Once again, a great cast supports Claudia's performance. When you watch her in this film, she shows no fear of anything, especially whether the audience likes her on-screen behavior or not. She is playing a cruel, sociopathic bitch and pulls it off perfectly.

In 1974, Hugh Hefner asked Claudia if she would do another pictorial. Claudia flat-out refused. She had been getting some television roles, and in those days, no one who posed for *Playboy* could appear on prime time TV for six months. It's hard to imagine a more cynical, hypocritical and sexist dictate than the one Claudia heard from

Hugh Hefner. There is no doubt that 99% of all the TV executives, board members and censorship commissioners bought and read *Playboy* regularly or were guests at the Playboy Mansion. Hef would not take no for an answer, according to Susan Miller:

> He told her she was being ungrateful, that she owed him her entire career and that he would just run with some older photos if she did not agree. At least this way she would get paid.

Bobby Hart confirmed this when interviewed for the *E! True Hollywood Story,* "The Fast Life and Untimely Death of Claudia Jennings."[24] Claudia always wondered whether posing was the right decision, but the danger was that if she refused, she wouldn't get paid and they would run the old photos anyway.

Hart would later comment that in his opinion *Playboy* took advantage of everything Claudia ever did. They gave permission for film producers to use their corporate name in advertising her movies, and they pressured her into pictorial after pictorial. Claudia was in a double bind as far as *Playboy* was concerned. She had decided as far back as 1974 she no longer wanted to be closely associated with the magazine. However, the threat of using her old photos without compensation put Claudia in an untenable position. She then had to choose the lesser of two evils, taking the money and continuing to do pictorials.

Remember, the model never owns her image, the photographer does. Hugh Hefner and *Playboy* could use images shot in 1969 for decades and never have to pay Claudia a single penny. Perhaps Claudia finally realized the downside to posing for *Playboy*. If in the future she attained the measure of success for which she had worked so hard, would the magazine embarrass her by printing old photos? Knowing Hugh Hefner's and Claudia's friendliness, it seemed unlikely to occur; but then again, his reaction to her initial refusal to pose in 1974 didn't bode well. Eventually Claudia caved in to Hefner's pressure and agreed to the pictorial, under the condition that she choose the photographers. She ended up picking five artists she felt comfortable working with, and the shoot went on.

Bobby Hart, the love of Claudia's life

A Biography

The happy couple: Claudia and Bobby

Constance Chesterton felt that if Claudia had seriously put up a fight against doing the pictorial, Hefner would have relented. She stressed Claudia truly admired Hefner and respected him. Constance said Claudia never tolerated mean people or abuse, and certainly would never befriend them as she did *Playboy*'s owner.

The 1974 pictorial would give the world a different view of Claudia. She was no longer the sugar-sweet teenage cheerleader first introduced in her Playmate of the Month pictorial. She wasn't even the sober, self-reflecting, ingratiating young woman from her Playmate of the Year spread. Mimi Chesterton had been buried, with the more sexual, ostentatious Claudia Jennings now vying for control, at least as far as the image she wanted the press and fans to read. From the start of the interview, Claudia seems to be unsure of which woman was the more dominant, and seemed to equivocate on what message she wanted to send.

Claudia had given clues in earlier interviews, as noted here, but in 1974 she told Bruce Williamson clearly how she felt about a great many subjects. The opening photo is a picture of Claudia with a champagne bottle, her legs encased in shiny silk thigh-highs, perched in the same Hispano-Suiza automobile used in *The Great Gatsby*. Her appraisal of that portion of the pictorial was, "Trash—with a bit of flash." She then went on to say, "This is the Hollywood me, not the real me; very camp, like so many movie roles I've played." Claudia's opinions about the next photographer, J. Fred Smith, were quite illuminating, as she said:

> He freaked me a little at first, talking about eroticism and nudity. But I soon got into his low-key style of shooting. Generally, I agree that pictures meant to be sexy shouldn't be too pretty. I'd rather show raunchy sex—it's much more honest.[25]

Somehow, it is difficult to believe Claudia meant that seriously. There is, after all, a difference between filming pornography and stylized nude photography. Whatever Claudia's message was, it marked a departure in her public discourse. Remember, in a 1971 interview with *New Woman* magazine, Claudia declared that her previous pictorials were only a necessary compromise to accomplish her goals. In the same interview, she declared it wasn't her aim to become a nude model or sexual object. The 1974 pictorial and subsequent interview certainly sent mixed messages about those sentiments.

The article continued with a series of rapid-fire commentaries and revelations quite different from Claudia's previous interviews. Claudia took pride at her performance in *Dark of the Moon*, and she reminded *Playboy* readers that Andy Warhol called *Unholy Rollers* the best trash movie of 1972; the movie critic from *Variety* said she delivered the year's best hard-boiled female performance. The interview then gives us Claudia's opinions on the many movies she was in between 1971 and 1974, with Williamson adding that they were the type of "schlock films" she wanted to avoid in the future. Claudia gives us her dramatic appraisal of *Truck Stop Women*: "I got so sick watching it I had to check into the UCLA hospital." This seems odd given that her performance was so magnificent, and she spoke of the film with pride in later interviews about her ability to drive an 18-wheeler.

It was even odder that her description of *'Gator Bait* was this: "*Swiss Family Robinson* in the Texas swamps ... I just run around jumping out of trees and skinning alligators." Considering her good friends Ferd and Beverly Sebastian had created the project just for her, this comes off as being a bit ungrateful. Likewise, *Group Marriage*, *The Love Machine* and *40 Carats* "are dismissed with a crinkled nose."[25]

One has to wonder to what good it served Claudia being so critical of her own films. It doesn't show Claudia in a good light, and one can only imagine what the casts and crew of those films thought upon reading her comments. Bobby Hart said when interviewed that Claudia never ever regretted a part or role in one of her movies or television appearances. She felt that each appearance was a learning experience and only made her a better actress. That sounds much more like Claudia than what she said in 1974 to Bruce Williamson.

Claudia also explains what she felt was her Hollywood image when Williamson noted her diamond and gold bracelet that spelled out "BITCH."

> That's what I always play in movies, though it's the total opposite of who I am, really. I'm cast as a spitfire—bad girl types—I suppose because being submissive is totally alien to me. There aren't many good female roles nowadays, so I figure I'll come into my own when I'm about 30. At this point, I can't play kids or hippies, and I sure as hell can't play the wronged wife ... because you wouldn't believe a man cheats on me.[26]

This portion of the interview is prescient in the saddest way possible, as Claudia would never live to see her day in the sun. It is at this point where Williamson makes a clever move by relating that Claudia had been out all night dancing with the patrons of the lesbian bar Le Jardin—clever because maybe Claudia was a little too tired to care what she was saying. The rest of the interview was a stream of consciousness commentary on her travels to Europe, casual drug use, men, Bobby Hart's and her relationship and an explosion of unexpected conspicuous consumption that is so extreme that it defies belief.

On Europe and related matters, Williamson writes:

> She prefers to discuss Europe: Having dinner with Bardot, meeting George Harrison, being photographed on the Riviera by David Hamilton, lounging in style between sessions at the Cannes Film Festival or at the fabulous Hotel du Cap in Cap d'Antibes, better known as Eden Roc.

Claudia then tells Williamson of a day spent skinny-dipping in the deep blue Mediterranean with some friends from the movie business, while tripping on psychedelic mushrooms. The story is awkward and rambling and it's curious why Claudia chose to

Claudia loved to read. Here she is with authors Will and Ariel Durant.

share it. For one, it contradicts her future interviews where she denies drug use; and second, it contradicts what many of her best friends said when interviewed about Claudia not even smoking a joint until after she and Bobby broke up.

The only theory that makes sense is that Claudia wanted to appear "cool" and "with it." The question remains, though: How much "cooler" could she be? Here is a movie star, a Playmate of the Year and one of the most beautiful women on the planet straining to convince everyone she's an amazing force of nature. Claudia was also intelligent and delightful, yet it seems she was always trying to convince some unseen eye or audience that they needed to legitimize her and give her validity.

Claudia then denies her rumored affairs with Bernard Cornfeld, Johnny Carson and others. However, it was true that Johnny Carson was infatuated with her. Claudia does go out of her way to praise Bobby Hart and declare that their agreed upon "fidelity pact" was her idea. Claudia does give a nice history of their relationship, including that Bobby's son Bobby, Jr., then 13 years old, was living with them. It would have been better if that point was emphasized, for in truth, Claudia made a wonderful mom.

Toward the end of the article, the reader is treated to a description of Claudia's whirlwind shopping spree. She spends $1,000 in under 23 minutes at the Yves St. Laurent store on gifts for Bobby. Then the tone changes as she reflects on purchases made at FAO Schwarz—two windup bathtub toy whales (a mama and a baby) plus a blue plastic hopping frog. Williamson notices the dual nature of the woman he has been interviewing. Claudia's words and descriptions have left two distinct furrows on your mind: Tough/soft, child/sex object, housewife/movie star, sweetheart/party girl; they swirl together and the ruts form where they intersect.

As the interview ends, Williamson wants us to remember two things. First, that Claudia is writing a novel ("I've always been a bit too cerebral for my own good, though in L.A. it's difficult to be an intellectual, since there's no one there to be an intellectual with."[28] That's a pretty strong comment, and on paper, comes across as being quite mean-spirited. Second, she is trying to learn patience, but probably won't. "When things become boring to me, I create situations. I get the crazies sometimes."[29]

The final thoughts we are left with in the article?

I'm not Cicely Tyson, who claims she's never done a thing professionally she can't be proud of. Well, I have. I've done everything the hard way and made a lot of money. Obviously, I'm bright. I'm also well educated, I'm wealthy, I'm photogenic and I'm a damn good actress.[30]

Again, for some reason, Claudia used a scream where a whisper would have been more effective. She was correct on all of her assertions, with the exception of being well educated in the traditional sense. Claudia had all the attention she would need by appearing in the pictorials. To add many of these self-proclamations and raw stories seemed beneath her. I don't know why there was such a dramatic difference in Claudia's attitude in this article. Perhaps it was too much nightlife, a few too many drinks at lunch or Bruce Williamson catching her on a bad day. There is no question in my mind that this woman doing the interview was not the real Claudia.

Claudia came back from Europe after the pictorial, and while there, according to Susan Miller, had one of her "flings." Apparently, this one did not work out well for Claudia, who returned home exhausted and depressed. She also felt let down by *Playboy* for the first time in her career.

Back at Woodrow Wilson Drive, Bobby and Claudia's love affair was floundering, and it seemed time was working against them. How can we explain why Bobby and Claudia could not work as a couple? Unfortunately, they had more things going against them than holding them together at this point. The fact they were both in the time-demanding business of the entertainment world would have been a strong impediment to a successful relationship. Both of them would be away from each other for long stretches, either filming or touring. The stress of this alone has torn many a Hollywood union to shreds.

It is also necessary to consider how young Claudia was when she met Bobby. Barely 22, she was living with an older man who was much worldlier and established; Claudia was swept off her feet. However, the longer the relationship continued, the differences that Claudia found so seductive initially began to become painful fissures. Many of their friends told me that Bobby's reluctance to have children and marry grievously hurt Claudia. This was a very sad set of circumstances. They loved each other, but Bobby simply could not give Claudia what she wanted the most. For her part, Claudia likely felt that a marriage and children were the solutions to her self-esteem problem and her experiences in Evanston. The two had trapped themselves in a world of desirable but mutually exclusive outcomes.

Bobby and Claudia also had different value systems when it came to money and the spiritual side of human existence. Hart had already achieved success and wealth, so the desire to pursue a more material lifestyle was not a priority. He was also fully committed to meditation and the Eastern religious practice of introspection after reading the teachings of various gurus.

Claudia, by contrast, was still at the beginning of her career, and the pursuit of wealth and fame was paramount. In *Psychedelic Bubble Gum*, Bobby says:

> In the early 1970s, my substantial income from The Monkees had taken a sharp decline. It was a momentary setback, until the royalties from my new hits would start to arrive. But Claudia had told me back then, "When I was still in school, I made a vow to myself that I would do whatever it takes, but I

would not be poor." Over the ensuing years she would remind me from time to time that she had a standing offer from real estate tycoon Stan Herman to set her up in a house in Beverly Hills.[31]

Bobby also contrasted the couple's value systems and spiritual sides.

There was a disparity in how we expressed our spiritual natures. Day after day, I would witness examples of Claudia's natural kindness, empathy, generosity and kindness to others ... her compassion had inspired me to be more open, service-oriented and caring. She was completely supportive of the alone time I required every day for my meditation practice ... but in spite of all her innate spiritual qualities, she had a non-negotiable aversion to organized religion.[32]

Bobby elaborated on his feelings for Claudia and the strains put on the relationship.

Claudia was, of course, a beautiful woman, but she had a funky, fun personality that was the real attraction. She was funny, full of energy, always upbeat and constantly smiling. I appreciated her not being resentful of my Transcendental Meditation or interest in Eastern religious thought. She simply had no interest in participating, and had not developed a spiritual side to her nature at that time. She never complained about them, but she thought my beliefs were BS.

One thing I truly admired about Claudia was her willingness to help other actors out. She would always give them the best advice she could, and that went for anyone, not just people in the film industry.

I think one of the things that broke us up was her schedule. She never took more than a month or two off when we were together. And it was all about money. She would rather have a nice paycheck as the lead in a drive-in feature than a walk-on role in an A-film. She once auditioned for *Once Upon a Time in the West*, but didn't get the part.

It is not difficult to understand Claudia's feelings on either money or religion. Her family had gone through some miserable times because of her father's unemployment. The move to Evanston only reinforced her sense of being a "have-not." It makes one feel quite sad for the young Mimi Chesterton, going from lower-middle-class life in a wealthy Chicago suburb to the worlds of *Playboy* and Hollywood, with their exaggerated, unrealistic opulence.

Claudia had also expressed her opinions on religion as far back as her *New Woman* interview. She rebelled against her strict Catholic upbringing, which she saw as personally harmful and demeaning. There is also no doubt that her rejection of Catholicism was also a rejection of her parents. It does pose a bit of a paradox that Claudia's actions were indicative of a highly religious person, yet her opinion of organized religion remained uniformly hostile, at least, until she was nearing the end of her life. Bobby valued his spiritual life, and it was an important part of his daily routine. However, Claudia's aversion to his beliefs—and sometimes her open hostility to them—must have created enormous tension.

She and Bobby would still enjoy time together. One day, Barry Richards relates, Claudia was asking Bobby why he never wrote any songs about her. Bobby responded:

Claudia, *all* of my songs are about you!" Always anxious to show his love for her, Bobby sat down and wrote a song called "Claudia," with her name in each line and chorus, along the lines of "Claudia, I love you/Claudia, I need you," *ad infinitum*. Hart recorded it, had it manufactured and presented it to Claudia with its own sleeve, with a picture of her face on the jacket.

Sally Kirkland was one of Claudia's first "big-name" friends in Hollywood. Sally is a giant of a figure of the movie business—literally. Standing almost six feet tall, she is blonde and statuesque even at 74. Her mother was a fashion editor at *Vogue* magazine, and Ms. Kirkland began acting in the early 1960s in off-Broadway productions. Noted for being the first actress to ever appear in the nude during a stage play, she spent 10 years doing theater before starting her movie career. Ms. Kirkland has

Another professional head shot of Claudia

appeared in over 140 movies, including *The Sting* and *The Way We Were*. Nominated for the Best Actress Oscar in 1987 for *Anna*, Ms. Kirkland ended up winning the Golden Globe for that category the same year. She has also appeared in countless television movies and shows. Ms. Kirkland is also an activist for the Democratic Party, AIDS research and LGBT issues. She is an ordained minister, and gave a moving speech at Claudia's celebration of life service. She is one of the most extraordinary Americans to have graced our time.

Following is my talk with Ms. Kirkland about when she met Claudia and how they became friends:

> We met through my manager Carl Parsons, who was also a friend of Claudia's. This was around 1973 or 1974. Now, I was so bored in Los Angeles, coming from New York. The only way I could think of to liven things up was to throw parties. Now, I only lived in a crappy little place at the time, so I asked Claudia and Bobby if I could throw a party at their house. Bobby had a huge home in Laurel Canyon, so we had it there. So many people would show up, and I introduced them all to Claudia. Now, a lot of them were my friends from New York and the Actor's Studio, like Robert DeNiro, Al Pacino, etc. Mama Cass [of the rock group The Mamas and the Papas] started coming by, and I had to hire armed guards because so many famous people were there. And Claudia was the quietest, most gracious hostess you would ever see. She was so sweet to everyone, and so happy just to meet all these famous people. These parties were written up in a column for the *Hol-*

lywood Reader. It gave all these new up-and-coming actors some free publicity. Claudia appreciated it too.

Bobby took such good care of her. She really had a fairy tale life. He gave her everything she could possibly want. I always wished they had stayed together, and I always wished someday they would get back together.

The best story I have about Claudia, to show you what kind of person she was one time my house had an electrical fire and burnt to the ground. I literally had nothing. I went over to Claudia's house and told her what happened. She literally took me by the hand and walked us into her enormous closet and said, "Take whatever you want." So I had clothes and a good friend to stay with. Nobody had ever been so generous to me in my life.

Claudia and I used to hang out at the Playboy Mansion. She introduced me to Marilyn Grabowski, who was their photo editor; so that's how I got into *Playboy*, through Claudia. As far as her relationship with *Playboy* went, I always thought she really appreciated everything Hef had done for her. She felt like she owed her career and fame to him. As far as posing for the magazine, she never thought twice about it. *Playboy* offered me a cover story, but since I had won a Golden Globe award and was nominated for an Academy Award, I thought it would hurt my career.

I think Claudia's values stayed the same from the time she was a teen through the time I knew her. She loved people. She loved to have fun.

Later on, she began to get a bit depressed about her career. She felt she wasn't being taken seriously as an actor. She told me she wanted to have the kind of career I had—more serious, maybe getting back into theater and going back to acting school. The thing I remember about her the most is that Claudia just loved people so much.[33]

Ms. Kirkland gives us a positive view of Claudia's life up to now. We have a portrait of a kind, accommodating, generous young lady who obviously thought of her friends first in any situation. There were certain things Claudia drew a line in the sand for, however.

The fairy tale was almost over, unfortunately. The time and distance apart from each other made both Claudia and Bobby restless. Bobby seemed to be the one compromising, and did whatever it took to calm or please Claudia. The more malleable Bobby became, the more Claudia demanded of him; however, he did not waver on his reluctance to marry or have children, which exacerbated the tensions present in the relationship. This issue would always be present like an unseen, malevolent spirit in the room. When Bobby decided to go back on tour with Tommy Boyce and former Monkees Davy Jones and Mickey Dolenz, Claudia hit the roof when she discovered the tour would take him away from home during Christmas. Unable to find any common ground, or unwilling to, Claudia moved out to her own place on Larrabee Street in West Hollywood. It was not that far geographically from the Mansion on Woodrow Wilson Drive, but it might as well have been on the other side of the globe from the comfort and stability she had enjoyed for the last five years.

This was a sad ending to Claudia and Bobby's love affair. The truth, unhappier still, is that it was most likely doomed from the start. Bobby could not recapture the idyllic

Actress and model Sally Kirkland fondly remembers Claudia

times of their early relationship or convince her she was heading down an uncertain path. Their different views of having children, marriage and spiritual values presented almost insurmountable obstacles to their long-term happiness.

Bobby was Claudia's one and only long-term romance. There is no question they loved each other deeply, and it is to Bobby's credit he remained Claudia's friend up until the day she died. Only a man who sincerely had Claudia's happiness in mind could have endured what happened over the next four years. While Claudia didn't flaunt her other affairs in front of Bobby, at the same time, it would have been impossible for him not to be aware of them.

As far as Claudia is concerned, her reasons for ending the love affair are murkier. Bobby represented everything she never had in a relationship. He provided emotional and financial stability and could give her the love she never received at home. There doesn't seem to be a convincing number of factors that would make Claudia leave Bobby Hart (but who really knows what goes on beyond closed doors?). The difference of opinion about marriage and children was perhaps the biggest wedge in the relationship. Strange that Claudia never actively pursued either of these goals with any of her other paramours. In fact, most of the men she dated after Bobby would have been overwhelmingly poor choices as far as marriage and starting a family are concerned.

Claudia simply may have stopped seeing Bobby as a romantic figure in her life; people do fall out of love, sometimes. Then again, perhaps the reasons were rooted in Claudia's psychological profile and had very little to do with Bobby. Claudia seemed to have a limited tolerance for lengthy relationships. Maybe her internal alarm clock went off after five years with Bobby, signaling it was time to move on. Perhaps she sabotaged the relationship herself because of her low self-esteem issues.

Whatever the reasons, cognizant or subliminal, the couple separated for a while, letting the dust settle a bit. The end of Claudia's most significant relationship marked a turning point in her personal history. Up to this point, her career and personal trajectory had moved forward in a consistent manner, despite a few bumps along the way. A new phase of Claudia's life was about to begin. Her rocket-like ascendency to stardom and a private life marked by peace and tranquility was now in jeopardy. The navigation system on her personal spaceship malfunctioned, and Claudia was heading toward unchartered territory.

After only a short time apart, Claudia decided to move back in with Bobby. The reunion did not last and soon Claudia was off, going on location to film one of her better movies, and meet some new friends.

The Man Who Fell to Earth (1976)

In 1975, Claudia began dating renowned Hollywood producer Si Litvinoff. He is one of the most respected individuals in the entertainment business. His best-known film is *A Clockwork Orange*, one of the most controversial and influential movies of all time. Litvinoff also produced *Walkabout*, directed by Nicolas Roeg—a film that made a star out of a young Jenny Agutter, an unknown who was 17 years old when the movie was shot.

Si Litvinoff began his career as a lawyer and agent in New York. He represented such artists as Andy Warhol, Joel Grey, Rip Torn and Beatrice Arthur. He was also responsible for more than 50 stage productions, including many for the Oakwood Playhouse, where Dustin Hoffman, Barbra Streisand and Peter Fonda began their careers. Among his many accomplishments was being executive producer for the Doobie Brothers' HBO special, *Listen to the Music*.

Litvinoff and Nicolas Roeg began work on *The Man Who Fell to Earth* that same year. They had considered Peter O'Toole for the lead role, but the director and producer both agreed that David Bowie more completely fit the profile of the alien stranded on Earth, and it turned out to be an inspired choice. Pale, with alabaster skin and a lithe unblemished body, Bowie—who never looked completely human—was a perfect choice for a being from another world.

Claudia knew Bowie, since she and Ava Cherry (one of Bowie's backup singers and part-time girlfriend) were friends. The three shared a house in Hollywood for a short time.

The production was notable as the first British film filmed in America with a British crew and with British financing. Roeg chose White Sands, New Mexico for his location.

Mr. Litvinoff generously shared his recollections of Claudia and the experience of making *The Man Who Fell to Earth*:

> I relocated to California after six years in London. I had an office on the Colombia Pictures lot, where I was developing two films, *Niagara Falls*, to be directed by Howard Zieff, and *Out of Africa*, to be directed by Nicolas Roeg.
>
> A very aggressive agent was apparently showcasing Claudia to various producers' offices, including mine. He did the same with Linda Evans. Sometime later, I was having dinner at *Mr. Chow* in Beverly Hills with my beautiful English girlfriend, who had just flown in from London. Claudia suddenly appeared at the table and requested that I come to her table and meet her parents and Bobby Hart.
>
> Very shortly thereafter, I was at a party in Beverly Hills that Tony Richmond took me to, and Claudia was there and came home with me. Apparently, her longtime relationship with Bobby Hart had just ended. I knew she and David Bowie were friends, so I asked her to do a small part for $15,000. She would also babysit my children while we were on location.

She loved to go to a private and popular backgammon club on La Cienega, *Pips*. I went only once with her and never again, as I did not enjoy backgammon. She liked to gamble, and en route to the New Mexico location, she would fly first to stop in Las Vegas and then arrive with gifts. She was always giving me gifts and photos of herself.

By the way, one of my memories is that I remember vividly her saying that all women wanted to be with musicians. Why she said it I don't remember.

I also remember her telling me that she was on a private jet once, and that she saved Keith Richards from an overdose. She was ambitious and had an aggressive agent during my time. If she had gotten *Charlie's Angels*, it all might have escalated. I guess the competition was stronger. Nevertheless, she was doing fine at her age, and the future may have been bigger, but …

Once in town for the shoot, Claudia Jennings was immediately recognized and received as much attention as did David Bowie. She was a cult figure, even in 1975. The film, however, had its challenges. A group of Hell's Angels happened to be camped nearby. Rip Torn, one of the film's stars, was apparently on some sort of alcohol or drug-induced mania and had to be constantly looked after. Bowie was staying up all night and took to snorting No-Doz to be alert during filming. Cameras jammed up unexpectedly, seemingly without cause. For Claudia, though, it was a dream come true. She was working with a respected veteran director on a major film. This is what she had been waiting for. The movie's troubles did not affect her.

The most daunting challenge *The Man Who Fell to Earth* faced occurred far away from the set, after the film was completed. According to one of the producers Michael Deeley, when Paramount executives saw the final cut, they refused to pay for a film that was different from their expectations. The studio pulled out of the project, and was

Bernie Casey and Claudia in *The Man Who Fell to Earth*

sued by British Lion, who managed to get some money out of the settlement. When they saw the movie Nicolas Roeg had created, they panicked and cut 30 minutes of the film. The movie was still beautiful but nearly incomprehensible. Because of all the legal squabbles and quarrels, the film barely made back its budget. The studio refused to pay David Bowie for the score he wrote, replacing it with music by John Phillips of The Mamas and the Papas. There was no soundtrack released because of more legal disputes between Roeg and the studio. One was eventually released in 2016.

Claudia's appearances in the film are limited. There is one striking scene where she is nude and lifted out of a swimming pool by her equally nude husband, Bernie Casey. They engage in a passionate embrace, both of their bodies so perfect it almost looks as if two Greek statues have come to life. A focal point of the shot is the image of Claudia's hands in a human silhouette, caressing his broad black shoulders with her impossibly long and perfectly shaped fingers. Her one line of dialogue comes shortly after, when the couple has put their children to bed; he asks her: "I wonder if we do and say the right things?" Claudia looks up and questions, "To the children?" Casey answers while looking at a picture of himself in his general's uniform. "Anything."

This is actually an important part of the film, coming right after Casey's character was duplicitous in the murder of Bowie's friend and partner Farnsworth, played by Buck Henry.

The film, sold to the distributor to recoup the production costs, disappointed at the box office. Eventually, Nic Roeg was able to edit the missing footage and release a director's cut, one of four versions in circulation. The restoration changed the film from a baffling mish-mash of scenes into a more coherent masterpiece. It remains a cult classic and a very influential piece of cinema.

Nicolas Roeg was gracious enough to share his memories of Claudia with me:

> I remember Claudia for the one little scene she agreed to do when we were on location. It was the scene where she is helped out of the swimming pool by a wonderfully fit African-American boxer,[34] which the two young people agreed to do. The tragedy of her death was quite shattering, but in a strange way perfection for the scene, upon reflection. There is nothing further I can say about them; in a curious way her tragedy has made the scene unforgettable. Personally, I only met her for the morning of the shoot—one day, virtually an hour in the day, at most.

The Man Who Fell to Earth might possibly be Claudia's most famous film. Mr. Roeg's comments on how perfect her scene was, in his recollection, fits with the themes of the film. All of us are mortal, no matter how perfect and beautiful we are in life. Viewers have a hard time wrapping their minds around the movie, but it is best enjoyed as both a commentary on the human race's fall from glory, man's relationship to technology and our perception of reality. The movie thoughtfully examines human desires and our cultural values. Visually stunning, there are no CGI effects present, but it is one of the most beautiful films ever shot. David Bowie was a perfect choice to play the alien, Thomas Jerome Newton, with his porcelain-plastic skin and gaunt face. If ever an actor was born to play a particular role, it was David Bowie in *The Man who Fell to Earth*. Musical persona Ziggy Stardust was the alien's doppelganger.

Thomas Jerome Newton, with the help of a patent attorney Farnsworth (Buck Henry), appears one day with a set of blueprints that revolutionize technology, as we know it. Newton soon becomes a billionaire and is planning to rehydrate his home planet, which is running out of water. His companions in this pursuit are Dr. Bryce (Rip Torn), a college professor, and Mary Lou (Candy Clark), Newton's only friend. She introduces him to alcohol, religion and sex. Newton builds his spaceship and starts preparations to go back and see his wife and family, who are dying.

Betrayed by Bryce shortly before he's about to journey to his home planet, Newton is imprisoned, and Farnsworth murdered. Kept in a torture chamber/hospital/apartment, he endures every type of medical test imaginable. Then, one morning, he awakes to find he is no longer a prisoner. Still youthful, everyone else he knows has grown old. He finds himself in a world where everyone he loves is either dead or dying. Newton slips into a haze of alcohol and memories.

Claudia and her two "children" from *The Man Who Fell to Earth*

It's easy to get overwhelmed by *The Man Who Fell to Earth*. It is a film that challenges the audience to appreciate a work that doesn't have a linear narrative or explain every situation. Best to relax and enjoy the show and let the film come to you.

There are some primary themes that are easy to discern, such as the literal fall of man. The viewer sees repeated scenes or suggestions of this throughout the film: Newton's original landing on Earth; Farnsworth murdered by being thrown out of a window; characters collapsing onto beds and into swimming pools; a glimpse of Breughel's *Landscape with the Fall of Icarus*; elevators descending and the like. The depiction of the conceptual fall of man, along with his physical fall through alcohol, wanton sex, greed, betrayal and murder, reinforces the theme.

Roeg's world presents us with a place where technology is a marvel, yet humanity is worse off despite all its perceived benefits. Newton morphs into a Dorian Gray character, except that the portrait is not present. Newton's mind and behavior are now monstrous because the more human he has become, the humanity that he brought as an alien has dissolved. As an alien, he was gentle, kind and caring; all of those qualities disappear quite literally the longer he is among us.

Claudia, despite her miniscule role, does show another theme of the movie. When we first see her and her husband, they are young, fit and passionate. In a scene many years later, Bernie Casey sits on a coach with a bloated belly and graying hair, while Claudia sits next to him seemingly without emotion. Although Casey has his arm around

her, she sits frozen; one of her hands is resting on Casey's leg, but with no warmth or love behind the gesture. These scenes and others show the loss of passion and beauty, leading inevitably to the loss of life.

I believe Claudia must have felt satisfied appearing in *The Man Who Fell to Earth*. She was able to play a mother, shown in one of her few scenes putting her children to bed. Nic Roeg was also an A-list director at the time, which is never bad for an actress' career. Unfortunately, due to contractual reasons her name does not appear in the movie's credits. Claudia never complained about it, and she enjoyed the overall filmmaking experience. The opportunity to work with a superb cast, director and earn $15,000 for one line of dialogue and three brief scenes was ample reward.

In a way, *The Man Who Fell to Earth* predicts our current time in an incredibly accurate manner. Surely one of the finest and most cerebral science fiction films of all time, it is a movie for the ages.

Si Litvinoff and Claudia split amiably, and Claudia soon found an interesting group of men to date. One of them was Skip Taylor, former manager of Canned Heat, also famous for being the agent who signed Sonny and Cher and the Rolling Stones to the William Morris Agency.

Taylor remembered:

> Claudia was just a beautiful girl with a heart of gold. She was chosen by Hugh Hefner to take new girls from the Mansion around L.A. and show them the sights, but only after Hefner and his friends had "broken them in." Claudia would bring them over my place and we'd party. Every so often. Claudia would come by and we'd have fun sex. No "I love you," no commitments. She was a wonderful, funny and really intelligent woman. And, man, did she know and understand men. If men understood women the way Claudia understood men, it would be a much different world.

Claudia found a more serious relationship with Chris Blackwell, founder of Island Records, the man who introduced the world to Bob Marley and the Wailers and heir to the Cross and Blackwell food conglomerate in Great Britain. According to her sister, Claudia really loved Chris Blackwell. In turn, he very much respected her. He told her mother Joan that she was the only woman in the entertainment business who he'd ever seen read a book.

Chris Blackwell also told the Chesterton family that Claudia was indirectly the blame for breaking up the rock band *Traffic* and getting him fired as their manager. It seemed that only Chris could calm Steve Winwood down when he would be angry or unhappy, which apparently he was, quite often. Evidently, one night, when Steve walked off the stage, the rest of the band was frantic, trying to call Chris to ask him to contact their AWOL band mate. Chris explained he was waiting for a call from Claudia, and that was more important. The next day the band fired Blackwell, and Traffic dissolved.

Unfortunately, Claudia and Blackwell's relationship didn't last long. He said he broke up with her, which may or may not be true. This dynamic would repeat itself in all of Claudia's future relations, with the male insisting he ended the affair, while Claudia stated she simply was bored or tired of the dalliance and needed to move on to greener pastures.

In 1973, Claudia gave a very interesting interview to her hometown paper the *Chicago Tribune*. The piece had the same feel that would be repeated in her future interviews, creating an unrealistic assessment of her career and false bravado. Whether she really believed what was said at the time, or whether it was to boost her image as a tough cookie, is hard to discern. Looking back, however, the Claudia giving the interview is completely different from the real-life person.

> I've done eight rotten roles in a row. If there's a bad girl in a B-movie, I get the part. But no more. I've just finished my last B-movie ('*Gator Bait*). From now on I'm only doing A-pictures or none at all. And I'm not uptight about it because you know what? I can afford to wait.

The unfortunate truth was Claudia could not afford to wait. What was even more regrettable, the only A-film she would ever get was the brief, un-credited appearance in *The Man Who Fell to Earth*. This interview and other subsequent interviews are difficult to interpret. We know Claudia never regretted any of her film appearances privately, according to Bobby Hart and others. Why she felt the need to proclaim the opposite in the media is frankly inexplicable.

The Streets of San Francisco

To keep herself busy and to have an income stream, she did appear on television several times during the mid-1970s. Despite the fact her appearances on shows like *The FBI* and *The Streets of San Francisco* were praised, Claudia never received any offers to appear in mainstream films outside the TV arena. To make matters worse, she didn't even land the role as TV's *Wonder Woman*, which would have given her career a more solid footing.

Time and circumstances began to work against Claudia, as the decade moved forward. She had ended her relationship with Bobby Hart and the financial security it provided. Claudia had also become a fixture on the L.A. party scene, which was not conducive to her career or personal success. With few alternatives, when a B-movie opportunity beckoned, Claudia accepted the part. The fact that it was a Roger Corman co-production made the decision somewhat more palatable.

The Great Texas Dynamite Chase (aka *Dynamite Women*) (1976)

This film still stands out as one of Claudia's best, an almost perfect example of how an exploitation film can be thought provoking, entertaining, artistic and fun. Claudia dominates the movie, appearing in almost every scene, much like *Unholy Rollers*, giving another measured, self-assured performance.

There is a copious amount of T&A in addition to "buffalo shots" of three male actors, but rarely has nudity been used in such a relevant manner to the narrative of a B-movie. The violence in the film is realistic and is consistent with the plot. Despite those limitations, it is a gorgeous spectacle. Honestly, I would categorize it as a B+ film.

Claudia's character avenges the death of Slim.

One of the movie's tag lines alluded to *Butch Cassidy and the Sundance Kid*, and this is definitely where the film's philosophical moorings come from. Some critics have suggested that *Thelma and Louise* owes its origins to *The Great Texas Dynamite Chase*, and the comparisons are certainly easy to make. However, *Thelma and Louise* is a more pessimistic, even nihilistic, look at feminism, whereas Claudia's film is gleefully subversive and a realistic look at a true feminist hero and establishes a plausible friendship between two women.

Roger Corman's New World studios put together a strong cast and crew for the film. As was his nature, Corman assigned a first time director, Michael Pressman, to the production. Craig Safan, a prolific composer, provided the music (he also composed the theme for the hit TV show *Cheers* and the score for *Thief*). There is even some subtle humor slipped into the film. About halfway through, Claudia robs a bank called the New World Bank, which, of course, was a nod to the name of Mr. Corman's production company.

Jocelyn Jones, who plays Ellie-Jo Turner, was a pretty young actress who looked remarkably like Claudia. Her biggest role before *The Great Texas Dynamite Chase* was in *The Other Side of the Mountain*. Raised in a family of successful actors and artists (her father won two Emmy awards), she started acting in her early teens.

Johnny Crawford plays Slim, a young man that the girls kidnap but who becomes their willing accomplice. One of the more amazing talents in Hollywood, Crawford started his career as one of the original Mouseketeers. He then became famous as Chuck Connor's son, Mark McCain, in the TV series *The Rifleman*. From there he had a successful singing career, with hits such as "Cindy's Birthday," "Rumors" and "Patti Ann." He even became a rodeo star for a while before doing movies and TV appearances. He is known as the first male model to pose for a full frontal nudity spread in *Playboy* magazine. To top it all off, he is now a popular bandleader in Los Angeles, playing music from the 1920s.

Claudia's co-stars Johnny Crawford and Jocelyn Jones noticed a change in her personality as the filming went on. Johnny Crawford noted his observations of Claudia:

> I had seen Claudia many times at the Playboy Mansion. She was always down to earth, friendly and of course exceptionally beautiful. She was very sweet to me and always came up to say hello. When we were filming *The Great Texas Dynamite Chase*, I noticed Claudia wasn't herself. She was very thin. It looked like she had lost 10 pounds since the last time I saw her. She was very hyped up. Jocelyn Jones and I noticed it most in one particular scene. Claudia was driving the getaway car, and Jocelyn and I jumped in. Claudia was driving very erratically, and frankly, we were scared. Claudia even missed the cue to stop the car. Jocelyn was able to talk with her a little, but I had trouble conversing with her. It was obvious something was wrong with her. She was not the same Claudia I had met before.[35]

The crowd Claudia was running with was increasingly seedy, and her ability to manage her recreational use of drugs was weakening. Whether it was depression over her career, or her split from Bobby Hart, the overall effect was decidedly negative. There is no doubt the demons Claudia had brought with her from Evanston—the self-esteem issues among them—were exacerbated by drug use. It is to her credit that she functioned as well as she did.

One day when filming a scene involving Claudia running into a bank, something went terribly wrong. She tripped and ran into a wall, severely injuring herself. Those on

Tara Strohmeier and Claudia from *The Great Texas Dynamite Chase*

the set recall that Claudia threw herself into the scene with more force than necessary, implying it was a self-inflicted incident. True to her nature, though, she finished the scene waiting for the ambulance to come.

Shooting was shut down for two weeks while Claudia recovered. When she returned, she was in poor shape, mixing the prescribed meds with the recreational drugs. Her injury and her fondness for street drugs fed off each other, and probably generated increased feelings of dislocation and disorientation.

Even with the occasional interludes of lucidity and the sentimental conversations with her co-star, the overall impression Claudia gave her director Michael Pressman was that of "an accident waiting to happen." Despite all of this drama, Claudia ultimately created a great performance.

Our story opens up with Candy Morgan (Claudia) running away from prison. Yes, Claudia is seen running hill over dale in her penitentiary duds (denim; no orange jumpsuits in this era). She's dynamited her way out of prison, using the knowledge she gained doing roadwork for the state. She arrives at the rendezvous point where her sister Pam (Tara Strohmeier) is waiting. After a brief reunion and a change of clothes, Candy borrows Pam's car to "run an errand."

Simultaneously Ellie Jo (Jocelyn Jones), asleep in bed with her latest boyfriend, gets a phone call from one of her fellow employees at the bank where she works. Realizing she's late (again), she pops up, in the buff, throws on a dress and brushes her teeth. When her boy toy tells her to come back to bed, she simply tells him to be gone when she gets back.

Ellie-Jo gets to work and the manager is not impressed with her excuse. He fires her for not only being habitually tardy, but also because the townspeople don't like their money being handled by a woman who, putting it delicately, likes to handle a lot of other things. Ouchy! That's getting a little personal, and if that bank had an HR department back then, it would have been his ass.

While the manager is berating Ellie-Jo, Candy bursts in with two dynamite sticks, one lit with a long fuse, the other, with a very short fuse, unlit. Ellie-Jo volunteers to collect the money for Candy, and even stops one of the tellers from triggering the silent alarm. All during this activity, Ellie-Jo has the biggest, most adorable shit-eating grin on her face, and who can blame her? After Candy grabs the money, she gives Ellie-Jo a sincere look of gratitude and says, "Thanks." It is a fine piece of acting, as the characters communicate almost entirely with body language and facial expressions. This is a well-shot scene in every sense.

As Candy makes her getaway, she strategically drops the lit dynamite stick as she tears off down the main drag, barely missing the town's only police car. The officer parks right over the TNT, then runs into the bank to ask what the hell is going on and is finally treated to the sight of his vehicle blowing up.

Meanwhile, back at the ranch—or more properly, the Morgan homestead—things aren't going too well. Unable to afford living on the ancestral dump any longer, Pam and her horny boyfriend are putting up a "For Sale" sign when Candy comes heading down the road. After an emotional reunion with her father, who makes it obvious he doesn't approve of her methods but can't argue about the results, Candy gives him the money she's just stolen to save the property. It's a regrettably brief reunion.

Pappy's advice turns into serendipity. Poor Ellie-Jo is thumbing a ride when a handsome young man in a fancy car picks her up. Unfortunately, Mr. Playboy only wants to feel up every portion of Elli-Jo's hot little body. When she takes exception, he throws her out in the middle of nowhere. Who should come along just then but Candy! She agrees to give Ellie-Jo a lift, but only until the next major crossing. There is a nice interplay here between the two leads as Elli-Jo talks a reluctant Candy into letting her be her partner. Claudia realizes the emotional turmoil of really being fond of this girl, and she is worried about a future that might end in prison or death.

The ladies' first attempt fizzles, literally. None of the dynamite they try to use on the job works, so they're forced to run for their lives. They snatch a nice blue pony car, which comes in very handy during an exciting police chase. Candy then drives to a small

Claudia, Johnny Crawford and Jocelyn Jones at work

mining operation, which is a natural place to shop for nice fresh dynamite. Claudia is dressed as provocatively as can be: a white shirt with no bra knotted at the waist and a pair of denim shorts that make Daisy Dukes look conservative. She takes the operator of the concern to a back room and lies down on some hay with legs splayed while removing her shirt. The man is impressed, to say the least. Not only is he willing to sell her dynamite illegally, but Claudia and he have a very tasteful and erotic sequence of hoochie-koo. This might be Claudia's most sensual scene in any of her films, and one wonders if the production had more resources to put into lighting and set design how beautiful this episode might have been. The gentleman is so nice that he gives Candy a shotgun, warning her she may need it someday.

The girls pull a clever variation on their usual robbery style at their next target. Ellie-Jo hides in the bank while Candy phones in a bomb threat. While everyone else in the bank runs away in terror, Ellie-Jo hides and blows the safe. Meanwhile, Candy asks if anyone has seen her sister, who had gone into the bank shortly before the bomb threat. When everyone realizes she must have been left inside, Ellie-Jo staggers out, looking like she just cleaned a chimney. Candy assures the concerned crowd her sister is fine, and they drive off with a major score.

After their escape, Ellie-Jo is pulled over by a horny Highway Patrol officer. She offers a certain sexual favor, and takes him into the brush for some privacy. Once he drops trou, Candy comes along and handcuffs him to a tree. As an added measure of terror and humiliation, the girls leave a lit dynamite stick at crotch level before they flee. It turns out to be a fizzler.

The next day, the ladies are at a posh resort having breakfast when Candy, to her shock, reads in the local paper that the girls are being blamed for the murder of a bank guard in addition to their other crimes. This is a game-changer, as now police won't be out only to capture them, but to kill them. Well, Ellie-Jo, being the naughty wench she is, can't stop misbehaving. The ladies stop at a convenience store, and while Candy

Candy in action, two-fisted sticks of dynamite at her call

is trying to maintain a low profile, what with half the state of Texas after them, Ellie-Jo can't resist shoplifting some snacks. Candy pulls a gun out and grabs a young man named Slim (Johnny Crawford), who also happens to be shoplifting. They all head out to the car and speed away.

Then we have another well-staged scene as the three thieves drive away. Ellie-Jo is on the far left looking at Slim like he's a 32-ounce medium rare porterhouse. Slim is in the middle, not particularly worried, and says to Candy, "Ma'am, would you mind putting that gun down, please?" Candy smiles and gradually lowers the piece. Then Ellie-Jo says, "I'm hungry." Slim smiles, pulls a bag out of his jacket and says, "I've got some pretzels." They all laugh and drive down the highway.

Slim convinces them to let him join the outfit, against Candy's better judgment. He does come in handy as a fake hostage, and the gang is soon making lots of dough. Now maybe it's me, but if you were trying to keep a low profile, the getaway car should probably be something unassuming, am I right? Well, not for our group; they're motoring around in a Rolls Royce.

Everything is going fine, and the group decides to bed down for the night in a fancy hotel near the Mexican border. The stuffy desk manager is a butthole, but when Candy pays him double for the bridal suite, he warms up to them. The three bank robbers are having quite a time at the party, drinking champagne and eating fancy Texas hotel food, when Ellie-Jo and Slim start feeling the mood of the bridal suite overtake them. Candy discreetly slips away, calls downstairs, and asks the cute room service waiter to bring up a fresh bottle of champagne. When he delivers it, Ellie-Jo directs him to the bathroom, where Candy is waiting for him in the bath. Before you can say rub-a-dub-dub, all four are splish-splashing around. Morning finds Slim, Ellie-Jo and Candy in naked bliss under the covers.

A nice bit of trivia is that a bedroom in Bobby Hart's Woodrow Wilson estate served as a set for some of the hotel scenes.

Down at the front desk, the rotten manager sees the newscast about the bank robbers and phones the police. The waiter calls the gang to alert them the law is on the

Candy (Claudia Jennings) and Ellie-Jo (Jocelyn Jones) are about to give the Texas lawman a big surprise.

way. They barely escape, and Slim is starting to have second thoughts about his career choice. He tells the girls he's out of there and goes to take a Greyhound to nowhere, but the bus pulls away with old Johnny still there, and much joy erupts.

Unfortunately, the girls' luck is running out. They keep running into people they've robbed, and the banks are better protected now. Slim even gets winged during one holdup. They decide to hole up for a while in a secluded cabin, driving their Rolls Royce, of course. One afternoon while Candy's in town and Slim and Ellie-Jo are playing grab-ass by the lake, the cabin's owner calls the police, who are definitely out for blood this time. Candy pulls up just as the cops draw a bead on Slim, who dives in front of Ellie-Jo, saving her life. Unfortunately for Slim, he is turned into ground beefcake, while poor Ellie-Jo screams bloody murder. Candy, a whole lot of pissed off at seeing her BFF's BMFF get wasted, pulls out that handy shotgun the cute dynamite man gave her and ventilates the two Texas troopers.

The next few minutes are a highlight of the movie, as Candy and Ellie-Jo drive away. There is not a word spoken between the two women, only the guilt, grief and weariness in their faces to tell the story. The gals soon find themselves in a funk, with no money and the law closing in on them. Candy suggests one more heist and then an all-out sprint to Mexico. They case a small bank in a town near the border and proceed to rob it. They are surprisingly not curious when the town and the bank seem deserted. I guess they never saw *The Wild Bunch*. The ladies get what little cash is there and walk out into a small army of combined law enforcement agencies. Candy gets her arm shot up and the women barely make it out of town, now heading for the border.

They come to a small hacienda and park their ride in the horse barn. When they ask the owners if they are in Mexico, they get a confused look and a finger pointing to some green hills a few hundred yards away. Ellie-Jo fixes up Candy's arm as well as she can, just as the police start pulling up.

The coppers have the front of the barn covered. I guess they thought the structure didn't have a rear door. Just then, the girls' car comes roaring out, with the last of their dynamite festooning the front grill. When everything goes boom, we cut to the back of the barn to see Candy and Ellie-Jo hauling ass on a couple of palominos, heading south of the border. The screen tells us Ellie-Jo married a coffee magnate in Mexico City, and Candy is going steady with a bank president in Buenos Aires. Good work, girls! Shame about Slim, though. The moral of the story? Stay out of jail and marry well.

Despite Claudia's injuries and depression, *The Great Texas Dynamite Chase* is an excellent film and one of Claudia's best efforts. Fine direction, good special effects, exciting chase sequences, and most importantly, lead actors who can dominate their scenes firmly place this movie among Corman and Claudia's all-time greats. Jocelyn Jones does a great job as Claudia's partner; the two women have a wonderful chemistry on screen. It's as if Claudia's character sees Ellie-Jo as the girl she could have been, had she not turned to a life of crime. Conversely, Ellie-Jo sees in Claudia the wild and non-conformist life she secretly desired. There are literally no weak moments in the film that might have taken away from any of the movie's strengths. Whatever Pressman thought about Claudia personally, his film would have been far less effective without her.

Claudia: Is it a smile or a frown?

Claudia's co-star in the film had an interesting interview with Ari Bass in 1995, where she talked about Claudia as an actress and a person. The daughter of esteemed actor Michael Jones, Jocelyn grew up in Sneden's Landing, New York, just north of New York City. The hamlet is renowned for its arts community and inspired Jocelyn to become interested in all things creative. After a career as an actress, she now runs an exclusive actors studio in Los Angeles, supervises scripts and personally coaches actors who are ready to begin filming major projects.

> I found Claudia very helpful because this was only my second film. I would say I was a trained actress and she was a very experienced actress. She assisted me with hair, shoes and make-up, and also gave me a lot of confidence for the sexual aspects of the movie.
>
> It seemed to me she was very unhappy at the time we made the film. She talked often about how much she missed home and a quieter life and that she missed her sisters terribly. She said I reminded her of one of them.
>
> There was no question Claudia was a star; the whole film revolved around her. She definitely had that aura about her. Claudia was a sweet woman, but

I didn't feel she had a lot of confidence, mainly because of *Playboy*. Although she was one of the most beautiful women I'd ever met, at the Mansion she was surrounded by women she felt inferior to. I think being associated with *Playboy* hurt her self-confidence as far as acting went. She made many films, but never got the break or roles she really wanted. I believe training and acting lessons would have made a huge difference in her career, and ultimately, her personal life. The idea of acting lessons are to help a performer "know what they know"—in other words, give that actor a rock to build their performance on. Perhaps Claudia was afraid to be criticized in front of her peers.

I think it was sad the path Claudia had gotten herself on by the time I met her. The 1970s were such a different time. Drugs were looked on favorably. There were no Betty Ford clinics in those days, and people didn't have the same enlightenment and sensitivity toward addiction that they do today. She had gotten into the fast lane both personally and professionally. There was no one there who could pull her out of it. It was so sad what happened to her. I have nothing but fond memories of her.

Claudia's smile could light up the entire state of Texas

The director was not particularly proud of the film, saying exploitation was not the genre that lay within his comfort zone. He told the *Los Angeles Times* that *The Great Texas Dynamite Chase* was a means to an end—that is, his way to make more "personal movies."[36] His strategy paid off, as he went on to direct some big budget A-movies like *Doctor Detroit*, *Some Kind of Hero* and the underrated *Those Lips, Those Eyes*. Pressman is still working today, with impressive television credentials such as *Justified* and *Law and Order: Special Victims Unit*.

There was a sprinkling of diamond-grade actors in the cast, which helped as well. Stefan Gierasch, who played the hotel manager, appeared in *Silver Streak*, *The Hustler* and *High Plains Drifter*. Christopher Pennock, who played the hunky mining operator Jake, was a near-permanent fixture on television, but was best known for playing Gabriel Collins on *Dark Shadows*.

Moonshine County Express (1977)

Roger Corman's New World Pictures once again called upon Claudia for 1977's *Moonshine County Express*. This was a role that surprisingly called for no nudity. Claudia gave one of her best performances, surrounded by a great cast, which included a very young Maureen McCormick (who played Marcia Brady on *The Brady Bunch*). Often called one of the best carsploitation-hicksploitation films of the '70s, the film is actually a very well-made Shakespearean-style revenge play set in the hills and stills of the South. The only exploitation elements are a small measure of feminine eye candy, high-speed car chases and some gun violence, none of it terribly graphic.

Everything works in this movie. It features an impressive cast of veteran actors who are trained enough not to chew the scenery, even when given the opportunity. The film's director, Gus Trikonis, does a marvelous job in keeping the action going from scene to scene in a logical fashion—unusual for a B-movie. The cinematography by Gary Graver is quite good, especially during several car chases that are very exciting and not the boring, repetitive sort that are the failing of many other exploitation movies. I suppose the word "professional" comes to mind to describe the production.

If you ever feel the need to impress someone with trivia, director Trikonis was a dancer at one point in his career, appearing in the 1961 film *West Side Story* as Indio. He also had the distinction of being Goldie Hawn's husband from 1969 to 1976.

The film also saw a few changes in Claudia's personal life. The film's location was Nevada City, California, north of Sacramento. It had been one of the earliest gold rush towns, and the quaint Victorian architecture fits the needs of the movie. The cast and crew settled into one of the old, classic hotels of the locale. Before long, both Maureen and Claudia began to get friendly with the film's cinematographer, Gary Graver. The only complication was that Claudia and Bobby had reunited shortly before filming began.

Graver was a talented man, and was best known for being the last cinematographer to work with Orson Welles before the great man passed away. A native of Portland, Oregon, Graver learned his trade in the military, serving in the Navy's Combat Camera Group. Back in civilian life, Graver collaborated with the famous exploitation auteur Fred Olen Ray on some of his greatest films, such as *Evil Tunes* and *Dinosaur Island*. He also filmed such schlock classics as *Frankenstein vs. Dracula* and *Satan's Sadists*.

Graver made mostly documentaries until he heard Orson Welles would be making a stop in the town where Graver was working. Graver dropped in unannounced,

Betty Hammer (Claudia) in *Moonshine County Wars*

and declared he wanted to work with Welles. Welles told Graver that the only person who ever told him they wanted to work with him was Gregg Toland, who was director of photography on *Citizen Kane*. The two became inseparable, with Graver serving as Welles' apprentice, collaborator, manservant, dresser, and gofer. It was the beginning of a close friendship and creative filmmaking partnership. In 1970 Graver, Welles and his collaborator, Oja Kodar, started filming a feature project, *The Other Side of the Wind*, eventually released in 2018. The production was to take place over a period of five years. Shooting was completed in Los Angeles in 1975 at the home of Peter Bogdanovich, after a marathon schedule that took the project to Arizona, France, Spain, Belgium, New York, Hollywood, Yugoslavia, Italy and England. Because of a series of legal entanglements, the film never made it through post-production, although Welles left an edited 45-minute version with editing notes.

During this period, in 1973, Welles, Kodar and Graver made a feature in Europe titled *F for Fake* (1973). After that, Welles and Graver worked on many projects, including *The Orson Welles Show* (1979) for TV syndication, with Burt Reynolds, Angie Dickinson and The Muppets. Other projects included *Orson Welles' Magic Show* (1985) and the essay film *Filming Othello* (1978).

At the end of one project, Welles gave Graver an object and told him, "Here, keep this." It was Welles' Oscar for co-writing *Citizen Kane*. The gesture would prove problematic later in Graver's life. Considering it as a gift, the cinematographer sold the award when he needed some extra money. Graver attempted to have it auctioned off at Sotheby's. When Welles' daughter Beatrice learned of the impending auction, she threatened to sue and eventually won back the Oscar.

Other than that glitch, Graver had a successful career in Hollywood as a cinematographer and director. He also had a not-so-secret life as a director and photographer

The Hammer sisters (front to rear): Dot (Susan Howard), Sissy (Maureen McCormick) and Betty (Claudia)

of pornographic films under the name of Robert McCullum, taking part in well over 100 features, and was eventually inducted into the *Adult Video News* Hall of Fame. Graver, whose original ambition was to be an actor, also appeared in over 30 mainstream movies.

The time Graver spent working with Welles—six years—came at a price. Graver did little else in that time, and according to friend Ari Bass, it contributed to his second divorce. When Graver was introduced to Claudia, he fell hard for her despite the fact she was trying to reconcile with her longtime boyfriend Bobby Hart. They had broken up and only recently gotten back together. Graver told Ari Bass in a *Femme Fatales* article:

> We were on location in a great hotel. That's where Claudia and I started going together. Albert Salmi didn't like his room, so Claudia and I moved in. She was a great girl, a real "un-movie star" kind of person—honest. If I'd say something, she'd go, "Oh, come on Graver, cut the shit" or something. A real regular girl.[37]

The cast of *Moonshine County Express* really sets the film apart. Susan Howard (Dot Hammer) had distinguished herself as an actress on *Dallas*, the popular television potboiler. John Saxon (as the hard driving, romancing J.B. Johnson) was a versatile actor, handsome, rugged and equally capable of playing a hero or villain. He appeared in over 200 television shows and movies, including *Enter the Dragon*, *Queen of Blood* and *A Nightmare on Elm Street*, and he appeared with Claudia in her last film, *Fast Company*. William Conrad, a veteran film and TV performer, plays the movie's villain, Jack Starkey. He was the star of *Cannon*, and appeared in such productions as the quintessential film noir *The Killers*.

Betty and Dot prepare for action with the family shootin' irons.

Dub Taylor, another well-known character actor, was cast in many A-list films such as The *Wild Bunch*, *Bonnie and Clyde* and *Pat Garret and Billy the Kid*; he played the girls' Uncle Bill. Starkey's henchman Sweetwater was played by Morgan Woodward, best known for his role in *Cool Hand Luke* as Boss Godfrey. It is not a stretch to imagine that the Coen Brothers took inspiration from Woodward's performance, when they created the character of Sheriff Cooley for *O Brother Where Art Thou?*

Len Lesser was a familiar face as well, never playing the leading role but always contributing, as in his memorable appearances in *Papillon* and *The Outlaw Josey Wales*, not to mention *Seinfeld*. He also appeared with Claudia in *Truck Stop Women*. I hope that you can see that I'm trying to make a case for *Moonshine County Express* to be thought of as an A-movie—or at least an A-minus effort.

The last two members of the supporting cast push the film beyond the B-classification. Jeff Corey (the drunken, corrupt preacher Hagen) was one of the most respected actors and drama instructors of his generation. Claudia would eventually take lessons at his studio, but she dropped out. Corey was a fixture in many Westerns and adventure films, giving outstanding performances in *True Grit*, *Little Big Man* and *Conan the Destroyer*. The most illustrious of the cast was Albert Salmi, who plays Sheriff Larkin. Salmi studied under Lee Strasberg at the Actors Studio, where Marlon Brando and Marilyn Monroe learned their trade among dozens of other fine actors. He originated the role of Bo Decker in *Bus Stop* on Broadway, but he declined the chance to be in the movie; Don Murray took the role and won an Oscar as a result. He was nominated for an Academy Award for his performance in *The Brothers Karamazov*, and won Best Supporting Actor from the National Board of Review; however, he didn't care for Hollywood and preferred the stage and television. Among his over 150 roles were *The Bravados*, *The*

Morning at the Hammer homestead

Ambushers, Empire of the Ants and *The Outrage*. Tragically, he died of a self-inflicted gunshot wound after killing his wife, an incident that still haunts and puzzles many in Hollywood.

The movie opens with a picturesque scene of men preparing moonshine, serenaded by an excellent soundtrack of bluegrass music. We see Pap Hammer working hard, making sour mash, wiping his brow and directing his crew. His dog's nervousness foreshadows trouble, and trouble, indeed, does arrive. Suddenly, as we say in the South, all Hail breaks loose as a group of assassins, hiding in the woods, start picking off Pap Hammer's men one by one. The dog runs to the Hammer homestead, where Dot and Betty (our girl Claudia) grab some shootin' irons and start running toward the commotion. Dot, the oldest sister, tells the youngest, Sissy, to stay put. Of course, as soon as Dot turns and runs off, Sissy grabs a piece and starts following. The scene is shot well with a lot of tension; however, it seems like it takes an awful long time for the girls to reach the stills—which is a good thing, because after the killers siphon off all the 'shine to haul away, they blow the place sky high. The three sisters reach the scene and find their father dead, and realize their means of earning a living is completely gone and there's no question that things are looking pretty crappy for the girls.

After the funeral for Pap Hammer, the preacher (Jeff Corey) tells the sisters they can always count on him for anything they need. He gently encourages them to leave town now that nothing is left for them. From there, he runs straight to the fellow who had their father killed, the local crime boss Starkey (William Cannon)—a foul-mouthed deep Southern menace who now controls all of the moonshine trade.

The sisters head into town after learning their father's lawyer left something for them. As they drive down the street, J.B. Johnson (John Saxon) pulls alongside in his stock car and asks Dot, rather suggestively, if she wants to see his trophy. He also comments on how pretty the youngest sister Sissy is, which is kind of creepy and ill-advised, since he's trying to impress her older sister and it's implied Sissy is under the age of consent—at least in most areas of the United States.

Well, it turns out Pap Hammer was keeping a secret all these years. Way back during Prohibition, Starkey's daddy set up Pap and got him sent to the pokey for a spell.

A Biography

Jeff Corey as Hagen (incidentally, Claudia took acting lessons from Corey)

However, Pap got his revenge by stealing the elder Starkey's stash of real bottled in-bond whiskey, not that nasty moonshine. The girls find the booze by following written clues left by their pappy. It's stored in an underground bunker with a cleverly placed escape tunnel that leads to a remote part of the forest. This is a great scene in the movie, as Betty (Claudia) is the first one to see if the goods are still … good. She and Dot soon sit down, share a bottle and talk about their strategy going forward. The interplay between the sisters is very natural throughout the film, with Betty always deferring to her older sister, and the two older women protective and gentle with Sissy.

Meanwhile, we learn J.B. does more than race cars. He delivers moonshine for Starkey and starts out on a run for our first real car chase of the movie. He roars off and soon draws the attention of a police car. The chase is filmed with quick cuts between the cars and J.B. turning the wheel, all to the sounds of insane banjo music and squealing tires. The only slight problem, and I'm being picky, is that tires don't generally squeal on dirt roads or gravel. J.B. forces the cops to crash and drives off to deliver his wares.

Dot hasn't wasted any time and is selling the good stuff to every general store, garage and anywhere else fine whiskey is sold in Moonshine County. When Tom Scoggins (Len Lesser) balks at purchasing her wares for fear of incurring Starkey's wrath, she seductively tells him it'll be worth his while, and that maybe just the two of them could get together and share a bottle, etc., and the fool falls for it. Dot leaves him a free bottle, and Tom acts as if he's won the lottery and is going off on a one-week trip to Hawaii with Taylor Swift.

Starkey, seeing his sales drop, decides to drive up to the Hammer's place and try to talk sense to them, bringing his goon Sweetwater (Morgan Woodward). The parley doesn't go well, and Sissy, showing some spunk, unleashes the family pooch on the two men. The dog bites Sweetwater on the leg, although that's probably not where he was aiming, and the two criminals drive off in a hurry.

That night, at the Fireman's Dance, Dot shows up alone as J.B. walks in escorting one of the town bimbos. He drops her like a sack of dog poo and goes right over to Dot. The two have a wonderful evening, dancing and drinking beer. When Dot's truck can't make it home, J.B. drives her and is invited in for a cup of coffee. Before Dot can tell her sisters to shut up and go to sleep, the house comes under attack—I mean, a Sonny Corleone-at-the-tollbooth type attack. Bullets fly everywhere, breaking every knick-knack, piece of china, window and furniture in the process, generally causing a big mess. Sissy runs and finds the poor doggy dead. J.B. tells the ladies that if Starkey wanted them dead, they'd be lying next to their canine friend right now. This was a warning, and the last one they'd get. J.B. recommends they leave, which pisses Dot off; she calls him another type of hound and a coward.

The next night, the girls go to pick up a car that one of the local mechanics had promised them in order to run their own product into the next large town. On the way there, they see Tom Scoggins' place blown to hell, and poor Tom along with it. Sweetwater is responsible. More bad news waits at the garage, as Starkey's men had removed the jack from under the car the mechanic was working on for the ladies. This turn of events flattens their hopes as well as the grease monkey.

This finally convinces J.B. he's on the wrong side, and he drives up to their house—in a canary yellow 1969 Ford Mustang Boss 302, no less. Dot decides to take a load of whiskey to the big city, and J.B. volunteers to ride along with her to show her the shortcuts. Now, let's think about this. He's a champion stock car driver. She drives an old farm truck. Homicidal maniacs and the police are on the lookout for them. So naturally, you let the less experienced driver take the wheel. Makes perfect sense to me!

They start out fine, but soon Sweetwater is on their trail. After a few minutes, we can tell J.B. and Dot are destined to become sweethearts. How do we know this? Because while they're trying to get away from a hired killer, they start screaming at each other like any other husband and wife would do. Dot tells him to stop screaming, which makes J.B. scream louder. The chase, however, is first rate, with many smooth cuts and exciting angles of the cars getting it on. At the climactic moment of the chase, J.B. says to turn left and Dot turns right, resulting in all three of them—the pony car, Dot and J.B.—going for a swim in the local lake. Sweetwater gets out and watches the car quickly sink, with only a few bubbles rising to the surface.

That's not the end for our couple, though. They emerge further down the edge of the lake, soaked but still screaming at each other.

> Dot: Why did you keep yelling at me?
> J.B.: Because I was trying to keep you from doing what you did!
> Dot: You made me nervous!
> J.B.: You almost made me dead!

Well, this just helps the couple bond. Starkey, in the meantime, thinks Dot and J.B. are dead. The girls' treacherous Uncle Bill (Dub Taylor) spies Betty going to the secret stash of whiskey, and the drunken, dirty old skunk tells Starkey, who shows his gratitude by pumping a few bullets into the lush-bucket's belly.

J.B. and Dot find the thought of being dead very liberating, and stimulating to boot, and they hatch a plan to screw Starkey and keep their whiskey. When Starkey's goons get to the Hammer's house, they steal the whiskey, make lewd comments about Sissy and tie her up in the bunker. Oh, they also put a bomb down there. I guess they didn't care for Maureen's acting in the film. They pay for not using a shorter fuse when Betty picks them off one by one, and Claudia never looked sexier shooting a rifle.

Dot saves Sissy and they hightail it out of the secret tunnel, emerging just as the dynamite explodes. Dot and J.B. take off to steal back the whisky, but Sweetwater, with the tipsy preacher by his side, starts following them. Another exciting car chase takes place, with J.B. being shot in the right hand, so Dot has to shift for him. After much maneuvering, J.B. shows that he's a better driver one-handed than everyone else is with two, and he forces Sweetwater over the edge of a cliff to a gruesome crash.

The happy couple drives into town, where Starkey is waiting for them with his goons. Sheriff Larkin (Albert Salmi), who has busted J.B.'s balls all through the film, turns out to be a good guy. He arrests Starkey and his men and even lets the girls keep their booze. Dot and her sisters, along with J.B., drive off happily to sell their wares and leave the miserable hills behind them.

The movie stays true to its carsploitation roots as well, featuring, besides the Mustang, a 1970 Dodge Challenger, a 1970 Plymouth Satellite and a 1970 Plymouth Road Runner. No Burt Reynolds' "chicken on the hood" Trans Ams, but sweet rides just the same.

In addition to the general quality of the film, the juxtaposition of the characters is fascinating. There are no dominant male characters in the film, extraordinary for the genre of rowdy car chase movies of this era. The Hammer sisters are the ones with strength and purpose. The men in the film all have major flaws, a collection of weak-willed, treacherous, evil and murderous scum. Even J.B. is shown as indecisive, amoral and vain. He ends up being somewhat of a hero, but more of an anti-hero.

Claudia does a great job in this movie. I wish her role was bigger, but she does everything we expect of her and more. She's incredibly beautiful, and it's refreshing that there is no nudity in this film, so viewers can concentrate on her acting. As always, she does great in the action scenes, and her performance is measured and honest. Perhaps out of all her films, *Moonshine County Express* showed her potential for improved mainstream roles.

Claudia had moved back in with Bobby before filming *Moonshine County Express*; however, when he visited her on the set, he found her with the film's cinematographer, Gary Graver. Bobby told me that after his visit, he realized the couple had no future. Bobby didn't give a specific reason, but said he knew things were finally over for them. Bobby, being a gentleman and ever protective of Claudia's memory, didn't give specifics, but one gets the impression Claudia didn't try to hide her relationship with Graver. Claudia and Bobby would remain friends until her death, but the beautiful princess and the handsome prince would not live happily ever after with one other.

Her former agent, Mike Greenfield, said:

Claudia had a great guy in Bobby Hart. He couldn't have been more supportive; he let her do whatever she wanted. He was a terrific person, and if anything, he was too good to her. Claudia was self-destructive. She always had a wild streak in her, and I think she was a lot wilder than even Bobby ever dreamed of and certainly would admit. Claudia's worst failing were the men she chose. Bobby was the best thing to happen to her.[38]

Claudia moved in with Gary Graver for a short while after *The Moonshine County Express* wrapped. Simone Boisseree remembers that Gary was deeply in love with her and wanted to have a serious relationship. Unfortunately for the handsome cinematographer, Claudia saw their time together as just another affair. Graver later said he was the one to end the relationship, but others, like Simone, refute that assertion. As you will read later on, his feelings for Claudia remained rather conflicted long after her death.

One thing that stands out in Claudia's life up to this point is that, as helpful as she was to others, she refused to seek help for herself. She seemed to prefer to suffer in silence than to deal with issues too painful to process. Some might argue that under the circumstances that was a foolish and selfish decision; however, when one thinks about Claudia, she was never in the habit of asking for help. She had always been the one to protect, comfort and help her friends and family. It's quite possible she simply didn't know *how* to ask for help.

It is troubling that in the years to come, all the people surrounding her never intervened in Claudia's obviously declining situation. That brings up uncomfortable questions as we move on in telling her story, such as where was her support system when she needed them?

Claudia was entering a new phase of her life. She was now an independent woman, but no less caring toward her friends and sisters. Was she as confident, intelligent and tough as her comments to the press suggested? The biggest question was how she would handle the freedom, pressure and temptations of the 1970s version of Sodom and Gomorrah, Hollywood, without her relationship with Bobby Hart and the support he provided.

[1] "Fast Life/Untimely Death: Playmate Claudia Jennings," *E! True Hollywood Story*, September 24, 2000
[2] Playmate of the Year," *Playboy* Vol. 17, No. 6, June 1970
[3] *Ibid.*
[4] *Ibid.*
[5] Bass, Ari, "Claudia Jennings' 'Lost Highway,'" *Femme Fatales*, Vol. 9, No. 2, July 21, 2000
[6] Phone interview with Victoria Hale, April 2016
[7] *Ibid.*
[8] Bass, Ari, "Claudia Jennings' 'Lost Highway,'" *Femme Fatales*, Vol. 9, No. 2, July 21, 2000
[9] Hart, Bobby with Glenn Ballantyne, *Psychedelic Bubble Gum: Boyce & Hart, The Monkees, and Turning Mayhem Into Miracles* (New York: SelectBooks, 2015)
[10] Dirks, Tom, "100 Most Controversial Films," *AMC Filmsite*, July 16, 2006
[11] Keeyes, John, *Attack of the B Queens* (Baltimore: Luminary Press/Midnight Marquee Press, 2003)
[12] Von Doviak, Scott, *Hick Flicks: The Rise and Fall of Redneck Cinema* (Jefferson, NC: McFarland and Company, Inc., 2004)
[13] *Ibid.*
[14] *Los Angeles Times*, Review of *Unholy Rollers*, 1972
[15] Phone interview with Paige Millard, February 2016

[16] Phone interview with Keith Jennings, March 2014
[17] Phone interview with Barry Richards, May 2014
[18] Sheppard, Eugenia, the *Tucson Daily Citizen*, "*Playboy* Playmate Chooses Carpentry over Hectic Life of Model/Actress," July 21, 1971
[19] Phone interview with Simone Boisseree, May 2014
[20] Phone interview with Susan Miller, May 2014
[21] Hart & Ballantyne, *op. cit.*
[22] *Los Angeles Times, Claudia Jennings in 40 Carats Role*, 1973
[23] Phone Interview with Robert Emery, July 2014
[24] "Fast Life/Untimely Death: Playmate Claudia Jennings," *E! True Hollywood Story*, September 24, 2000
[25] "Claudia Observed," *Playboy*, December, 1974, vol.21 no.12
[26] *Ibid.*
[27] *Ibid.*
[28] *Ibid.*
[29] *Ibid.*
[30] *Ibid.*
[31] Hart & Ballantyne, *op. cit.*
[32] Hart & Ballantyne, *op. cit.*
[33] Personal Interview with Sally Kirkland, May 23, 2015
[34] Author's Note: Casey was actually a professional football player.
[35] Phone interview with Johnny Crawford, June 2015
[36] Bass, Ari, "Claudia Jennings' 'Lost Highway,'" *Femme Fatales*, Vol. 9, No. 2, July 21, 2000
[37] *Ibid.*
[38] Phone interview with Mike Greenfield, July 2015

Chapter 5:
It's Snowing in Los Angeles 1975-1977

"Drugs were everywhere. You'd go over to someone's house for dinner, and afterwards they'd bring out a big wooden box. Inside were 30 to 40 pre-rolled joints. Then someone else would bring in a sugar bowl filled with coke. Everybody did this. It was a social thing."[1]—Keith Allison

Life in Los Angeles in the 1970s was comparable to the most decadent eras that have existed in modern history. Fueled by unlimited amounts of cash, the drug scene found its way into the most respectable offices and homes of the entertainment elite. The 1960s were a time of frivolous marijuana and introspective LSD consumption; the next decade brought the more serious onslaught of cocaine, Quaaludes and heroin. In a matter of a few years, serious drug consumption was the norm, not the exception. As the late comedian Robin Williams would say after the death of John Belushi, "Cocaine is God's way of saying you have too much money." There is a depressing list of celebrities and entertainers who either overdosed or committed suicide during the decade.

Sex has always been a part of the Hollywood scene, a fact that continues to the present day and will continue until California falls into the sea. In the 1970s all things sexual seemed to explode, with everything from explicit, mainstream pornographic magazines and films like *Behind the Green Door* attracting middle-class audiences to individual sexual experimentation. Hugh Hefner's dream had come true, although it would come back to haunt him later when his empire faced challenge after challenge. It was considered natural by many to have as many sexual partners as possible, especially among the beautiful people of Hollywood. As the censors of motion pictures and television relaxed their standards, nudity and sex acts, real and simulated, proliferated across all media.

Claudia wasn't naive, certainly, yet she previously had Bobby there to shield her from the wolves. Now that she was unattached, she fell back on her survival instincts. When every man in Hollywood and beyond is hitting on you, what is your defense?

Claudia moved out of the big house on Woodrow Wilson to the condo on Larrabee. She decided to have a little fun, and took Ava Cherry's advice to get out of town for a while. The ladies went on tour with the Rolling Stones. This is when Claudia allegedly saved Keith Richards from an overdose, as she told Si Litvinoff. Cherry said on the *E! True Hollywood Story* episode on Claudia that she went a bit too far on the trip.

> I warned her that if she got with one of them, to stay with him. So Claudia got with Ronnie Wood. Then she decided to get with Keith Richards—and that started trouble.[2]

Knowing the dynamics of the Stones' past relationships and plain common sense makes this scenario highly unlikely. The Stones were notorious for stealing each other's girlfriends since the band's beginnings. Keith Richards took advantage of Brian Jones' hospital stay to woo Anita Pallenberg. It does take two to play, and if Claudia was breaking such a taboo, Keith could have told her off, which was his usual manner of dealing with

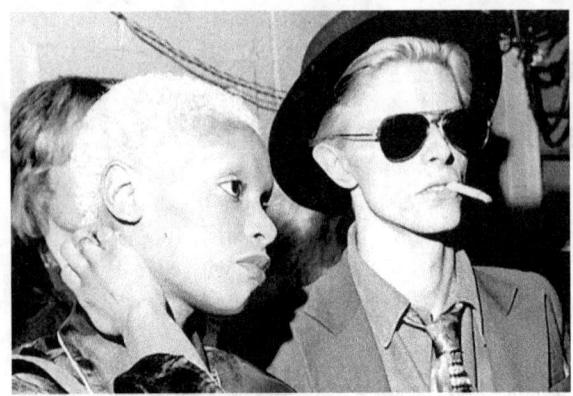
Ava Cherry and David Bowie

such distractions. I somehow think finding temporary female company, even someone as lovely as Claudia, was not a problem for the Stones. Perhaps Cherry was the only one truly disturbed by this.

Later that year, David Bowie and Cherry took up residence with Claudia, who was house-sitting at the time. Friends say it had more to do with Bowie and Claudia's common preference for drugs than a real romance. Of course, both of these people had a curiosity for members of the opposite sex, and it seems unlikely the two wouldn't have satisfied that inquisitiveness.

Bobby Hart actually had an amusing footnote to this story. One day, when he was at home, Claudia came in and ransacked his closet for a variety of outfits. She barely said a word as she streaked through the closet grabbing shirts, pants and shoes. When she was satisfied, she took off just quickly as she came, explaining Bowie had a television appearance that evening.[3]

Claudia was taking a break from moviemaking at this time. She made some TV appearances, but nothing steady. Appearances on *Caribe*, *The Manhunter* and *Movin' On* got Claudia some exposure, but those programs were not huge hits.

Claudia's neighbor and friend from Woodrow Wilson, Simone Boisseree, had split up with her husband and moved in with her. Simone remembered how kind Claudia was to provide a place to stay for her. The house was not only a place of shelter for Simone, but also all of Claudia's new party friends hung out there.

As Simone, a flight attendant at the time who was unable to partake of the activities at the house, recalled:

> The house was always full of the most beautiful people imaginable. Playboy Bunnies, young actresses and actors, the sons of all these Hollywood millionaires—no one was doing much sleeping. But Claudia remained a true friend to me through everything. If I needed clothes, she would give me hers. When I was poor, she would reach in her pocket and give me money. She never expected anything in return. She was the best friend anyone could have. I felt badly for Claudia. She was such a good-hearted person, but I could see her going sideways.[4]

There was an incident that would eventually haunt Simone, but at the time seemed sweet and playful.

> I was there the day Claudia bought her convertible white VW Bug. We bought matching cars. Such a girly thing to do, but it was fun. Just like Claudia. Simone eventually moved out after about eight months.

I could see where Claudia's life was going, and it wasn't a place I wanted to follow. I loved her sincerely, but my lifestyle needed to be quieter.

Simone moved to calmer confines out in the Valley but still remained friends with Claudia.

Claudia was so wonderful to me. She's the one that got me started as a stuntwoman, through her contacts in the film industry. Later I met an amazing man on one of my shoots who was the stunt coordinator. His name was Hal Needham and I was shocked to find out he was one of the best in the business. We dated for a few years, and he taught me so much about how to be a stunt performer.

Simone went on to have one of the most successful careers in the stunt business of all time. She has appeared in *Bruce Almighty*, *Titanic*, *Planet of the Apes*, *Nurse Betty*, *The Last of the Mohicans* and, of course, *Deathsport* with Claudia Jennings. Since retiring from the entertainment industry, she has started her own very successful business producing portable bedding for the luxury jet market.

Simone poignantly said:

I still miss Claudia. There's not a day goes by where I don't think of her.[4]

Claudia and Simone

Not long after Claudia and Bobby Hart parted ways, Claudia's longtime manager Mike Greenfield severed his relationship with her. Greenfield had been one of the foremost agents in Hollywood, and is still a major player in the movie business, although not as an agent. He very generously agreed to speak about his memories of Claudia:

I was always a little depressed I couldn't have taken Claudia Jennings where she should have been. Of all the actresses I've represented, she was one of the great tragedies. She was a dynamo, and a lot of fun. She had the whole package; she could act and sing, she had that great look and she was so vibrant. Claudia was one of the most intelligent and quick-minded people I've met. But she had some qualities I did not understand. With the exception of Bobby Hart, she made terrible choices in men, and that really hurt her personally and career-wise. She also put forward no effort to bolster her career. She stopped her acting lessons with Jeff Corey, for instance. Claudia chose to do it her own

A Biography   173

way. She was smart, but stubborn on some matters. One of her best attributes was also one of her biggest faults. Claudia would always dive right into things, sometimes without thinking things through. She should have dipped a toe into some of these waters. She was very brave, but could also be careless. You ask me if her association with *Playboy* hurt her career—no, I don't think so. Claudia hurt her career more than *Playboy.* To me, it seemed as if she was self-destructive. She had a good man in Bobby Hart. Maybe he didn't understand fully how wild Claudia was. I also represented Linda Evans at the same time I represented Claudia. I will tell you that Linda Evans is the most wonderful, beautiful woman I have ever known in my life, no exception. I think Claudia had that potential. I wish her life and career had gone better.[5]

Greenfield was quoted on the *E! True Hollywood Story* Claudia episode as saying, "Claudia was best when she was playing herself—hot-blooded, naughty, sexy and wild." There is no doubt that she was all of these adjectives. However, Claudia was passionate, naughty but nice, definitely sexy and wild as far as her willingness to do and try almost anything.

Claudia found a new agent—Jim Hyde, the son of Marilyn Monroe's agent, Johnny Hyde. That relationship did not do much for Claudia's career. He found her a few spots on television shows, but the one movie role she got was courtesy of her boyfriend at the time, producer Si Litvinoff: *The Man Who Fell to Earth.*

Claudia formed another relationship with fellow actress Maureen McCormick, while filming *The Moonshine County Express*. Shockingly, McCormick did not recall meeting Claudia on the set of *The Brady Bunch* during the "Adios, Johnny Bravo" episode.

These two beautiful stars spent a lot of time together doing increasingly large amounts of cocaine and partying in all the Hollywood hot spots, like the Candy Store and Carlos 'n' Charlie's, according to McCormick's autobiography. The two became just like sisters, according to mutual friends like Keith Jennings. Which is why Jennings and others in Claudia's circle were perplexed with the tone toward her in Maureen's book. It seemed to them that McCormick ignored all of Claudia's virtues and instead focused on one primary vice. Indeed, when I read the book, it felt that there was a sub-current of feminine jealousy running throughout, as Maureen cites several instances where Claudia is a romantic rival.[6] It leaves the impression that the two women had only one thing in common, which is sad and untrue.

McCormick does mention one episode where she was able to pour her heart out to Claudia about her self-doubts and mixed feelings concerning her *Brady Bunch* past. She acknowledges that despite Claudia's own heartbreak over losing out on the *Charlie's Angels* role, Maureen found a friend to turn to. McCormick goes on to mention Claudia gradually gave up drugs and straightened up, only to die shortly thereafter.[7]

Unfortunately, that was the extent of Maureen's praise for her friend. Regrettably, McCormick declined the opportunity to be interviewed for this book.

Keith Allison is one of the most admired musicians in America. Best known as a guitarist for Paul Revere & the Raiders, Keith's career has spanned over five decades. He has been a solo artist and a studio musician for the Monkees, and has played with such legends as Waddy Wachtel, Al Kooper, Jerry Lee Lewis, Kenny Rogers, Alice Cooper, Rick Nelson and a host of others. If that wasn't enough, he was the musical director for Ringo Starr and His All-Starr Band.

Allison has also had an impressive acting career, appearing in *Gods and Generals*, *Sgt. Pepper's Lonely Hearts Club Band* and the cult classic *Phantom of the Paradise*.

Keith and Claudia met when she and Bobby Hart saw him perform in Las Vegas. They remained close friends even after Bobby and Claudia were no longer living together. Keith was very generous in sharing his time and recollections for this book.

Keith Allison and Jackie DeShannon ham it up in an ad for *Where the Action Is*.

I was introduced to Claudia when Bobby came to see Paul Revere & the Raiders at the Flamingo Hotel in Las Vegas. She was open, warm and charming. We got along from the start. After she and Bobby split up and she moved out, we used each other as arm pieces. If I needed a date, I'd call Claudia, and she would do the same.

One time, some producers threw a dinner for Mae West at Chasen's. Now at this time, Claudia was driving a Rolls Royce, and I had a VW van that I had put a Porsche engine into. It wasn't the most beautiful ride, but it was fast as hell. Well, Claudia said no way she was going to a fancy party in my van. So she would drive to my house, scoot over to the passenger side and have me drive us.

She was such a joy to be around. I took her as my date to my son's Autumn Carnival one year. She seemed so much at home with the kids. You could tell she loved children. But what I remember most was this little ribbon she had twirled in her hair for the Carnival. I found it later. It had fallen out at my place

A Biography 175

and still had a few strands of her hair in it. I kept it for a long time. She was such a sweet kid. She would set me up with girls all the time. I didn't complain, believe me! I remember after my divorce, I had gotten this bachelor pad on King's Road. I didn't even have a bed. I used to go out and actually ask girls would they like to go to floor with me tonight. Well, Claudia thought I should have something proper to sleep on. She bought me a king-sized bed, and her old roommate Allison bought me designer sheets. I couldn't believe the two of them did that. Then again, Claudia was always doing things like that for people. She was very generous.

She was also completely uninhibited. I'd come over to her place and she'd yell, "I'm in the bathroom!" Well, I'd walk in, and she'd be taking a bath. It didn't faze her a bit. She'd say, "Keith, would you mind getting me a glass of wine?" or "Keith, would you mind handing me that lotion?" Claudia would just continue getting ready for a dinner date, completely oblivious to the fact she was naked and I was sitting there. That's the way she was. It was all very matter-of-fact.

Since you asked where she got exposed to the harder drugs, it's easy to answer. Drugs were everywhere. You'd go over to someone's house for dinner, and afterwards they'd bring out a big wooden box. Inside were 30 to 40 pre-rolled joints. Then someone else would bring in a sugar bowl filled with coke. Everybody did this. It was a social thing. I remember being at this party and someone sat down with two unopened containers of Merck pharmaceutical cocaine. So it was pervasive. I think Claudia did it at first to fit in.[8]

Constance Chesterton validated what Keith Allison said about the strange days of Hollywood in the 1970s.

We'd go out to eat with Claudia and be joined by her rock star friends and other glitterati of the music and movie business. It was like dining with Roman emperors. They would order hundreds of dollars of food that went untouched—that is until they passed out and fell face first into their plates. I think most of them spent more time in the men's room doing coke and gobbling down Quaaludes than they did at the dinner table.

If we go back to her Evanston high school days, Keith Allison's comment was a perceptive and plausible explanation. Claudia most likely kept that insecure piece of the old "Mimi" inside her. She had a need to fit in at a new school, where she felt inferior to wealthier classmates. Not only were they wealthier, many of them most likely felt and acted superior to her. Claudia was not anxious to have those feelings revived. Cocaine not only became a social activity, but obviously, a shield against issues arising from her past. She decided, just like her other activities, that drug use would make her more popular among her peers.

Claudia began a period in her life where men and drugs were her main concerns. She met cinematographer Gary Graver on the set of *The Moonshine County Express* and moved in with him for a brief time; she got restless and moved out. She and Maureen McCormick, whom she also met on the set, became best friends and roommates.

Claudia met James Caan at the Playboy Mansion one night, and allegedly the two became lovers and spent weekends at his ranch in the Las Vegas desert getting blasted, according to McCormick's autobiography. It was not the last of the gentlemen Claudia met at the Playboy Mansion who could offer her wealth and other perks.

Claudia had a fling with actor Michael Brandon, which was ironic since Maureen McCormick had an intense affair with him a few years earlier. Brandon's marriage to actress Lindsay Wagner was falling apart at the time and the two had an immediate attraction to each other.

Michael Brandon agreed to speak about Claudia for this book. He is an excellent and prolific actor, having made well over 100 television appearances in the United States and Great Britain. His film credits include *Goodbye, Columbus*; *Four Flies on Grey Velvet* and *Lovers and Other Strangers*. He is also one of the American narrators for *Thomas & Friends*, the much-beloved children's cartoon series.

> I knew Claudia Jennings. She was a terrific girl—a hip, charismatic woman with a great sense of humor and a hearty laugh. Easy to be with, she was very popular and well liked. She knew everyone and had a very varied and active social life. She was a dear friend I was privileged to know.

It should be noted that even when Claudia was in her own little snow globe, she was still a faithful friend and a wonderful person. Although it seems contradictory, if one looks at Claudia's overall character, it is not. All of us have our ways of dealing with pain, loss, frustration and sadness. Claudia expended an incredible amount of energy to keep up the image of a tough, self-sufficient devil-may-care Hollywood sex symbol. The effort needed to maintain this image had to have a cost. Once cocaine provided a sturdy foundation of self-confidence, Claudia let her libido run wild to reinforce her self-esteem.

Somewhere in her mind, somewhere in her past, Claudia somehow learned that sex was power. By seducing men—and she didn't need much effort to do that—Claudia

'Playboy Likes Girls With Baby Fat'

A Biography

gained control over the act of intercourse and at the same time built up her flagging self-confidence. She was not the first human being to equate beauty and sex with self-esteem, but somehow she stopped believing in her other virtues along the way.

Claudia was so full of innate kindness that she went out of her way to please people. Keith Jennings, who Claudia befriended at Bobby Hart's home, remembered several times where she did whatever she could for him, convenient or not.

> I was in high school at the time and I took some girls over to her house and Claudia happened to be cleaning out her closet that day. The girls were gawking at Claudia as well as the clothes, when suddenly Claudia asked them if they would like any of them. The girls all went home with t-shirts and blouses, and I looked like a hero.
>
> One birthday, Claudia offered to take me out to dinner at a wonderful Mexican restaurant on Sunset. Here I was with this incredibly beautiful movie star, and I'm just a teenager. Well, there was a table of these drunken guys sitting there, and they recognized her. They started talking very loudly about her, not all of it rude but certainly not appropriate. I was embarrassed, but Claudia acted like it was no big deal. When our table was ready, she took my arm firmly in hers and she stared at them as we walked away. She made me feel so wonderful and honored by that small gesture.
>
> Claudia also practiced tough love. You did not want to piss her off. One time I was very upset emotionally and I called to tell her I was going to kill myself. Her response was, "Go ahead. But if you do, I will not go to your funeral. I will never even think about you again. So if that's what you really want, do it." Well, needless to say, that was the last time I ever thought about doing that again.[9]

Claudia was now drawn to wealthy older men who had plenty of drugs. She found one in Las Vegas: Dean Shendal, a former rodeo cowboy. In the *Femme Fatales* article he's described as "a Sands Casino pit boss turned interest-holder in Caesar's Palace." Shendal had taken the fall for an alleged member of the Outfit by holding onto a gun equipped with a silencer and an erased serial number. He was represented by, of all people, so-called mob lawyer (and eventual mayor of Las Vegas) Oscar Goodman, who provided a solid defense. He was sentenced to five years' probation. Mr. Shendal soon found himself running the Palace's casinos. Shendal had many friends in the entertainment industry, a circle in which he was renowned for both his hospitality and the highest quality coke around. Since Las Vegas was a frequent destination for Hollywood's elite, he made a lot of friends like Tony Curtis (who gave the eulogy at his funeral), Dean Martin, Frank Sinatra, Sammy Davis, Jr. and James Caan.

His hospitality was legendary, entertaining guests at his huge ranch outside of the Strip. According to Ari Bass' article, Shendal had many good things to say about Claudia.

> I used to see her at Hefner's or at the Hollywood disco, the Candy Store. She was a roommate of Maureen McCormick's at the time. She loved to have a good time. We'd dance, go horseback riding or go to shows. We attended many rodeos with friends. I think I have some pictures with all of us in cowboy hats.

Claudia and her mother in 1977

I didn't know a single person who didn't like her. Claudia was one of the nicest people I've ever met. Maybe she had a few bad habits, but who didn't in those days? I'd never do or say anything to damage her reputation.[10]

I think it is important to mention that Shendal noted those so-called "bad habits" were the norm in those days. As 1977 ended, Claudia was spending time with Shendal, as well as multi-millionaire Jim Randall, writer Jonathan Axelrod, and movie producer David Niven, Jr.—all men she met at the Playboy Mansion. She would also become involved with two men who were to play prominent roles in the last years of her life.

[1] Phone interview with Keith Allison, September 2014
[2] "Fast Life/Untimely Death: Playmate Claudia Jennings," *E! True Hollywood Story*, September 24, 2000
[3] Phone interview with Bobby Hart, April 2016
[4] Phone interview with Simone Boisseree, July 25, 2014
[5] Phone interview with Mike Greenfield, February 2015
[6] Maureen McCormick, *Here's the Story*, pages 106-107,121 (Harper Collins, 2008)
[7] *Ibid.*, page 114
[8] Phone interview with Keith Allison, September 2014
[9] Phone interview with Keith Jennings, May 2014
[10] Bass, Ari, phone interview with Dean Shendal, March 1994

Chapter 6:
Utopia to Dystopia 1977-1979

On Christmas Eve 1977, Dr. Jack Garfield answered a knock on his door. It was Claudia, asking if a woman was there she was supposed to meet. Dr. Garfield, completely shocked, said there wasn't anyone else there, but she was welcome to come in.

Dr. Garfield knew who Claudia was. He was *Playboy*'s resident dentist, as well as having a successful practice in Beverly Hills. He had just broken up with his girlfriend, actress Jillian "Candy" Kesner. Jillian's career highlight was playing Fonzie's girlfriend on *Happy Days*. In a very odd twist of fate, Ms. Kesner would end up marrying Gary Graver; the couple became frequent visitors at Dr. Garfield's home.

Dr. Jack, as he was commonly referred to, generously allowed Claudia to stay the night. The one night ended up being a year-and-a-half-long involvement. Dr. Garfield even proposed marriage at one point. The story of their relationship is a compelling chapter of the most turbulent years of Claudia's life. Dr. Garfield was very honest, and he frankly discussed his relationship with Claudia and the other men she surrounded herself with during that time.

> Claudia took my heart. She was the most interesting woman I've ever met. She did a lot of things I didn't care for, but I would always forgive her. I had met her before the night she showed up at my house; I was at Carlos 'n' Charlie's one night. Claudia was with some friends and I joined them at their table. Well, all of a sudden, Stevie Wonder walks in, and the whole place was staring at him as he was shown to a table right next to ours. But as soon as everyone saw Claudia sitting there, they all stared at *her*.
>
> I was a practicing dentist when I met Claudia, but I was also a photographer. I will tell you something about her: I could never take a bad picture of her—not even when she was hung over, skinny or had no make-up on. The camera always captured her true beauty, inside and out.
>
> Claudia showed up on Christmas Eve, 1977. I was in a slump then, personally, after breaking up with Candy Kesner. I suspected later that Jillian might have told Claudia that I could write prescriptions for Quaaludes. Jillian enjoyed the high from them, and she idolized Claudia. Claudia knew that Jillian and I had broken up, so looking back, it probably was no coincidence she appeared at my house. She spent the night, and we talked and got to know each other better. The next evening we went out to see the movie *Saturday Night Fever*. John Travolta was a patient of mine, and he convinced Olivia Newton-John to become a patient of mine, too. Well, after the movie, we were just having fun singing the songs, and then I put the album on. We went to bed and didn't leave until the end of the weekend. I fell in love with her that weekend. We had a real relationship. We went to the movies, had dinner at home; Claudia loved simple foods in particular. One of her favorite meals was peas, gravy and mashed potatoes. No meat, just good plain food.

Claudia and Dr. Jack Garfield

Frankly, I think another reason Claudia was drawn to me was my drug license. I could get any drug that wasn't illegal, so I purchased Quaaludes, Valium and other drugs for my dental practice. I slowly became aware of her drug use. She would get up in the morning and, instead of smoking one joint, she would smoke three. Unfortunately, she did the same with stronger pharmaceuticals. It was painful for me to watch. She would tell me, "I'm going to Dean Shendal's for the weekend, don't try to call me." She would come home looking dead.

By the time Claudia came into my life, she was immersed in the drug culture. All of her friends were doing it. Coke, Quaaludes [Author's Note: Quaaludes were not illegal at this time; the drug did not become a Schedule 1 pharmaceutical until 1984], pot and ketamine, a type of powerful tranquilizer, were all readily available. Crack cocaine was just starting to be popular. If you didn't do drugs, you were shunned. That's just the way it was. Claudia would disappear for weeks with her millionaire friends, where God knows what went on, and then come back looking like she hadn't slept. I didn't want to make waves. I simply was afraid to screw up the relationship. The truth is, when she was home with me, Claudia was a perfect lover. We had great times together, and once she was a few days removed from her binges, she was back to her old self. She'd be cleaning the house, singing to herself, cooking and being perfectly happy.

Claudia loved being naked around the house. She would do her household chores, lay by the pool and, everything else, without wearing a stitch. I even snapped a picture of Claudia and my mom hula-hooping in the nude.

A Biography

I was best friends with Barry Goldwater, Jr., and knew his father well. He was my housemate for a while, and he was the United States Congressman from where we lived. One evening he was over, and Jack Kemp, then a congressman from New York (and later a vice-presidential candidate), was visiting and stayed with Claudia and me. We sat around one evening discussing politics well into the early morning. To the astonishment of all, Claudia pretty much won our little debate. Here she was with two of the most brilliant political minds of our time, and she was able to more than hold her own. Of course, the more playful side of Claudia showed up later in the weekend. Claudia and I were in bed one night and Jack Kemp came into the room to say goodnight. She was smoking a joint, just looking at him and making small talk. I could tell Congressman Kemp's mind was spinning in circles as he looked at Claudia.

Claudia, for many reasons, was an enigma. She had a deep horror of getting old. I would tell her, that's why you have a relationship with someone who loves you for whom you are, not what you look like. Then at other times she would say, when confronted with some of her self-destructive behavior, "No. I'm a survivor. I'm going to be an old lady with grandchildren." She would also do some incredibly wonderful things for people. She wrote to prisoners in places like Folsom and San Quentin—lifers. She would send autographed pictures and letters just to let them know another person cared for them.

I decided to ask Claudia to marry me. I took the diamonds from my father's ring, and had the engagement ring custom made. On the inside, I it had inscribed: "To Mary Eileen "Mimi" Chesterton." I was one of only a very few people to even know that was her real name. Even fewer called her Mimi. I was hoping that I could win her heart. The way I put it, I won Mimi's heart, but not Claudia Jennings'. No one ever did that.

Things went well for a while. Eventually, Claudia got anxious again. Claudia had a real problem managing her money. She would spend thousands of dollars on shoes, clothes and accessories, and then have no money for food. She was always giving gifts to everyone. She had such a heart of gold, but not a lot of common sense about her personal finances. I remember when she sold her white Mercedes. I warned her not to, because it was a safe car. But she did anyway, and leased her VW Bug. With the money she got from the Mercedes, she bought me some beautiful paintings and a ton of clothes and shoes for her. She spent it all.

Claudia's inability to manage her money was a real warning sign to me. I had to be able to trust this woman with my checkbook.

I remember Roger Corman wanted Claudia to promote *Deathsport*, so she was set to appear on *The Tonight Show*. I sat in the green room eating shrimp and enjoying myself while Claudia did the show. Now, I knew Claudia and Johnny had a fling years before, when the show was still based in New York. The next morning the doorbell rang, and a deliveryman had this huge gift box for Claudia. She tore it open and there were three hundred pairs of sexy panties from a shop called Trashy Lingerie. Inside was a note from Johnny Carson: "Thanks for doing the show. I love you, see you at the beach house later, as usual." Well, Claudia just kept going on and on about how much she

Claudia appeared on *The Tonight Show* to promote *Deathsport*.

loved Carson, and Johnny this and Johnny that. Well, we went over to Carson's Malibu beach house, and as we got there, he came walking up from the ocean. We went into his house, and there was a huge crystal bowl of cocaine on the dining room table. I don't know, coke was so pervasive, even if Claudia had wanted to get away from it, the fact everyone was doing it would have made it nearly impossible.

Claudia always had the greatest friends. One day I told a young doctor who was interning with me I had a blind date for him. He came to my house to find Maureen McCormick sitting on the couch with Claudia. You should have seen the look on his face. Maureen loved to party, and she especially loved to party with Claudia.

The end of our relationship started when *Playboy* asked her to do yet another pictorial. Claudia really liked and admired Hefner. She honestly believed he always had her best interests in heart. Well, this pictorial didn't work out so well for me. It was on location in Greece on the beautiful island of Mykonos. Marilyn Grabowski from *Playboy* was there, and the photographer doing the shoot was a guy named Tony Kent. The first thing that went wrong was on the flight over there. I had brought some Quaaludes as a sleep aid. Claudia got a hold of them and took a few too many. She got sick on the plane. Then we arrived in Greece, where things went well for a time. I even got to be a model in a few of the shots. It was Claudia's way of including me in her world. I deeply appreciated that, but Claudia and the photographer started doing drugs one night. She kind of wanted a fling with him, so they stayed up all night partying and missed the call for the next day's session. Marilyn Grabowski stormed over to me and started cussing, blaming everything on *me*! At that point, I had enough. I told Claudia I was going back home. She reacted rather flippantly, and I left. Her behavior shocked and hurt me.

Soon after she returned, we decided to go our separate ways. We stayed friends, but the engagement was off, and as much as I wanted to be with her, I knew it wasn't meant to be.

Claudia changed my life. She gave me so much confidence, almost a transfer of some of the qualities she possessed.[1]

Deathsport (1978)

If there was ever a movie that more aptly represented Claudia's personal and professional life during the late 1970s, it was the Roger Corman production *Deathsport*. Corman originally envisioned this as a sequel to *Death Race 2000*, and promptly signed two of the biggest B-movie stars to participate: David Carradine, who had appeared in *Death Race 2000*, and Claudia. This film could take up an entire chapter on its own, with its violence, drama and outright insanity—in front of and behind the cameras.

Nic Niciphor was hired practically right out of USC film school to direct. Niciphor impressed an agent enough to put in a call to Corman, who gave him a chance. Corman had tremendous success with novice directors in the past and had seen something promising in the young man's school projects. He hired the first-rate Gary Graver, still pining over Claudia, as cinematographer. The cast had several veteran actors, such as Jesse Vint and the always-perfect Richard Lynch, to support the two leads. What could go wrong, right? Just about everything, as it happened. The movie, though it turned out to be an artistic and logistical disaster, actually made a little profit. However, getting to that point was hardly pleasant. Niciphor started behaving oddly from the beginning. According to cast members, he would talk about his days in Vietnam and speak graphically about the atrocities he had witnessed. Jesse Vint said that it seemed Nic was obsessed with dead bodies. Evidently, the director also packed a gun and would wear a ski parka in the middle of the desert while filming. If that was not enough, he started calling Claudia at night to harass her. Of course, according to professionals like Carradine and Vint, Niciphor's worst vice was that he couldn't direct.

Although Claudia looked amazing in this French ad, *Deathsport* was not her best film

The movie also had mechanical difficulties from the start. The principal vehicle, upon which a good portion of the plot revolved, was a modified dirt bike. The problem was the modification—an enormous attachment to the handlebars, an aluminum shield with sharp edges—made the bike virtually impossible to handle. Now, I'm not trying to criticize the thinking of the screenwriter, but it's the freakin' year 3000! You've got death rays and all this highly developed shizzle hanging out, and your ultimate weapon turns out to be a stinkin' dirt bike with a shield on it?

In certain scenes, there are visible cables and wires that were used to trigger explosive effects. There are enough continuity errors to fill the Grand Canyon; to whit, in one scene Jesse Vint's character rides out with a sidecar on his "death scooter," and in the next scene, the side car is gone. A few frames later, presto! The sidecar is back again. Thus, the movie had a ridiculous plot, a senseless script, which went through at least three revisions, an erratic director and poorly thought out props. The crew immediately sensed this and did what any group of professionals would do under the circumstances: They relaxed and stopped taking the film seriously. Some of them partied  in excess, particularly Carradine and Claudia—ostensibly because they recognized a turkey when they saw one. Carradine really doesn't seem like his heart was in it, and one has to feel sorry for Richard Lynch, who is a fine actor and always plays a quality villain.

There is one widely circulated story stating that at one point Claudia was thrown off the set for being drunk and high on coke. David Carradine refuted this, as did Jesse Vint and Simone Boisseree, who was a stuntwoman on the film. There was trouble on the set, but Claudia had no part in the shenanigans.

It was only a matter of time before this toxic mix would boil over. One day, while Claudia was attempting a scene on one of the dirt bikes, Nic Niciphor felt she was not trying hard enough. According to eyewitnesses, he started screaming: "I thought you knew how to ride one of these things. You said you could ride!" Claudia was getting a little upset, and said, "I'm sorry, I don't know what you want. I don't understand the scene."

At this point David Carradine wandered over to see what the commotion was about. Niciphor was still screaming at Claudia and suddenly told her to get off the bike. Before anyone could stop him, he physically removed her from the monstrosity and appeared to be ready to either kick or strike her. Claudia ran to her trailer in tears.

David Carradine then confronted Niciphor, and after a heated exchange, delivered a karate kick that knocked the director down. By this time, someone had called Roger

Corman, who took Claudia's side and relieved Niciphor of his duties; Allan Arkush was brought in to finish the film.

According to Carradine, interviewed in the Headpress book *Cult People: Tales from Hollywood's Exploitation A-List* by Nicano Loreti, shared:

> *Deathsport* was a fiasco. Nic Niciphor had written a brilliant script, but he was a madman—quite literally—and didn't know how to direct. He quit the picture before it was over. After he attacked Claudia Jennings and was thrown down and kicked by me, his heart really wasn't in it. Some of it, though, is almost great. The final swordfight with Richard Lynch is excellent. Gary Graver's camerawork is sometimes breathtakingly beautiful. We all loved Claudia. She was a great lady and afraid of nothing. Roger Corman became a great friend of mine. On each of the films I did with him, he would drop by once to compliment my performance, and over the years he's given me good advice. I didn't always take it, as when he offered to let me out of my contract for *Deathsport*.

The film's cinematographer, Gary Graver, said of Claudia:

> She was a real, honest person, not a movie star type. Niciphor was mean to her, no question. Claudia had this daredevil reputation, but the motorcycles for *Deathsport* were not balanced right. They had so much armor and other things attached that they were difficult for even an experienced rider to handle.

While it's true Claudia was a daredevil, she did not have a lot of experience riding motorcycles. She could handle horses, speedboats and 18-wheelers, but modified dirt bikes were not her strength, especially ones as screwed up as these particular bikes were. After all, a leading lady is supposed to act, not be a stuntwoman. That's the stuntwoman's job. A well-known female motorcycle rider was a stunt actor in the film and was quoted as trashing Claudia's abilities to handle the problematic bikes. Everyone I spoke with on the set explained this person was very jealous of Claudia, and was fairly spiteful towards people in general. Simone Boisseree told me that person was a cancer on every set she worked on and the bikes were difficult for even experienced riders to handle.

Allan Arkush took over as director, but as Jesse Vint said in *Shock Cinema*:

> David Carradine told me, when he met Arkush, "out of the frying pan, kid." I knew the film was a lost cause. There was not enough money to make a quality film. We all knew what was happening, but there was nothing to fret about, because no one was going to see the movie anyway.

Claudia handled the awful scene with Niciphor like a pro and immediately went back to work. Unfortunately, she had to do several gratuitous nude scenes for *Deathsport*. Even more disturbing, those particular scenes involved torture as well. She looked lovely, but she had worked hard to get way from these types of scenes. They were full frontal nude shots with pubic hair, some of the most graphic of her film career.

Dr. Garfield and Keith Jennings told me that Claudia was very upset about having to do these scenes. In one instance, Carradine agreed to disrobe as well in an effort

An iconic publicity shot from *Deathsport*

to show solidarity with Claudia. However, his nude form was never shown in the final print. Most likely, Claudia agreed to do them because of the respect she had for Roger Corman. Of course, her contract legally obligated her to do the scenes, so she was quite aware of them beforehand.

I think I can sum up the film as follows: Take a movie with *Star Wars* ambitions and add an Ed Wood budget and a nervous, novice director, and you have a candidate

for the *Mystery Science Theater 3000* Golden Raspberry of the Millennium award. Do you think it's a coincidence this film takes place in the year 3000?

The film starts out with a narration that tells us that during the Neutron Wars just about all life on Earth was greased, and humanity has been reduced to three kinds of people. We have the inhabitants of two city-states who control just about everything (one of the cities being nice and the other pretty mad-dog mean), the guides who ride horses and fight the city guys and the mutants, who are cannibalistic and hate everybody.

Remember what I told you about how movies need to create a suspension of disbelief? Personally, I don't think any human being can suspend their disbelief to the extreme this film requires.

There are some nifty trivia nuggets in this gem. Andy Stein, who played fiddle for Commander Cody and the Lost Planet Airmen and the Prairie Home Companion Orchestra for Garrison Keillor, was the musical director. In addition, none other than Jerry Garcia of the Grateful Dead contributes some guitar licks. As an extra bit of trivia, an unbilled Scream Queen Supreme Linnea Quigley appears as a courtesan.

The film starts out with the bad guys, the Statesmen (sounds like a 1950s doo-wop band) riding these motorcycles that shoot death rays. I mean, you don't burn up or get blown to pieces; you *vaporize*. Kaz Oshay (Carradine) is a guide, who rides horses and uses swords called "Whistlers." The swords are very effective against mutants, who are really messed up, but the swords are pretty useless against the Statesmen. Come to think of it, the bad guys look like the techs on Dark Helmet's ship in *Spaceballs*. The guides, on the other hand, look like neo-cave people with cool hoodie-type capes. Good thing for the guides that the death rays can be set on "I'm gonna knock you out," as Kaz is soon stunned and captured. Seems that Ankar Moor (Lynch) has an old grudge to settle with Kaz. As a matter of fact, Ankar offed Kaz' mom. So I suppose it's really Kaz that has the grievance. The Statesmen also capture another guide, Deneer (Claudia), who was trying to rescue one of the guides' daughter from the mutants. Well, I suppose we know what will be on their menu tomorrow.

The ruler of this crazy city-state, Helix, is Lord Zirpola (David McLean)—a weak, impotent old pervert who gets his jollies by torturing naked women. I truly felt sorry for Claudia during these scenes because, while it's no disgrace to reveal her beauty, it's a crime to do it in a somewhat sleazy setting such as a torture chamber.

In between scenes of torture and Ankar telling Kaz he's going to kick his ass very soon, Deneer and Kaz have this mystical bond thing going. They sit across from each other and chant this ridiculous dialogue, which makes me wonder if they were indeed stoned during the filming of the movie. On the other hand, if I had just burned one, there's no way I'm keeping a straight face while reciting my lines. Of course you just know, by the end of the movie, Deneer and Kaz are going to knock sandals.

Lord Zirpola is also a bit of a putz as well as a creep, and he ends up zapping himself during one of his sex games. That's the good news. The bad news is that Ankar has now assumed power, and his first order of business is to sentence Kaz and Deneer to death by motocross. Yes, for what seems the next two hours, Ankar and his men chase Deneer and Kaz around the Bronson Caves area outside Los Angeles. I will say that the cinematography by Gary Graver helps dramatically, because any thrills in this sequence are due to his excellent work. Unfortunately, how many times can you watch the same guy blow up, get thrown from his motorcycle or ride the same dirt bike down a very steep slope?

After trashing most of the Statesmen and blowing up a lot of things, Deneer and Kaz escape, with Ankar and a few Staties hot on their trail.

Then it's off to rescue the child before the googly-eyed mutants can make BBQ baby-back ribs out of her. In a priceless scene, Deneer sets one of the mutants on fire, who then sets another mutant on fire. Nice two-for-one, except rumor has it that wasn't in the script. If you look closely, it almost seems you can see a crewmember frantically trying to extinguish the flames on the unwilling human s'mores. Let's hope the poor fellow was a member of SAG. The Rangers rescue the little girl and split.

Happily, it comes down to Kaz and Ankar fighting to the death with Whistlers. This a very well-choreographed fight, but I figure by that point in filming they all must have been, exhausted, physically and mentally, so it, too, becomes a bit tedious. Eventually, Kaz gives the bad guy the *coup de grace* by lopping off his head.

Deneer, with child in tow, reunites with Kaz, and rides off into the sunset of a beautiful dystopian future. The film was supposed to be a follow up to *Death Race 2000*, also starring Carradine, which was a very good film and deserving of its cult status. Even though *Deathsport* was a critical failure, it actually made back its meager budget and earned $400,000 worldwide. Therefore, it can't be termed a true disaster. I think it's important to point out that of all the people involved in *Deathsport*, Claudia did her best to make the film work. She was obviously in an uncomfortable situation for many reasons, was embarrassed by the director and had to perform a plethora of nude scenes, but she didn't fold. She kept her composure and finished the film like a professional, despite what Nic Niciphor would say later. He told the media he had to remove Claudia from the set one day because she was too drunk and coked up to perform.

Given what others present observed this does not seem likely. She was known for her professionalism on the set, and Roger Corman certainly would not have tolerated such behavior, because it would have cost money to postpone a day's shooting.

As for Mr. Arkush, he insists to this very day that *Deathsport* is the worst film he's been associated with. He was charitable in his overall assessment of Claudia's performance, however. Arkush stated in his January 28, 2014 *Trailers from Hell* segment that Roger Corman pulled him away from directing *Rock and Roll High School* to finish *Deathsport*. The director was taken aback by the cheap special effects, such as the ping-pong balls used for the mutant's eyes. The whistler swords, which looked like toys to begin with, were so

Publicity still of Carradine and Jennings

Jesse and Alan Vint in *Macon County Line*

poorly constructed that the blades fell out of the handles when swung.

Arkush also emphasized the fact that the motorcycles were nearly impossible to drive and stuntmen were falling all over the place. He did mention Carradine got high on the set, but that he was also very helpful assisting with some of the pyrotechnics. Arkush states, "The stunning Claudia Jennings got naked," but not even that could save the picture.

Jesse Vint is a veteran actor and comes from a family of performers. His brothers Bill and Alan were both actors and attended Lee Strasberg's Actors Studio as observers. He has appeared in over 100 movies and television shows during his career and has acted alongside Jack Nicholson, Dustin Hoffman, and James Garner, among others. Jesse acted in such notable films as *Chinatown*, *Little Big Man* and *Silent Running*. He is a lifetime member of both the Academy of Motion Pictures Arts and Sciences and the American Academy of Television Arts and Sciences. His most famous leading role was in 1974's *Macon County Line*, in which he co-starred with his brother.

In addition to his acting, screenwriting, and directorial accomplishments, Jesse is the reigning champion of the World Celebrity Chess Championships. Mr. Vint was kind enough to tell us about *Deathsport* and his relationship with Claudia:

> Even though *Deathsport* was a bad movie, it was a great experience for me. I met Claudia on the set during the filming in late 1977, and I saw her frequently for several months. I was in a stormy relationship with another actress at the time,

and she was seeing someone too, so Claudia and I were secretive. She came to Seattle to visit me for a weekend when I did a pilot for Universal—a spinoff of *Emergency*. We had great times, but I had a problem with her drug use. To this day I am completely bewildered by seemingly intelligent people doing things that they know are blatantly destructive. I said this to her: "When you know the outcome of taking this road, and that outcome is the destruction of your looks, health, happiness, bank account, relationships and all that is important to you in this life, why do you choose to travel it? Why would you even take the first step down that road?" It wasn't the first time, or the last, that I put that question to people that I cared about.

She promised me that she would stop, but I don't think that she really wanted to. I think she saw it as part of an exciting lifestyle. I felt helpless. Our exchanges were in every way fun, intense and electric until she did drugs, and then she went from being one of the world's most fascinating women to being a monkey in a tree chattering mindlessly away—and that was in a matter of minutes.

These things were outside of my world. Because of this, I knew that our time was limited. It was intense and it was fun, but I knew that it was a dead end for me because I had seen this before—several times.

Claudia was a beautiful, exciting, fun, down-to-earth stunning redheaded hometown girl who never fully understood her enormous potential as a talent; but that's all it was—potential. She had enormous potential, but she allowed her body to rule her mind instead of the other way around, so she never really developed her abilities to their fullest.

Here was a girl that is one of the most beautiful women in the world—and yet Claudia Jennings had a severe case of low self-esteem. Oddly, I have seen this over and over and over with some of the world's most beautiful women. I think it's because they are always told by the world that they should be a reigning queen, so no matter how well they do, by comparison they always feel like they are failing, so they turn to substance abuse as a way of compensating. Maybe that's it. I have known a number of them, and this seems to be the common denominator—but I could be wrong.

In the spring of 1978 I went into production on a film that I had written. It was around that time that we drifted apart. Our time together was less and less frequent, and then nothing.

Claudia Jennings, to this day, remains as one of my life's most enduring and cherished memories. On that same highway where Claudia met her end, we used to fly up and down the Malibu coast on my Triumph Tiger 750 motorcycle, usually stopping off at the Paradise Cove restaurant or Neptune's or the beach at Leo Carillo State Park. We were always laughing. At the time, everything seemed perfect.[2]

The affair went on despite the fact Claudia was engaged to Dr. Jack Garfield, and Jesse was involved with the beautiful actress Karen Carlson.

The public's reception to the film was lukewarm. In some theaters it was literally laughed off the screen. *Variety*'s review stated:

The best thing that can be said about Carradine's acting and part is that he doesn't say much. The best thing that can be said about Ms. Jennings' part is that she takes her clothes off, twice.[3]

Ouch.

I hate to sound like a hypocrite, but although I'm no fan of *Deathsport*, Carradine's and Claudia's performances were not the worst things about the movie. The film was tainted by so many problems, one can easily say the acting by Carradine, Claudia and Richard Lynch were some of the few highlights. Still, *Deathsport* has a certain tacky charm and has quite a few admirers. The film has morphed over time from an all-out turkey to a campy cult favorite. The fact that many people consider it worth viewing nowadays is a tribute to Claudia. Her star power and status as a cult icon gives the film some much-needed credibility. Of course, perhaps sadly, the main attraction is still her body, not her acting.

Claudia considered it one of her worst films, and even Roger Corman admitted it wasn't one of New World Pictures' best efforts. Nic Niciphor was given credit as co-writer and co-director under the name of Henry Suso. He later went on to become a successful screenwriter, penning such efforts as Alejandro Jodorowsky's *Tusk* and Joseph Ruben's *Our Winning Season*. *Deathsport* was his one and only directorial effort.

The Importance of Roger Corman to Claudia and the Motion Picture Industry

When writing about Roger Corman, one runs out of superlatives. One of the most prolific producers and directors ever, he has no comparison in the history of motion pictures. His vision and abilities are remarkable and nothing short of uncanny. There have been at least 12 books written about him, his production companies, his films and his influence on the industry.

It is difficult to choose what quality about Roger Corman is most impressive. He entertained us with such cult classics as *The Little Shop of Horrors*, inspired us with *Boxcar Bertha* (directed by young Corman protégé Martin Scorcese) and distributed magnificent

International films such as *Fitzcaraldo, The Brood, The Harder They Come, Amarcord* and *Cries and Whispers.*

After graduating from Stanford, Corman started his career in the early 1950s, working in the mailroom at 20th Century Fox. He was promoted to script reader for the studio; then, disenchanted when he wasn't credited for his contributions, he quit. After studying at Oxford, Corman returned to Los Angeles, and by 1953, began to dabble in producing and screenwriting.

In 1955, Corman started directing ultra-low-budget films, his initial effort being *Swamp Women*. During the mid-1950s, he produced and directed up to nine films a year, all of them finishing within budget—and in less than a week, in some cases. He began to produce films for other film companies, and formed his own with his brother Gene, Filmgroup.

Roger Corman

Filmgroup was successful in making double feature, drive-in and other black-and-white features. However, by the time the 1960s came, color features were becoming more popular, so the Cormans closed Filmgroup and started working with American International Pictures. This move turned out to be most propitious for Corman, as he soon made a series of films based on the writings of Edgar Allan Poe.

The films featured collaborations with many talented individuals in the United States and Britain and won Corman critical praise and financial success. Vincent Price's career was defined by the movies he made with Corman, and noted author Richard Matheson , who was the primary scenarist for the Poe series. Few horror films at that time achieved the spectacle of the Poe adaptations by Corman: brilliant acting with superior camera work, featuring moody Gothic sets and shot in vivid color that were superior to their competition.

Corman's films of the later part of the decade would reflect many counterculture themes. Always the innovator and pioneer, Corman made the first serious biker movie since *The Wild One* with *The Wild Angels* in 1966, starring Peter Fonda and Nancy Sinatra. Of course, this started a trend, and more biker-themed movies followed. Naturally, dozens of imitators copied Corman's formula. Corman also gave us some films exploiting the psychedelic craze with *The Trip*, written by Jack Nicholson and starring his favorite antihero Peter Fonda.

Following a less than happy experience making the big-budget movie *The St. Valentine's Day Massacre* for 20th Century Fox, Corman once again formed his own production company in 1970 called New World Pictures. For the next 14 years, New World dominated the exploitation market with a combination of excellent up market fare and plenty of down market movies as well. Roger's wife Julie was an integral part of the operation, producing many of the features for New World. It is impossible to list all the Corman films that have become cult classics from this time period. He had made his mark in the industry, and eventually sold New World in 1983, forming his present company, New Horizon Pictures.

Roger Corman is still active today, and not showing signs of either slowing down or retiring. At the most recent count, he has produced well over 300 films and directed 55 more. His most recent directorial effort came in 1990 with *Frankenstein Unbound*, starring Bridget Fonda, the daughter of one of his early discoveries. He continues to produce films, many of them for the SyFy channel, including *Dinoshark* and *Sharktopus*.

The list of film industry professionals he mentored is incredible. Besides the aforementioned Martin Scorsese, directors Joe Dante, Paul Bartel, Peter Bogdanovich, Jonathan Demme, Francis Ford Coppola, Ron Howard and James Cameron—to name but a few—all began their careers with Corman. When you consider the careers these individuals have had, it is a staggering tribute to Corman's ability to cultivate talent.

Corman's method of filmmaking can be described as a style of marvelous economy. He worked with minuscule budgets, shot movies in weeks (not months) and often used sets left over from previous films. His propensity for using undiscovered talent was no doubt another way to limit expenditures on a particular project. He was able to use legendary horror film star Boris Karloff in *Targets* because the actor owed him several days' work from a previous film.

Corman carefully examined all scripts so his directors had a solid road map to follow. The director of *Night Call Nurses*, Jonathan Kaplan, recalled Roger's concise list of requirements for the film, all in a 10-minute meeting. They were the exploitation of sexual fantasies; plenty of action and violence; two subplots—one of them comic and the other reflecting liberal and left of center values; frontal nudity from the waist up, total nudity from behind and no pubic hair; and the exploitation of the title within the film.[4]

Corman enjoyed working with actors he employed in his earlier films. David Carradine and Peter Fonda were favorite leading men, with character actors Dick Miller, Roberta Collins, Alan Vint, Barry Primus, Candice Rialson, Mary Woronov, Don Steele and Robert Carradine providing quality supporting roles. Many veteran performers also appeared in Corman's films, such as Angie Dickinson, Cloris Leachman, Sally Kirkland, Ben Gazzara, Sylvester Stallone, William Shatner, Barbara Steele and Kevin McCarthy. It should be noted that Stallone, Shatner and Kirkland were not the household names they would become in a few years.

One of the many actresses whose career was helped by Corman was a 23-year-old beauty named Claudia Jennings. She auditioned for his 1972 roller derby epic *Unholy Rollers* and Corman was immediately impressed. One of the requirements for the role was physical loveliness, but Claudia also had a screen presence, the ability to act without dialogue and a strong athletic prowess. Despite the fact that the film is a lurid, exploitation film to its core, Claudia, the cast and the plot elevate it above most others in the subgenre. Technically, while not completely flawless, it is well crafted. *Unholy Rollers* would establish a pattern between Corman and Claudia for their future collaborations. The film gave her a firm character foundation to utilize for subsequent roles. Corman also made sure to surround Claudia with veteran actors and a competent crew to give her the best chance to shine. The formula worked fine until the last movie they would make together.

What's fascinating about *Unholy Rollers* is that Claudia's character is completely different from her subsequent parts in Corman's films. They all share common traits, which were toughness, a willingness to fight for survival and a pursuit of happiness, even if the means to that end was illegal. However, Corman was instrumental in shaping the screen image that would propel Claudia to the top of the genre.

The next film Claudia did for Roger, although he co-produced it, was not really his creation. His production company, New World Pictures, released it, but did not make the film. *The Great Texas Dynamite Chase* had all the elements of an excellent exploitation movie. On top of the nudity, violence, car chases and explosions, it featured a real plot, dynamic performances, taut direction and marvelous cinematography. The picture was a victory for all concerned, except that it didn't do well at the box-office. It is ironic that one of Corman's most critically praised releases could not replicate the financial success of his lesser films. As mentioned earlier, it is frequently compared with *Thelma and Louise*. I may be in a small majority, but I feel *The Great Texas Dynamite Chase* is a superior film in many ways. When viewed simply as cinema, Claudia's film has better acting and doesn't rely on broad stereotypes. Considering the budgets of the two films, *The Great Texas Dynamite Chase* definitely gives more bang for the buck. Finally, if one compares the two films as feminist fables, Claudia's work comes out way ahead by virtue of the fact the hostile men lose, while the smarter, tougher women win.

Moonshine County Express was an anomaly for Claudia, a hicksploitation/carsploitation film where she remained fully clothed. Corman set her up for success once again with a great crew and cast. Although the film had its share of violence, car chases and just a flash of nudity, it contains a well-done romantic sub-plot and some endearing, realistic family bonding. Corman was very proud of this film, in part because it showed Southerners in a positive light and not as bigoted Neanderthal stereotypes. Also atypical for

Deathsport

Claudia at that time, she is part of an ensemble cast, instead of being the lead character.

The last movie Claudia and Corman would collaborate on, *Deathsport*, was the least successful of their films. Despite the fact Claudia's body was on display in several scenes, it was not enough to draw audiences in. Roger had her in mind when he cast the film, and tapped David Carradine for the leading role. Corman figured the pairing of these two B-movie stars would be box-office gold. Carradine had starred in *Death Race 2000*, a successful and popular movie.

The film should have worked, as it capitalized on the novelty of having the two most popular stars of the genre in the same vehicle, and it was touted as the semi-sequel to *Death Race 2000*. Roger decided to turn the directorial duties over to a film school graduate with no prior professional experience. This turned out to be one of Corman's very few miscalculations, and his instinct for finding raw talent did not pan out in this case. Niciphor had problems with Claudia and alienated much of the cast. As a result, Roger felt he had no choice but to replace the director in the middle of the shoot. Veteran director Allan Arkush was brought in to finish the film. Claudia also supposedly balked at some of the nude scenes, but she was eventually convinced to proceed with the filming.

If Claudia seriously objected to her nude scenes, she did not hold a grudge against Roger. Publicly, she was very proud of her films with Corman, and bragged that she was his favorite leading lady. Roger has indeed faced some criticism for the nudity and perceived misogyny in some of his films. Just after *Deathsport* was completed, New World produced a film called *Humanoids from the Deep*. Roger, exercising his right as the producer, had the second unit add some scenes of women being assaulted by the title monsters. He felt the movie was good but was too tame; however, the director, Barbara Peeters, and the female lead, Ann Turkel, went berserk when they saw the finished film. According to Peeters, Corman had told her that some additional footage was added, but only filler scenes. Both women demanded their names be removed from the credits, though they were unable to force Corman to comply. They did battle in the court of public opinion as well.

Here is where the dichotomy between so-called legitimate film and exploitation movies is again vividly illustrated. I have to favor Mr. Corman in the controversy over *Humanoids from the Deep*, which is one of my favorite films. It is, in fact, a very complex movie that deals with serious issues of bigotry, the environment and whether careers or the preservation of the natural world come first. That these questions are even explored in such a horror spectacle is an amazing achievement. I sympathize with Ms. Turkel and Ms. Peeters, who felt rape was being trivialized and exploited. However, is the rape scene in *Straw Dogs* any more palatable? That film was a major studio release and had a distinguished actor in Dustin Hoffman as the leading man. Keep in mind a horror film is, by nature, supposed to tap into psychological as well as physical fear.

I honestly don't believe Roger Corman meant to titillate his audience as much as scare them. The offensive scenes are filmed in a manner where the male viewers can't possibly identify with the huge, disgusting fish-men. In the screenplay, the assaults did occur, but they were off-camera and implied rather than graphically shown. By filming them, the attacks increase the film's tension and sense of dread.

To Ms. Peeters' credit, I feel she made one hell of a movie. The added scenes don't destroy the continuity or interfere with the narrative. The film is quite gory and suspenseful, both admirable qualities in my opinion. Although most of the women we see are victims, the two strongest characters in the film are female. One, the sheriff's wife, manages to fend off two of the beasts when attacked in her home, while at the same time defending her child. The other lead, Ann Turkel, is a no-nonsense scientist who more than holds her own against the men, most of whom act like primitive savages. So there's a valid argument to be made that the movie isn't nearly as misogynistic as one might think.

As for Mr. Corman, he said:

> I find that most critics who discuss such things [whether the film was misogynistic] in their reviews felt *Humanoids* was a strong feminist statement in the guise of a horror movie.[5]

I agree with him wholeheartedly. His job as producer was to release the best film possible and one that would make money. As it turned out, the negative publicity that surrounded the film proved to be a bonanza for the production, as its receipts were another impressive victory for New World. Most film critics despised the film—not a great shock, mind you—focusing almost exclusively on the rape scenes and overlooking the positive aspects of the movie. Among those was the incredible special effects work by a very young Rob Bottin, who would go on to fame and widespread admiration for his work on *The Howling*, *The Thing* and *Legend*.

It makes for an interesting question that if Claudia, as an actress, was willing to appear completely nude for her torture sequences in *Deathsport*, why would Peeters and Turkel object so vehemently to the sexual violence in *Humanoids*? As a director, she had already filmed two exploitation films, *Just the Two of Us* (about a lesbian relationship) and *Bury Me An Angel*.

When I was a young boy, my world revolved around monsters. I collected toy monsters and I read Forrest J. Ackerman's *Famous Monsters of Filmland*, but I predominantly watched monster movies. By age 10 I had seen *Dracula*, *Frankenstein* and *The Wolf Man* 20 or 30 times each.

When the new wave of horror films swept over America in the 1950s and 1960s, *Attack of the Crab Monsters*, *Creature of the Haunted Sea* and the Edgar Allan Poe adaptations entranced me. As I laughed out loud at *The Little Shop of Horrors* or gazed in awe at *The Masque of the Red Death*, little did I know that one man was having such an effect on my intellectual upbringing. I didn't simply stare at these spectacles, I went a step further and read their source material—Poe and H.P. Lovecraft, for example. My fascination with monsters led to a love of film and then to a love of literature. Roger Corman was the individual responsible. Pure ecstasy is the only way to describe the feeling when Corman's assistant said that he had agreed to my request for this interview.

Claudia Jennings loved Roger Corman, and the feeling was mutual. He appreciated her talents and she appreciated his gentle manner and professionalism.

Still making movies at age 90, Roger Corman has already firmly established his legacy as one of America's all-time cinematic geniuses. The British Film Institute and the Cinémathèque Française have also recognized his work, where Roger was the youngest filmmaker so honored. He was also presented with the first ever Producer's Award at the Cannes Film Festival, and in 2010, the Academy of Motion Picture Arts and Sciences presented him with an honorary Academy Award.

Beyond his numerous talents, perhaps the best accolade I can heap upon his many others is that Roger Corman is a true gentleman in every sense of the word.

Eric: First, a little housekeeping. Constance Chesterton, Claudia's sister, wanted me to tell you how much she appreciated your handling of an interview with Leonard Maltin. She saw it after a showing of *Deathsport*, and Maltin was trying to bait you into saying something negative about her sister, but you just said she was a great actress and a beautiful woman who would have gone on to great success. She said she's always loved you for that.
Roger: Well, Claudia *was* a great actress and a beautiful woman. There's no doubt she would have gone on to stardom.
Eric: Also, Jesse Vint wanted me to send his deepest thanks and appreciation for everything you did for his career. He was one of many that you mentored who went on to do great things in the industry.
Roger: Well, they were all good, which is why I hired them—Ron Howard, Martin Scorsese and the others. So the fact they went to later success was no surprise to me.
Eric: Well, you're probably being too modest, but let's go on to each picture Claudia made for you. I remember seeing you interviewed and saying Claudia got the part for *Unholy Rollers* 50 percent because of her acting ability and 50 percent because of the way she fit in the uniform.
Roger: Gosh, Eric, I hope you'll nuance that better in the book (*laughs.*) But I had a very high opinion of her work before she auditioned for the part. She was, of course, a beautiful woman. But she came to the audition with some stills, and read for the part. Then I always have the actors do a few improv scenes. She did very well in the improvs,

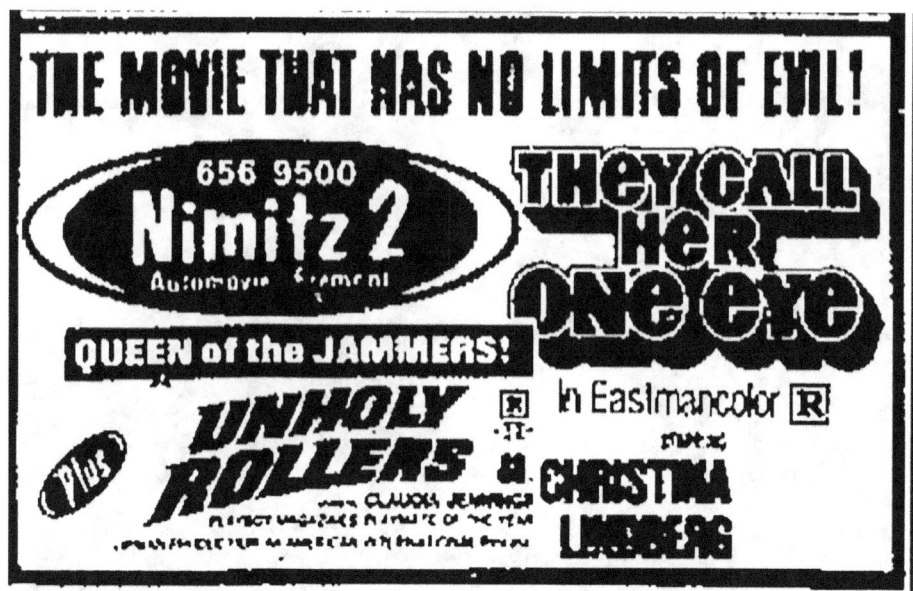

so she got the part. I've always been a strong believer in the improvs. Yes—and Martin Scorcese did the editing for the movie, so we had a strong cast and a strong crew.
Eric: Did Claudia surprise you with her athleticism in the film?
Roger: Well, she had roller-skated since she was a girl, but we did bring a roller derby professional and gave her a little rehearsal time before shooting. But she was a very good athlete.
Eric: Claudia reportedly said the extras on the set were pretty rough on her. Any recollections of that?
Roger: Well, in an action movie there's a chance of that happening. Claudia was a very tough girl and pretty physical herself.
Eric: Let's talk about one of my favorite films, *The Great Texas Dynamite Chase*
Roger: Yes, I was co-producer and distributed this movie. We had a great cast, a great crew and Claudia did one of her best jobs of acting in this film.
Eric: Claudia injured herself on this film, didn't she?
Roger: Yes, we had to shut down production for a week or so. Claudia probably came back too early from her injuries, but she was always a trooper.
Eric: I really felt Claudia showed her great chemistry with the camera in this film. She's in practically every scene and pretty much steals them.
Roger: Yes, Claudia could take direction well and improvise when needed. She was so beautiful your eyes were naturally drawn to her. That's what you want out of your leading lady.
Eric: Then you made *Moonshine County Express*. Claudia acted with an impressive cast and really held her own. Some say it was her best acting performance.
Roger: Yes, she was excellent in that film. We had a veteran director in Gus Triakonis, who really brought out a splendid performance from Claudia. The cast was full of veterans like John Saxon and William Conrad.
Eric: Maureen McCormick talked about a lot of drug use on the set, as did the cin-

New World Pictures Presents
DEATHSPORT
NSS 780019

ematographer Gary Graver. Claudia also started a relationship with Graver on the set. Did you sense any of this in the final result of the movie?
Roger: No, I was the producer, so I never went to set unless I was asked to be. I do know the film was a big hit in the South because we treated them as people, not caricatures.
Eric: Now we move on to the most controversial film Claudia did for you, Deathsport. Gary Graver said he told you to hire Claudia for the lead because he wanted to try to get back together with her. Any truth to that?
Roger: No, I don't think so. I knew I wanted Claudia from the start. I thought pairing her with David Carradine would be perfect.
Eric: So what is your memory of the circumstances of Nic Niciphor being fired? I've heard several stories.
Roger: What versions have you heard?
Eric: Well, first, Jesse Vint and others mentioned Nic behaved rather erratically from the beginning. He talked about the dead bodies he had seen in Vietnam, that he was hassling Claudia at night and basically behaving in a bizarre manner. Then one day when Claudia was trying to maneuver the dirt bikes modified for the film, he ended up throwing her off the bike and screaming at her. Then the stories go, David Carradine either kicked him in the chest right then or waited during a take later.
Roger: Well, I was sitting in my office when I got a call saying, you better come down here, there's trouble. So I got to the set and there was no shooting going on, which was costing us money. So it was obvious Nic and David were about to have a physical confrontation. When I heard what happened, I felt it was clearly Nic's fault, and I told

him this is your leading lady, you can't treat her like that. So I replaced him with Allan Arkush, and we finished filming. Claudia took it better than anyone. She just shrugged it off and went back to work. You have to remember it was Nic's first film. I had seen a short he had done in school. He just wasn't quite ready.
Eric: Looking back, do you think the change of directors and the incident with Mr. Niciphor impacted the quality of the finished film?
Roger: Yes, I think so. *Deathsport* was not a great film.
Eric: I look at *Deathsport* as a step back for Claudia's career, because of the somewhat gratuitous nudity. Any thoughts?
Roger: Well, Claudia never had a problem with nudity. She wasn't afraid to show off her body.
Eric: Well, perhaps in terms of the types of films she wanted to do in the future.
Roger: Well, then, I suppose, yes. Claudia definitely wanted to move into more A-type productions. But she did do a great job in *Deathsport*. The movie's lack of success had nothing to do with her performance.
Eric: Had Claudia lived, would you have used her again?
Roger: Absolutely. She was a fine actress.
Eric: Of the films she did for you, which are your favorites?
Roger: Definitely *Unholy Rollers*, followed by *The Great Texas Dynamite Chase*. Those were films where I felt Claudia did a particularly great job, but she performed well in all of them. I think people forget how talented she was.
Eric: Did you ever get to know Claudia socially?
Roger: No, we only saw each other on the movie set and during rehearsals.
Eric: Do you feel she is in danger of being forgotten as an actress?
Roger: Not really. She always had cult status, and cult stars will always have their audience. There are a lot of her fans who haven't forgotten her or her films.
Eric: I always thought that if she had arrived on the film scene in the 1990s or even the late 1980s, the improvements in technology and film production would have given her films a better look—less low-budget.
Roger: There's no question that with the use of digital cameras, lighter cameras, cheaper film and overall improved equipment, less expensive films can now have the production values of more expensive movies. In Claudia's day, we only had the big, clunky immobile cameras.
Eric: Any last thoughts on Claudia, Mr. Corman?
Roger: Only that she was a great actress, always professional—and, of course, she was a beautiful girl.

One can see from Roger's answers why he is so highly thought of in the movie industry. He has never said a bad word about anybody, and refuses to engage in what he perceives to be gossip or innuendo.

In February of 1978, Claudia was interviewed for the *Los Angeles Times* in order to promote *Deathsport*. The article probably gives us the clearest view into what Claudia honestly thought of her life and career. She would repeat many of the same sentiments stated in her last *Playboy* interview a year later. The piece was titled "Claudia Jennings: A Hard Boiled Persona" and it gives us, in her own words, one of the links between Evanston and Hollywood. It also shows very clearly the rise of the female action villain or hero.

They are not too common, but there have always been at least a few evil females on screen—Faye Dunaway in the *Three Musketeers* and Louise Fletcher in *One Flew Over the Cuckoo's Nest*. But the for the most part, characters like this are too much of a risk for the people who produce, direct and finance the vast majority of films. Along with the men in the audience, they're probably more comfortable seeing women in non-threatening roles. Another reason for the dearth of female heavies is that typecasting can be an even greater problem than for their male counterparts.

Finally, to hear Claudia Jennings tell it, there aren't many actresses to match her claim of "doing more Roger Corman films than anybody."

"You name it, I've done it," says the star of *Truck Stop Women*, *Unholy Rollers*, *The Great Texas Dynamite Chase* and the upcoming sequel to *Death Race 2000*—*Deathsport*. "I know my way around motorcycles, horses, cars, guns; I can do karate or drive a truck. You give me one of those 18-wheelers and I can turn it around right in the middle of the street."

Jennings claims by observing some of the people she's met on location she's been able to create her hard-boiled acting persona. "In *Unholy Rollers* those were some real dirty skaters, you know. Their idea of a really funny joke was to kick your skates out from underneath you when you weren't looking."

"No, no, I was a bookworm, totally school-oriented," she protests to a suggestion that she might have been a tomboy when she was younger. Her childhood was a normal one, spent mainly in the Midwest, but she recalls that her mother stressed academic achievement and middle-class values. It was concern for her parents and sisters that compelled Mimi Chesterton to change her name to Claudia Jennings when she was photographed in a Playmate of the Month pictorial (1970). "I did it for the money, you know. A quick $5,000. I didn't even know there was a Playmate of the Year."

"People are always surprised to see that I'm really healthy, well educated, well bred," she says. "The casting directors have seen my movies and they expect me to be some six-foot-tall raging Barbarella." Jennings is no demure young thing. "I'm a character actress, not an ingénue, a Bette Davis type.[6]

Fast Company (1979)

Claudia's final film, released in March of 1979, was another anomaly for Claudia. Its Canadian director David Cronenberg, and others in the cast and crew stepped out of their usual celluloid comfort levels. For Cronenberg, it was the first film for which he didn't supply the screenplay, and it was not a horror or body-destruction celluloid spectacular. However, in my opinion, it is very much in keeping with the Cronenberg philosophy.

Claudia's part is very small; in fact, she has less screen time than the featured actress, Judy Foster, who plays Candy. Claudia never appears bare, despite the ample nudity in the movie; she just parades around in a filmy see-through camisole and panty ensemble. She does play a tough world-weary woman, unwilling to follow her racecar driver boyfriend, William Smith, any longer. She's sweet, but not overly so; tough, but not bitchy. She's also sexy without being slutty. The shame is that she doesn't have more to do. It's scary to think how much better this movie would have been if Claudia had more screen time.

If possible, get the Blue Underground Blu-ray. It has the most extra features, including a disappointing bio of Claudia, but the film itself is sharp as a razor and clear as glass. The sound, so important to a drag racing film, is magnificent.

The back-story of the film is interesting. David Cronenberg loves racecars, but not the fuel dragsters and nitro-burning funny cars that form the narrative for *Fast Company*. Cronenberg is a fan of classic British racing vehicles. He decided, however, to make an all-American exploitation movie, partially as a tribute to Roger Corman, who had distributed some of his previous films. He signed three Roger Corman veterans—William Smith, John Saxon and Claudia—to star in the vehicle (no pun intended). The rest of the cast is practically all-Canadian, as were the crew.

Fast Company

The film was shot on location in Edmonton, Alberta, which stood in for Montana and Spokane. There are some scenes where it actually is supposed to be Edmonton. The primary set was an abandoned airfield with few lights, meaning most of the racing sequences were shot day for night. The announcement towers were, well, control towers and the landing strips served as the racetracks and highways.

The movie had a very low budget, but it doesn't look cheap. Many critics and fans of Cronenberg say this movie is his weakest, and one does get the sense he hedged on whether to go to one extreme or the other. Some simplify it, saying it was a basic good-guy-versus-bad-guys Old West morality tale with the funny cars taking the place of the horses.

I see it as something more Cronenberg-esque. Let's look at the cars, and specifically the scenes where the cars are being worked on. It's very reminiscent of an operation, with the gaskets, tubes and pipes being removed or put into place, much like a doctor would remove or transplant organs. The fuel, the very lethal and potent nitro-methane, is the life's blood of the vehicles. Then we have the drivers themselves, wrapped in flame-retardant suits, with alien-type goggles for eyes. They are strapped into fragile dragsters, completely surrounded by the machine. It is a dehumanizing ritual, and it's almost impossible to tell where man ends and machine begins. Instead of the typical Cronenberg theme of destruction of the human body, we have the rather novel concept of man and machine morphing into a single organism—a little bit of Frankenstein monster merged with an ominous future vision of the Borg. Then the driver hurls down the quarter-mile track at over 200 miles per hour, in a little over six seconds. Of course, that was then. Today's dragsters go much faster.

The next concept to watch is the effect that noise has on the spectators. The noise these monsters belch out is fiercer than NASCAR-type vehicles. In the movie, you'll see a motor oil representative wince in pain when the cars take off. This is quite accurate, as the sound of the funny cars is not only heard, but also felt, much like a bomb explosion. The sound waves travel through the body and impact its organs. There are many shots of the crowd showing its pain and discomfort when the engines roar.

For the benefit of the uninitiated, here is a very brief primer on the cars in the movie. A funny car is a modified production car (i.e., a regular car, like you'd buy off the lot) with a fiberglass or carbon fiber body dropped over a conventional chassis. This lightens the vehicle, in order to increase speed. A fuel dragster has a specially designed, elongated chassis, lighter than a funny car and aerodynamically engineered to increase speed. Both vehicles use a nitro-methane fuel, which is extremely explosive since it requires little oxygen to ignite.

The movie opens with gorgeous views of mountains, rivers and the racing team trucks of FastCo's Lonnie Johnson (William Smith). He gets top billing, with Claudia next and John Saxon third. We watch the credits roll by to the tune of what sounds like a Bruce Springsteen tribute band.

The first scene is before a big race, where the crew is installing a supercharger onto Lonnie's engine to boost its output up to 2,000 horsepower. During the race, however, a fuel line ruptures, causing Lonnie's dragster to burst into flame. Lonnie escapes without injury, but the car is ruined.

Phil Adamson (John Saxon), the sponsor's representative, comes over to Lonnie's lead mechanic, Elder (Don Francks), telling him it's the crew's fault that the car was

Claudia in a pensive mood in *Fast Company*

ruined. Then Lonnie and Phil have a come-to-Jesus meeting, where it's made clear the racing team is just there to sell FastCo. oil and not necessarily win. Reasonable, I'd say, but Lonnie doesn't take it that way.

Back in his trailer, a glum Lonnie is watching replays of his fiery crash on the news. He decides to call his lost love, Sammy (Claudia), who lives in Seattle. Claudia looks alarmingly thin, and although her natural beauty disguises it, there's no doubt she could use a few baked potatoes. She must work in a head shop, too, because I swear there are like a zillion bongs lined up on the shelf behind her. Or perhaps they're auto parts that look like bongs. Lonnie asks her to join him, but she politely refuses. She does tell him she'll try to meet him in Spokane, where he'll be racing in a few weeks.

While on their way to the next race, the crew gets a flat and discovers they forgot to pack a spare. A racecar crew? No spare? Really? Along come their rivals, led by driver Gary "The Blacksmith" Black (Cedric Smith). You can tell Gary is unsavory because his right eye is somewhat droopy. Well, despite the fact that he hates Lonnie, Gary loans them a spare, and even has one of the guys, Stoner (David Graham), help them change the flat. Gary saunters over to Lonnie, trying to make nice, but Lonnie tells him he's a loser, in essence, which puts the kibosh on the party, so to speak. Gary angrily tells his grease assistant to remove the spare and load up. Can't blame him.

Next, we see Adamson flying into Helena with the new Miss FastCo, Candy (Judy Foster). He starts telling her about this great hotel with a heated swimming pool, a whirlpool and a sauna. Then he starts massaging her upper thigh. She replies, coolly, "Sounds great. Just book two rooms." *Burn!*

A little later on, there's a quick shot of the security policemen at the raceway. One of them is wearing a cap with a Maple Leaf on it! Snap! Oh well, everything else looks American, eh?

Shortly before race time, we see Adamson visit the owner of the racetrack. In addition to his other bad habits, Phil is ripping off the venue managers by demanding a cut of the gate.

Fortunately, we are rescued from his sleaze by the best sequence in the film. During one of the time trials, there is a scene with no dialogue. All the viewer sees are the actions of the crew and the unsettling ritual of the driver entering the vehicle to the point where he becomes part of the machine and loses his humanity. The seating area is terrifying and claustrophobic, sucking the breath out of the audience until the car takes off in a roar with nothing but the visible timer to contrast with the ride. At the end, we hear the faintest exhalation of breath by the driver.

This is a perfectly shot scene, the camera being behind the driver so the audience has his vantage point. It's a medieval torture device updated to the 20th century. It stands out because there are no scenes even close to it in the movie. It is a silent distillation of one of modern man's deepest fears: Will I end up in an iron lung or a dialysis machine? What does a claustrophobic think when being slid into an MRI machine? This is why I think *Fast Company* does fit quite neatly into Cronenberg's unique philosophy of body destruction or assimilation.

Well, just when you think Adamson couldn't get any lower, he does. Since Lonnie would typically drive the fuel dragster, and his up-and-coming driver Billy "The Kid" Brooker (Nicholas Campbell) pilots the funny car, this leaves FastCo one car short. Adamson explains it would help FastCo get publicity if Lonnie would let Billy drive, with the switch benefitting everyone.

Lonnie just doesn't have a way with folks—except for Sammy, I guess, because he sure screws up telling Billy why he can't drive anymore. If the film has one weakness, it is the script, and the scene just comes off as Lonnie bullying the poor kid.

As luck would have it, Lonnie gets to race against Gary Black that night, who's pissed because Lonnie isn't supposed to drive funny cars anymore, God damn it. Of course, Lonnie smokes him, and to add insult to injury, Lonnie tells him it felt weird to drive so slowly. So now Gary really hates Lonnie's ass.

One cute production note before I forget: Although, Canadian and Montana accents are not that different, you can discern a Canadian twang in the extras' voices. After all, it is their home and native land! Please don't accuse me of belittling Canada or its people. I married one of them.

The crew then heads off to another race, this time in Spokane. At this point there hasn't been much exploitation aspects in the film, except for the obvious carsploitation angle. The boys spot two comely hitchhikers, with high heels and cut-off shorts, providing a decent view of their butts. They climb in the back of the trailer with Billy, and you have to feel good for the kid after getting the shaft the night before. Then, as the three of them lay there in post-coital bliss, Billy grabs a can of FastCo and pours it over one of the young ladies' breasts and torso; therefore, we get some nudity to spice things up. Completely unnecessary to the narrative—but hey, remember this is an exploitation movie.

CLAUDIA JENNINGS as Sammy and WILLIAM SMITH as Lonnie "Lucky Man" Johnson in FAST COMPANY.

WILLIAM SMITH · CLAUDIA JENNINGS ... JOHN SAXON

Meanwhile, in Spokane, Adamson is up to no good again. He tells the company's owners that Lonnie is a drunk, unreliable and over the hill—all lies. He neglects to notice that Candy has walked into his room and hears the whole conversation. He then tells her to mind her own business, and that he's hooking her up with one of FastCo's execs that evening. She refuses, telling him directly she won't do it—only to have Adamson fire her on the spot.

All this and we've only seen less than a minute of Claudia in the entire film!

Adamson, being the jerk that he is, then approaches Gary Black and asks him to be FastCo's new driver. He also asks Meatball (George Buza) to help out with a little sabotage on Lonnie's car.

Poor Candy wanders over to Lonnie's trailer, which Billy is using while Lonnie's looking after some business. Hopefully he cleaned up the combined oil and skank-dew from his bed, as he and Candy get real friendly real fast.

In the morning, who should come pulling up but Sammy in her black Camaro, to the sound of a screaming guitar riff, expecting to jump Lonnie's bones ASAP. She bounds up the stairs to the trailer and sees two bodies lying there. Our girl goes apeshit, kicking Candy figuratively and literally in the ass and hurling expletives at the person she thinks is Lonnie. Fortunately, the real Lonnie shows up, and everybody's friends again. Then Lonnie throws Candy and Billy out and tosses Sammy in the bed. After a nice mid-morning of bumping the uglies, the couple has a serious discussion. It's obvious Lonnie still wants to go on racing, and Sammy makes it clear she will never go back to the days where she followed him around track to track. The simple scene demonstrates Lonnie's world-weariness, yet at the same time shows he can't let go of his passion for racing. Claudia, by contrast, clearly shows her passion for Lonnie, but not at the cost of having to live a nomadic life.

A Biography

Of course, Adamson shows up to spoil the party by walking in on a half-dressed Sammy and a furious Lonnie. Lonnie tells him to get out, mainly because Adamson didn't knock, and then lectures him on the proper way to treat people. I guess Adamson didn't notice the huge guns and rippling forearms that Lonnie's wife beater tee reveals, but makes the following ill-advised comment: "First you turn my trailer into a whorehouse; now it's an insane asylum!"

In a brilliantly executed scene, Lonnie cracks Adamson one upside the head, knocking him out of the trailer, down the stairs and onto the ground below. Perfect editing, perfect cinematography and a perfect stunt.

During the first time trial, Lonnie's car explodes due to Meatball's sabotage. Then Adamson comes to confiscate the car and the trailer, telling Lonnie he's fired. When Lonnie objects, Meatball comes up behind him and administers a whack on the noggin with a large metal object. Lonnie goes down like a sack of garbage, bleeding profusely, so Cronenberg has now added at least a bit of the old ultra-violence to the film.

The team, now carless, has to drive up to Edmonton for the next race and get its vehicle back from Adamson. Along the way, we see some more beautiful scenery, and it's a nice contrast between the natural and mechanical world, as the highway snakes along majestic rivers and mountain ranges.

Once in Edmonton, Elder and P.J. (Robert Haley) are walking through a car show when they see Lonnie's car on display. The crew comes up with a plan to steal it back. Later that night, after the show is closed, Billy and Candy distract the security guard by doing some very heavy petting in Billy's car. While the guard is getting an eyeful of Candy's abundant charms, Lonnie sneaks in, fires up the car and drives it through what must be a very flimsy door.

Lonnie, along with his crew and the girls, work all night getting the car ready to race. There is almost a clinical feel to this scene, with wrenches and sockets laid out like surgical instruments on stainless steel tables, sparkplugs arranged like spare body parts and a distributor cap placed like a second skull.

During this part of the film, Claudia has nothing to do, literally. She doesn't even get to be bait for the guard. However, she doesn't have to take her clothes off, either. I imagine that is the reason, besides working with Cronenberg, that she took the part.

Just before the final run, Lonnie surprises everyone by letting Billy take the wheel, proving he's a really good mentor after all. Unfortunately, no one is aware Adamson has told Meatball to rig a fatal accident for Lonnie. Not even Gary is aware of their plans, although he does get suspicious when the race officials make Billy change lanes before the start of the race.

Meanwhile, that devilish Meatball is down at the finish line, pouring a hundred gallons of fuel in Billy's lane, which will ignite as soon as his funny car hits it. The race begins and Gary smells a rat, so he speeds up and passes Billy, only to hit the fuel and get French-fried. Billy hops out of his car and sees Meatball trying to run away. In his panic, Meatball, soaked in fuel, gets too close the flames and becomes a human tiki torch.

Adamson understandably freaks, grabs his money and attempts to fly his way out of this mess. Lonnie, however, jumps in his car and races Adamson's plane down the runway. Lonnie's timing is perfect, as he literally clips Adamson's wings, sending the plane into the FastCo trailer with a great, fiery crash. That's a lot of serious mayhem in the last few minutes of action.

In the morning, the gang is talking about what they're going to do now that all the excitement is over. Curious, that there's not a cop, coroner or other investigator around to ask why there's three dead burnt bodies lying there, eh? Not to mention an exploded airplane!

But our group is all casual, in good moods and probably already drinking a few Molsons. Billy and Candy are fixing to spend some QT together, Elder and P.J. are off to work in a fuel dragster shop and Lonnie and Sammy are going to Seattle for a week. He's thinking it'll take one week to convince Sammy to go back on the racing circuit with him, and she's thinking it'll take one week to convince Lonnie to settle down.

It's been a fun ride for everyone—except for the three dead guys, of course—and all the audience is left with is the Bruce Springsteen tribute band blaring on the soundtrack.

Fast Company is distinguished by the quality of its cinematography, which truly makes this film rise above others of its kind. I was fortunate to be able to interview the cinematographer of the film, Mark Irwin, for this book. If the name sounds familiar, it should be. He was the cinematographer or director of photography for many David Cronenberg's masterpieces, including *The Brood*, *Scanners*, *The Dead Zone*, *Videodrome* and *The Fly*. In addition to the films Irwin made with Cronenberg, he was the cinematographer for such landmark films as *Scream*, *There's Something About Mary*, *Dumb and Dumber*—and the list goes on.

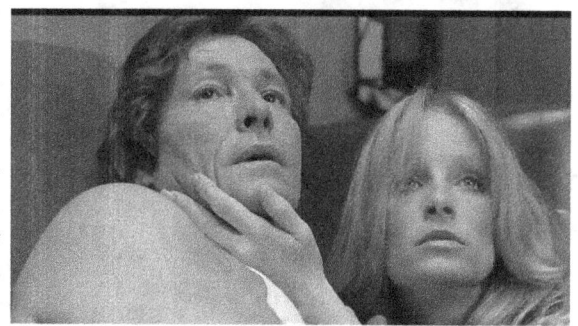
Claudia and Will rudely interrupted

Mark told me how he came to work with Cronenberg for the first time on *Fast Company*:

Well, I had known producer Peter O'Brian from working on the film *Blood and Guts*, which starred William Smith, coincidentally. David's usual cinema-

A Biography   209

tographer, René Verzier, was set for *Fast Company* but dropped out at the last minute to take a job in Italy. Peter asked me to step in, and in two days I was in Edmonton getting ready to shoot.

It was the summer of 1978, and most of the filming was done in an abandoned airbase. David wasn't into funny cars or dragsters. He had one vintage British racing car at the time, and didn't really have a deep interest in American racing. However, he did want everything to scream "America" in the film. So we had a lot of red, white and blue sets and costumes.

I will tell you, Claudia brought her A-game to the film. There was something so natural about her as an actress and a person. She had definitely learned how to "act for the camera." If I had to shoot a scene where she stood up, she stood straight up instead of leaning forward, which would have forced me to change the shot. She and William Smith were both great to work with, and those two got along nicely. Everyone really enjoyed working with her. The only time I was concerned was when she was helping me out on a shot. I was filming using a hand-held camera, and she was driving the car. She took two Quaaludes to relax before we started driving. Other than that, she was a perfect actress to have on set.

David was not an actor's director. He spent most of his time with the crew and getting the photography right. However, he respected Claudia. Usually, when shooting a scene, he would signal his need for an actress by yelling, "Bring in the girl." I think he saw something different in Claudia.

Like all of us who worked with her, we couldn't believe it when we heard she died. The movie was released only a few months before her death. I think *Fast Company* will always be memorable for me—my first film with David, and several of the crew as well like Nick Campbell, who went on to star in several of his films. And sadly, I'll always remember it was Claudia's last film.[7]

Fast Company would suffer from distribution problems, much like several of Claudia's other films. The movie opened in only a few theaters in the United States, and virtually nowhere else worldwide—an unfortunate fate for such a well-crafted movie, which is now considered a minor cult classic.

John Saxon appears as the villain, and had worked with Claudia in *Moonshine County Express*. Mr. Saxon was kind enough to share his memories of Claudia:

She was a beautiful lady, and always very professional. I starred in two movies with her—*Moonshine County Express* and *Fast Company*. My main memory of Claudia is that she seemed so very young. I think she died right after *Fast Company* was released. It was an awful shock to everyone who worked with her on the picture. It was so sad.[8]

Even David Cronenberg himself, recognizing the film wasn't his usual style and not usually impressed with actors, said in his book *Cronenberg on Cronenberg*:

It doesn't seem to fit in with the rest of my work now, but it does. It has to fit; it's all coming from me ... I enjoyed making the movie and working with Bill Smith, Claudia Jennings and all those B-movie actors.

Despite the fact her fellow cast and crew adored her, the city of Edmonton did not agree with Claudia. When she arrived back in the United States, Bobby Hart remarked she was nothing but skin and bones.

Even though Claudia was fighting personal battles on several fronts, she always had time to make a new friend. Debra Jo Fondren was an incredibly beautiful blonde from Texas, who made it into the world of *Playboy*. She went through a period after her Playmate days were over where she struggled like Claudia had; however, she's successful now and living back in Texas. She was generous enough to share her memories of Claudia.

I was a new Playmate, and Playmate of the Year in 1978, and unfortunately I didn't get to meet Claudia until 1979, when I moved from Texas to L.A. I lived in a West L.A. condo briefly, and she and I met on several occasions when she visited her friend there. I always admired Claudia; she was a superstar in my eyes, and more importantly, she seemed unimpressed with her celebrity—not stuck up and a genuinely nice gal. [9]

Claudia also made an impression on another gorgeous lady who led an interesting life. Barbara Leigh was an actress from Georgia who found herself way out in Hollywood. She became Elvis Presley's mistress and dated Steve McQueen and Jim Aubrey, the infamous head of MGM and CBS. She wrote a book titled *The King, McQueen and the Love Machine*, detailing her relationships with those men.

Barbara would often see Claudia at parties and at the Mansion. She told me she could tell how much in love she and Bobby were in by the way they behaved around each other. One evening, at a Hollywood soiree, a self-important VIP type decided to insult Leigh in front of most of the guests. Although Leigh wasn't a good friend of Claudia, it didn't stop the fiery redhead from standing up for her so vehemently that the offending oaf left the party.

Leigh would go on to work for *Playboy* for 17 years as Marilyn Grabowski's assistant.

Claudia ended her relationship with Dr. Jack Garfield and moved on. Maybe he reminded her too much of Bobby; perhaps she had not really convinced herself that a domestic life was really what she wanted. Both Hart and Garfield let Claudia do what she wanted; both were afraid of losing her, and both felt helpless when faced with her questionable decisions.

Claudia and Stan Herman

Claudia had also gotten a taste for dating extremely wealthy men. Dr. Garfield and Bobby were comfortable, but Claudia decided that she needed a higher level of economic strata to be comfortable. She didn't waste time in finding one.

Stan Herman was king of the Hollywood real estate business. He had made a fortune buying and selling homes to the entertainment community's elite. Herman was also a gracious host who threw fabulous parties for clients, most of whom became friends. He was a fixture at the Playboy Mansion and became very good friends with Hugh Hefner. Stan Herman was considered a bit of a playboy himself, according to the Hollywood community, and did not have a good track record with relationships, even before he met Claudia. He had been married once, for only three months. Then he met Linda Evans, arguably one of the few women as beautiful as Claudia. They were married in 1976. They seemed to have great marriage; they threw outrageous parties for the Hollywood set and were quite the Hollywood power couple. Linda was devoted to him, and all seemed perfect. It is important to keep in mind that Linda had been dumped by her husband, John Derek, for a teenaged Mary Cathleen Collins, nicknamed "Bo" Derek; the 46-year-old man fell for the 16-year-old actress while she was still in high school. Shortly afterwards, Linda and John divorced.

While Linda was on location in Europe filming *Avalanche Express* in early 1979, Stan was enjoying himself. He was allegedly observed one night having sex with the younger sister of a family friend.[10] Soon, Linda received a phone call describing the infidelity, and she decided to divorce Stan.

Stan was known for high living and having extramarital involvements. When Claudia and Dr. Jack broke up, she went straight to Stan Herman's Malibu beach house. A few of Claudia's girlfriends stayed there regularly, so Claudia was certainly familiar with the high-profile realtor. Remember, he had actively pursued her during their trip to the Hamptons years earlier, and no doubt lusted after her, seeing Claudia frequently at Pip's and at the Mansion.

After Claudia's death, Stan Herman then married Canadian model Denise Vandenberg. This union lasted a little longer, but ended in divorce as well. Stan's last wife Sheila remained with him until his death from leukemia in 2002.

Apart from being famous as a realtor, Herman was immortalized because he was involved in a landmark legal case. In the early 1990s, Herman impregnated a high-school dropout named Lori McGinley. She claimed they had a relationship; Herman argued they did not. Under California law at that time, it was a moot point, since both parents are obliged to provide financial support. Since McGinley had a negative cash flow, the court looked at Herman's finances. His CPA showed the court Mr. Herman had a negative cash flow as well. Ms. McGinley's attorneys then showed the court documents proving Mr. Herman's net worth was in excess of 11 million dollars; however, at that time, under California law, the compensation for the mother and child was not based on the wealth of the father, but only on a formula determined by computer that only took into account monthly income and expenses.

The court ruled Ms. McGinley was due $2,150 a month in child support, plus $750 a month for the child's college fund. Her attorneys appealed, and the lower court's decision was overruled. The court's finding, which is the basis of present-day custody and divorce law in California:

> Where the supporting parent enjoys a lifestyle that far exceeds that of the custodial parent, child support must to some degree reflect the more opulent lifestyle even though this may, as a practical matter, produce a benefit for the custodial parent.[11]

This case set a precedent that is still followed today. It is known informally as "the style in which they are accustomed to" ruling.

Debbie Chenowith was a good friend of both Claudia and Stan Herman. She spent a lot of her time at Herman's Malibu beach house with Claudia, and got to know both of them well. She was kind enough to share her recollections of those last few months of Claudia's life:

> God, I loved Claudia so much. Like many of the younger girls, she was like a big sister to me. She would take me to the Mansion for movie nights on Fridays. There was a huge buffet with great food. For all of us girls, it was paradise—great food and the Who's Who of Hollywood. I met so many actors, athletes, producers, writers and directors; it was like being at an Academy Awards show every Friday. Barry Goldwater, Jr. and Dr. Garfield were always there, along with Stan Herman.
>
> I think Stan liked the idea of who Claudia was rather than liking Claudia herself. She was another notch in his belt, a trophy like Linda Evans and a lot of other women. Stan was allegedly into threesomes; I really don't think Claudia was into that scene at all. That created some tension between them. They fought a lot, I remember. I was staying at Stan's house, and Claudia spent less time there after she purchased her home. Of course, there were always a lot of drugs around at the Malibu house. I think maybe that's why Claudia hung out there, frankly.

But that's not what Claudia was about. She started to ease off that stuff a lot that summer. She was just the best friend you could ever have. She taught me so many things about life, how to handle myself and how to treat people. I've never met a person who cared so much about others, and she would always give you the best advice on any subject. Boy, she was tough, though! If she felt you were screwing up, she would let you know instantly. I got many a reprimand from her, but she always did it for your own good, and she did it with love.

It's not an exaggeration when I say I never met anyone like her, and I never have since she died. The day of her accident, I was in London. A friend called me to tell me what happened. I didn't believe it. I didn't want to believe it. I screamed and broke down. Even to this day, I have a hard time believing she's gone.[12]

Another girl Claudia befriended around that time was Gayle Gannes-Rosenthal. She was the daughter of the founder of Gayle's Sweet and Sassy BBQ Sauce, one of the best barbecue sauces in the country. She is now president and CEO of the company.

Gayle was a teenager when she hung around with Claudia's circle of Hollywood friends. She shared her memories of her friendship with Claudia:

We were all drawn to Claudia. She had just an amazing personality. You couldn't help but love her. She was always a kind and a gentle person. Claudia was always protective of me. I was in with her partying crowd, but she made sure I was never a part of the activities. I knew all of her boyfriends and hung out with them. Dr. Jack Garfield became my dentist. I would spend a lot of time at Stan Herman's house in Malibu. Claudia would take me out to Dean Shendal's ranch in Las Vegas, where we'd go horseback riding. A lot of famous people would be there as well, from Hollywood and all over; but when the drugs came out as they always did at Dean's, and other stuff started going on, Claudia made sure I wasn't any part of it. I was also a friend with Skip Taylor. I do know that Claudia was not on her way over to Stan's the morning she was killed to break up with him. She was going over there to tell him the good news that she had gotten a role in a great film. Claudia had been up most of the night celebrating with friends. I still think about her almost every day.[13]

One of Claudia's escorts at this time was another very wealthy individual. Jim Randall was not your prototypical Hollywood personality. His business was rivets and fasteners for airplanes. His father had invented some ingenious patented parts, which made Allfast Inc. one of the largest companies in Southern California.

The young Randall enjoyed the Hollywood scene, and in particular enjoyed Hugh Hefner's hospitality. Jim Randall's background was not without controversy. In 1976 he and actress Marisa Berenson were married in what was called at the time, "The Wedding of the Year." However, by 1978, things started falling apart rapidly. Randall filed for a no-fault divorce and moved into one wing of his Beverly Hills mansion, while Berenson moved into the opposite wing. Things deteriorated to the point where Berenson filed a restraining order citing Randall's uncontrollable temper, alleging he bruised her arms while dragging the actress across a room while she was holding their daughter, Starlite Melody. Berenson also said Randall changed the locks on the mansion, and ordered the security guard to ban her friends from the property.[14]

When reached by phone for his comments on Claudia, Randall would only say that he met her at the Playboy Mansion, and that she was a wonderful, fun and great girl to be around. When pressed for further details, he replied he needed to get off the phone. Attempts to reach him by other means were unsuccessful.

Ms. Gannes-Rosenthal and other friends of Claudia's show via their interviews the paradox that her life had become. The two images of her, self-indulgent and guardian angel, are in vivid contrast. There are more questions than answers, unfortunately. How does a person with so much self-confidence, caring and intelligence seemingly become a gold digger and an addict nearly overnight? The simple answer is she could not. For Claudia, it must have seemed like there was no escape. Everyone told her how wonderful she was, but she couldn't internalize it. Men threw themselves at her, yet it created doubts in her mind whether they only wanted her body and not to share her dreams. The drugs she consumed to push away the pain, and the money spent on expensive clothes, only started the nightmarish cycle again. Claudia now needed to jump off the carousel before it started to spin so fast that escape was impossible.

Her adopted brother and friend, Keith Jennings, was adamant about what he saw in Claudia's behavior:

> Claudia did everything she could to shelter me from all the bad things in her life. I only saw her smoke cigarettes the entire time I knew her, and I wasn't happy about that. It was only after she died that things came out about what she and Maureen McCormick were doing. I never knew any of her boyfriends besides Bobby. I did meet a few of them, because I stayed at her house and her condo. Claudia was my angel and my sister. She always will be.
>
> I want people to know the real Claudia. Look at people today and look at most of Hollywood back in the 1970s. They were doing much worse things than Claudia did. I know in my heart she did not lie to me when she said she was cleaning up her act about drugs, her career and being bound to *Playboy*.[15]

[1] Phone interview with Dr. Jack Garfield, June 15, 2014
[2] Phone interview with Jesse Vint, February 20, 2014
[3] "Claudia Jennings, A Hard Boiled Persona," the *Los Angeles Times*, February 5, 1978
[4] Cross, Robin, *B Movies*, page 26, 1981, St. Martin's Press
[5] Koetting, Christopher T., *Mind Warp!: The Fantastic True Story of Roger Corman's New World Pictures* (Baltimore, Maryland: Midnight Marquee Press, 2013)
[6] *Los Angeles Times* interview with Claudia Jennings, February 4, 1978
[7] Phone interview with Mark Irwin, November 19, 2015
[8] Interview with John Saxon, March 25, 2014
[9] Personal interview with Debra Jo Fondren, April 1, 2014
[10] Interview with Sharmayne Leland-St. John-Sylbert, September 2017,
[11] The Lifestyle to Become Accustomed To, The Law Offices of Makupson & Howard, September 29, 2013
[12] Phone Interview with Debbie Chenowith, April 28, 2014
[13] Personal phone interview with Gayle Gannes-Rosenthal, April 23, 2014
[14] Kalter, Suzy and Allison Rahel, "It Was the Wedding of the Year in 1976—Now Marisa Berenson Loses a Husband and a Plum Role," *People* Magazine, Vol. 9, No. 21, May 29, 1978
[15] E-mail interview with Keith Jennings, September 2017

Chapter 7:
Summer of 1979: The Small Screen

Although there is no doubt Claudia wanted to star in major motion pictures, she rarely passed up an opportunity to appear on television. The fact she was willing to perform in any medium shows a dedication to her craft and a desire to keep improving her acting abilities. Bobby Hart said she would go to almost every casting call, whether it was for movies, television or even commercial work.

A look at Claudia's television work is fascinating, because it brings together so many facets of her life and the hypocrisy of the entertainment business in the 1970s. Many people felt Claudia's film roles were just extensions of her Hollywood bitch-goddess/sex symbol personality; however, the characters she played on television were for the most part mainstream and middle class in keeping with the show and sponsor's demands. She could not dress nor behave provocatively, and the violence allowed in exploitation films would not have made it past the censors. Anyone who thought Claudia was limited to one stereotyped part would only need to look to her entire body of work to see her versatility and depth.

It is a shame, therefore, that with one notable exception her television career is more famous for the roles she didn't get than for the ones she did.

Claudia turned in very professional performances on *Barnaby Jones*, *The F.B.I.*, *Cannon* and *The Streets of San Francisco*. Claudia held her own with some veteran actors, such as Karl Malden, Michael Douglas, Harvey Keitel, William Conrad and Buddy Ebsen.

Her most successful appearance was in the most unlikely of forums. The former Playmate of the Year would guest star on the beloved, wholesome, middle-class fantasy *The Brady Bunch*. The 1973 episode, "Adios, Johnny Bravo," would attract the most viewers in the show's history. The cast and crew would be captivated as well: Barry Williams would later tell E!, "Claudia made quite an impression on me. The crew would think of excuses to do another take to keep her around the studio." Susan Olsen, who played Cindy Brady, remembered Claudia as a very special woman who treated her and the rest of the cast as family.

Claudia plays a talent agent, Tami Cutler, who tells the Brady's she wants to represent them. Secretly,

The Brady Bunch, "Adios, Johnny Bravo"

however, she only wants Greg (Barry Williams) for a solo act. While the rest of the family stews over this humiliation, Greg's newfound glory clouds his better judgment. He gets brought back to earth when Tami tells him it wasn't his talents that won the new name of "Johnny Bravo," but the fact he looked good in the ridiculous suit he was supposed to wear.

One cast member who did not remember working with Claudia was Maureen McCormick, who played Marcia Brady. The two would later work together again on *Moonshine County Express* and become close friends and roommates.

Warner Bros. provided Claudia with a chance to break into prime time TV by optioning a pilot for *Wonder Woman* in 1975. Claudia did very well, but ironically, she and the statuesque Joanna Cassidy came in second to Lynda Carter. Ms. Carter was a good actress, but Claudia was the more polished presence. The part could have gone to Claudia, but the size of the taller Ms. Carter's bust was judged more suitable for the role. Of the two, Lynda did appear more Amazonian, but at least Claudia made it to the final three considered..

This was a little bit of television studio hypocrisy at its worst, especially when we look at what happened with *Charlie's Angels*, another role Claudia missed. If Lynda Carter had shown another two inches more of her breasts, her appearance would not have been any different than the poses Claudia did for *Playboy*—the only difference being Lynda looked a bit kinkier in her costume. In fact, the *Wonder Woman* costume was reminiscent of the Playboy Bunny outfit, with high cuts up the hips of Ms. Carter.

Unfortunately, there was a worse incident to come. It could not have happened at a poorer time in Claudia's life, and many people wonder if she still might be alive today had things turned out differently.

In the spring of 1979, Aaron Spelling was looking for a new Charlie's Angel, because Kate Jackson was leaving. Claudia was asked immediately to audition. Barbara Bach, Michelle Pfeiffer, Melanie Griffith and Bo Derek were also considered. In fact, Michelle Pfeiffer borrowed a pair of Claudia's shoes for the audition. Everyone was impressed with Claudia's reading, and the general feeling was she had nailed it and the role was hers. She was asked to come back and do a second and third reading. Claudia was positive she had earned the role, and was told nothing to dissuade her from that feeling.

Then Claudia got a call that she did not get the part. Unfortunately, the network executives and sponsors were a bit nervous about Claudia's *Playboy* background. As pointed out earlier in the book, this was an outrageous decision that defies logic and business sense. They overruled Spelling's decision and gave the part to Shelley Hack. Ms. Hack was a lovely model, but an inexperienced and somewhat limited actress.

The decision not to hire Claudia was Hollywood hypocrisy at it most transparent. *Charlie's Angels* was about sex and male fantasy, with a token drop of female empowerment thrown in. Most of the episodes featured standard TV crime solving plots, with the three female investigators providing eye candy. When you threw in David Doyle's Bosley character, with his incessant leers and borderline off-color jokes, the show was hardly a bastion of middle-class morality.

Mr. Spelling later told Claudia he was writing a part for her in the new show he was producing, *Dynasty*. One would have to wonder whether the TV executives would have changed their minds in so short a time about Claudia's background. The only possible explanation is that, despite evidence to the contrary, *Charlie's Angels* was perceived as a "family show," whereas *Dynasty* was strictly adult entertainment.

A Biography

Claudia took it well on the outside, even joking about it to *Playboy's* Bruce Williamson in the interview that accompanied her 1979 September pictorial. Bobby Hart and Sally Kirkland said, despite her brave face, Claudia was terribly hurt by the decision. In one respect, some good did come out of it. Claudia began to question her life and career choices.

As Sally Kirkland noted:

She was depressed after she got the news about *Charlie's Angels*. She was thinking maybe she could have handled her career differently. She told me she wanted a career more like mine.

That's exactly what Claudia decided to do, as she began taking acting lessons again and auditioning for parts in quality movies.

Claudia was not finished with television, and made two more appearances, including one in *Lucan*, a pilot that starred Kevin Brophy. He recalled:

She worked for three days, and played a nurse. Claudia was fun and funny; I can't say enough good things about her. We would lunch together. She made working and life on the set so much better. She was unforgettable.

Her last television appearance was in *240-Robert*, a police drama starring Mark Harmon and Joanna Cassidy. Claudia told Keith Jennings she was particularly excited about the part, because for the first time on TV she would play a mother. It must have been a cathartic experience for the actress, who was now nearing 30 and had always desired a family of her own.

Claudia had bought a home in Laurel Canyon formerly belonging to superstar Ava Gardner, what she called a "fixer-upper." She showed she could be independent if she wanted to. The way her relationship was going with Stan Herman, it was a good hedge. Stan had shown a very possessive and jealous side when he was with Claudia. Not all of the attributes he had loved about her were endearing now that she was his girlfriend. Claudia gathered a lot of attention, dressed provocatively and was for all intents and purposes just being herself. Mr. Herman did not take it well. He and Claudia would have spectacular and very public fights. Here were two people very much used to getting their own way. One incident in particular sent Stan over the edge; he found out Claudia was going to appear in the September

A sultry pose

issue of *Playboy*. The couple would establish a pattern: They would have an argument, split up and then reunite.

At one point during these months, a very bizarre incident occurred. Claudia sought out her old friends the Sebastians for help. She showed up at their boat in Marina del Rey requesting sanctuary. Ferd Sebastian shared his memories of that time:

> Claudia had told us about her involvement with drugs, and that she was scared. She wanted to hide, and so we let her stay on our motorsailer at Marina del Rey. She stayed there about a month, and shortly after she left, she was killed. She never told us very much after she moved in with us. She was just scared. She just did not want us to be involved. She never really told too much about her involvement. She wanted to protect us from whoever was chasing her. Claudia would talk about a few things with us; she talked about her sisters and how much she loved and missed them. She showed us pictures of them. She almost never spoke about her parents. You asked me before about how Claudia and Mr. Hefner got along; I think he wanted her to succeed more than anything. He would have felt he was part of that. They had a very personal relationship, I believe. I do not think she was afraid of him at all, but despite the fear and the tension, Bev and I were glad we were there for her. When the three of us were together, we were living in the world of now, as I call it. They say the past is gone and the future may never come. That is why they call today the present. So it was the present, or the gift, when we were all together. The three of us loved each other very much.[1]

Constance Chesterton recalls one of the last conversations she had with Claudia:

> We talked for a short while. I asked her how she was doing with her cocaine use. She replied that there were a lot of good days, but some bad ones, too. I got the impression she was more concerned about me and our other sister, which was typical of Claudia. Overall, I felt she was handling things better and making progress.

The few of Claudia's friends who knew of the incident were not sure of the reasons she hid herself away in Marina del Rey. Speculations ranged from her owing a drug dealer a lot of money to wanting to stay away from the drug scene entirely.

Dr. Jack Garfield discounted the latter theory:

> Once Claudia and I became friends again, I used to help fix up her house. I was putting in track lighting one day when James Caan, Tony Curtis and Claudia were sitting around doing coke. After they had a good buzz going they indulged in what I called "drug babble." The three of them would talk about all these projects and films they would plan, and all these great ideas they had. Of course, none of them were ever realized.

Dr. Garfield had started dating Cheryl Ladd, even before he and Claudia ended their relationship. He managed to make the undisputed sex symbol of her time a little jealous, as well.

I remember one time Claudia had a dental appointment. Well, it just so happened that day I had four other Playmates in the office waiting. Claudia disappeared into the restroom and came out with more make-up and her hair done a little more exotically. She got so jealous, she called Hefner and asked him to ban me from the Mansion. Hugh calmed her down and said that was unreasonable, and that she should work things out with me.

Claudia and Dr. Jack, note how thin she is.

Most likely, when Claudia thought about the situation, it was a tremendous tribute to her that all her Playmate friends were curious about Dr. Jack. After all, she was first among equals in the *Playboy* hierarchy. They all admired Claudia, envied her relationship with Hugh Hefner and respected her. Their thinking was, if they could have the man that loved Claudia, they would be able to have a piece of her glory.

Claudia herself even fanned the flames with this quote from the 1979 pictorial about her and Dr. Garfield's relationship: "That was a hot affair … very."[2] (Dr. Garfield said the mention in Claudia's article did do wonders for his social life.)

The article refers to other men Claudia dated, such as Jim Randall, but when asked about her current man, Claudia demurred. She said coyly he was "big," and a professional tennis player, which was nonsense. The gentleman she was referring to was Stan Herman. The interview in her September pictorial tells one quite a lot about Claudia. Reading it today, it's difficult to discern whether it is more PR posturing on her part, or a sincere attempt to describe the previous 10 years of her life. In previous interviews, she seemed to prevaricate and give at least plausible deniability to her own decisions—and the consequences they generated. In the *Playboy* article, she perfectly describes her experience at points but attributes them to others. For example:

> I've seen what's become of people who started out when I did, and it's absolutely frightening. There are so many things to divert your energies. You can stay high, party every night. There are a thousand traps.[3]

While the quote is true, there is no question it could be applied to Claudia. Again, under the circumstances, with a career comeback hanging in the balance, and with the possibility of obtaining a valuable role on television after she'd lost the big prize, the PR part of Claudia was undoubtedly at work. It would have been unwise to admit she had been ensnared in some of those traps.

The article also shows, quite vividly, the sweet and vulnerable side of Claudia. She admits to being more fragile and reserved after 10 years of non-stop Hollywood machinations. She expresses her admiration for Hefner and Roger Corman for supporting her emotionally and professionally. Claudia singles out Corman for praise, since he was one of the first to cast women in leading roles. She ends the interview with what Keith Jennings said was a message to him as much as to herself:

> Never compromise; always stay true to yourself. Don't do anything the whole world can't know about. Above all, hold yourself in the highest esteem.[4]

Claudia finishes the interview with a poignant allusion to the role she didn't get, made more poignant by what was to follow in a few weeks—and, looking back, an incredibly sad comment. She tells Bruce Williamson:

> My God. I've led my life this way because it's important to me. Maybe I *am* an Angel.[5]

It is rather inexplicable why she decided to do this final pictorial for *Playboy* and agree to the one scheduled for Mykonos. As the interview in the article continues, she loses the role for *Charlie's Angels*. Claudia recognized her *Playboy* past had at least a part to play in the TV executives' decisions. We do know, according to Keith Jennings and others, that Claudia had told Hefner this was definitely her final appearance in the magazine. Sadly, it turned out to be a tragic prophecy. Had Claudia lived, it's impossible to say whether she would really have stayed away from *Playboy*. All evidence points to the contrary. If she had become a successful movie actress, Claudia would have been asked to appear again, without a doubt. There is probably no way she could have said no to Hugh Hefner or Marilyn Grabowski, for that matter.

One day at an audition, Claudia met Sharmagne Leland-St. John-Sylbert. The two would bond quickly and become inseparable the last summer of Claudia's life.

Leland-St. John-Sylbert is a seven-time Pushcart Prize nominee and winner of a 2013 International Book Award, as well as many other prestigious poetry awards. She has performed for live audiences and was the last fashion model signed by Wilhelmina Cooper before the prestigious talent manager passed away.

Ms. Leland-St. John-Sylbert was very gracious and shared her memories of meeting Claudia and sharing the last few months with her before she died:

> I had just spent the last 15 minutes in the bathroom of a casting agency on Sunset Boulevard repeating, in front of a mirror, the insipid lines I would soon have to deliver to a group of ad reps. Someone was impatiently tapping on the bathroom door. When I opened it, I encountered a stunningly beautiful green-eyed strawberry blonde. I remember thinking "Oh, my God, this is my competition!"

She took one look at me and said "I know you." I narrowed my eyes and tried to place her as she continued: "I'm Claudia Jennings, Bobby Hart's girlfriend. You are the only woman whose photograph I've allowed him to keep in the house."

Later, Bobby told me it was bullshit; she made him remove the photographs of *all* his old flames. I wound up getting the commercial, and Claudia didn't.

A few weeks later, I invited Bobby to my annual birthday bash at La Fontaine, and that was the next time I saw her. She was fun and added a lot to the gathering. She came to several birthday parties after that.

We also ran across one another at casting calls and in the homes of mutual friends, but I really got to know her and bond with her when she began dating my dear friend Stan Herman. He was also my broker. I got my real estate license in 1976, and immediately went to work for him. When Stan's wife, Linda Evans, filed for divorce, I started spending my weekends at his Malibu beach house.

One Sunday morning, David Janssen and I were doing the *New York Times* crossword puzzles; the door to the master suite opened and Claudia came bouncing down the stairs. I was surprised to see her. I didn't know she and Bobby had broken up. Stan came out a few minutes later and suggested we "girls" go shopping together. He handed Claudia a wad of bills and off we went.

When we returned with our packages and shopping bags full of beachwear, he took me aside and asked me if she had treated me properly and had shared equally. I told him that she had. He said, "Hmmm, this one might be a keeper!"

Claudia and I became very close, and spent much time together, either at the beach house, my apartment or our friend Jacqui Cohen's.

One weekend we decided to go swimming in the ocean. Vince Edwards showed up just as we were discussing whether or not I should go in topless. Claudia said, "Well it depends if you drown on how you want them to find you when they pull you out." There was an incident with Stan that explains a lot about his personality. Stan and Claudia had flown in from somewhere. He had picked up this woman on the plane; she may have been a flight attendant. He invited her home and wanted to do a threesome with Claudia. The woman's name was something like Denille or Danielle.

Claudia wasn't thrilled about it, and we sat around my room plotting what we could do to this woman. We decided to treat her to a bikini wax. Do you have any idea how much that hurts, or how irritating and annoying it is when it grows back? We finally got rid of her, and Claudia settled back into her domestic bliss with Stan.

The list of guests read like a Who's Who of Hollywood. For the most part, it was an incredible summer, full of Piña Coladas, mushrooms, parties and fun. The kind of fun we had as kids, but there were no parents to call us home.

The more time Claudia spent with Stan Herman, the further she moved away from the woman Bobby Hart had known. Her new friends, most of whom hadn't observed her behavior around Bobby, assumed she had always been a wild, uninhibited partier. Now it seemed Claudia was falling in love with Stan, which drew her closer to his lifestyle.

Sharmagne Leland-St. John-Sylbert continued her account of the summer of 1979.

Claudia liked me because I always helped avoid the "scenes" Stan wanted to arrange. She was really turned off by his attempts to bring another woman into their bed. The only men I ever knew her to be with were Bobby and Jack Garfield. Stan, as it turned out, was definitely a bad choice. He flirted with and had sex with other women while he was with her, just as he did with all of his wives and girlfriends.

I think Jack Garfield was a good match and a good person. And of course, I can't say anything negative about Bobby, because there isn't anything negative to say. He is an honest, kind, caring and humble person.

Claudia's relationship with Stan began to fray as the summer went on. There would be short stretches of happiness followed by sudden, unexpected tiffs that left her confused and frightened; yet Claudia remained devoted to Stan through all the emotional storms.

Later that summer, Hefner hosted the famous Midsummer's Night party at the Mansion. All the female guests traditionally wore negligees and similar attire. Stan and Claudia allegedly had one of their worst fights in their short relationship; the more people who came up to congratulate Claudia on her pictorial, the angrier Stan became.

The situation exploded when Herman saw Claudia speaking with a well-known African-American athlete. A furious Herman stormed over and began swearing and hurling racial epithets, according to one of Claudia's close friends. Claudia ended up leaving—some say in tears—and spent the night at the home of her friend, heiress Jacqui Cohen.

Sharmagne remembered the incident vividly and recorded the event and its aftermath in her diary:

> Despite the fact Stan had plenty of money, a Beverly Hills mansion and a beach house—all the things Claudia wanted in a husband—she was not a gold digger. She had her own money from doing *Playboy*, modeling and her films. She had her own home and a reliable car. Stan may have been a rebound from Jack Garfield, or maybe it was the coke Stan had in generous supply. Where Jack and Bobby lived quieter lives, Stan lived right out loud. Claudia was in love with Stan, as most women are until they really get to know him and his quirks—and what I consider sexual aberrations.
>
> She was terribly hurt and blindsided when he publicly admonished her for her *Playboy* layout. It was a truly ugly scene, right there in the tent at the Mansion in front of everyone. The racial slurs he used were uncalled for, and caught all by surprise. Keep in mind, Stan was one of my closest male friends, but I will never take the side of a friend if I think they are wrong.
>
> I later had a conversation about the incident. He knew going in that Claudia was a nude model. You don't suddenly get all prudish the first time she disrobes for a layout after you are together. It was okay for him to want to do a *ménage à trios* in real life, but it wasn't appropriate for her to do a fantasy layout in a well-respected magazine? Go figure.
>
> He might have been angry about something else and used that as an excuse to blow up at her.[6]

Shortly after the confrontation at the Mansion, Claudia stepped back from the relationship with Stan—never ending it, but making less frequent visits to his beach house.

It was beginning to dawn on Claudia that her lifestyle and relationship with Stan Herman could not go on forever.

Claudia turned her energies to reading for roles in A-list movies, or at least more respectable fare. The work was different from the movies she was accustomed to starring in, where nudity and exploitation were the first priority.

Claudia always expressed admiration and gratitude for Hugh Hefner and Roger Corman. Both men made a lot of money selling Claudia's body; at least in Corman's case, he displayed her acting talents for the most part. This is why many take issue with Hefner's philosophy. It is a disproportionate transaction for the woman. Claudia did make some money from modeling, and it gave her publicity and opened the door to a movie career. However, Hefner and *Playboy* made a lot more money than Claudia ever did.

Give credit to Claudia in all of this: She remained true to her internal values. The loss of the *Charlie's Angels* role seemed to invigorate her. She moved on with her life; she took positive steps, even if they weren't a clean break from all of her past problems; and she gained weight and slowed down on her drug consumption. Friends said she was sincerely evaluating the role men played in her life. In retrospect, it is not surprising that her relationships with Bobby Hart and Dr. Garfield fell apart. Marriages—Hollywood marriages in particular—are prone to extreme stress, exacerbated by time away from one another. Claudia also seemed to do as much as she could to sabotage her relationship with Dr. Garfield. She probably cared for him a great deal, but simply could not let herself share true intimacy where it was essential. Being a spectator to her own parents' divorce was no doubt a driving force in her inner feelings of avoiding commitment. Her self-esteem issues compounded all of this, too. In other words, if Claudia thought so little of herself, why would someone worthy be interested in her?

Claudia continued to show conflicting sides of her personality. Sharmagne had invited her to a birthday party in late May of 1979. Claudia then inadvertently invited a "friend" from Chicago, known by his Runyonesque *nom de guerre* of Eddie the Hat.

Sharmagne was a bit put off, saying that the party was only for close friends. Claudia pleaded that he really wanted to come, and she felt badly he would be disappointed. Since the party was the next day, Claudia needed an answer immediately so Eddie would have time to book a flight to get him to Los Angeles in time for the party.

Sharmagne tells what happened next:

> I hated to see her in that sort of predicament, because of her kindness and caring nature, so I relented. Eddie booked a new flight and got to L.A. in time for the party.
>
> His original flight, American Airlines 191, crashed shortly after takeoff, killing everyone aboard. Had it not been for Claude's insistence, he would have been on that flight.
>
> After the party, we discovered something had disappeared. A beautiful red and white cotton scarf belonging to my friend Mary Garcia was missing. Since Eddie was the only stranger, I was certain he had it. Claudia called him and he pretended not to know anything about it, so we got into my little Mercedes sports car and drove to his house, and she stormed in and went directly to his closet, where we found the missing scarf. I remember her saying, "I can't believe

I saved your effing life, and you stole from my best friend!" He still pretended as if he hadn't a clue how it got there. [7]

All in all, with the exception of her strange interlude on the Sebastians' boat and her problems with Stan Herman, the summer of 1979 finally seemed to be the time when life was turning in Claudia's favor. Her career was on the verge of taking off, and her dependence on drugs had dropped to recreational levels. Claudia was achieving some independence by purchasing a home and having Keith Jennings plan to move in, where they could support each other. It was almost like she was Mary Eileen Chesterton again, on that first day of school at ETHS. She had taken some rough shots from life; however, just like in Evanston, she was ready to straighten up and go after what she wanted.

[7] 240-Robert "Bank Job Officers Thibideaux and Applegate are endangered while diving for stolen bank money when an attendant trips a valve drawing them towards a huge drain Claudia Jennings Art Kassul and Gerald McRaney guest

Claudia's last TV appearance was in *240-Robert* "Bank Job"

The calendar turned from summer to fall, and Claudia was ready for the next chapter of her life. She still had plenty of friends who loved her. Bobby was still a part of her life and offered to teach her Eastern meditation techniques. Claudia thought perhaps she had a spiritual side after all. She had every reason to be optimistic. Twenty-nine is still relatively young for an actress. Of course, she was still beautiful, not looking much different than 10 years earlier when she first came to Hollywood. One of Claudia's greatest qualities was to live in the moment; she didn't look back with regret upon her wounds of the past, even the self-inflicted ones. Of course, as has been stated frequently in this book, she never used any internal or external rage as a pretext to mistreat another human being.

In *Psychedelic Bubble Gum*, Bobby Hart remembers the surprising change he saw in Claudia as autumn began in Southern California.

> One beautiful Monday morning in late September, Claudia stopped by the house unexpectedly. Right away I noticed a change in her demeanor. Over the last four years, her party life had taken its toll. But she had put a little weight back on, she was clear-eyed and she looked good. Claudia told me she was studying and taking her acting more seriously, "And I've made up my mind to break it off with Stan for good," she volunteered.
>
> "I bet you thought you'd never hear me say this, Hart, but I've come to you for some help. I've cleaned up my act. I'm trying to do all the right things, but I just don't know what to do. All those years I watched you meditating and trying to become a better person. I just couldn't admit to myself that you knew something I didn't. But I'm ready to listen and I know you can help me."

Bobby asked her to control her breathing, and then sit in his meditation room for a while. He described what happened next:

> In 10 minutes' time, she opened the door. There was a miraculous serenity on her face I had never seen before.
>
> She obviously had a deep experience and did not want to talk. "Paper and pencil," she whispered. I found Claudia something to write with, and she spent the next 10 minutes transcribing her thoughts. We hugged and then she left. Then I looked at the journal that she had placed in my hands. It began, "Hart, you knew, you always knew."[8]

That day is important to understanding Claudia as a person. She didn't go over there to beg him for money, shelter or anything material. Claudia was looking for something that couldn't be bought, worn or snorted. She wanted Bobby's help to find a way back from the pain she felt, and the hollow existence she had been living.

Bobby said he felt that the last year of Claudia's life was one of her worst; that she was unhappy, terrified of turning 30 and still in the grip of cocaine abuse. He felt helpless because Claudia seemed unable to get a grip on her life. He told me, "There's nothing you can do for someone out of control."

However, seeing her that day gave him renewed hope that perhaps Claudia was successfully fighting back the demons. This was a woman who was always tough, and willing to do whatever was necessary in order to come out on top. Always resourceful and brave, there was now cause for Claudia to be optimistic.

The calendar moved from September to October. Nothing could prepare anyone for what was to come. It would have the effect of dropping a huge stone in the middle of a calm lake—the initial smack and splash giving way to unstoppable ripples that still emanate outward, even today.

[1] Personal interview with Ferd and Beverly Sebastian, September 14, 2015
[2] "Claudia Recaptured," *Playboy* Vol. 9, No. 9, 1979
[3] *Ibid.*
[4] *Ibid.*
[5] *Ibid.*
[6] E-mail interviewwith Sharmayne Leland-St. John-Sylbert, September 2017
[7] *Ibid.*
[8] Hart, Bobby with Glenn Ballantyne, *Psychedelic Bubble Gum: Boyce & Hart, The Monkees, and Turning Mayhem Into Miracles* (New York: SelectBooks, 2015)

Chapter 8:
October 3, 1979 and the Aftermath

Claudia was doing much better, physically and mentally, according to most of her friends, as the summer turned to fall. She was still seeing Stan Herman, but not as frequently. The renovations on her house were coming along well. She decided her adopted little brother, Keith Glass, would soon move in with her.

The best things that were happening to Claudia had to do with her career. She finally had a potential television series, *Dynasty*, in her grasp. More importantly, she had four firm movie offers: *Used Cars*, *The Postman Always Rings Twice*, *Fade to Black* and *Blood Beach* all wanted Claudia for major roles. Claudia knew the director of *The Postman Always Rings Twice*. Bob Rafelson had directed several episodes of *The Monkees* TV show and Claudia worked with the director of *Fade to Black*, Vernon Zimmerman, before appearing in *Unholy Rollers*. There was also some talk that John Landis was interested in her for a role in *1941*.

Keith had driven to Claudia's house on the afternoon of October 1. He was going to speak with her about his plans for moving in. When Keith pulled in, he noticed Stan Herman's vehicle parked out front. He tells what he observed and heard:

> Stan was outside the house, and Claudia was inside sticking her head out the window. It was not a friendly conversation. They were yelling at each other when Claudia noticed me. I was sitting there, not knowing what to do, when she gave a look that seemed to say, "Not now, Keith!" So I took off. That's the last time I saw her alive.

The next evening, on October 2, Claudia had dinner with her old friend Barry Richards at one of their favorite restaurants, the Caioti Cafe in Laurel Canyon. The landmark restaurant has since moved to Studio City:

> She was in a great mood, telling me about the plans she had for her house and the movie offers she'd been getting. It looked as if the old Claudia was back. She

Barry Richards and Claudia

Body of Claudia Jennings lies covered with sheet in convertible.

Crash kills Claudia Jennings

MALIBU, Calif. (UPI) — Actress Claudia Jennings, 29, former Playboy magazine "Playmate of the Month," was killed Wednesday in a traffic accident.

Miss Jennings' car drifted across the center divider of Pacific Coast Highway near the intersection with Topanga Canyon Boulevard and smashed head-on into an oncoming truck, California Highway Patrol officers said.

She has appeared in several motion pictures, including "Truck Stop Women," "Unholy Rollers" and "The Great Texas Dynamite Case."

The truck driver, Craig Bennell, 19, of nearby Rancho Palos Verdes, was hospitalized.

looked healthy, and was very happy. Claudia told me she was going to have some friends over to celebrate—probably stay up all night and then go to Stan Herman's to sleep on the beach for a while.

It would be the last time Barry Richards would see Claudia Jennings alive as well.

That night, Claudia and her friends stayed up very late partying and celebrating, according to some of her friends. On the contrary, though, Ari Bass quoted some of them as saying she called them that evening very distressed about Stan Herman and the state of their relationship. They described the general mood of the gathering as somber, not celebratory. Unfortunately, there is no one who would corroborate either version.

Claudia left her house on the morning of October 3 at approximately 8:45 a.m. What has been established is that she was going to Stan Herman's beach house in Malibu. The reason she was going there that morning is a matter of disagreement among her friends. Bobby Hart, Dr. Jack Garfield and several of Claudia's friends maintain she was driving over there to finally sever the relationship and pick up her remaining belongings. Other friends of Claudia are adamant she was merely driving over there to tell him about the good things happening in her life, grab a nap and enjoy a day at the beach. A few of Claudia's friends were not positive either way. After all, Claudia and Stan's relationship had been on and off for months.

Claudia had the top down on her white VW Bug. She had turned on to the Pacific Coast Highway, a beautiful but dangerous roadway. There are only two lanes, with no divider. Dozens of accidents occur along the busy thoroughfare every year; however, Claudia had driven this road countless times. Sometime around 8:50, near the intersection of Topanga Canyon Road, her vehicle crossed into the oncoming lane and was instantly struck head-on by a pickup truck driven by 19-year-old Craig Bennell. Witnesses said the accident happened so quickly, it appeared that Claudia swerved into the oncoming truck deliberately. Bennell was taken to the hospital and released later that day.

In an odd twist, a few people on that stretch of PCH that day said it appeared there was a movie shoot going on at the time, off to the side of the highway. Some speculated that Claudia might have been curious about the activity and decided to pull over to check it out. It is not out of the question, but it was never confirmed either.

Claudia was trapped in her car for nearly 15 minutes while the police and paramedics were summoned. After they arrived, a sheriff managed to ease her out of the vehicle, and held her. Barry Richards spoke to the sheriff a day later and was told she murmured a few words and was declared dead at the scene. He also found a picture of Claudia and her mother spattered with blood in the backseat of the car.

The news quickly spread through the community of Claudia's loved ones. The initial feeling was one of acute pain. For most, it was not only an emotional reaction, but also a very real physical response. Bobby Hart, in what was most likely one of the worst days of his life, bravely called Claudia's family and made arrangements for her "Celebration of Life" service. He also notified the Neptune Society, which supplies cremation services.

In *Psychedelic Bubble Gum*, Bobby remembers that day and the days that followed:

On October 3, 1978, the phone rang. "Is this Bobby Hart?" a female voice inquired. "Yes, it is. Who's calling?" "I'm one of the secretaries here at *Playboy*," she answered. "Mr. Hefner asked me to call to make sure you knew that Claudia Jennings was killed this morning in an automobile accident."

A shudder of cold anguish shot through my body. The shock of the news instantly drained the strength from my legs and I quickly sat down ... my dad had come to stay with me when Claudia died. He had accompanied me to the morgue for the sad and uncomfortable task of identifying the remains ... On a sunny October day, as gentle breezes blew the fragrance of pittosporum blossoms like incense through the mountain air, 300 mourners made a pilgrimage up my driveway. Movie stars, bit actors, girlfriends, boyfriends, doctors, lawyers, gaffers and grips stood on a green grassy terrace to say goodbye to a girl whose soul had touched each of their lives in extraordinary ways.[1]

Jesse Vint recalls his reaction when he found out about Claudia's death:

One early morning in October of 1979 I was sitting in a coffee shop and turned the *Los Angeles Times* newspaper to page three, when Claudia Jennings' face suddenly and without warning leaped out at me. She had been killed on the Pacific Coast Highway in Malibu in a traffic accident. I won't try to describe to you what happened to me at that moment, because I am not capable of it. I will say that there were no tears (perhaps because I wasn't surprised), but there was a total numbness followed by an excruciating pain, and then the question that has never completely left me: Could I have done something more? When a person doesn't want help, I have found that it's a true challenge to continue.[2]

Dr. Jack Garfield was with Cheryl Ladd when they received the news:

We were both so shocked we didn't do anything for a moment. Then we cried for hours. We just held each other and cried. I don't think we moved, spoke or did anything else. We were devastated for days.[3]

Keith Allison, 34 years later, remembered vividly when he heard about Claudia's death:

I was working on a song, and when a musician is doing that, you're very focused. I was trying to get the thing written and finished and the phone kept ringing. I didn't want to lose my train of thought, so I ignored it. It turned out to be Allison Granno, Claudia's old roommate, trying to reach me. She had heard Claudia had been killed. I went through the whole day not knowing what had happened. The next day I got a call first thing in the morning from my ex-wife. She told me Claudia had died in an automobile accident. I had a feeling of disbelief and grief. I was struck numb for hours and thought she was either kidding or mistaken. I was numb for days.[4]

Beverly and Ferd Sebastian found out in a particularly painful way:

We only found out about Claudia's death when the morgue called us asking us to claim her body. We were so shocked and saddened. It was horrible to find out she had been killed, but then to be notified in that fashion! We thought it was horrendous that she was so alone no one was there to take care of her. When we got to the morgue we found out Bobby had taken care of the arrangements.[5]

The Sebastians went on to make more movies before retiring from the entertainment business. Beverly created a greyhound rescue program called Second Chance for Life that works in conjunction with the penitentiary system. The prisoners take care of the canines until they are adopted. The benefits of the program are awesome, as the prisoners learn responsibility, spend less time idle and receive unconditional love from the dogs. The program helps save thousands of greyhounds per year that would otherwise have nowhere else to go except an animal shelter. The Lifetime Network has recognized Beverly for her efforts.

Beverly Sebastian now rescues greyhounds

Ferd, after suffering a severe health crisis, founded his own ministry. He is now a pastor and believes in the healing power of Jesus Christ and the value of faith and prayer in everyday life. The Sebastians are a remarkable couple, and it is a testament to Claudia that they loved her unconditionally.

Sharmagne Leland-St. John-Sylbert told me about what she heard from her friends concerning the circumstances surrounding Claudia's death:

> To the best of my knowledge, Claudia was on her way to Stan's beach house to fetch her belongings. She was definitely well on her way to breaking up with him.
>
> David Niven, Jr. told me she had been up all night, along with a young man who was staying at her home, doing some construction work. Evidently, she fell asleep behind the wheel of her Volkswagen, crossed over the line and impacted with the pickup truck on the Pacific Coast Highway.
>
> I was in New York on a modeling assignment when she died. My neighbor had seen it on the news and called to tell me. I immediately called Nivey, and his first words were "Claudia's dead."
>
> I was crushed, and October 3 is a sad spot on the calendar even to this day. I wrote in my diary that evening, "Jennings died today ... she who swore she'd never go away." [6]

Mimi Chesterton's old boyfriend from Evanston, Wisconsin reflected upon the news of her death and his overall impression of her life:

> The news of her death was deeply troubling to me. She came into my life and brightened it during a very dark time. Our relationship was mostly sweetness and light. The other, later, tawdrier stuff came to trouble me almost to the point of wanting to scold her, though I was hardly a paragon of homespun virtue myself. I just had to let that go, partly as concern about my own hypocrisy. I really wasn't very interested in the cast of characters accruing to her West

Coast legend out here in the Midwestern homeland. She was what she was to me. I liked her very much, respected her drive and spunk, was amazed (along with many others) at her rapid ascent into the national limelight in the pages of *Playboy*—had heard whiffs of her affairs before that (and reports of other shabby, debased behavior), but hadn't seen or followed her exploits other than an accidental sighting of her on *The Dating Game*. Maybe one late-night spot on *The Tonight Show*? I caught a glimpse of her that one time in the basement of Wieboldt's department store. She was speaking to one of her sisters, looking very un-Claudia-like—that is, no make-up, and hair pulled back. When I got news of her death, I could imagine the emotional "dead zone" she was living in, driving through. That was upsetting to contemplate. It made me very sad.

Joan Chesterton spoke for the family when she said, "It seemed as if the color had gone out of all of our lives."

Marilyn Grabowski spoke of the anger she felt at Claudia for leaving her so prematurely. It was an anger born out of helplessness, loss and the knowledge that a person who had been such an important part of her life was gone forever.

Many of Claudia's friends spoke of feelings that were similar—the shock, then an eruption of anguish and inconsolable grief.

Understandably, questions were raised almost as quickly as the news of Claudia's death reached the media. A majority of them centered on whether Claudia was doing drugs at the time of her accident. The coroner's tests for alcohol and drugs came back negative. A few of her good friends said they had heard she was up all night partying and must have fallen asleep at the wheel. Some of her other friends suggested she was distracted by something, such as putting on makeup or turning the radio dial.

It would be comforting to know the absolute truth, mainly because it would provide a measure of closure, at least on these points. Despite three years of research and interviews, there are no definitive answers as to what went on the night before or why she was going to Stan Herman's beach house.

The truth is, as bitter a pill it is to swallow, it makes no difference in the overall view of Claudia's life. Like in all tragedies, she was meant to be at that place at that exact time. Suppose she had left five minutes earlier or stopped to get gas! Unfortunately, she did not. Although the incident was incomprehensibly sad for her friends and family, Claudia achieved immortality in that moment. She will remain eternally beautiful and kind.

We are a society that looks for answers, thinking there must always be a rational resolution or a conspiracy behind unanswered phenomena. What is far more important than questions about Claudia's death is what we learn from her life. She was put on this Earth for a reason, as we all are. Her passions, her personality, her trials and her death were her inescapable fate. Claudia was a beautiful child, and she was taken from the world—for what purpose we can never hope to understand, although we try.

A celebration of Claudia's life was held at Bobby Hart's house on Woodrow Wilson. Hugh Hefner generously flew in Claudia's immediate and extended family and put them up at a very posh L.A. hotel, all at his expense. Over 300 friends of Claudia from all aspects of the entertainment business and all walks of life attended, including old friends like Marcia Wallace, Polly Bergen, Sally Kirkland and many others from Hollywood's elite. Danny Bonaduce of *The Partridge Family*, and famous actor David Jansen, also paid tribute to a woman who had touched all their lives. Of course, most

of the *Playboy* family was there. Ed Begley, Jr., Danny Janssen and others were there to support Bobby and say goodbye to Claudia. Stan Herman showed up, and according to Bobby Hart, the other attendees did not make him feel welcome and he left quickly. Before he did, Constance Chesterton remembered he went up to her, took one look and started crying. Dr. Jack Garfield brought Claudia's good friend Cheryl Ladd with him, which raised a few eyebrows. Some thought of it as a betrayal when the two got together shortly after Dr. Garfield and Claudia broke up. Under the circumstances, this all seems quite petty. There is little doubt Claudia herself didn't care what Dr. Jack and Cheryl Ladd were doing.

The guests were invited to come up and speak about their time with Claudia. In her role as ordained minister, Sally Kirkland presided the service. She told me about the experience when interviewed:

> Bobby asked me to conduct the service. It was also very healing for me to give the eulogy. Claudia meant so much to so many people. Her death left a void that nothing could ever fill, and the fact I could speak about her helped heal that wound.

Many other others got up to speak, from celebrities to everyday people to whom Claudia had shown kindness. One dear friend of hers could not speak; Keith Jennings took Claudia's death particularly hard. She had been his sister, his friend and his savior. Keith told me it took him almost five years to fully recover from Claudia's death.

After the Memorial was over and all the sad goodbyes and condolences were spoken to the Chestertons, a strange sense of reality crept back into everyone's life. It's the sense that life will never again be the same. Many people were stung by the fact that all that was left of her were memories. These memories carried with them barbs of regret and bitterness, in many cases.

Stan Herman wasted no time in approaching Claudia's family about a small business matter. He had lent Claudia $21,000, apparently to help purchase her home, and wanted it back. The Chestertons paid him out of Claudia's estate. Perhaps he was angry about an incident that took place several days earlier. Claudia's youngest sister Julie had gone to Herman's beach house to collect her possessions. When she tried to enter the house, a confrontation ensued, and Julie literally had to force her way in to gather her sister's belongings. Among them were some dresses, shoes and the record Bobby Hart had made for her, its sleeve portrait of Claudia now torn and faded.

Claudia's ashes, per her request, were scattered in the waters of the Pacific by the Neptune Society.

Claudia's longtime friend Sally Kirkland wrote a tribute to her in the *Los Angeles Times* a few weeks after the accident. She kindly allowed me to reprint it for this book.

To Claudia Jennings:
Memories of a DareAngel
by Sally Kirkland

I remember, while acting in an off-Broadway play in New York in 1969, reading a review by the infamous John Simon about a girl named Claudia Jennings. The play was *Dark of the Moon*.

"She is a completely lovely girl with something sensitive, vulnerable perhaps, even haunted in her eyes and around her mouth. She makes the spotlight light up as no wattage could do it. At all times, she makes you forget the dismalness of the play she is trapped in and such a shot in the arm can set an un-fabulous invalid like our theater dancing."

She couldn't have been more than 19, had apparently graduated from a straight-A honor student from Evanston High, Illinois (top cheerleader and all) and Mimi Chesterton had already changed her name to Claudia Jennings (to not embarrass her younger sisters) to do the centerfold of *Playboy* magazine. She spent four months off Broadway, flew to L.A., met and moved in with songwriter-producer Bobby Hart and moved into Gower Champion's old house on Woodrow Wilson Drive—and took off again to do the road company of *Lenny*. While hugging her after the show in San Francisco, Mrs. Lenny (Honey) Bruce told her, "Thank God it was you!" Her performance, from those who saw it, was "stunningly good." In 1970 she was named Playmate of the Year and began a film career that ultimately pegged her "Queen of the Bs." She began a string of starring roles for Roger Corman and somewhere in that period, between 1972 and 1973, I met her.

Our relationship began when she asked me to come over and "teach everybody yoga." I was just out from New York, and even though I had a year of plays involving "nudity," I was resistant and suspicious of any girl who would do a Hefner centerfold. She was only one of the most devastatingly beautiful women I had ever met, and at first I tried to be jealous. Here she was, starring in films (B-films though they be), Playmate of the Year, living with a gorgeous and talented man, sharing his mini-mansion, making money hand over foot herself. But it was impossible to be jealous of Claudia because she would love you too much.

She took me in as if I was a long-lost child. She dressed me for auditions in her finest silks, took me out to dinner with Bobby Hart, invited me to Thanksgivings and Christmases at their house and basically gave me my first L.A. home.

When a lot of my New York Actors Studio friends started "making it"—à la Al Pacino and Bobby De Niro—she gave me her house to celebrate their success and "L.A. arrival," and provided what became for me a social sanctuary, for me and all my displaced New York actor and musician friends.

When my own house burned down in 1975 and I lost all my possessions, except the suit on my back, she took me into her walk-in closets and said, "Take anything you want." I said "You can't be serious—anything?" She said, "Anything." I'm still wearing her dresses and silk suits.

She and Bobby created something of an ashram with the house they shared for the six years they were together. They had a special synergy together. Their love spilled over to hundreds of people. Judging from the day of the memorial service at Bobby's house, Claudia affected many people—all of her "strays," from myself and Marcia Wallace to the 13-year-old ex-groupie, and the grocery boy fired the same day he met Claudia, and the 20 or so others who stood up and cried unabashedly as they shared her unconditional generosity and love, and the other 300 (mostly industry) who cried and laughed and cried along with those of us speaking.

No character she ever played could be as colorful as she was herself. Every time I talked to her she had just jetted back from Europe, where she had dinner with Brigitte Bardot or had been photographed by the five most important photographers of beautiful women, or she was recovering from professional roller-skating in *Unholy Rollers*, learning how to drive 18-wheeler trucks in *Truck Stop Women*, driving speedboats through the swamps of the bayou in *'Gator Bait*, having accidents on a motorcycle in *Deathsport*, then going off to sell some condos and buy Ava Gardner's old house to remodel it, and doing some art directing and styling with Marilyn Grabowski on the side.

Her mother, Joan Chesterton, told me, "We as a family feel we have lost a part of ourselves: The daring part. The part that loved the center of the stage. We feel like we have lost the color of our lives. She made everything so vivid around her."

Just before Claudia died she lost out to Shelley Hack in what was purported to have been a brilliant screen test to replace Kate Jackson in *Charlie's Angels*, and she was up for starring roles in four films: Stephen Spielberg's *Used Cars*, Bob Rafelson's *The Postman Always Rings Twice*, Irwin Yablans' *Fade to Black*, and Jeff Bloom's *Blood Beach*. And she died October 3, 1979, at age 29, in a car wreck on the Pacific Coast Highway.[7]

Ms. Kirkland's tribute captured Claudia's story and spirit while appropriately avoiding any hint of her troubles. It sums up Claudia's kindness and generosity and gives a sense of how much good she did while alive. The end of the article is quite abrupt, and gives a perfect sense of the terrible speed and devastation of her death.

Todd McCarthy, her old classmate from Evanston Township High School, wrote an obituary for her in *Variety*. He admitted he wrote a fairly generic piece, leaving out

the personal relationship he had with Mimi back in high school and sticking to her career data. He would note later that very few media outlets reported on Claudia's death, and those that bothered did so in a cursory manner.[8] Was this because of her *Playboy* background, the fact her movie career was in a slump at that point or because she had acquired a reputation as a partier? It might have been all of those, including the fact there was no social media at that time, no E! network or *Entertainment Tonight*.

Bobby Hart lived with his pain and his own set of memories, then met current wife Mary Ann and eventually married the lovely and wonderful lady. He still wrote and performed music. By 1983, he penned an Oscar-nominated song for the film *Tender Mercies*. Unfortunately, Bobby lost another dear friend when his partner Tommy Boyce died shortly after suffering a brain aneurysm in 1994. Mr. Hart, however, is still going strong and still touring and working today, primarily with Mickey Dolenz of The Monkees.

Of all the people I've interviewed for this book, Bobby Hart is the individual who, in particular, stands out. His courage, compassion and inner peace seem beyond what most human beings are capable of in the face of the anguish he has faced. He kept a quiet, cool demeanor in Hollywood, surrounded by sordid personalities, decadent lifestyles and every possible excess known to man. I believe he loved Claudia long after she was taken away. He and Claudia were a good couple. They were both one of a kind: compassionate and caring, with Claudia's wild streak balanced by Bobby's contemplative nature.

As for the rest of Claudia's friends and family, there's always that appalling shock that strikes one when a person we love is taken away from us so young and so suddenly. Most of them never had a chance to say goodbye, and we will always be left wondering if there was anything that could have been done to prevent the accident.

Barry Richards told me of some eerie coincidences that happened after Claudia died:

> One night my girlfriend and I were asleep in Bobby's house. All of a sudden, she woke up terrified and screamed. She had dreamt she was Claudia, driving in her car just as the accident happened.
>
> I had bought Claudia an antique crib as a gift one year. I thought she might like it, because she wanted children someday. Well, after she died, I took it and had it my house. One night a storm came by and knocked down a bunch of things on top of it, crushing the crib. It was eerie.
>
> However it wasn't as eerie as what happened to a portrait of Bobby and Claudia I had given them as a gift. Shortly before he married Mary Ann I brought the portrait to my place. I put it in a spare room and propped it up against a bookshelf. Well, right after Bobby and Mary Ann's wedding, somehow the bookcase, despite the fact it was bolted into the wall, had fallen over and destroyed its picture frame.

With the advent of VHS, DVD and Blu-ray, many of Claudia's films are now available. Some of her more obscure titles are out of print. She still has an enormous Internet and cult following. Claudia is mentioned in books about movies of the 1970s, B-movies, drive-in movies, the films of Roger Corman and similar subjects. It is through her films that she lives on, just as all of our celluloid chimeras do.

[1] Hart, Bobby with Glenn Ballantyne, *Psychedelic Bubble Gum: Boyce & Hart, The Monkees, and Turning Mayhem Into Miracles* (New York: SelectBooks, 2015)
[2] E-mail interview, May 2014
[3] E-mail interview, May 2014
[4] Phone interview, June 2014
[5] E-mail interview, May 2014
[6] E-mail interview, September 2017
[7] Kirkland, Sally, "Memories of a DareAngel," *Los Angeles Times*, November 11, 1979
[8] McCarthy, Todd, "Claudia Jennings: Before the Beginning and After the End," *Film Comment*, Vol. 15, No. 6, November-December 1979

Chapter 9:
The Good is Oft Interred With Their Bones

Hypocrisy seems to be the common denominator that has imbued our culture, more than money, sex, charity and every other noble or ignoble human desire or trait. Society tends to build up our icons with dizzying speed then take delight in their fall, whether the unfortunate idol is guilty or innocent.

The media and now social media help feed this frenzy by giving multiple opportunities to praise, malign or distort any individual's life. A careless post on Facebook can now come back to haunt that poster, even it were first written 10 years ago. It is ridiculously easy to cast the first stone and then run away, without consequences.

The previous chapters have demonstrated that Claudia Jennings was a person who positively impacted all who knew her.

Long after she died, however, the media, in various forms, sometimes shone an unfavorable light upon Claudia's life. These stories created perhaps a false narrative that was contrary to those who were closest to her and how they believed her to be. The result of these stories infuriated Claudia's family and friends. As stated earlier, it was their outrage that in part motivated me to tell her story in a more positive manner.

During her lifetime very few people, if any, had a negative word to say about Claudia as a person. Movie critics as a whole did not think much of her acting abilities, of course, but the vast majority of people separated her personal and professional life.

Over 300 people attended Claudia's celebration of life memorial service; yet in the years that passed, it seemed her legacy became intentionally sullied. In most instances, these unfortunate portrayals of Claudia reached only limited audiences. However, one spectacle in particular was a nationally televised dagger to the heart of Claudia's reputation.

Of course, there were people who emphasized Claudia's many fine qualities. The most notable has been Roger Corman, who has been completely consistent in his admiration of Claudia, and has been her advocate since she passed away. Bobby Hart has also been an honest commentator on her life, remaining remarkably objective about some memories that are no doubt painful.

'B-movie queen' killed in crash

MALIBU, Calif. (UPI) — Actress Claudia Jennings, 29, the 1970 Playboy magazine Playmate of the Year who transferred her pinup talents to motion pictures as "Queen of the B-movies," was killed Wednesday in an auto accident in California.

Miss Jennings, who specialized in playing tough women who lived hard and drove fast, died after her small car swerved across the center divider of Pacific Coast Highway and smashed into an oncoming truck.

She died as she was being removed from the wreckage. The truck driver, Craig Bennell, 19, of Rancho Palos Verdes, was treated at a hospital and released.

Miss Jennings was proud of her skill as a driver, which she said she had learned watching the professionals in making action-oriented movies such as "Truck Stop Women" and "Deathsport."

"YOU NAME IT, I've done it," she once said.

"I know my way around motorcycles, horses, cars, guns. I can do karate or drive a truck," she had said, adding, "You give me one of those big 18-wheelers, and I can turn it around right out in the middle of the street."

Born Mimi Chesterton, she changed her name — to protect her parents in the Midwest from embarrassment, she said — when she appeared in Playboy as "Miss November" in 1969.

Miss Jennings was later chosen Playmate of the Year, an honor that brought in lucrative prizes and helped her get movie roles.

PLAYBOY ALSO featured her in subsequent layouts — including one last month that dubbed her "Queen of the B-movies" for her appearances in films such as "Unholy Rollers," "Fast Company" and "The Great Texas Dynamite Case."

She was unmarried but said she lived with song writer Bobby Hart for five years.

THE BODY OF ACTRESS Claudia Jennings, right. She died in a collision with a truck Wednesday on lies covered with a sheet in a mangled convertible. the Pacific Coast Highway in California.

Although Claudia is beloved by her many fans, and they of course worship her as a cult queen, chronicles of her life have ignored her virtues. This is not difficult to understand. Claudia's life was exciting; she was a Playmate of the Year, she appeared nude in many of her films and she is deceased. She cannot defend herself, which makes her the perfect target for anyone seeking to sensationalize her life.

Apart from the obituaries that were published after her death, very little information about Claudia's life was made public. All that changed in the mid- to late-1990s when a movie, a television special and two seminal articles appeared.

Todd McCarthy, the well respected film critic for *Variety* and an award-winning filmmaker, put together a documentary on his former classmate called *Claudia Jennings*. The film used clips from her movies to explore her career and her tragic death, but not much more.

In early 1999, Keith Jennings, upset that there was very little favorable information about Claudia and very little information at all, decided he would let the world know the real Claudia Jennings. Remember, Claudia felt obligated to keep Keith in the dark about her partying activities because of his relative youth and innocence.

Jennings started out by sending letters to the programs and networks that used biographies and documentaries as part of their programming: the E! Network, Biography and A&E. Keith was initially turned down by all of them. A few weeks later, a producer from E! called back and said they were now interested in doing an episode on Claudia for the *E! True Hollywood Story*. He told them he had to be a part of the production, or he could not get Bobby Hart and few of Claudia's other best friends to participate.

Keith, given assurances he would have input on content and the individual interviews on the program, was satisfied despite being leery of the show's tabloid reputation. Unfortunately, in his enthusiasm over the fact the project was green-lighted, Jennings felt he could control the show's producers and show a side of Claudia previously unknown to the public. He would find out to his regret that he was mistaken and naïve. The truth is the *E! The True Hollywood Story* segment on Claudia would be appealing to the worst instincts of its viewing public. Keith arranged for Marcia Wallace, Bobby Hart, Barry Richards, Roger Corman, Keith Allison and Sally Kirkland to be interviewed, and felt the program was progressing well.

What happened next is a disturbing example of best intentions gone wrong. Instead of being a sweet tribute to the most beautiful and kind individual Keith had ever known, the show painted an incredibly dark portrait of Claudia. Gossipy, salacious and lacking balance, the show portrayed Claudia as a drug-addicted train wreck. Horrified, Keith Jennings went back to the executives and complained he never intended the program to be such a hatchet job on Claudia's life. The producers dismissed his efforts and told

E! CLAUDIA JENNINGS: THE E! TRUE HOLLYWOOD STORY Playmate Claudia Jennings was turning her life around after tumultuous times, until a tragic accident in 1979 ended it all. (In Stereo) ⓒ him the show would air without further alteration. Then, the show's producer, Charla Smith, informed Jennings that they were cutting him out of the production. She emphasized that if Jennings became a public nuisance or tried any legal action, the program would delete all the interviews from Claudia's friends and his participation.

When word got out how Keith had been treated, many friends of Claudia's refused to participate. The program had already alienated her family, who declined to have anything to do with the show. To add insult to injury, the story of how close Keith and Claudia actually were was changed to strongly imply that Keith was just a crazed fan, so enthralled with the beautiful actress, that he took her name as his own legal one. This was a very personal and humiliating slap in the face to a young man who only wanted to show the world what an extraordinary and sweet individual Claudia was. However, documentaries about the positive aspects of sweet, young mid-Western girls who move to Hollywood was not the story that E! wanted to tell.

The Chesterton family was so upset they refused to speak to any media until this book. Joan Chesterton did not want to cooperate with the producers, and was profoundly shocked when she saw the program. She even cut off all communication with Bobby Hart because he appeared in it. This was despite the fact Bobby said only positive things about Claudia. To Joan, the show was so offensive, no one who cared about Claudia should have appeared in the program lest, they give the impression of endorsing its point of view. It must be remembered that these people were simply interviewed about Claudia's life, but they did not see the editing of how their participation was used in the actual narrative until the show was aired. And by that time it was too late to back away. Apparently, Bobby tried to convince Joan by saying if the people who cared about Claudia refused to do the show, it would only leave the pulpit to her detractors.

"The Life/Untimely Death: Playmate Claudia Jennings" *The E! True Hollywood Story* does not start well, beginning with the title, emphasizing her association with *Playboy* and not stressing her extensive acting career. The narrator then solemnly intones, "Her personal life was outrageous as her films" and that she was just another girl attracted by the "lure of Hollywood, and suffered the fate of those who get mesmerized by it." [1] Her longtime friend, Marilyn Grabowski, calls her a "sexual predator" while the narrator says self-righteously, "She seduced her way across Hollywood."[2]

The producers then run a smarmy sound bite from David Carradine, who respected Claudia immensely, but states, "She liked to take her clothes off." Moreover, we hear the narrator intoning, "Her addiction to cocaine cost her a career."

The host of the show is Ari Bass, given credit as Claudia's biographer because, for a while, he considered writing a book about her and other cult film stars; however, the closest he got was an article in *Femme Fatales* magazine. Bass, to his credit, was the first one to look into Claudia's fascinating life with any depth. Bass does keep his objectivity throughout the program; unfortunately, he functions mostly as a bridge between the people with unsavory comments about Claudia and those who remembered her fondly.

The show deliberately edits interviews to put Claudia in a bad light. Ava Cherry, who spent time with David Bowie and Claudia for a while, strongly implies in essence that she was a drug-consuming trollop. Cherry's comments were mostly limited to which of *The Rolling Stones* Claudia had slept with and how much noise she made when making love. It's a shame the producers didn't ask more interesting questions of Cherry, who is a fabulous entertainer, and who I'm positive could have given us better insight into Claudia's life.

After David Bowie died, Jake Malooley interviewed Ava Cherry in the *Chicago Reader* on January 13, 2016. Nearly 17 years after the E! program was televised, Ms. Cherry's memories of Claudia appeared to have altered. Her response to a question of what happened when she and Bowie broke up was as follows:

> So then what happened was I was hanging out with my girlfriend who was a *Playboy* playmate, Claudia Jennings—she was a model and an actress, but she died in a car crash in 1979.
>
> Claudia said, "Come on, let's go to Jamaica until you figure out what you're going to do. Truthfully, I really felt like someone had come and rescued me. Claudia had a nice house in the Hollywood Hills with Bobby Hart.

After a short while, Bowie and Cherry reunited, and with Bowie having nowhere to stay in Los Angeles, she asked Claudia for help:

> I asked Claudia if he could stay. She said, "Yeah, no problem." Well, it turns out she had the use of Robert Wagner and Natalie Wood's apartment in Century City. So that's where the three of us went.

A little later on in the interview, Cherry was asked about a coke spoon that was part of an exhibit of Bowie artifacts at the Museum of Contemporary Art:

> Everybody was doing it. The thing that got him into coke was Hollywood.

Ms. Cherry's comments on the E! program did not reflect how kind Claudia was at her time of need, nor did they give the perspective on drug use at the time, as her more recent comments reflect.

However, the single worst segment is the so-called interview with Hugh Hefner. In essence more a series of brief sound bites than an interview, Hefner comes across as self-aggrandizing and a dark, unsympathetic character. The observer listens to Hef say at least three times:

> She told me I was the first man to make love to her ... I have no idea whether it was true or not.[3]

It seems odd he would have nothing else to comment on besides a sex act (of course his other comments could have been edited out). For all the stories of how much Claudia respected him and felt she owed him her career, Hefner did not reciprocate on the E! program. If he did, the producers did not include it in the documentary. As for the quote, we know that Claudia was not a virgin when she encountered Hefner for the first time, rendering his statement even more fatuous.

A Biography

The show also allows Hefner to have the last word, another major mistake on the producers' part. It strongly implies that posing for *Playboy* was the only thing Claudia had accomplished in her brief life. His final words, "I miss her"—ring hollow and give the piece a suitably depressing denouement.[4]

It is curious that, except for Ava Cherry—who, to her credit, is brave enough to admit doing cocaine with Claudia—no other person who spoke negatively of Claudia would confess to any indiscretions. Are we to believe no one else did drugs or had sex in Los Angeles during the 1970s?

Fortunately for Claudia, Keith Jennings speaks about the person he knew and loved. His is the kindest and most gentle appraisal of what Claudia meant to other people. Marcia Wallace and Sally Kirkland have the opportunity to say something positive about her, although Marcia Wallace does mention Claudia's affair with Warren Beatty. The interviews with Barry Richards, Roger Corman, Keith Allison and, of course, Bobby Hart attempt to balance out the negative. Other than that, it is a very depressing and sleazy spectacle. The producers also rather underhandedly stack the deck against Claudia by emphasizing interviews with people who barely knew Claudia, as opposed to those who knew her best.

As for Keith Jennings, he has lived these many years feeling the guilt of, as he put it, "Serving Claudia's head on a platter to E!" Although the program briefly reminds viewers at the end that Claudia was cleaning herself up and receiving better scripts for consideration, but the damage was complete, and the show had fulfilled its mission. All Keith had from the experience was credit as creative consultant. E! piled enough dirt on Claudia's reputation to obliterate the sweet, caring, generous person that her friends in Hollywood knew her to be.

Keith blamed himself, but truthfully, it was not his fault. He had the best intentions, but was not ready to battle the power of a network. It's also difficult to blame E! entirely, although the show was a character assassination. A leopard cannot change its spots, and E! did what was in their nature. They found an irresistible victim, one incapable of defending herself, and they pounced without mercy in telling Claudia's story as sordidly as possible. E! was responsible for steering the production in the direction it went. Tabloid TV will always produce something that is negative, sensational and exploitative, pushing every button that will appeal to prurient interests, and this should not be surprising. The producers never intended to put Claudia in a positive light. That wasn't the story they wanted to tell, and that wasn't the story that would sell the program and get them ratings. Unfortunately, Claudia was victimized yet again. But this should not be surprising since ratings are the be all and end all of television. Perhaps, Keith was naïve, however, but there is no question he was a good person who was played by the producers.

The article by Ari Bass in *Femme Fatales*, published in July of 2000, though seen by a smaller number of people, has superior research, crisp prose and gives a better account of her life. It is the most comprehensive story of Claudia's life we have had until now. The producers at E! probably felt confident in calling Ari Bass Claudia's biographer because of what Bass told *Femme Fatales*. The editor, Bill George, states Bass spent six years researching Claudia's life, and was preparing to release a biography soon.[5]

Bass analyzes Claudia in this manner:

> I think she was someone who didn't know herself and created an alternate personality—someone who could tear through men and be a powerful person, at least on-screen. She seemed to have a habit of falling for older men of some power and means, who would not challenge her to find out who she really was. The only one who did was Bobby Hart, and she discarded him after five years.[6]

Bass certainly makes a strong argument for his theories in the article and does give a fact-filled, colorful, concise condensed version of Claudia's life, from being born Mimi Chesterton, to noting her films and *Playboy* pictorials and includes many short interviews with her friends, lovers and show business associates. He does a fine job of assessing her career, including her television appearances and her films. He gives a good account of the time, late in her life, when Claudia must have thought about the path she was heading toward. Bass recognizes this as her epiphany, and chronicles how she begins to reclaim her soul. Bass does give more copy space to her detractors and to the crowd with whom Claudia enjoyed partying. Bobby Hart, once more, is her champion, giving earnest, heartfelt testimony to her kindness.

The last portion of the article very nearly ruins the work, however, as he creatively concocts a graphic picture of the day she died. He states that Claudia fell asleep at the wheel of her car, which was never proven as absolute fact. Bass then provides a fictional account, in somewhat graphic detail, of what went through her mind the instant she woke up in the mini-seconds before colliding with the other vehicle. Considering how well-written and researched the rest of the article is, it is a shame this portion had to be included, as all I really needed to hear were the facts, not imaginative supposition. It is difficult to read, for obvious reasons, and is disturbing; however, it certainly gives a dimension to the absolute horror and nightmarish aspect of the accident, despite the fact it is pure conjecture. Overall, considering the paucity of written research about Claudia, Bass' article is a great achievement.

There was one other seminal article—the one that inspired this book, written for the *Chicago Reader* in September 2000 by an old Evanston Township High School classmate, Albert Williams. The article appeared around the same time the E! program and the *Femme Fatales* piece came out. Mr. Williams is a gifted writer and by all accounts a wonderful man, and he paints a flattering portrait of Mimi Chesterton. The article's tone gets progressively unforgiving as it discusses her transformation to Claudia Jennings. He also quotes a line from the Beatles song "A Day in the Life": "He blew his mind out in a car" when discussing the context of the year when Todd McCarthy filmed *Mimi*. Considering the manner in which she died, it shows questionable judgment. The article's overall tone is baffling, because another ETHS grad interviewed for this book stated that Williams adored Mimi, and Williams even states in the piece, "She was one of the nicest kids I knew."[7]

Therein lies the problem with Mr. Williams' article. It gives the impression that Mimi Chesterton was the only legitimate manifestation of the girl they knew in high school. The article makes it appear that as soon as Mary Eileen deviated from the cheerleader/National Honor Society image, her status as a good person dropped considerably. The mood of the article changes, with relatively harsh quotes from former lovers and high school classmates. But how would any of us fare if we were judged by the comments of our high school classmates many decades after the fact?

It is most confusing, then, that Williams is also highly ambivalent about the E! program and of Bass' intentions. He rightly takes offense at Hugh Hefner's quotes casting them as "grating" when the show revealed he used the threat to publish old photos of Mimi in the magazine if she did not do a fresh pictorial. Williams also looks sourly on E!'s and Bass' attempts to capitalize on Claudia's fame; Bass with his proposed book on B-movie icons and E! with their video catalogue of her movies.

Williams occasionally praises the *E! True Hollywood Story* program, noting it isn't bad for "tabloid TV," but that's the point. The episode *was* tabloid TV, and though it may have shown the briefest glimpse of Mimi's wonderful attributes, it emphasized her darkest days while painting the facts of her life only in the ominous hues. The show's purpose seemingly was to focus on the alleged lasciviousness and moral turpitude of Claudia's final years.

Mr. Williams also praises the show for putting Claudia's supposed personality conflict into perspective:

> It juggles contradictory assessments of her personality to suggest—I think accurately—that she was a conflicted person torn between self-sufficient sex goddess "Claudia Jennings" and eager-to-please, slightly insecure Mimi Chesterton.[8]

The article also has a brief interview with Joan Chesterton, the final time the family would speak to the media before now:

> The producer of the E! segment sent me a tape, and it was one of the smarmiest things I'd ever seen. It showed some child actress dead on the floor from drugs. The only reaction you could have possibly had was "yuck." There was very little interest in my daughter as a person and much interest in her as a Playmate, God save us all. We had a daughter who was such a straight arrow until she wound up with *Playboy*.[9]

Albert Williams ends his article with a somewhat dubious conclusion. He states that Ari Bass and Charla Smith, the producer, were sincere in their efforts to put Mimi's life into a cultural context. Yes, Claudia threw herself into the swinging 1970s, the world of *Playboy* and Hollywood, but the method E! used was more about sleaze and ratings than cultural anthropology.

Williams' final comments also come off as a mild putdown of Claudia's life. He speaks of people making mistakes in their 20s, learning from them and then regretting them; yet he adds that no one would want to be remembered for them. In this context, Williams has made it difficult for the reader to create the proper assessment of who Claudia/Mimi is, given the contrasting arguments presented in his article. He also ignores the fact that hundreds of entertainers, politicians and even chefs have made millions of dollars by reminiscing about their youthful transgressions, and even reveling in them. Almost none of them have ever apologized or said publically they regret a single moment.

The final statement also implies Claudia should have had much to regret. The only reason Claudia might be remembered for the less savory times in her life is directly because of programs such as the *E! True Hollywood Story*. While it's true those that loved her weren't swayed by the show, it's equally true the ones who thought ill of her only had their worst instincts about Claudia confirmed. What goes unanswered is what the person unfamiliar with her story and life would think if this was their one and only source of information.

One other book has come out that offers a deeper glimpse into Claudia's life: Bobby Hart's *Psychedelic Bubble Gum*, co-written with Glenn Ballantyne in 2015.

Bobby Hart's book is insightful, painfully honest at times, and conveys the deep relationship he and Claudia shared. The book does not delve into Claudia's career as much as it describes an incredible woman who made life better for those around her. By the end, one has to marvel at the strength of character and the vast ocean of faith that Bobby Hart must possess to have endured such trying times. Their relationship lasted almost six years, which is remarkable when one reflects back on how challenging their lives must have been. Claudia was gone almost constantly, making movies or traveling, and despite being very much in love, forces both internal and external were tearing at them. It may be a cliché, but in life, timing is everything. Although only 10 years separated them, the couple came from two different generations. As Claudia grew older into her own personality, Bobby was quite comfortable in his own, and he had settled into a quiet life of meditation and service. Claudia felt conflict from two opposing desires—wanting to settle down and start a family of her own and the natural urge to take advantage of the life of a Hollywood starlet. The book is not entirely devoted to his relationship with Claudia, but gives us some never-before-revealed insights into the complex individual that was Claudia Jennings.

Daredevil Movie Actress Killed in Car-Truck Crash

BY RICHARD WEST
Times Staff Writer

Actress Claudia Jennings, who specialized in hard-boiled roles and high-speed chases in the movies, once told an interviewer that she could do just about anything with a car, a motorcycle or even a truck.

"You give me one of those big 18-wheelers and I can turn it around right out in the middle of the street," said the star of such films as "Truck Stop Woman," "Unholy Rollers," "The Great Texas Dynamite Chase" and "Deathsport."

But Miss Jennings' luck ran out at 9:15 a.m. Wednesday as she was driving her little Volkswagen convertible north on the Pacific Coast Highway in Malibu.

At Topanga Canyon Blvd., the California Highway Patrol said, Miss Jennings' car swerved across the center line for some unexplained reason and crushed head-on into a pickup truck.

The 29-year-old actress died as she was being removed from the wreckage.

The driver of the pickup truck, Craig Bennell, 19, of Rancho Palos Verdes, suffered minor injuries. He was treated at Santa Monica Hospital and released.

I did find one other book that gave me no actual insight into Claudia but spoke volumes about the times she lived in and one of the biggest influences on her life. I cited it in Chapter 3, but I offer it here as an exhibit of everything negatively written or said or shown about Claudia.

The book was *Mr. Playboy: Hugh Hefner and the American Dream*, written by Dr. Steven Watts of the University of Missouri. His other books have been about other American cultural and corporate icons such as Henry Ford, Dale Carnegie and Disneyland. I was eager to read the book, positive that I would find some valuable information about Claudia courtesy of Hefner himself. To my shock, there was not a single mention of Claudia in the entire volume. Here was a woman, the *de facto* den mother to his Mansion's Bunnies, his magazine's most popular model in the 1970s, a movie star and one of the most charismatic people in Hollywood being completely ignored in a comprehensive story about his life. Of course, this doesn't even take into account her tragic death and the effect it had on hundreds of people in Hefner's organization.

I began a correspondence with Dr. Watts to see if there was some reason, or if there had been an oversight in the work responsible for Claudia's exclusion. He simply replied that Mr. Hefner felt he could only mention those people who were instrumental to his story, that he never mentioned her in any interview and that she seemed, at best, only a marginal part of his life.[10]

I don't think it's possible intellectually for him to have forgotten her; he was, after all, a brilliant man with a razor-sharp mind. *Playboy* has continued to profit from her likeness, including her image in many Playmate of the Year anniversary collections over the years. The continued use of her photos contradicts Claudia's seeming unimportance to the empire. While Hefner and *Playboy* have venerated lesser lights in both the beauty and entertainment world, Claudia remains an orphan ghost.

Her absence from Hefner's story seems like an aberration. There are literally hundreds of Playmates and Playmates of the Year mentioned in Watts' book, in some cases with minute details from over 50 years ago. Hefner also mentions dozens of Playmates who had brief, superfluous acting careers, appearing in only one or two films. Therefore, it is inconceivable that Hugh Hefner would leave Claudia out of his story and the history of *Playboy*, considering what we know about the man and the organization—unless a clear reason existed that severed the ties between the two. Claudia was never banned from the Playboy Mansion, which would have been a sign that her relationship with Hefner was compromised. What seems to make the most sense was that Hefner had a cold and ruthless personality. Despite the fact Claudia saw him as a father figure and as one of her biggest supporters, he most likely used her in a personal and business sense and then quickly tossed her aside. Or, perhaps she was never as important to Hefner as Hefner was to her? Or did Claudia burn bridges with Hef? Why else then couldn't he even say a few kind words about her in his biography?

Perhaps it was because of all the above reasons that Hefner and *Playboy* declined the opportunity to speak with me about Claudia, or cooperate in telling her story. Perhaps part of the *Playboy* philosophy is never to speak ill of the dead.

In a way, Claudia's absence from Dr. Watts' book sums up the way the entertainment community has treated her. Outside of her friends, loved ones, a few cult movie writers and a hardcore group of fans, the memory of Claudia is fading a bit more each year, like a wraith, or a piece of some exquisite but worn lace.

There is one more story, an incident that occurred after Claudia's death, which speaks volumes about how she was viewed as a woman and a professional. Constance Chesterton was at Chicago film critic Roger Ebert's home watching one of Claudia's movies. Constance, who had become very good friends with the Eberts (her husband had stood up at Roger's wedding), was becoming a bit uncomfortable viewing the film. Ebert, whom she described as being one of the kindest individuals she'd ever met, stopped the movie at one point, sensing her anxiety, and said, "Isn't it wonderful that your sister got the opportunity to do what she always wanted to do at age 21?" Constance explained that from that moment on, she looked at Claudia and her career in a new light, a triumph of her will and discipline. After all, this is what Claudia's life was about. She loved to entertain people and it took amazing courage to accomplish what she did.

Keith Jennings told me:

Bruce Kimmel and Ann Gibbs, writers of *The Facts Of Life* TV series, were going to be working with me on a movie based on Claudia's life. I had met them through my friends actress Lisa Whelchel (Blair) and Geri Jewell (Cousin Geri).

We put quite a few hours of work in on the project. But when they approached Claudia's mom Joan about the film, she had her attorney send a cease and desist letter. So the project died. Now you also have to remember this was about 1982 or 1983, and Claudia's family was still in mourning.

Keith spoke of meetings he had with several prominent Hollywood producers after Claudia died:

> I met with three very powerful men that Claudia worked with: Quinn Martin, Aaron Spelling and Sherwood Schwartz. I also had the opportunity to speak with Roger Corman. Each one said they loved her and her work and wanted to keep using her in their productions. She did many Quinn Martin television shows (he was a very nice and open man) and Aaron Spelling ones as well. Of course during our meeting [Spelling] told me about *Charlie's Angels* and about wanting her for *Dynasty*. As a tribute to her, after Claudia's death, he named Linda Evans' character Crystal Jennings. Sherwood wanted to work with her again and said they just loved and admired her on the set of *The Brady Bunch* episode, "Adios Johnny Bravo."

The above statement only reinforces the fact that Claudia's career might have thrived and grown. She was not at a dead-end in her career. Claudia was neither hopeless nor helpless.

The sad fact is that it's all too easy to judge Claudia; we think her immune to pressure and that her beauty guaranteed happiness. No doubt Claudia felt she had to live up to expectations that were in reality unreasonable for any human being to achieve.

My opinion is that Mimi Chesterton simply grew up and became an adult. Unfortunately, she had to undergo her rite of passage in a situation that would put immense pressure on her, not to mention present an extraordinary volume of temptation from her peers. As Claudia, she underwent a culture shock, going from a strict middle-class home to the rarefied air of Laurel Canyon. The 1970s were also a unique time in American history. Cocaine and the drug scene were more prevalent than at any other time, even the 1980s.

These days the bar is set much lower. When comparing modern Hollywood actors and some of their indiscretions to Claudia's, she was mostly a paragon of virtue by comparison. The royalty of the entertainment and sports industry seem to miraculously rebound from multiple stints at rehab, sexual assault charges, spousal abuse, accusations of theft and a surfeit of DUI.

In my heart of hearts, perhaps the best way I can describe Claudia is that she was complicated. Some point to her altruism and say it was a ruse to mask her materialism. Others suggest her drug use as being indicative of self-destructive behavior. Her critics say her sex life was out of control, and showed signs of some mental instability or abnormality.

I disagree with all of these assumptions. Claudia's life was like a puzzle, only with a few key pieces missing. Locked within her was a deep pain, possibly the result of some unknown trauma or abuse that will never be revealed. It would explain a lot about this wonderful woman. Claudia had several traits in common with other victims of abuse. Of course, this does not guarantee she was subject to such a horrible event. She was not self-destructive, as others have labeled her behavior. Claudia was asking for help towards the end of her life, and was helping herself. Her love and generosity were genuine and yes, as real as her fondness for shopping, so there was no personality conflict. As you read in some of the interviews, some of Claudia's friends spoke both favorably and unfavorably about her. There was only Mary Eileen "Mimi" Chesterton, who changed her name to Claudia Jennings for show business purposes—a talented, beautiful and yes, troubled woman at times, who wanted to be a star.

I have tried to give you the clearest picture of Claudia Jennings that I could. My opinion is that you should consider her whole life, not just a relatively small portion of it.

This book is my answer to all her critics—those who denigrated her career, and the few vindictive individuals who spoke ill of her personal life. The forgotten tragedy is all the horrible things that have been said about Claudia do not bother her. She is in a place where the cruel words and acid comments can't hurt her. Instead, it is her friends and family that have borne the pain and humiliation of the thoughtless and insensitive remarks all these years.

When you remember Claudia, think about her life story. How many women did the things she did, saw what she saw and experienced an incredible life so dramatic that if you read about in a magazine you would scarcely believe that it was all true? She was a true icon for women and for all of us.

I believe love for her sisters, friends and Bobby kept her focused and determined up until the end of her life. I think she wanted more than anything to regain the spark of her early days in Hollywood. I know she wanted to be there for her sisters. Moreover, there is no doubt that as unlikely as it may seem, Claudia wanted a family of her own. Those are all powerful incentives for a woman like Claudia to find her way home. If you are aware of the dynamics of individuals caught in the grips of an addiction illness, you know one can only let go and hope they land softly before it is too late. I believe that is what Bobby and her friends were waiting for, and I believe that is why Claudia went to Bobby that early autumn day, to ask for guidance.

In terms of her movie career, there are a number of fans that are dedicated to keeping her memory alive. However, movie stars—even icons—can fade, and the further we go forward in time, the more difficult it is to see them. It is almost as if Claudia stands on a seashore covered in fog, and as our boat recedes, her image becomes fainter and fainter.

She will always look at us with her incredible green eyes, the remarkable features and wry smile. There will never be another actress like her, who had the combination of looks, style and attitude that dominated a genre and charmed her fans. She was confident and graceful, with her striking posture and imposing "take-charge" attitude; Claudia showed American cinema what women were capable of.

Each one of you will remember Claudia in a different manner. Some of her admirers will never get beyond her alluring images from *Playboy*. Others will imagine her as Venus with a bandolier, a Valkyrie in torn denim shorts, and a cult goddess speeding on roller skates blazing a fiery red glow across the heavens, the immortal super woman who will never age another moment, who will remain tough as stone and feminine as a tea rose.

I will remember her in a different manner. Mary Eileen "Mimi" Chesterton is my dream and becomes my reality of the actress Claudia Jennings. The pretty girl with the red hair, the brilliant student reading Hemingway and J.P. Dunleavy, the cheerleader and the budding actress who dreamed of success tells her story. A kind soul with a ready smile, as multi-textured and full of hope as a crisp, autumn afternoon.

---

[1] "Fast Life/Untimely Death: Playmate Claudia Jennings," *E! True Hollywood Story*, September 24, 2000
[2] *Ibid*.
[3] *Ibid*.
[4] *Ibid*
[5] Bass, Ari, "Claudia Jennings' 'Lost Highway,'" *Femme Fatales*, Vol. 9, No. 2, July 21, 2000
[6] *Ibid*.
[7] Williams, Albert, "But She Was A Cheerleader," *Chicago Reader*, September 21, 2000
[8] *Ibid*.
[9] *Ibid*
[10] E-mail interview with Dr. Steven Watts, August 20, 2015

Chapter 10:
Claudia's Career in Perspective

In any endeavor, whether it is acting, professional sports, art or writing, everything is relative. In order to fairly and properly judge Claudia's place in movie history, relativity is one very important factor, but not the only one. I believe Claudia's career was more than the sum of her body of work and her individual performances.

Claudia's roles sometimes seemed as if they bordered on objectifying women rather than empowering them. However, when one digs deeper into the individual characters, the sexuality of her characters always has a purpose. In the films where she is merely exploited, as in *Deathsport*, it is not her flaw, but the character's flaw. The majority of Claudia's performances reflect the qualities that any male star would have, such as courage, strength and an iron will. If we think of the male sex symbols of the 1960s and 1970s, the James Bond character is a perfect model for many of Claudia's roles. Although male stars weren't asked to disrobe to the extent female stars were, it is difficult to distinguish the difference between Sean Connery's bare chest writhing on top of his distaff co-star and Claudia moving sinuously beneath her paramour.

The double standard in male and female behavior extended to the screen, to Claudia's detriment. John Wayne was widely admired as an actor, yet his character's behavior was often reprehensible. Many critics, even those who acknowledge his unmatched place in American film, consider him more a presence than a great actor. The Duke had some very impressive performances, particularly in *The Searchers* and *The Man Who Shot Liberty Valance*, but it is difficult to argue against the proposition that he played the same character over and over again. As far as personal behavior, Wayne's antics never caused a scandal. Claudia was similarly assigned an equal appraisal, with the addition of a blatant condemnation of having the gall to remove her clothes on camera. It will be an enduring question about Claudia's life and career whether the shadow of *Playboy* and Hugh Hefner obscured Claudia's brilliance. There is no doubt it affected the beginning of her career, and, unfortunately, we will never know if she would have found her way out of the gloom and into the sunshine.

Claudia's place among the long list of Hollywood talents depends on several objective and subjective judgments. For example, can we assume she was destined for a traditional stardom—one that entailed major roles in big budget films, with a first class crew and cast? On the other hand, do we accept that Claudia, although stunning and possessed of rare charisma, had plateaued as far as her abilities went? Had she gotten as much out of her talent as possible, and would she be relegated to B-movie roles and bit parts for the remainder of her career?

I think the most compelling argument that Claudia might have gone on to major success in mainstream movies was the number of roles she was competing for when she died. It is more than likely that she would have won parts in *Blood Beach* and *Fade to Black*. A lead or featured appearance in *1941* was quite possible, while starring in *The Postman Always Rings Twice* seems a reach, but not impossible.

There are many conflicting opinions in the entertainment community. The *Hollywood Reporter*'s head movie critic, Todd McCarthy, said the following to Ari Bass in 1996 when he looked back at Claudia's career:

> She wasn't a great actress. Her appeal was in her unique look, her red hair and chiseled features. She certainly couldn't be mistaken for anyone else. But she did show in films like *Unholy Rollers* a willingness to throw herself into the action. On stage, her personality never boomed over the floodlights, and she wasn't as funny as others in high school theater. She had a certain magnetism though, which was her trademark.[1]

When Bass mentioned the excellent review John Simon gave Claudia for *Dark of the Moon*, McCarthy dismissed the reference without comment. Indeed, other than Roger Ebert of the *Chicago Sun Times*, Claudia did not garner many favorable reviews. Of course, we all know tastes and perspectives change over time as far as movie criticism is concerned. *Night of the Living Dead*, when it premiered in 1968, was excoriated by an outraged media, with one reviewer famously calling it, "amateur night in the butcher shop." Since its initial debut, the movie is now considered a masterpiece of modern horror, and given credit for creating the "new zombie" genre. Claudia's career, and the way her acting is viewed, has changed over time as well.

Claudia is a cult figure, yet people don't consider her roles mere caricatures. Her movies, and the women she played in them, weren't campy. Claudia did not employ a self-conscious acting style.

There is a large group of movie business professionals who admired Claudia's abilities and work ethic. Every director who worked with Claudia spoke about how seriously she took her acting. Many said that before each scene she would ask for clear instructions on her character's motivations, and what the director's expectations were for the scene. When the sequence was finished she always asked if she had performed up to expectations and asked for feedback. This hardly sounds like a B-movie actress who wanted to remain mired in low-budget films.

Claudia also excelled in the technical aspects of acting. She knew how to hit her marks, learned her dialogue and acted quite effectively with her eyes, facial expressions and gestures. When she moved or pivoted, she did so in such a manner as to make the shot easy for the cinematographer to capture on film. The fact that she had a good grasp on her craft was aided by her intangible qualities. Going back to when she was a young girl, until her last film, the camera loved Claudia. The cameraman was always able to capture her every mood, nuance and physicality.

The one and only time Claudia had trouble on a set was during the filming of *Deathsport*. The actions ascribed to Claudia might be considered libelous and slanderous; however, they appear in every story about her. The situation is even more corrosive, because people on the set said Claudia had no part in the difficulties including the producer, Roger Corman. There were only two people on the set who complained about Claudia: The immature first-time director and an embittered stuntwoman. If Claudia

Ahhh, for the old days of B-flicks

Perhaps in that environment, Sen. Gramm could profit from film follies

IAN SHOALES
SYNDICATED COLUMNIST

Sen. Phil Gramm has been forced to engage in some Q&A recently involving a T&A flick called "Truck Stop Women" (the 1974 movie that made Claudia Jennings a star). When Gramm's then-brother-in-law, George Caton, showed him the movie in the early '70s, Caton claims the senator was "titillated." (As if being titillated by Claudia Jennings is a bad thing.)

Whatever his testosterone level was at the time, Gramm admits that he later invested $7,500 in a project by the director of "Truck Stop Women," a movie called "Beauty Queens," which never got made. Instead the director took the money and made a spoof of the Nixon administration, which wound up getting released the day Nixon resigned, and stiffed big-time. Poor Phil.

But that's show business. If the author of "Forrest Gump" has yet to see his share of the profits of the movie they made of it, Phil Gramm is certainly guaranteed never to see a penny from his 20-year-old investment in a Nixon burlesque.

But does this make him a failed porno merchant, as some anti-Grammites have gleefully claimed, or just a fool from Texas with money to throw away?

I tend to lean toward the latter, not because I have any sympathy for Gramm, but because I too have seen "Truck Stop Women" (at a drive-in, where the good lord meant us to see Claudia Jennings movies), as well as her later "Gator Bait" (1976, same drive-in). I don't remember anything about either movie now, but at the time if I'd had 7,500 bucks, I'd have laid it at Claudia Jennings' feet.

So maybe Phil Gramm and I have something in common. In fact, I'd urge Sen. Gramm to join me (and his fellow Texan Joe Bob Briggs) in supporting B movies everywhere. I realize this is hard.

It might be too late, now that Claudia Jennings and drive-in movies are no longer with us, but we can sure make a stab at reviving a wonderful art form. A women-in-prison picture is a good bet if you're looking for a return on your investment. I'd like to see a movie featuring bikini-clad women riding Harleys. I'd pay a buck to see a movie about bikini-clad anti-terrorists. I suspect Sen. Gramm would too, in his heart anyway.

Sure, most major motion pictures these days are already B movies with a budget of a quarter billion dollars, but I for one would have enjoyed "Jurassic Park" twice as much if the makers had left out the computer-animation, and represented dinosaurs the old-fashioned way: iguanas with spikes glued to their backs.

Sure, the producers wouldn't have made as much money, but if they'd spent a hundred dollars on the movie instead of a kazillion, their profit margin would have remained the same.

We keep seeing audioanimatronic aliens in 70mm and Dolby Sound; what's wrong with using a stuntman in a monster suit? I don't even mind if the zipper is showing. Whatever happened to gorilla suits? What was wrong with showing the wires on flying rocket ships?

And why do we have this compulsion to blow up buildings every time we make a new action picture? Haven't we ever heard of stock footage?

And who would be the new Queen of the B's? Who's worthy to step into the shoes of the glorious Claudia Jennings, Yvonne Craig and Faith Domergue? Who in the '90s can compare?

Actresses today: They can't twotime, they can't scream, they can't shoot, they can't faint. Put a modern actress in a room with a stuntman in a gorilla suit, she'd probably just yawn.

But if we do succeed in breaking the back of the sleek Hollywood Tax cats, and bring back the producers of my youth, a cigar in one corner of their mouth, a "More cleavage!" snarled from the other, I believe America would be better off.

A revival of B movies isn't part of the Contract With America, but it should be. So get in that gorilla suit, Phil. Please. Put your mouth where your money was.

(To receive a complimentary Ian Shoales newsletter, call 1-800-989-DUCK or write Duck's Breath, 408 Broad St., Nevada City, CA 95959.)

---

could work with Nicolas Roeg, David Cronenberg and Roger Corman, why would she deliberately cause trouble for a novice director? Whatever ultimately happened on the set did not affect Claudia and Corman's relationship. He would have happily cast her again in another film had she not been taken from us.

An often-overlooked aspect of Claudia's résumé is her work on television. She made frequent appearances on such shows as *The Brady Bunch*, *Cannon* and *The F.B.I.* It may not seem that important an achievement, but television has been the springboard for many future A-list Hollywood movie stars such as Tom Hanks, Robin Williams, Clint Eastwood, Bruce Willis and scores of others. It makes perfect sense, then, that at several times during her career Claudia auditioned for a high-profile role in a television series. Looking at it from the performer's point of view, a starring role in a hit series would provide many benefits. The prospects of steady work, endorsements, residuals and other goodies certainly outweighed any negative ramifications; the most insidious of these would be typecasting.

Claudia had these thoughts when she auditioned for the role of Wonder Woman. Out of 200 women who auditioned, the three top candidates were Claudia, Joanna Cassidy and Lynda Carter. Cassidy was the oldest of the group, and had a modest background in acting and modeling. Carter was the youngest, had won the Ms. World America title, was an accomplished singer and had some acting experience as well. Claudia had the most acting experience by far, and was used to doing her own stunts. Obviously, all

> **Video of the Week:** *Truck Stop Women* (1974) One of the gooliest Mafia movies ever made, starring Claudia Jennings, the only Playmate-of-the-Year who could ever act and the woman who would of been the greatest drive-in actress in history if she hadn't been killed in a car accident. Soap opera star Lieux Dressler runs Anna's Truck Stop in New Mexico, which is a front for a whorehouse, truck-theft operation and stolen-goods fencing outfit, but the Eastern mob finds out that her daughter Rose (Claudia Jennings) is jealous of Mama and will do anything to get control of the business for herself. Rotten to the core, Claudia is a spoiled country girl who thinks of herself as royalty. "Jackie Onassis wouldn't eat a chicken-fried steak!" she screams, slammin' her dinner plate on the counter. So she offers up her body to whatever sleazeballs might help her get what she wants. Filmed at the height of the CB craze, it features a couple of decent truck chases and eight or nine Bobby Hart country-western songs, includin' *I'm a Truck* ("There'd be no truck drivers if it wasn't for us trucks") and *Big Bull Shippers*. Exceptional breast count for this kind of movie, 23. Four stars.
>
> **Joe Bob Briggs review**

three women were beautiful and physically qualified, being in excellent shape. However, Carter and Cassidy were 5'9", while Claudia was a relatively short 5'6". The two other ladies were bustier than Claudia, and Carter eventually got the part. The next time Claudia auditioned for a major role on television was for *Charlie's Angels*. As discussed earlier, this incident is potentially where Hollywood hypocrisy, *Playboy* and perhaps some personal antipathy towards Claudia all came together. All of the facts of the process are indisputable. Claudia went through multiple auditions and supposedly killed all of them. She was told by the show's producer she was practically guaranteed the part. She had beaten out the competition, which included some formidable actresses. The show had already lost its franchise actress, Farah Fawcett, and needed a "name" to invigorate the show. Then, without warning, they pulled the rug out from under Claudia, selecting a model with no acting experience for the role. Perhaps not getting the *Wonder Woman* role was understandable; however, this was a travesty. The reason given for not giving Claudia the part was her *Playboy* background. How in the world did the network executives not know of this from the first day the auditions started? To my mind, it is a horrendous blot on what little integrity the entertainment business has as a whole. I wish I could say it was the last time a double standard would be applied to Claudia.

As I have noted, it is my opinion that Claudia's association with *Playboy* damaged her career from the beginning. Although she never stopped giving Hugh Hefner credit for her successes, the preponderance of evidence suggests his patronage was self-serving at best. None of Hefner's protégés had anything remotely resembling a successful film career, with the exception of Stella Stevens in the 1960s. Ms. Stevens was already a trained actress, and while her *Playboy* appearance did not harm her career, it most likely did not boost it all that much. Barbi Benton, while musically gifted, never achieved any success as an actress. The Playmates that had limited film careers in the 1970s never came close to achieving Claudia's status. Beauties like Victoria Vetri, the Collinson twins, Susan Denberg, Connie Mason and others enjoyed moderate film and sometimes-broader television success, but they never achieved leading lady status.

Even when Hefner found his elusive Marilyn Monroe surrogate, Dorothy Stratten, the situation exploded in murder and madness.

If one looks at the films *Playboy*'s acolytes were drawn or pushed to, they were all B-films, filled with nudity and as much simulated sex as the 1970s censors would permit. In my research, I could find no concrete evidence that *Playboy* paid for or even urged the girls to take acting lessons. It seems that this would be mandatory for any serious actress! Of course, the question can be asked: Did these women want a serious film career? With *Playboy* arguably at its peak in the early '70s and films that kept pushing the boundaries of sex and violence, producers and directors no doubt leapt at the opportunity to cast one or more Playmates. For the young women of *Playboy*, it was easy money.

What Claudia didn't fully understand—and most likely Hugh Hefner neither—was that no serious producer would place a multimillion-dollar film in the hands of a relative newcomer with no solid acting background and whose claim to fame up to this point was appearing nude in a men's magazine. If the film was a light sex comedy, perhaps; but Hollywood was filled with accomplished actresses who were just as sexy as Claudia without the ball and chain of *Playboy* dragging behind. Don't forget, Ann-Margaret, Shirley MacLaine, Janice Rule, Julie Newmar, and yes, even Joan Collins were around, and although older than Claudia, all were still potent sex symbols.

Claudia found herself in this rapidly changing world of cinema and public morality. She was quite comfortable with nudity, on and off stage; whether this was a confidence instilled in her by her experience at *Playboy* or a natural tendency for a dedicated actor to perform in any manner required, I do not know. Friends and associates told me this was part of her personality—that she was comfortable nude in almost any situation. This tendency certainly made Claudia an ideal choice for a typical B-movie, with the added cachet of her Playmate of the Year title. Of course, the downside was the possibility of being typecast in the same sort of roles forever.

Looking back at the A-list actress of the 1970s, one notices a lot of familiar names. Although the list of Oscar winners and nominees does not necessarily represent the most talented performers, it does indicate who were getting the best parts. Jane Fonda, Diane Keaton and Glenda Jackson were the actresses most frequently cited for individual excellence. Faye Dunaway, Ellen Burstyn, Marsha Mason and Julie Christie had their share of nominations and awards. Other actresses popular, prolific and praised in the era were Barbra Streisand, Liza Minelli and Vanessa Redgrave. Does Claudia compare with any of these accomplished actresses? In general, the British actresses are a tough comparison. They invariably have a regimented and highly organized background in the performing arts, and practiced classical along with method acting. Since the cornerstone of British theater is Shakespeare, actors from the United Kingdom had to learn comedy, tragedy and complex historical dramas. Claudia does not measure up when compared with Helen Mirren or Glenda Jackson. However, given that Claudia had significant stage experience, she was not that far away from reaching a level of excellence that Diane Keaton, Faye Dunaway or even Jane Fonda enjoyed.

Claudia was as lovely as these other performers. The question is, if given the chance, could Claudia have handled the lead in *Looking for Mr. Goodbar*, *Bonnie and Clyde* or *Klute*? I believe that she could have, without any problems. It's easy to dismiss the suggestion that she was capable enough to do well in these roles; however, consider the parts and films that showcased Claudia's talents. These were not Hollywood blockbusters with generous budgets and, perhaps most important of all, a lengthy shooting schedule. Claudia's movies had to

be shot and in the can in a couple of weeks, at most. I'm not exaggerating when I say that Stanley Kubrick probably spent more time on one take than it took to shoot an average Claudia Jennings film. It's unlikely that the most practiced actress could do her best work in that situation. However, Claudia did her best, doing a scene in one take, while doing her own stunts and make-up.

Suppose we flip the scenario and put Faye Dunaway in one of Claudia's roles. Would she have been as effective as Claudia in the *The Great Texas Dynamite Chase* or *Truck Stop Women*? Without the advantages an A-movie provides, most accomplished actresses would have a difficult time making their characters believable working under the pressures of B-moviemaking.

So while Margot Kidder, Cybill Shepherd and Candice Bergen were getting choice roles, Claudia was left the scraps, which, not surprisingly, she accepted. However, in an era of disaster movies, organized crime sagas and upmarket horror films, one is puzzled that she didn't land at least a supporting role in a larger production. It is also curious that with the resurgence of European cinema during the decade, Claudia didn't just pack a suitcase and try for some opportunities across the Atlantic. I remember what one of Claudia's agents told me about her stubbornness, and wonder if she deliberately stood in the way of her own success.

It is intriguing to compare Claudia to Cybill Shepherd. Almost the same age as Claudia, Cybill had the looks of a classic blond beauty—a girl-next-door wholesomeness. Her early performances were very well received, being nominated for a Golden Globe Award as Most Promising Newcomer for *The Last Picture Show* directed by Peter Bogdanovich, who romanced her on the set.

She then received critical praise for *The Heartbreak Kid* and *Taxi Driver*. When one considers her entire career, I feel Ms. Shepherd's best work was on television's *Moonlighting*. Although she was a lovely young woman in her early roles, she did not hit her stride until the mid-1980s, nearly 15 years after the premier of *The Last Picture Show*. In that film and others, she's rather wooden and appears uncomfortable with moving her body while reciting lines. Claudia could have handled the role in The *Last Picture Show*, in my opinion. She looks more the small-town rural rich girl than Ms. Shepherd, who is portrayed as if she appeared by magic straight from the Cotton Bowl parade.

Cybill was the perfect choice for *The Heartbreak Kid*, as the blonde WASP girl that every Jewish lad ever fantasized about. Claudia certainly didn't look like the co-ed envisioned by the screenplay.

I believe if Claudia had lived, she might have had a chance at *Taxi Driver*. Martin Scorsese was familiar with Claudia from *Unholy Rollers*, and although the role wasn't physically demanding, it did require intelligence and a certain eloquence. She would have been a more appropriate choice than Cybill in playing straight woman to Albert Brooks. *Taxi Driver* also had the heart and soul of a B-movie. But of course this is only supposition.

Let's go back to my comparison of Marilyn Monroe and Claudia. Keep in mind, Marilyn was the ultimate symbol of sex, Hollywood entertainment and the *Playboy* philosophy, to Hugh Hefner's thinking. He had an obsession to find the reincarnation of his idolized platinum-blonde goddess, and pursued it well into the 21st century. What made Marilyn so successful, and why wasn't Claudia the successor Hef desperately wanted? Both women started as models, although Claudia had extensive theater training as well. Both eventually turned to nude modeling for financial considerations. Here is where their paths diverge somewhat. Marilyn was one of the most industrious cheesecake models of the 1940s, appearing on over 30 magazine covers. In time, Hollywood noticed, and she spent a few years going through short-term movie contracts, none of which panned out. Marilyn's career stagnated as she played bit parts in B-movies and romanced studio executives to earn a break.

In 1948, Marilyn began dating agent Johnnie Hyde, vice-president of the William Morris Agency. She still didn't get any major roles, so she went back to modeling and agreed to her now-infamous nude calendar photographs that Hugh Hefner used to turn *Playboy* into the most popular men's magazine in history. Eventually, Hyde was able to get her a large contract with 20th Century Fox, and her career began to bloom. By the mid 1950s, Marilyn was a superstar and the first modern sex symbol. Monroe's career seemed secure, and critics began to praise Marilyn for her acting and not her looks. Unfortunately, Marilyn went into a downhill spiral of drug use, depression and that severe lack of self-esteem that had haunted her since she was a child. Her choice of men, whether casual affairs or two celebrated marriages to baseball star Joe DiMaggio and writer Arthur Miller, were disasters. To some extent, this parallels Claudia's story. It took Marilyn almost eight years before she was considered worthy enough to be cast in major roles. Claudia was just about to reach her 10-year anniversary of filmmaking, still young and beautiful enough to play a variety of decent parts.

One tremendous difference between the two women is how natural Claudia's beauty was, and the effort it took to manufacture Marilyn Monroe. The most Claudia ever did was dye her hair blonder. She never augmented her breasts, which she always felt were a bit smaller than the usual Playmate, but neither did she feel the need. Claudia did envy the physiques of her fellow *Playboy* Playmates, which contributed to her already-exaggerated low self-esteem. Marilyn, on the other hand, had her hairline raised by electrolysis, had silicon prosthesis implanted in her jaw and had a rhinoplasty. Of course, this doesn't include gradual lightening of her hair until it was platinum blonde.

The saddest thing the actresses shared was how they were seen after their deaths. Today, Marilyn's talents as an actress have become overshadowed by the lurid details of her personal life. She was manipulated by many of the men she associated with, which only exacerbated all the emotional tumult of her childhood. Her reputation grows increasingly lascivious, to the diminution of her positive qualities.

Both actresses are now icons, the motion picture industry's sad sacrifices to immortality. The quantities of their tragedies cannot be measured by any comprehensible method, and our only comfort is that they live on our computers, DVDs and televisions.

Just consider if Marilyn, with all the people she knew and all the friends she had, could have relied on just one person to guide her along another path.

Another powerful example of the significance of Claudia's career was how often she was asked to carry a film. The movie that she dominated from start to finish, *Unholy Rollers*, was her *tour de force*. Present in almost every frame, she confidently puts the movie on her shoulders. Although it's arguably her best performance, only her friend, film critic Roger Ebert, praised her acting. The film was widely panned—and unfairly, since the movie was superior to *Kansas City Bomber* (IMDb gives *Kansas City Bomber* a 5.5 rating and *Unholy Rollers* a 5.7 rating). Claudia also triumphed in *'Gator Bait* (despite being given few lines of dialogue*)*, *Truck Stop Women*, *The Great Texas Dynamite Chase* and *Sisters of Death*—the last a classic case of her performance being the best thing about a bad movie.

There were too many movies where Claudia was underutilized, which was a shame. However, in *The Single Girls* and *Group Marriage*, Claudia showed she could be part of a successful ensemble cast. In a few other films, her role was never meant to be more than a glorified walk-on. The one example that I think her fans were most disappointed in was *The Man Who Fell to Earth*. As I discussed earlier, many people were under the impression that most of Claudia's work was cut from the film. Although a small portion was removed from the original release, in truth, her role was not that large to begin with. There was only one significant female character, and that role went to Candy Clark.

Claudia's Place as Queen of the Bs and the Ultimate Cult Siren

The term "B-movie" has taken on a pejorative connotation since it was first introduced as part of the cinematic lexicon. Originally the term was used for the second film in a double feature by 1930s Hollywood—the A-movie being the main attraction. These B-films often had much lower budgets, used lesser or unknown actors and frequently employed sets from A-movies. The Western was the most popular genre, being relatively cheap to film and popular with audiences, with familiar characters and themes.

What enabled the B-system to work was a business practice that the studios employed to their great advantage. Most of the big filmmaking conglomerates also owned movie theater chains, thus controlling content, price and a *de facto* distribution monopoly.

Independent theaters were required to block-book a studio's production for an entire year; in addition, the B-movies were rented at a flat fee set by the studios, practically guaranteeing profitability of even the poorest-quality film. By contrast, A-movies were billed at a box office percentage of the receipts.

It is relevant to note that a B-movie designation did not infer an automatic seal of cinematic cheese upon the film. Future stars, both actors and crew, got their first experience in these films. John Wayne first came to prominence in *The Three Mesquiteers*, and in the 1940s, noted directors Val Lewton and Jacques Tourneur, respectively, created such horror masterpieces as *I Walked with a Zombie* and *The Body Snatcher*. Perhaps the most prominent example of a B-movie was Orson Welles' *The Magnificent Ambersons*.

It was the 1950s that brought about a wave of change that swept over Hollywood. A Supreme Court decision ruled against the major studios, which were forced to divest their theater holdings and end the practice of block booking. This provided a boon for smaller, more flexible filmmakers and studios, which could produce movies for considerably less money than the major studios. By this time, the average cost of an A-movie was $1 million. As revenues decreased and resources were pinched, the majors had no choice but to leave the B-market business.

What followed was an explosion of more sensational, thought provoking, crude and morally challenging films that were the harbingers of the exploitation era. There were some brilliant film noir projects made, such as *Kiss Me Deadly*, and many films managed to slip social commentary in between the thrills and monsters. The most important of these was *Invasion of the Body Snatchers*, directed by Don Siegel of *Dirty Harry* fame. *Invasion* was effective as film noir, as science fiction and as a detective story. Many people read all manner of political messages into the film; some saw it as an allegory against McCarthyism, some as an anti-communist statement and others as a warning against blind conformity. Ironically, the author of the source novel and the filmmakers all denied the movie had any political message.

The next watermark of the B-film was the debut of a talented, bright novice filmmaker from Detroit. In 1954, he scraped together $12,000 to produce his own horror film, *Monster from the Ocean Floor*. With an ambitious title and lurid lobby art, the auteur Roger Corman shot the film in six days. When all was said and done, the movie grossed $850,000, a spectacular return and the beginning of Corman's legendary reputation. The significance of Corman's accomplishment was not lost on his fellow producers and directors; as the new decade approached, the B-movie was to enter a brave new world, even less inhibited than ever thought possible.

Alfred Hitchcock filmed Robert Bloch's novel, *Psycho*, in 1960, based on the real-life cannibal killer Ed Gein. Gein would also inspire *The Texas Chain Saw Massacre*, among a host of other films. What Hitchcock accomplished was to bring the down-market sensibilities of the B-movie to an upmarket A-list quality. Shooting in black-and-white and framing his scenes with finesse, Hitchcock made the slasher movie into an art film. *Psycho* had all the components of a modern horror film—graphic violence, blood, nudity and a general sense of decay, not only of the spooky old house but also of Marion's morality and Norman Bates' schizophrenic mind. In this one spectacle, Hitchcock created cinematic tropes that endure to this day.

Hitchcock had opened Pandora's box. As soon as filmmakers realized mainstream audiences could be attracted to the unsavory, all manner of depravity was unleashed on the screens of America's theaters. The ingenuity of these purveyors of poor taste was nothing short of brilliant. When Herschell Gordon Lewis found that other directors were co-opting his nudie films, he desperately searched for another genre to titillate audiences. What he invented was the gore film. His movies are no more than *Grand Guignol* stage plays brought to the screen, with less convincing special effects; however, for 1960s' audiences, the spectacle of having a beautiful woman's tongue ripped out or a beach bunny's brains scooped into a receptacle was a little off-putting. American cinema didn't fully embrace gore (or "splatter films," using the modern vernacular) until fairly recently, but since the 1980s they have become more popular, to the point where almost every horror film has a few scenes of inventive, dynamic body destruction.

B-films have a delicate recipe, and one mandatory ingredient is the female figure, often in its full, unclad display. Some movies only had one primary female lead, while others had an ensemble cast. Women in groups could be in prison, part of a biker gang, nurses, teachers or slaves. An interesting observation is that most B-films that featured a sole female lead were generally of the "damsel in distress" type, requiring a man to rescue her from some horrible fate. In general, the women who were collectively sequestered or grouped by some occupation did better when threatened by men, by uniting against the common threat—not that they always escaped unscathed, or with their virtue intact.

Besides Roger Corman, Russ Meyer's movies became enormously popular. Films like *Faster, Pussycat! Kill! Kill!* and *Beneath the Valley of the Dolls* were two examples of his unique art. Considering Meyer's reputation, *Pussycat* has no nudity, but is violent and lurid. The dialogue and acting make even Roger Corman's weakest efforts look like *Hamlet*, however. *Beneath the Valley of the Dolls* is more like the Russ Meyer we love. It has plenty of violence, what can only be described as an insane plot, naked women and the sense we are watching some Hollywood executive's nightmare after a particularly bad drug-fueled night on the Sunset Strip.

As the motion picture codes relaxed, it wasn't difficult to find actresses willing to appear nude and suffer all forms of degradation. The rougher the films became, the tougher the women who acted in them had to become. There soon developed a sorority of actresses who specialized in the sex, violence and general sleaze of the B-film. Even that appellation was becoming outdated, as production companies such as Roger Corman's New World Pictures, New Line Cinema and Cannon Films began to churn out dozens of features. The lines began to blur between A- and B-films. In 1964, Corman directed and produced an adaptation of Edgar Allen Poe's *Masque of the Red Death*. An oddity for Corman, the film was made in England over the course of five weeks. Corman shot the film in Great Britain to take advantage of certain tax laws, which earned the film a subsidy.

Masque has all the trappings of an A-film. The cinematography by Nic Roeg is stunning, with the color and set design impeccable. The cast is first-rate, with classically trained actors in all the lead roles—Vincent Price, who cut his teeth on the London stage; Hazel Court, later to become a familiar figure in both Corman and Hammer; and finally, Patrick Magee, a favorite of both Corman and Stanley Kubrick. Corman stated in several interviews that although the *House of Usher* was his most successful Poe adaptation, *Masque* was one of his favorite films. If one were unaware of who directed the film, a natural guess might have been a disciple of Ingmar Berman or Federico Fellini, someone who possessed a genius for inventive color photography.

By the time the 1970s rolled in, the term B-movie was becoming passé. Since the late 1950s, many films were now made for the drive-in market, seeing as a more prosperous America could afford family automobiles. The cars also gave the rising number of teenagers an opportunity for social and sexual exploration, a personal freedom previously beyond their grasp. The operators of these facilities needed as many attractions as possible to build business. Although some would still run the big budget A-list films, most made their living off of two, three or sometimes four or five features in one evening. A couple could spend a cozy evening steaming up their windows and occasionally watch what was transpiring on the huge screen.

Then, in 1972, Roger Corman was casting for the lead in a roller derby movie and met Claudia Jennings. She embodied everything that the New Wave of B-movies was all about. She was smart, sexy and more than willing to kick anyone's ass, male or female. She was versatile enough to be convincing in and out of her clothing, and was cast in a variety of roles, not strictly the horror/exploitation films that were Corman's specialty. Claudia was one of many talented actresses to work with Roger, but none ever reached the level of adoration she received. Pam Grier came close, but never received the credit she deserved until Quentin Tarantino's *Jackie Brown*. I cannot mention *Jackie Brown* without referring to another talented actress, Bridget Fonda; Claudia and Bridget were as close to doppelgangers as can be found in Hollywood. They had almost identical looks, similar acting styles and of course, uncommon beauty. Had Claudia lived, they probably would have competed for some roles, and perhaps co-starred in some films.

The list of Corman's discoveries is impressive, including Talia Shire, Luana Anders, Beverly Garland, Sandra Bullock and Sherilyn Fenn. All have their niche in Hollywood history, with Sandra Bullock in particular showing that she was capable of being an action hero, mirroring some of the physicality Claudia demonstrated in her films.

As far as her being crowned Queen of the Bs, Claudia didn't mind that, and took that title as a compliment. It would have been more accurate to call her, as Roger Corman described his style of filmmaking, the Queen of the Low-Budget Exploitation Film, because to his mind, he didn't feel he made B-movies. Naturally, it's a lot easier to say Queen of the Bs, so I suppose that's why the name stuck. Claudia, though, wasn't typical of the other B-movie actresses. In her performances, she was never raped, eaten by a crocodile, had her head split with an axe, set on fire, thrown off a cliff, impaled by a stake or any of the other grisly fates that befell the lovely ladies of 1970s cinema. She was unique because of this quirky serendipity. Actually, she did die once, but it was a relatively clean way to go, and of course, she had been a very bad girl in the film. Then again, it would have been heresy to her fans to see her portrayed in any way other than the strong, smart, tough women she played.

What is forgotten by modern audiences today is that Claudia did her own stunts and used her feminine wiles to lure men to an ass-kicking, or to her bed. The 100-pound models that throw adversaries through windows or jump out of buildings onto moving cars in today's films are absurd compared to Claudia's realistic stunts. The feminine heroes (excluding the ones with superhuman powers) of today are cartoonish, and it's difficult to take them seriously. Watching Claudia's movies, though, it is quite believable to see her killing without wire effects, stunt doubles and image manipulation.

Shortly after she passed, Todd McCarthy, then chief film critic of *Variety*, wrote an article for *Film Comment*. The piece talks about how he first met Claudia at Evanston Township High School, but there is some significant discussion of her career. There is also a strange linkage between her personality, her career and her death that McCarthy fashions in the piece. In the article, McCarthy ponders whether Claudia's death was a suicide.

> One acquaintance immediately thought of Billy Wilder's *Fedora*, guessing that Claudia might have done it on purpose. After all, she had recently lost out on the job of Kate Jackson's replacement on *Charlie's Angels* after having been led to believe she might get the part. But she was too tough for that, too levelheaded to be plunged into depression over not winning a role. Despite my rejection of the notion of suicide, I shuddered to think that perhaps she had come to the same realization as her most cynical detractors: That she was indeed washed up. Where, after all, can a Queen of the Bs sexpot go once she hits 30? All the answers are depressing.[1]

It is to McCarthy's credit that he recognized Claudia's toughness and that she was grounded enough not to succumb to hopelessness and despair. She loved her sisters and friends far too much to be that selfish. She used her toughness and level-headedness to bounce back from the disappointment of not getting the *Charlie's Angels* role.

As far as her being washed up at 30, that however shows a fundamental misunderstanding of the woman and of the movie industry itself. Even if Claudia, by some curse of bad luck, stayed in the exploitation end of the film industry, there were plenty of roles for an actress of her age and even older. As examples, Pam Grier and Sybil Danning continued to make films well into their 50s, and both are still striking-looking ladies.

McCarthy's words also bring up an interesting point. At what age is an actress over the hill, or too old to play a part requiring a vibrant, life-loving woman? Jane Fonda, Katharine Hepburn, Meryl Streep, Diana Rigg and Helen Mirren defy the notion that the older an actress is, the less appealing she becomes.

This also seems to be a sexist observation, as no one ever accused Cary Grant, Robert Redford, or Paul Newman of being too old to be effective actors—and indeed, they were powerful sex symbols well into their later years. There is also the fact that some performers didn't reach their peaks until much later in their careers. Among the stars who didn't reach their achieved recognition until their 30s or 40s are Jessica Chastain, John Hamm, Christoph Waltz, Jane Lynch, the late Alan Rickman and Kristen Wiig.

It's obvious McCarthy did not anticipate, along with his "cynical" associates, that the 1980s would bring an explosion of better roles for women, but also hundreds of action and exploitation films that would have been perfect for Claudia. Her experience, affinity for the camera and her unique beauty would have made her a wanted commodity in Hollywood—and probably abroad.

If we look at some of films that were made in the 1980s, it isn't difficult to imagine Claudia playing the lead female role in *Flash Gordon, Raiders of the Lost Ark, Conan the Barbarian, Sheena, Streets of Fire* (where she could have done her own vocals) and other adventure features. She would also have enjoyed opportunities in the horror genre in films like *Maniac*. Claudia was far from being washed up in the motion picture industry. Despite the fact *Deathsport* was a poor film, people still turned out to see Claudia in the buff. All she needed was some fine-tuning as an actress, a decent director and a well-written script, and Claudia could have crossed the boundary to legitimate stardom.

Even if Claudia did not thrive in the motion picture world, there was still television. Aaron Spelling all but promised her a part on *Dynasty* after the fiasco with *Charlie's Angels*. At worst, Claudia would have had a nice career combining television, film and an occasional theater appearance. She was more capable than a majority of actresses at starring in all three mediums.

I think McCarthy's comments also show a fundamental cynicism. Without any empirical evidence, he uses buzzwords that are pejorative and designed to eliminate any positive view of Claudia's career. While Queen of the Bs is not inherently prejudicial, when combined with sexpot, the entire phrase is demeaning and vulgar. There is a difference between sexpot and a sex symbol, and it is not mere semantics. One has a crude meaning and is exclusively directed at women. The term "sex symbol" is non-gender specific and implies the subject is attractive and sensual.

The most disheartening aspect of McCarthy's article is his judgment that Claudia had no possibility of growth as a performer. He admits in his piece that he had not spoken with Claudia for years. Therefore, his conclusions were no doubt tainted by his last contact with her, which, according to him, was unpleasant because she didn't go out of her way to assist him. He felt because they were longtime acquaintances she owed him some special consideration, for old times' sake. In general, whenever McCarthy was interviewed or wrote a piece about Claudia, with the exception of the obituary, there was a distinct bitterness flavoring it—one that faint praise or the infrequent off-handed compliment could not disguise.

There is certainly a nexus where the private and public life of an actress collide. I believe this is where Claudia became misunderstood, and in some cases she had only herself to blame. Any

WITH GIL HOEL
photo courtesy Gil Hoel

Mimi, meanwhile, became known as the "Queen of the Bs." She changed her name to Claudia Jennings—in part so as not to embarrass her family and in part, according to retired ETHS drama teacher Bill Ditton, because she thought "Mimi" sounded too girlish—and debuted her saucy, sensual new persona in a November

No one can say what path Mimi's career might have taken as she grew older. "I figure I'll come into my own when I'm about 30," she once said in a *Playboy* interview. She might have made a crossover to mainstream success. She might have parlayed her sex-kitten image into a serious acting career. She might have ended up doing public-service spots

A Biography   263

actress who appears in *Playboy* takes a risk of not being taken seriously. In Claudia's case, she appeared in four pictorials and was photographed for a fifth, which was not run because of her death and she was featured in a few other random photos for the magazine. The individuals I interviewed told me Claudia agreed to participate out of her loyalty to Hefner. I wonder where was her loyalty to herself. She was a complete angel, but she could be feisty. Her frequent arguments with Bobby Hart and other boyfriends attest to that. It seems that she was too eager to please in some cases. On a set with a director, the willingness to surpass expectations is a virtue. However, in the pages of *Playboy*, with the knowledge it might damage her career, that trait was a definite vice.

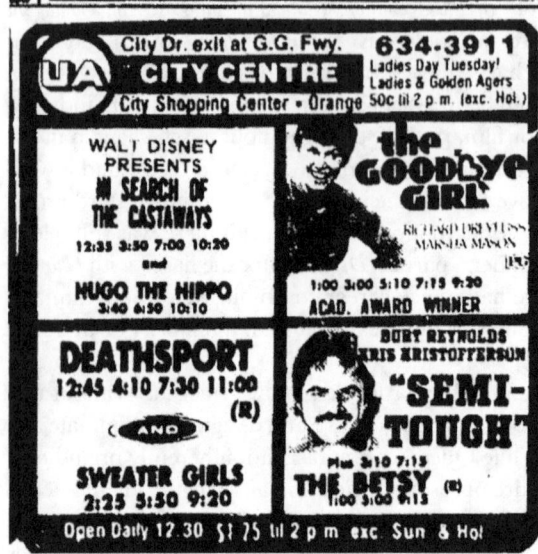

There have been some notable actors and actresses who have appeared in *Playboy*. One cannot speak for their motives, but they had an advantage, whereas Claudia had none. Sarah Miles and Kris Kristofferson were seen performing a rather blatant sex act in *Playboy*, an outtake from *The Sailor Who Fell From Grace With the Sea*. Kristofferson later said the pictures were the last straw in breaking up his marriage to Rita Coolidge. Sarah Miles, a free spirit since she was a young girl, didn't care. She embraced nudity as much as Claudia, feeling her body was a natural part of her acting skill. The major difference was that Miles had built up some serious credibility as an actress, with an Academy Award nomination and several Golden Globe nominations to her credit prior to her appearance in the magazine.

Claudia's seeming embrace of *Playboy* and everything Hefner did had the result of alienating the film community. It was a case of guilt by association, with the critics and the majority of entertainment executives unwilling to give her a fair chance. As mentioned several times in the text, there occurred a self-sustaining and self-fulfilling cycle where Claudia could not escape the stigma of her *Playboy* appearances. The cycle started with her first pictorial, and then picked up steam immediately upon being named Playmate of the Year. Her first movie, *Jud*, and her New York stage appearance in *Dark of the Moon*, both exploited her exposure in the magazine.

Then, at a critical juncture in her career and personal life, Claudia agreed against her better instincts to another pictorial. This was after her movie career was beginning to blossom and earn limited yet tangible respect. Actresses are usually forgiven for being somewhat iconoclastic, but Claudia came off as being rather peculiar. She stubbornly agreed to continue her role as *Playboy*'s leading lady, incrementally chipping away at her credibility as an actress while engaging in a radical lifestyle change. This digression from Bobby Hart's sweet and charming partner to a caricature of a Hollywood hellion alarmed her friends and gave ammunition to her detractors.

It is puzzling, also, that despite her many connections in the film industry, Claudia could never get the prize role that she sought. The many studio executives, directors, cinematographers, writers, and outstanding actors she knew were never able to secure a part that would have vaulted her out of the B-movie world. Outside of a few exceptions, which seemed more personal than professional, those in the business spoke highly of her abilities and work ethic. Was there a rational explanation for this, or was it the dark forces of American Gothic at work, with poor decisions, bad timing and the abhorrent nature of fate all playing a part?

While this doesn't absolve Claudia for her alleged offenses, such as missed auditions and the like, it does place her behavior in the context of the times. Furthermore, it illustrates that Claudia, as has been suggested by others, allowed herself to be surrounded by people that certainly didn't have her welfare in mind.

Claudia took a brief hiatus from acting to concentrate on the more rambunctious aspects of Los Angeles nightlife. However, upon her return, she took a one-two-three combination that sent her reeling. She took the role of Deneer in *Deathsport*, which, while it showed off her talents as an actress and proved that she was still a remarkable beauty, became an embarrassment to all concerned. The dialogue was preposterous, and even Sir Laurence Olivier would not have been able to make it sound less juvenile and stilted. This was followed by another pictorial in *Playboy*, which eroded her credibility further. Those in the industry began to question how serious she was about her career. The final blow was her role in *Fast Company*—a good film, but one that received no distribution, and in which her part was very limited. All of this, taken as a whole, along with the notorious drama that her relationship with Stan Herman engendered, made her life seem like a train wreck when viewed from afar.

Claudia certainly deserved the same respect from the critics that they were more than happy to lather on to other actresses. Talia Shire received justifiable praise for *Rocky* and *The Godfather Part II*, but those were groundbreaking films—the former having unprecedented technical achievements and an "everyman" universal story, and the latter being one of the greatest films ever made.

When you consider women like Raquel Welch, Farrah Fawcett, and Jane Seymour, who earned some parts in borderline A-films strictly on the basis of their looks, it's tough to argue that Claudia's acting was an impediment to her getting good roles. I mean, I believe Claudia could have filled out the bearcat bikini Raquel wore in 1966's *One Million Years B.C.* just as nicely. I suppose timing is everything.

A considerable amount of film criticism is objective. For example, one can easily recognize bad acting; but past that point, what constitutes good acting? This is where the subjective nature of criticism meets the objective. Even among the elite film critics, disagreement is standard among film reviews. Let us take Alejandro Jodorowsky's *El Topo* as an example: Vincent Canby of the *New York Times* and Gene Siskel of the *Chicago Tribune* disliked it, the former calling it "all guts, with nobody to give the guts a particular shape or function," and the latter saying, "It is enough to make one yawn." In contrast, Peter Schjeldahl of the the *New York Times* called it "a very strange masterpiece" and Roger Ebert included it in his "Great Movies" series.

If we look at the history of criticism, there are many examples where the artist was eventually vindicated after first being denigrated. Van Gogh, Thoreau, Vermeer, Gauguin and Bach were all considered failures in their times, most dying forgotten and in poverty. Tastes change with the times, whether the subject is food, art, music or acting.

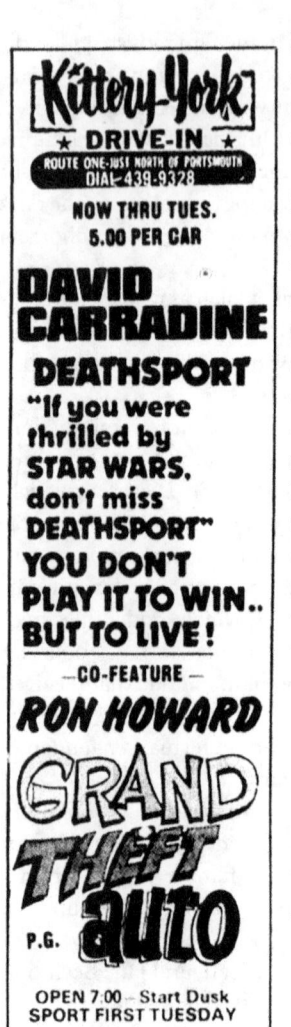

I believe there is already a subtle shift in the way Claudia's acting career is viewed. Some audiences and critics now recognize the subtleness in her craft and the intangibles that made her performances memorable.

All things being considered equal, the motion picture industry is about one thing, and that is entertainment for profit. Art has its place in the equation; the experience of watching a film connects with the human mind and body in so many ways that it is impossible to truly judge a movie or performance without taking into consideration a staggering amount of psychological data, such as the life experience of the viewer, their ethnic background, their political views and the education of the subject. Claudia entertained us in her movies. It didn't matter if they were illogical, shallow or well made. She connected with many people who felt disenfranchised and ridiculed in 1970s America, such as people from the South. Women also responded to her characters, which seems counterintuitive but shows us how the average woman felt about her status in America at that time. They didn't care if she enjoyed sex, or metaphorically and sometimes literally castrated men.

Lost in Cyberspace

I believe that if it were not for the age of social media and the Internet, Claudia's legend would have been lost forever. After all, I would have never seen *The Great Texas Dynamite Chase* nor read "But She Was a Cheerleader" if not for the personal computer.

Unfortunately, with but a few exceptions, many of the Internet search engines will bring you to pages that have no interest in telling Claudia's story. The sites that do show interest in her life only give us a snapshot of the person. It is comparable to a thunderstorm in a darkened house; when the lightning flashes, we see glimpses of the person, but no real detail.

The other problem with material found on the Internet is its unreliability. One can publish anything without corroboration or citation, and most people will believe whatever they read. I have read basic errors in fact about Claudia's life, everything from where she was born to the road on which she met her end. There was one article in particular, from a so-called comedian from Atlanta. He claimed to have worked as a stuntman on *Deathsport*. Besides being full of outright lies, the article is scatological and crude. Disrespectful of Claudia's acting abilities, the author even makes light of Claudia's death, an unforgivable act. There is no attempt to put what went on during filming in perspective, and as a result it appears that Claudia was to blame for all the problems on the set.

That story was but one example of how one film, *Deathsport*, poisoned Claudia's reputation. Despite the fact that Roger Corman and the film's co-stars stood up for Claudia. She drew all the ire of the incompetent director and is blamed for all of the problems that beset the production. So it went with almost every online review of *Deathsport*. The positive effect the Internet had, though, was to keep interest in Claudia and her films alive. Even though many of the reviews, especially of the films where she disrobes, have a bit of a wink to them, they still have a positive cast. Remember, an overwhelming majority of these reviews are from fans of the genre, not professional critics. This demonstrates how Claudia connected with her average followers. Her acting may not have been what mainstream critics thought was acceptable, but her fans were loyal and appreciated her skills.

Another aspect of Claudia's cyber-popularity is the availability of her movies. If you do a search on "Claudia Jennings," the majority of sites offer you the promise of her nude photos. However, the second-largest hits are about her films and her status as a cult icon. The reviews of her movies, often by fans and not paid critics, are glowing and understand her appeal and abilities. There are practically no websites or blogs about her, and the occasional ones that appear are vulgar or intellectually dishonest, as well as factually incorrect. Recently, many of Claudia's films have finally been released on DVD after decades of exile on VHS tapes. I believe the availability of an enhanced Blu-ray version of Claudia's movies will give her works a polished, less B-movie feel. Today's fans have expectations that are greater than the viewers of the 1970s, as far as quality and clarity of film.

I've tried to think of the best arguments I can about Claudia's place among our country's greatest film stars. Suddenly, her performance in *'Gator Bait* came to mind. I thought of Ferd Sebastian's comments that the movie showed the real Claudia; then it dawned on me what made her so effective as an actress. Think of the silent movie stars, who had to rely on facial expression, body language and physical movement to create characters; stripped of dialogue, the actor still connected with the audience through non-verbal skills. This was the essence of a Claudia Jennings performance. She could say more with a brief eye movement or a gesture than any 10 pages of dialogue. Do we consider the actors of the silent film era ineffective or marginalized? Those performers made us laugh, cry, lust and feel inspired by the power of their physical gifts. I would put a performance by Charlie Chaplin, Louise Brooks or Buster Keaton up against those of any modern actor.

So it was with Claudia Jennings. Roger Corman called her his favorite leading lady, which is a common phrase but implies an actress having uncommon qualities. No other

Claudia Jennings

performer dominated a film like Claudia, and even when surrounded by other lovely women, your eyes were naturally drawn to her.

My part in Claudia's narrative ends at this point. She had a career that was difficult to understand in many ways. I have tried to explain and make sense of it; however, the answers are complex and probably only known to Claudia herself. She was talented and successful, but the answer as to why her career went down the path it did eludes me. However, she did what she wanted to do—act in films. More than that, she made many people, including me, happy.

I have been fortunate to watch thousands of movies in my lifetime. Seeing a movie is like being whisked away to another world, if only for a few hours. Films like *Casablanca*, *King of Hearts*, *The Lady from Shanghai* and others continue to amaze and inspire me. The actresses in film are like angels, with a divine light between their image and our eyes. Claudia was one of those angels, who brought their luminescence and grace to those of us watching in the dark and dreaming, perpetually dreaming.

[1] McCarthy, Todd, "Claudia Jennings: Before the Beginning and After the End," *Film Comment*, Vol. 15, No. 6, November-December 1979

Chapter 11: Connie's Poem

I believe the final words about Claudia should come from her family. Her sister Constance wrote this poem, entitled "For Mary Eileen," a short time after her Celebration of Life memorial service.

1.
Los Angeles—we drive
on roads curling through
hills dripping with
flowers. Outside her home
my father stands, talks
to her friends beneath
the green-winged click
and whir of dragonflies.
"Remember the best, forget
the worst," in a dried petal
voice. I listen to the
porch door, banging open,
shut, open. My younger sister
has risen, blinking, speaks
to the group, clenching
and unclenching her fists.
The sky is acutely blue.

2.
Ornate sanctuary, gold
and blue painted beams, ash
of roses. Mary, an old priest:
"Whither shall I flee
 from thy spirit? At evening
mass we remember her.
Mother lights candles
cupped in red glass.

3.
Turning to me
hopefully: "She loved you,
you know," and twisting
toward the window—thirty
stories down the lights: dime-
store jewels in neat rows.

Chin in hand, I can
see wide nets of
light thrown
over buildings.
Bright shapes waver
in their mesh, pulled
from the water—green glass,
quartz, a silver barrette.
But the lake is a cracked
ice-tundra. Frozen waves
hulk at the shoreline
like mammoths. There's not
been a winter so cold
in fifty years. Snow falls
and falls, down-
whirling spirals, winter city

Chapter 12: Author's Notes

When Claudia died, she was cremated, and her ashes were scattered at sea. Joan Chesterton placed a marker in a cemetery located in the Midwest where Claudia's friends and family could go to remember her. The marker has her given name, then Claudia in quotation marks as a sign of respect to those that loved her and knew her by that name, like Bobby Hart, Barry Richards and Keith Jennings.

Mary Eileen Chesterton
"Claudia"
December 20, 1949-October 3, 1979

However, she will be always be Mimi.

Filmography

Jud, 1971
Credits—Producer: Igo Kantor; Director: Gunther Collins; Writer: Gunther Collins; Production Manager; John "Bud" Cardos; Cinematographer: Isidore Mankofsky; Music: Stu Phillips; Music Supervisor: James Nelson
Cast—Joseph Kaufmann (Jud); Robert Deman (Bill Arness); Norman Burton (Uncle Hornkel); Claudia Jennings (Sunny)

The Love Machine, 1971
Credits—Producer: M.J. Frankovich; Executive Producer: Irving Mansfield; Director: Jack Haley Jr.; Writer: Jacqueline Susann (from her novel); Screenplay: Samuel A. Taylor; Cinematographer: Charles B. Lang; Music: Artie Butler; Costume Supervisors: Seth Banks, Edna Taylor.
Cast—John Phillip Law (Robin Stone); Dyan Cannon (Judith Austin); Robert Ryan (Gregory "Greg" Austin); Jackie Cooper (Danton Miller); David Hemmings (Jerry Nelson); Jodi Wexler (Amanda); William Roerick (Cliff Dorne); Maureen Arthur (Ethel Evans); Shecky Greene (Christie Lane); Claudia Jennings (Darlene).

The Stepmother, 1972
Credits—Execuitve Producer: Lenke Romanszky; Associate Producer: Marlene Schmidt; Producer: Hikmet L.Avedis; Director: Hikmet L. Avedis; Writer: Hikmet L. Avedis; Director of Photography: Jack Beckett; Film Editors: Tony de Zarraga, Ralph Hall; Sound Mixers: Don Cahn, Jim Cook; Title Song "Strange are the Ways of Love," lyrics by Paul Francis Webster and music by Sammy Fain.
Cast—Alejandro Rey (Frank Delgado); John Anderson (Inspector Darnezi); Catherine Justice (Margo Delgado); Larry Linville (Dick Hill); Duncan McLeod (Chief Inspector) ; David Renard (Pedro Lopez); Marlene Schmidt (Sonya Hill); Claudia Jennings (Rita); John D. Garfield (Goof).

Unholy Rollers, 1972
Credits—Executive Producer: Roger Corman; Director: Vernon Zimmerman; Screenplay: Howard R. Cohen; Story: Vernon Zimmerman and Howard R. Cohen; Music: Kendall Schmidt and Bobby Hart (uncredited); Cinematography: Michael Shea; Film Editor: George Trigoroff; Supervising Editor: Martin Scorsese; Musical Director: Bobby Hart.
Cast—Claudia Jennings (Karen Walker); Louis Quinn (Mr. Stern); Betty Anne Rees (Mickey); Roberta Collins (Jennifer); Alan Vint (Greg); Candice Roman (Donna); Jay Varela (Nick); Joe E. Tata (Marshall); Kathleen Freeman (Karen's mother).

Group Marriage, 1973
Credits—Associate Producer: Paul Rapp; Director: Stephanie Rothman; Screenplay: Stephanie Rothman, Charles S. Swartz and Richard Walter; Cinematography: Daniel Lacambre; Film Editor: John A. O'Connor; Music: Michael Andres; Sound Editor: Leonard Corso.
Cast—Victoria Vetri (Jan); Solomon Sturges (Sander); Claudia Jennings (Elaine); Zack Taylor (Phil); Jeffrey Pomerantz (Dennis); Aimee Eccles (Chris); Jayne Kennedy (Judy).

40 Carats, 1973
Credits—Producer: M.J. Frankovich; Director: Milton Katselas; Screenplay: Leonard Gershe; Stage Play Adaptation: Jay Allen; Play: Barillet and Grédy; Music: Michel Legrand; Cinematography: Charles B. Lang; Film Editing: David Blewitt; Production Design: Robert Clatworthy
Cast—Liv Ullman (Ann Stanley); Edward Albert (Peter Latham); Gene Kelly (Billy Boylan); Binnie Barnes (Maud Ericson); Deborah Raffin (Trina Stanley); Nancy Walker (Mrs. Margie Margolin); Natalie Schafer (Mrs. Adams); Claudia Jennings (Gabriella).

The Single Girls, 1974
Credits—Producers: Beverly Sebastian, Ferd Sebastian; Directors: Beverly Sebastian, Ferd Sebastian; Cinematographer: Ferd Sebastian; Screenplay: Ann Cawthorne
Cast—Claudia Jennings (Allison); Jean Marie Ingels (Phyllis); Chéri Howell (Shannon); Joan Prather (Lola); Greg Mullavey (George); Albert Popwell (Morris); Victor Izay (Andrew); Mercy Rooney (Cathy); Robyn Hilton (Denise).

Truck Stop Women, 1974
Credits—Executive Producer: Peter S. Traynor; Producer: Mark L. Lester; Director: Mark L. Lester; Screenplay: Mark L. Lester and Paul Deason; Director of Photography: John A. Morrill; Film Editing: Marvin Walowitz; Music: Big Mac & the Truckstoppers
Cast—Claudia Jennings (Rose); Lieux Dressler (Anna); John Martino (Smith); Paul Carr (Seago); Dennis Fimple (Curly); Gene Drew (Mac); Jennifer Burton (Tina); Len Lesser (Winter); Speed Sterns (Rusty); Uschi Digart (Truck Stop Woman).

'Gator Bait, 1974
Credits—Producers: Beverly Sebastian, Ferd Sebastian; Directors: Beverly Sebastian, Ferd Sebastian; Original Story and Screenplay: Beverly Sebastian; Cinematography: Ferd Sebastian; Film Editing: Ron Johnson; Music Department: William A. Castleman and William Loose (Music Arrangers), Lee Darin (Singer).
Cast—Claudia Jennings (Desiree Thibodeau); Sam Gilman (T.J. Bracken); Doug Dirkson (Leroy Bracken); Clyde Ventura (Deputy Billy Boy); Bill Thurman (Sheriff Joe Bob Thomas); Dan Baldwin (Pete Bracken); Ben Sebastian (Ben Bracken); Janit Baldwin (Julie); Tracy Sebastian (Big T).

The Man Who Fell to Earth, 1976
Credits—Executive Producer : Si Litvinoff; Producers: Michael Deeley and Barry Spikings; Associate Producer: John Peverall; Director: Nicolas Roeg; Novel: Walter Tevis; Screenplay: Paul Mayersberg; Music : John Phillips and Stomu Yamashta; Director of Photography: Anthony Richmond; Film Editing: Graeme Clifford; Special Photographic Effects: P.S. Ellenshaw.
Cast—David Bowie (Thomas Jerome Newton); Rip Torn (Nathan Bryce); Candy Clark (Mary-Lou); Buck Henry (Oliver Farnsworth); Bernie Casey (Peters); Captain James Lovell (Himself); Claudia Jennings (Peters' Wife, uncredited).

Sisters of Death, 1976
Credits—Producers: Gary Messenger and Gustaf Unger; Director: Joseph A. Mazzuca; Screenplay: Elwyn Richards and Peter Arnold; Original Story: Elwyn Richards; Director of Photography: Grady Martin.
Cast—Arthur Franz (Edmond Clybourn); Claudia Jennings (Judy); Chéri Howell (Sylvia); Sherry Boucher (Diane); Paul Carr (Mark); Joe Tata (Joe); Sherry Alberoni (Francie); Roxanne Albee (Penny).

The Great Texas Dynamite Chase, 1976
Credits—Producer: David Irving; Director: Michael Pressman; Screenplay: David Kirkpatrick; Photographer: Jamie Anderson; Film Editing: Millie Moore; Music: Craig Safan.
Cast—Claudia Jennings (Candy Morgan); Tara Strohmeier (Pam Morgan); Jocelyn Jones (Ellie-Jo Turner); Tom Rosqui (Jason Morgan); Johnny Crawford (Slim); Chris Pennock (Jake).

Moonshine County Express, 1977
Credits—Executive Producers: Doro Hreljanovic and Paul Joseph; Producer: Ed Carlin; Director: Gus Trikonis; Screenplay: Hubert Smith and Daniel Ansley; Cinematography: Gary Graver; Film Editing: Gene Ruggiero; Music: Fred Werner.
Credits—John Saxon (J.B. Johnson); Susan Howard (Dot Hammer); William Conrad (Jack Starkey); Morgan Woodward (Sweetwater); Claudia Jennings (Betty Hammer); Jeff Corey (Hagen); Dub Taylor (Uncle Bill), Maureen McCormick (Sissy Hammer); Albert Salmi (Sheriff Larson); Len Lesser (Scoggins).

Deathsport, 1978
Credits—Producer: Roger Corman; Directors: Nicolas Niciphor (as Henry Suso) and Allan Arkush; Story: Frances Doel; Screenplay: Nicolas Niciphor (as Henry Suso) and Donald Stewart; Cinematography: Gary Graver; Film Editing: Larry Bock; Music: Andrew Stein.
Cast—David Carradine (Kaz Oshay); Claudia Jennings (Deneer); Richard Lynch (Ankar Moor); William Smithers (Dr. Karl); Will Walker (Marcus Karl); David McLean (Lord Zirpola); Jesse Vint (Polna).

Fast Company, 1979
Credits—Executive Producer : David M. Perlmutter; Producers: Michael Lebowitz, Peter O'Brian and Courtney Smith; Director: David Cronenberg; Story: Alan Treen; Screenplay: David Cronenberg, Phil Savath, and Courtney Smith; Cinematography: Mark Irwin; Film Editing: Ronald Sanders.
Cast—William Smith (Lonnie "Lucky Man" Johnson); Claudia Jennings (Sammy); John Saxon (Phil Adamson); Nicholas Campbell (Billy "The Kid" Brocker); Don Francks (Elder); Cedric Smith (Gary "The Blacksmith" Black); Judy Foster (Candy); Robert Haley (P.J.); George Buza (Meatball); David Graham (Stoner).

Television Appearances
Ironside, 1971: "The Professionals," Maralyn
Barnaby Jones, 1973: "To Denise, With Love and Murder," Denise Frazer
The Brady Bunch, 1973: "Adios, Johnny Bravo," Tami Cutler
Cannon, 1974: "Lady in Red," Susan Williams; "Bobby Loved Me," Lenora Wilson
Movin' On, 1974: "Ransom," Ann
The Manhunter, 1974: "The Truck Murders," uncredited
The F.B.I., 1974: "Deadly Ambition," Judith Grinnell
The Streets of San Francisco, 1976: "Underground," Evie
Lucan, 1977: "Nightmare," Debbie
240-Robert, 1979: "Bank Job," Barbara Rice

A Completely Arbitrary Rating of Claudia's Films from Best to Not-So-Best

I have not included films where Claudia's screen time was limited. This list is for the films in which she was actually given an opportunity to act.

A little bit of trivia: Claudia is frequently credited with appearing in a film *La Trampa Mortal*, which was the Spanish name for *Sisters of Death*. She is also frequently credited as appearing in *Invasion of the Bee Girls*, which is incorrect. It starred the lovely and talented Victoria Vetri, but not Claudia.

1. *Unholy Rollers*: Still her best overall performance, combining acting and action. Made all the more astonishing by her relative youth, inexperience and that she was required to carry almost every scene.
2. *The Great Texas Dynamite Chase*: Claudia's film all the way; she commands the viewer's attention in every shot.
3. *Truck Stop Women*: I believe Claudia did a magnificent job in creating a true femme fatale, a film noir character updated to the exploitation genre. The only true villain Claudia ever portrayed.
4. *'Gator Bait*: Effective, non-verbal physical acting; Claudia plays a believable swamp girl.
5. *Moonshine County Express*: One of her best movies; it's too bad she didn't have a larger role.
6. *Fast Company*: Underrated film, and Claudia doesn't have enough on-screen time, but I highly recommend it.
7. *The Single Girls*: Good performance in an ensemble cast.
8. *Group Marriage*: Another fine movie where Claudia was part of a larger group of actors. A shame Stephanie Rothman couldn't have given her some comedic lines. She's very serious in the film.
9. *Sisters of Death*: Claudia does her best in a bad film.
10. *Deathsport*: Claudia tries, but the dialogue and a screwed-up plot makes this a lost cause. Best viewed by 15-year-old boys who are stoned (or those who think like them).
11. *Jud*: Depressing film, depressing filmmaking, not enough Claudia.
12. *The Stepmother*: This film has a unique quality; it is both irritating and interesting simultaneously. Unfortunately, more of the former than the latter.

I have not seen *Willy and Scratch*; therefore, I cannot rate the film. Likewise, Claudia's scenes in the rest of her films were quite limited; however, her appearance in *The Man Who Fell to Earth* was very memorable, and her one line was significant and well delivered.

Bibliography

Bass, Ari, "Claudia Jennings' 'Lost Highway,'" *Femme Fatales*, Vol. 9, No. 2, July 21, 2000

Carpenter, Teresa, "Death of a Playmate," the *Village Voice*, November 5-9, 1980

Colander Pat, "The Life and Death of Bobbie Arnstein, The First Funeral Hugh Hefner Ever Attended," *Chicago Reader*, August 15, 1975

Hart, Bobby with Glenn Ballantyne, *Psychedelic Bubble Gum: Boyce & Hart, The Monkees, and Turning Mayhem Into Miracles* (New York: SelectBooks, 2015)

Kalter, Suzy and Allison Rahel, "It Was the Wedding of the Year in 1976—Now Marisa Berenson Loses a Husband and a Plum Role," *People* Magazine, Vol. 9, No. 21, May 29, 1978

Keeyes, John, *Attack of the B Queens* (Baltimore: Luminary Press/Midnight Marquee Press, 2003)

Koetting, Christopher T., *Mind Warp!: The Fantastic True Story of Roger Corman's New World Pictures* (Baltimore, Maryland: Midnight Marquee Press, 2013)

Von Doviak, Scott, *Hick Flicks: The Rise and Fall of Redneck Cinema* (Jefferson, NC: McFarland and Company, Inc., 2004)

Watts, Dr. Steven, *Mr. Playboy: Hugh Hefner and the American Dream* (Hoboken: Wiley & Sons Inc., 2009)

Williams, Albert, "But She Was a Cheerleader," Albert Williams, *Chicago Reader*, September 21, 2000

Williamson, Bruce, "Claudia Jennings," *Playboy* Magazine, Vol. 21, No. 12, December 1974; "Claudia Recaptured," *Playboy* Magazine, Vol. 9, No. 9, 1979

The Lifestyle to Become Accustomed to, Law office of Makupson & Howard, posted on September 29, 2013

"Acting Playmate," *Playboy* Magazine, Vol. 16, No. 11, November 1969

"Playmate of the Year," *Playboy* Magazine, Vol. 17, No. 6, June 1970

Index

40 Carats, 178, 188, 277
1968 Democratic Convention, 105

A

Acapulco, 154
Acting Playmate, 140, 280
The Actor's Studio, 191, 203
Adios, Johnny Bravo, 210, 237, 278
A&E Network, 252
A-films, 190, 196
Agatha Christie, 174
Albee, Roxanne, 167, 170, 278
Alberoni, Sherry, 168, 170, 278
Albert, Edward, 178, 277
Alessandrini, Goffredo, 146
A-list actress, 264
Allen, Jay, 277
Allison, Keith, 112, 210, 212, 214, 246, 253–54
All-Starr Band, 211
Amarcord, 221
The Ambushers, 203
American Academy of Television Arts and Sciences, 220
American Gothic, 113–15, 124, 271
American Gothic literature, 113–15
American International Pictures, 113, 222
A-movies, 110–11, 197, 203, 223, 251, 264, 266–67, 273, 279
A&M Records, 143
Anders, Luana, 268
Anderson, Jamie, 278
Anderson, John, 276
Andres, Michael, 277
Ann-Margret, 264
Ansley, Daniel, 278
Antibes, 188
Antoni/Weitz Productions, 113
Arabesque, 177
Archibald Leach, 133
Argento, Dario, 183
Arness, Bill, 275

Arnold, Peter, 278
Arnstein, Bobbie, 279
Arthur, Beatrice, 193
Arthur, Maureen, 275
Attack of the 50-Foot Woman, 109–10
Attack of the Crab Monsters, 225
Aubrey, Jim, 233
August Underground, 151
Austin, Judith, 275
Avedis, Hikmet L., 154, 275

B

Bach, Barbara, 237
Baker, Rick, 151
Baldwin, Janit, 180, 278
Ballantyne, Glenn, 149, 166, 257
Banks, Seth, 275
Bardot, Brigitte, 188, 250
Barnaby Jones, 237, 278
Barnes, Binnie, 178, 277
Barris, Chuck, 145
Bartel, Paul, 222
Bass, Ari, 107, 113, 122, 139–40, 147, 200, 202, 207–8, 213–14, 245, 253, 255–56, 260, 262, 279
Bava, Mario, 183
The Beatles, 119
Beatty, Warren, 143, 254
Beckett, Jack, 275
Belushi, John, 208
Bennell, Craig, 245
Benton, Barbi, 129–30, 133, 138, 263
Berenson, Marissa, 235
Bergen, Candice, 264
Bergen, Elizabeth, 167
Bergen, Polly, 249
Berman, Ingmar, 268
Best Actress Oscar, 191
Best Original Song Oscar, 154
Best Supporting Actor, 203
Beverly Hills, 140, 150, 159, 165, 170, 190, 193, 214, 235, 242
Blackwell, Chris, 195–96

Blackwell food conglomerate, 195
Blair, Nicky, 183
Blazing Saddles, 175
Blewitt, David, 277
Blood Beach, 245, 262
Blood Sucking Freaks, 152
B-movies, 110, 141, 152, 159–60, 166, 172, 174, 178, 181, 196, 201, 251, 264–69, 273
Bobby Hart & Glenn Ballantyne, 251, 279
Bobby Hart's and Claudia's relationship, 143, 145–46, 149, 155–56, 160, 162–67, 174, 188–92, 201, 207–8, 211, 233, 236, 240–44, 246, 249–51, 253, 257, 259
Bob Newhart Show, 146
Bock, Larry, 278
Bogdanovich, Peter, 137, 222, 265
Boisseree, Simone, 112, 165, 207–9, 214, 217–18
Bonaduce, Danny, 249
Borsari Images, 113
Bottin, Rob, 151
Boucher, Sherry, 167, 170, 278
Bowie, David, 193–94, 209, 254, 278
Boxcar Bertha, 221
Boyce, Tommy, 143, 156, 166, 170, 192
Boyce & Hart, 166, 207, 244, 251, 279
Boylan, Billy, 277
The Brady Bunch, 210, 237, 258, 263, 278
Brando, Marlon, 203
Brandon, Michael, 113, 212
Breughel's Landscape, 195
Bright Lights Film Journal, 135, 140
Brill Building Group, 143
British Film Institute, 225
British Lion Film Corporation, 113
Broadway, 115, 155, 170, 178, 203, 249
The Brood, 221, 232
Brooks, Albert, 265
Brooks, Louise, 273
The Brothers Karamazov, 203
Bruce Almighty, 209
Bryce, Nathan, 278
Bullock, Sandra, 268
Burger King, 111

Burstyn, Ellen, 264
Burt Bacharach-Hal David, 147
Burton, Jennifer, 184, 277
Burton, Norman, 275
Bus Stop, 203
Butch Cassidy and the Sundance Kid, 196
Butler, Artie, 275
Buza, George, 278

C

Caan, James, 212–13, 239
Caesar's Palace, 213
Caffaro, Cheri, 150
Cahn, Don, 275
Caioti Cafe, 245
California, 103, 140, 146, 163, 172, 193, 201, 208, 234
Callaway, Tom, 145
Cameron, James, 222
Campbell, Nick, 230, 232, 278
Canby, Vincent, 271
The Candy Store, 210, 213
Canned Heat, 195
Cannes Film Festival, 188, 225
Cannibal Holocaust, 150
Cannon, 148, 202, 237, 263, 278
Cannon, Dyan, 147, 275
Cannon, William, 203
Cannon Films, 268
Captain James Lovell, 278
Caribe, 209
Carlson, Karen, 221
Carnegie, Dale, 257
Carr, Paul, 168, 170, 185, 277–78
Carradine, David, 216–18, 222, 226, 253, 278
Carradine, Robert, 222
Carson, Johnny, 189, 216
Carspoitation films, 206
Carter, Lynda, 237, 263
Casablanca, 273
Casey, Bernie, 194–95, 278
Cassidy, Joanna, 238, 263
Castleman, William A., 277
Cawthorne, Ann, 277
CBS, 233

Centerfold, 131, 133, 136, 249
Century City, 254
CGI effects, 152, 194
Champion, Gower, 155, 250
Chandler, Jeff, 143
Chaplin, Charlie, 273
Charlie's Angels, 138, 143, 193, 237–38, 240, 250, 258, 263, 269–70
Charlie's Angels role, 243, 269
Chastain, Jessica, 269
Chenoweth, Deborah, 112, 234, 236
Cher, 195
Cherry, Ava, 193, 208–9, 253–54
Chesterton, Joan, 111, 115–19, 132, 140, 163, 187, 246–47, 249–50, 253, 256, 258, 274
Chesterton, Mary Eileen, 106, 113, 115, 117–19, 124, 129, 215, 256, 259–60
Chesterton family, 111, 113, 115–16, 120, 129, 138, 145, 187, 196, 212, 225, 239, 249, 253, 258
Chestertons, The, 115–20, 124, 129, 133, 186, 215, 249, 259–60
Chicago, 105, 118, 124, 126, 128, 134, 145, 155, 162, 165, 243
Chicago Carton Company, 128
Chicago Playboy Club, 130, 133
Chicago Reader, 107, 113, 118, 124, 255, 260, 279–80
Chicago Sun Times, 262
Chicago Tribune, 196, 271
Chinatown, 220
Christie, Julie, 264
Christy, Karen, 130
Cinémathèque Française, 225
Citizen Kane, 111, 202
Clatworthy, Robert, 277
Claudia, 103–18, 120–22, 124–26, 129, 132–51, 153, 155–57, 159–68, 170, 172–98, 200–204, 206–21, 223–66, 268–74, 279
Claudia's abuse of drugs, 107, 114, 208, 210, 212–13, 215–17, 220, 226, 239, 254, 259, 265
Claudia's auditions, 121, 140, 155, 172, 226, 237, 240, 250, 263

Claudia's career, 106–8, 125–26, 132, 134–36, 138, 141, 143–44, 165, 170–71, 189–93, 196–97, 200–201, 210, 220–23, 238, 254–55, 258–63, 265, 269–71, 273
Claudia's cyber-popularity, 114, 200, 236, 247, 250, 273
Claudia's Death, 103, 107, 110, 148, 151, 154–55, 167, 170, 180–81, 183, 185, 207–8, 219, 232, 234, 247–49, 251, 266, 269–70, 278–79
Claudia's film roles, 108–10, 116–17, 140–43, 146–47, 153, 155, 160–61, 182, 196–97, 201, 203, 222–23, 235, 237, 240, 243, 245, 261–66, 268–69, 271
Claudia's private life, 107–8, 111–15, 117, 134, 136, 144–45, 147, 162–63, 165, 177–78, 192, 207, 209, 234–35, 237, 239–40, 244–49, 251–60, 272, 274
Claudia's professional life, 108, 135, 146, 155, 160, 178, 186, 210, 221, 227, 257–58, 260, 262, 264, 266, 269–70, 273
Cleopatra Jones, 175
A Clockwork Orange, 150, 173, 193
Coca-Cola, 130
Cocteau, Jean, 173
Coen Brothers, 152, 203
Cohen, Howard R., 160, 277
Cole, Michael, 140, 143
Collins
  Gunther, 141
  Jo, 145
Collins, Joan, 264
Collins, Roberta, 150, 222, 277
Collinson, Madeleine, 148
Collinson twins, 263
Columbia Pictures, 113, 178, 193
Commander Cody and the Lost Planet Airmen, 218
Connery, Sean, 260
Connor, Chuck, 197
Conrad, Kimberly, 129
Conrad, William, 202, 226, 237, 278
Cool Hand Luke, 203

Coolidge, Rita, 270
Cooper, Alice, 211
Cooper, Jackie, 275
Corey, Jeff, 203, 210, 278
Corleone, Sonny, 204
Corman, Roger, 111, 113, 150–51, 155–56, 159, 167, 171, 197, 200, 216–18, 220–25, 227–28, 240, 243, 250–54, 258, 262, 267–69, 272–73, 277–78
Corman films, 197, 222, 267–68
Cornfeld, Bernard, 189
Corso, Leonard, 277
Cosby, Bill, 133, 144
Costa, Don, 143
Cotton Bowl, 265
Court, Hazel, 268
Craven, Wes, 150
Crawford, Johnny, 113, 197, 199, 208, 278
Cronenberg, David, 152, 228, 230–33, 262, 278
Cronenbergesque, 228
Cronenberg philosophy, 228
Cronenberg theme, 229
Crosby, David, 166
Crystal, Billy, 174
Curtis, Tony, 213, 239

D

Damn Yankees, 170
Danning, Sybil, 150, 269
Dark Shadows, 201
Davis, Sammy, 213
Death Race 2000, 216, 219, 224, 227
Deathsport, 103, 156, 209, 216–21, 223–27, 250, 260, 262, 270–72, 278–79
Deeley, Michael, 194, 278
Deep Purple, 133
Deliverance, 179, 181
Deman, Robert, 275
Demme, Jonathan, 222
Denberg, Susan, 263
DeNiro, Robert, 191
Derek, Bo, 154, 237

Dickinson, Angie, 222
Digard, Uschi, 185, 277
DiMaggio, Joe, 265
Dimension Pictures, 113
Dinoshark, 222
Dirkson, Doug, 277
Dirty Harry, 174, 267
Disneyland, 257
Ditton, Bill, 121
Doel, Frances, 278
Dolenz, Mickey, 192, 251
Douglas, Michael, 237
Dracula, 225
Dressler, Lieux, 184, 277
Drew, Gene, 184, 277
Dunaway, Faye, 227, 264
Duque Films, 113
Dura Corporation, 118
Dynamite Women, 196
Dynasty, 238, 245, 258, 270

E

Earlham College, 116
Eastwood, Clint, 174, 263
Easy Rider, 173
Ebert, Roger, 262, 272, 279
Ebsen, Buddy, 237
Eccles, Aimee, 171, 277
Edgar Allen Poe film adaptations, 126, 222, 225, 268
Edwards, Vince, 241
Elias, Justine, 151
Elm Street, 202
El Topo, Alejandro Jodorowsky, 271
Elwyn Richards, 278
Emergency, 220
Emery, Robert, 113, 182, 208
Emmy awards, 197
Entertainment Tonight, 251
Ericson, Maud, 277
Esquire magazine, 127–28
Europe, 105, 112, 118–19, 121–24, 132–33, 138–40, 145–46, 188–90, 197, 212, 227, 243, 247, 250
Evans, Ethel, 275

Evans, Linda, 193, 210, 234–35, 241
Evanston and ETHS (Evanston Township High School), 118–22, 243, 251, 269
Exploitation films, 149–54, 170, 179–80, 182, 196, 223, 225, 237, 269
Exploitation movies, 103, 149–50, 152, 168, 177, 181, 184, 186, 201, 222, 224, 230, 243, 265, 268–69

F

Fain, Sammy, 275
Falcon Crest, 153
Famous Monsters of Filmland, Forrest J., 225
Fantasy Island, 138
FAO Schwarz, 189
The Fast and the Furious, 152
Fast Company, 202, 228, 230, 232–33, 271, 278–79
Fawcett, Farrah, 271
The FBI, 196
Femme Fatales article, 107, 112, 121, 202, 207–8, 213, 253, 255, 260, 279
Fenn, Sherilyn, 268
Fideler, Lew, 112, 121
Field, Sally, 153
Fimple, Dennis, 184, 277
Fitzcaraldo, 221
Flash Gordon, 270
Fletcher, Louise, 227
Fonda, Bridget, 268
Fonda, Jane, 177, 264, 269
Fonda, Peter, 193, 222
Fondren, Debra Jo, 112, 233, 236
Ford, Harrison, 163
Ford, Henry, 257
Foster, Judy, 228–29, 278
Francks, Don, 229, 278
Franju, Georges, 173
Frankenstein, 178, 180, 225
Frankenstein Unbound, 222
Frankovich, Mike, 178
Franz, Arthur, 168, 170, 278
Frazer, Denise, 278

Freeman, Kathleen, 277

G

Gannes-Rosenthal, Gayle, 112, 235–36
Garcia, Jerry, 219
Gardner, Ava, 250
Garfield, David, 153
Garfield, Jack, 112–13, 214, 221, 233, 235–36, 242, 245–46, 249
Garfield, John D., 277
Garland, Beverly, 268
Garner, James, 220
Gator Bait, 157, 174, 178–83, 188, 196, 250, 266, 273, 277, 279
Gauguin, 272
Generals, 211
Gerard Alfred Chesterton, 115
Gershe, Leonard, 178, 277
Ghouls, 181
Gibb, Maurice, 163
Gibbs, Ann, 258
Gierasch, Stefan, 201
Gilman, Charlotte Perkins, 114
Gilman, Sam, 179–80, 277
Glass, Keith, 161–62, 244
Glen Miller Park, 116
The Godfather, 111, 183
The Godfather Part II, 271
Golden Girls, 146
Golden Globe, 191
Golden Globe Award, 265
Golden Globe nominations, 270
Golden Raspberry, 218
Goldwater, Barry, 215, 235
Goodman, Oscar, 213
Grabowski, Marilyn, 134, 140, 165, 191, 216, 233, 240, 247, 250, 253
Graeme Clifford, 278
Graham, David, 229, 278
Gramercy Place, 143, 145
Grand Canyon, 217
Granno, Allison, 143, 246
Grant, Cary, 133, 269
Grateful Dead, 133, 219
Graver, Gary, 201–2, 207, 218–19, 226,

278
Gray, Erin, 106
Grease, 177
Great Britain, 195, 213, 268
The Great Gatsby, 187
Great Texas Dynamite Chase, 107, 156, 160, 181, 196–97, 200–201, 223, 226–27, 264, 272, 278–79
Great Texas Dynamite Chase and Deathsport, 103
Great Texas Dynamite Chase and Sisters of Death, 266
Greece, 140, 145, 216
Greene, Shecky, 275
Greenfield, Mike, 113, 116, 207–8, 214
Greenspun, Roger, 148
Grey, Joel, 193
Grier, Pam, 150, 268–69
Griffith, Melanie, 237
Grinnell, Judith, 279
Group Marriage, 170–71, 173, 188, 266, 277, 279
Guiding Light, 153
Gunilla Hutton, 138

H

Hack, Shelley, 106, 238, 250
Hale, Victoria, 112, 143–44, 146, 165, 207
Haley, Jack, 143, 147–48
Haley, Robert, 278
Hall, Ralph, 275
Hamilton, David, 188
Hamm, John, 269
Hammer films, 268
Hamptons, 165, 234
Hanks, Tom, 263
Hannibal, 170
Happy Days, 214
Hard Boiled Persona, 227, 236
Harris, Crystal, 129
Hart, 143, 146, 148, 156, 163, 174, 187, 190–91, 233, 244, 251, 279
Hart, Bobby, 112, 139, 141, 143–45, 149, 155–56, 162–64, 166, 186–88, 192–93, 196–97, 207, 209–11, 213–14, 236, 243–46, 248–55, 257, 270–71, 277
Hartman, Mary, 174
Haskell, Jimmie, 186
Hawn, Goldie, 201
Hayes, Allison, 108
Headpress book Cult People, 217
Heartbreak Kid, 265
Hee Haw, 138
Hee Haw Honeys, 138
Hef, 125, 127–40, 149, 165–66, 187, 191–92, 195, 201, 233–34, 236, 239, 242–43, 254, 257, 263
Hefner, Cooper, 131
Hefner, Hugh, 105, 108, 113, 124–40, 148–49, 186–87, 195, 208, 213, 234, 239–40, 242–43, 246, 248, 254, 256–58, 260, 263, 265, 270–71
Helena, 229
Helix, 219
Hellfire Clubs, 125
Hell's Angels, 193
Hemingway, Ernest, 260
Hemmings, David, 148, 275
Henry, Buck, 194, 278
Hepburn, Katharine, 269
Herman, Stan, 165–66, 234–35, 238–39, 241–45, 248–49, 271
Herman Melville's Moby Dick, 114
Herrera Jr, Rudy, 153
Hick Flicks, 159, 207, 280
High Plains Drifter, 201
Hilton, Robyn, 277
Hitchcock, Alfred, 141, 185, 267
Hoel, Gil, 122
Hoffman, Dustin, 193, 220, 224
Hollywood, 106–7, 113–16, 120, 132–33, 140, 146–47, 190–91, 193, 202–3, 207–10, 212, 233–36, 242, 244, 251, 253–57, 259, 261, 264–68, 270
Hollywood hypocrisy, 238, 263
Hollywood's Exploitation A-List-by Nicano Loreti, 217
Home Improvement, 146
Howard, Ron, 222, 225
Howard, Susan, 202, 278

Howell, Chéri, 167, 170, 175, 277–78
Hull House Theater Company, 123, 132
Hustler Magazine, 201
Huston, John, 141
Hyde, Jim, 210
Hyde, Johnny, 210

I

Illinois, 127–28, 164, 249
Ingels, Jean Marie, 175, 277
Iowa, 115
Irving, David, 278
Irwin, Mark, 113, 232, 236, 278
Island Records, 195
Ittenbach, Olaf, 151
Izay, Victor, 175, 277

J

Jackie Brown, 268
Jackson, Glenda, 264
Jackson, Joe, 170
Jackson, Kate, 237, 250, 269
Janssen, Danny, 143, 156, 186, 249
Janssen, David, 241
Japan, 127, 280
Japanese Pinky Violence, 151
Jardin, 188
Jennings, Claudia, 103, 111, 113, 123–25, 131, 133–34, 146, 148, 159–60, 181–82, 207–9, 221, 227–28, 245–46, 249, 256–57, 259–60, 273, 275, 277–80
Jennings, Keith, 112–13, 161–62, 208, 213–14, 218, 236, 238, 240, 249, 252–54, 258, 274
Jimi Hendrix, 119
Johnson, Ron, 277
Jones, Brian, 208
Jones, Charlene, 158
Jones, Jocelyn, 197–98, 200, 278
José Mojica Marins, 280
Joseph, Paul, 278
Josie and the Pussycats, 143, 268
Jud, 141–42, 144, 153, 271, 274–75, 279

Justice, Catherine, 276
Justice, Katherine, 153

K

Kansas City Bombers, 159
Kaplan, Jonathan, 222
Karl, Marcus, 278
Katselas, Milton, 178
Katselas, Milton, 178, 277
Kaufmann, Joseph, 141, 275
Keaton, Buster, 273
Keaton, Diane, 264
Keitel, Harvey, 237
Kellerman, Sally, 163
Kelly, Gene, 178, 277
Kemp, Jack, 215
Kennedy, Jayne, 171, 173, 277
Kent, Tony, 216
Kesner, Candy, 214
Kidder, Margot, 264
Kimmel, Bruce, 258
King, Carole, 143
King's Road, 212
Kinsey, Alfred, 127
Kirkland, Sally, 113, 164, 191, 223, 238, 249, 251, 253–54
Kirkpatrick, David, 278
Klute, 264
Koetting, Chris, 112
Kristofferson, Kris, 270
Kubrick, Stanley, 150, 264, 268
Kulcsar, Mike, 154

L

Lacambre, Daniel, 277
Ladd, Cheryl, 143, 239, 246, 249
Lake Michigan, 117
Lake Shore Drive, 123, 133
Landis, John, 245
Lane, Christie, 275
Lane, Frankie, 127
Lang, Charles B., 275, 277
Langdon, Harry, 113
Larrabee Street in West Hollywood, 192

The Last House on the Left, 150, 181
Las Vegas, 143, 193, 211–13, 235
Latham, Peter, 277
Laurel Canyon, 162, 191, 238, 245, 259
Law, John Phillip , 147–48, 164, 275
Leachman, Cloris, 223
Lebowitz, Michael, 278
Ledger, Jason, 175
Lee Strasberg's Actor's Studio, 220
Legrand, Michel, 277
Leigh, Barbara, 112, 233
Lenny, 166, 250
Leo Carillo State Park, 221
Lesser, Len, 184, 203–4, 277–78
Les Theatre du Grand Guignol, 151–53
Lewis, Herschell Gordon, 150, 267
Lewton, Val, 266
Li'l Abner, 135
Lindeland, Liv, 148
Linville, Larry, 153, 276
Litvinoff, Si, 113, 192–93, 195, 208, 210, 278
Loose, William, 277
Lopez, Pedro, 277
Loren, Sophia, 177
Los Angeles, 112–13, 125, 130, 133–35, 140, 142–43, 145, 165, 191, 197, 200, 208, 219, 221, 243, 254, 271, 273
Los Angeles Playboy club, 175
Los Angeles Times, 113, 160, 178, 201, 208, 227, 236, 246, 249, 251
Lost Highway, 207–8, 260, 279
Lou, Mary, 194
Lovecraft, 225
Loy, Myrna, 177
LT Productions, 113
Lucan, 238, 279
Lulu, 163
Luminary Press/Midnight Marquee Press, 207, 280
Lynch, Jane, 269
Lynch, Richard, 217–18, 221, 278

M

Macbeth, 147
MacGyver, 153
Macklin, Tony, 135
MacLaine, Shirley, 264
Macon County Line, 220
Magee, Patrick, 268
Magic Eye of Hollywood Productions, 113
Magna Carta, 128
The Magnificent Ambersons, 267
Makupson & Howard, 236
Malden, Karl, 237
Malibu, 103, 113, 174, 235, 245–46
Maltin, Leonard, 225
Mangnani, Anna, 146
Manhunter, 209, 279
Maniac, 270
Mann, Barry, 143
Mansfield, Jayne, 135
Margolin, Margie, 277
Marley, Bob, 195
Marquette University, 115
Martin, Dean, 213
Martin, George, 163
Martin, Grady, 278
Martin, Quinn, 258
Martino, John, 183, 277
Mary Eileen Chesterton, 105, 113, 243, 274
Mason, Connie, 263
Mason, Marsha, 264
Masque of the Red Death, 167, 225, 268
Matheson, Richard, 222
Mayersberg, Paul, 278
Mazzuca, Joseph A., 167, 170, 278
McCarthy, Kevin, 223
McCarthy, Todd, 120–22, 251, 262, 269–70
McCartney, Paul, 163
McCloud, Duncan, 153
McCormick, Maureen, 162, 212, 214, 216, 226, 236–37, 278
McCullum, Robert, 202
McGinley, Lori, 234
McLean, David, 219, 278
McLeod, Duncan, 276

Memories of a DareAngel, 251
Merci Montello, 175
Messenger, Gary, 278
Meyer, Russ, 268
Midnight Marquee Press, 113, 236, 280
Miike, Takashi, 151
Miles, Sarah, 270
Millard, Paige, 112–13, 208
Miller, Dick, 222
Miller, Susan, 112, 165, 187, 189, 208
Milwaukee, 115
Mimi Chesterton, 103, 106, 115–24, 129, 131–34, 140, 155, 187, 212, 215, 247, 249, 251, 256, 259–60, 274, 280
Mimi Chesterton All-American, 118, 131, 140, 190, 228, 255–56
Mimi's ambitions, 106, 111, 115, 117–18, 120–24, 132, 186, 215, 256
Mimi's desire for children of her own, 115–17, 120, 123, 126, 128, 134–36, 143, 148–49, 151–52, 160–62, 164, 166, 180, 189–90, 192–95, 219, 224, 234, 251, 265
Minnesota, 108, 113, 115
Miracles, 166, 207, 244, 251, 279
Mirren, Helen, 264, 269
Mocsary, John, 182
The Mod Squad, 140, 143
Monroe, Marilyn, 128, 133, 135–36, 165, 177, 203, 210, 263, 265
Montello, Merci, 175
Moonlighting, 265
Moonshine County Express, 103, 156, 201–3, 207, 210, 212, 223, 226, 233, 237, 278–79
Moore, Millie, 278
Morrill, John A., 277
Motion picture industry, 105, 138, 221, 266, 270, 272
Mourguet, Laurent, 151
Murray, Don, 203
Mykonos, 216, 240
Mystery Science Theater, 218

N

NBC Universal, 113
Needham, Hal, 209
Nelson, James, 275
Nelson, Jerry, 275
Nelson, Rick, 211
Neptune Society, 246, 249
Nevada City, 201
New Horizon Pictures, 222
New Line Cinema and Cannon Films, 268
Newman, Paul, 269
Newmar, Julie, 264
New Woman Magazine, 187, 190
New World Pictures, 113, 150, 155, 221–25, 267
New York, 128, 132, 143, 145–46, 160, 165, 186, 191, 193, 200, 207, 215–16, 244, 247, 249–51, 279
New York Times, 146, 148, 241, 271–72
Nicholson, Jack, 222
Niciphor, Nicolas, 216–18, 221, 224, 226–27, 278
Nilsson, Harry, 163
Niven, David, 247
Norma Jeane Mortenson, 133
Northwestern University, 118–19, 122, 128
Nurse Betty, 209

O

Oak Creek Canyon, 163
O'Brian, Peter, 278
Olsen, Susan, 237
One-Eyed Jacks, 180
O'Toole, Peter, 193

P

Pacific Coast Highway, 103, 107, 113, 245–47, 250
Papillon, 203
Paradise Cove, 174, 221
Paramount Television, 113
Parkin, Judd, 121

Parsons, Carl, 191
The Partridge Family, 249
Paso Robles, 167
Paul Revere and the Raiders, 210–11
Peckinpah, Sam, 141
Pennock, Chris, 278
Pennock, Christopher, 201
Penthouse Magazine, 131
People Magazine, 236, 279
Perkins, Anthony, 163
Perlmutter, David M., 278
Per Se, 111
Petty, George, 127
Peverall, John, 278
Pfeiffer, Michelle, 237
Phillips, John, 194, 278
Phillips, Stu, 141, 275
Pictorials, first Playboy, 120, 141
Playboy appearances, 107, 110, 132, 134–35, 140–41, 144, 209, 237, 251, 263, 271
Playboy Magazine, 103–4, 106–8, 124–38, 140, 144, 148, 165, 181–82, 186–87, 191, 197–98, 233–34, 236–38, 240, 242–43, 256–58, 260, 263–65, 270–71, 280
Playboy Mansion, 125, 136, 139, 160, 187, 191, 197, 212, 214, 234, 236, 258
Playboy philosophy, 126, 136–37, 265
Playboy pictorials, 138, 141, 255
Playboy Playmates, 108, 124, 129, 133–34, 136–38, 140–41, 144–45, 147–48, 163, 165, 174, 187–88, 228, 233, 239, 250, 252, 256–57, 263–65, 271
Playboy's owner, 122, 125, 130–31, 134, 136–37, 140–41, 147, 149, 164, 182, 187, 227, 238–39, 242, 249
Playboy's Playmate, 111, 113, 132, 135, 137, 140, 144–45, 148, 161, 164–65, 171, 175, 207, 214, 233, 237, 280
Playmate Claudia Jennings, 129, 134–35, 138, 140, 144–45, 148, 164, 186–89, 207–8, 214, 216, 239, 242, 260, 270–71

Plymouth Road Runner, 206
Poe adaptations by Corman, 222
Polanski, Roman, 133
Pomerantz, Jeffrey, 277
Popwell, Albert, 174, 277
Prather, Joan, 175, 277
Pressley, Elvis, 233
Pressman, Michael, 197, 278
Price, Vincent, 222
Primus, Barry, 222
Psychedelic Bubble Gum, 190, 207, 244, 246, 251, 279
Psychics, 146
Psycho, 153, 185, 267

Q

Quaaludes, 208, 214–16, 232
Quadrant Films, 113
Queen of the Bs, 104, 106, 250, 270
Quinn, Louis, 277
Quinn Martin Productions, 113

R

Rafelson, Bob, 245, 250
Raffin, Deborah, 178, 277
Rahel, Suzy & Allison, 279
Rand, Ayn, 128
Rand, Jess, 143
Randall, Jim, 235, 239
Randazzo, Teddy, 143
Randy's Donuts, 157
Rapp, Paul, 277
Recaptured, Claudia, 244, 280
Redford, Robert, 269
Redgrave, Vanessa, 264
Rey, Alejandro, 153, 276
Reynolds, Burt, 151, 206
Rialson, Candice, 222
Rice, Barbara, 279
Rich, Buddy, 133
Richards, Barry, 112–13, 143, 149, 160–61, 163, 190, 208, 246, 251, 253–54, 274
Richards, Keith, 208

Richmond, Alan, 154
Richmond, Anthony, 278
Richmond, Indiana, 112, 116–19
Richmond, Tony, 193
Richmond High, 118
Rickles, Don, 148
Rigg, Diana, 269
Roach, Hal, 141
Robbins, Harold, 107
Roeg, Nicolas, 113, 193–95, 262, 268, 278
Roerick, William, 275
Roger Corman's New World Pictures, 197, 201, 236, 268, 280
Rogers, Kenny, 211
Rohmer, Sax, 126
Rollerball, 159
The Rolling Stones, 195, 208
Roman, Candice, 156, 277
Romanszky, Lenke, 275
Rooney
　Marcy, 277
　Merci, 175
Rosqui, Tom, 278
Roth, Eli, 151
Rothman, Stephanie, 171, 173, 277
Rowe, Misty, 138
Ruben, Joseph, 221
Ruggiero, Gene, 278
Rule, Janice, 264
Ryan, Robert, 147, 275

S

Safan, Craig, 197, 278
Salmi, Albert, 202–3, 206, 278
Sanders, Ronald, 278
Sands Casino, 213
San Quentin, 215
Santa Barbara, 167
Savage Soldier, 144
Savath, Phil, 278
Savini, Tom, 151
Saxon, John, 113, 202–3, 226, 228–29, 233, 236, 278
Schafer, Natalie, 277
Schjeldahl, Peter, 272

Schmidt, Kendall, 277
Schmidt, Marlene, 153–54, 275, 277
Schwartz, Sherwood, 258
Scoggins, Tom, 204
Scorsese, Martin, 159, 222, 225–26, 265, 277
Screen Actors Guild, 179
Sebastian, Beverly, 174, 178, 188, 244, 277
Sebastian, Ferd, 112–13, 176–77, 179, 238, 246, 277
Sebastian, John, 171, 173
Sebastian, Tracy, 180, 278
Sedaka, Neil, 143
Segal, Fred, 166
Seinfeld, 184, 203
September pictorial, 238–39
Serato, Massimo, 146
A Serbian Film, 151
Seymour, Jane, 271
Sharktopus, 222
Shatner, William, 223
Shea, Michael, 277
Shendal, Dean, 213–15, 235
Shepherd, Cybill, 264–65
Shock Cinema, 218
Siegel, Don, 267
Silent Running, 220
Silverado, 180
Silver Streak, 201
Simmons, Gene, 138
Simon, John, 146, 249
Sinatra, Frank, 213
Sinatra, Nancy, 222
The Single Girls, 167, 174, 177, 277, 279
Single Girls and Group Marriage, 266
Sir Arthur Conan Doyle, 126
Sir Douglas Quintet, 133
Sir Laurence Olivier, 271
Siskel, Gene, 271
Sisters of Death, 167, 170, 175, 266, 278–79
Six, Tom, 151
Skil Power Tool, 118
Smith, Bill, 233
Smith, Cedric, 229, 278

Smith, Charla, 253, 256
Smith, Courtney, 278
Smith, Fred, 187
Smith, William, 228–29, 232, 278
Smithers, William, 278
Sneden's Landing, 200
Snider, Paul, 136
Spacek, Sissy, 163
Spartacus, 111
Spelling, Aaron, 237, 258, 270
Staebler, Tom, 134, 140
Stallone, Sylvester, 223
Stanley, Trina, 277
Starr, Ringo, 211
Steele, Barbara, 223
Steele, Don, 222
Stein, Andrew, 278
Stein, Andy, 218
Steinbeck, John, 280
Stephen Spielberg's *Used Cars*, 250
Steppenwolf, 133
Stevens, Stella, 135, 138, 140, 175–76, 263, 280
Stewart, Donald, 278
St. James, Susan, 144
St.John-Sylbert, Sharmagne, 240, 242, 247
Stomu Yamashta, 278
Stoppelmoor, Cheryl, 143
St. Paul, Minnesota, 108, 113
Strasberg, Lee, 203
Stratten, Dorothy, 136, 138, 263
Straw Dogs, 224
Streep, Meryl, 269
Streisand, Barbra, 193, 264
Strohmeier, Tara, 198, 278
Studio City, 245
Sturges, Solomon, 171, 277
Sujac Productions, 113
Sunset Strip, 240, 268
Susann, Jacqueline, 107, 147–48, 275
Suso, Henry, 221, 278
Swartz, Charles S., 277
Swift, Taylor, 204
SyFy channel, 222

T

Tata, Joe, 159, 168, 170, 278
Tata, Joe E., 277
Tate, James M., 170
Tate, Sharon, 133
Taylor, Dub, 203, 206, 278
Taylor, Edna, 275
Taylor, Liz, 181
Taylor, Samuel A., 275
Taylor, Skip, 112, 195, 235
Taylor, Zack, 277
Tender Mercies, 251
Tevis, Walter, 278
Thief, 197
Thomas & Friends, 213
Thompson, Linda, 138
Thoreau, 272
Thorne. Dyanne, 150
Thousand Oaks, 162
Thurman, Bill, 179–80, 278
Titanic, 209
Todd, Lisa, 138
Toland, Gregg, 202
Topanga Canyon Road, 245
Tourneur, Jacques, 266
Trampa Mortal, 279
Transcendental Meditation, 190
Travolta, John, 214
Traynor, Peter S., 277
Treasure of the Sierra Madre, 179
Treen, Alan, 278
Triakonis, Gus, 226
Tribute, to Claudia, 221, 228, 239, 249, 258
Trigoroff, George, 277
Trikonis, Gus, 201, 278
True Grit, 203
Tucson Daily Citizen, 164
Turkel, Ann, 224
Tusk, Alejandro Jodorowsky, 221
Tweed, Shannon, 129, 138

U

UCLA, 130, 140, 188

Ullmann, Liv, 178, 277
Unholy Rollers, 103, 155, 159–60, 174, 179, 183, 188, 196, 223, 226–28, 245, 250, 262, 265–66, 277, 279
USC film school, 154, 216

V

Van Gogh, 272
Varela, Jay, 157, 277
Vargas, Alberto, 127
The Velvet Vampire, 173
Vermeer, 272
Verzier, René , 232
Vetri, Victoria, 174, 263
Videodrome, 232
Vietnam, 105, 142, 144, 217, 226
Vint, Jesse, 113, 156, 217–18, 220, 225–26, 236, 246, 278
The Virgin Spring, 150
Von Doviak, Scott, 159
Vonnegut, Kurt, 280
VW bug, 209, 216

W

Wagner, Lindsay, 212
Wagner, Robert, 254
Walker, Nancy, 277
Wallace, Marcia, 146, 249–50, 253–54
Walowitz, Marvin, 277
Walter, Richard, 277
Waltz, Christof, 269
Warhol, Andy, 188, 193
Warner Brothers, 237
Warwick, Dionne, 147
Watergate, 105
Watts, Steven, 113, 126, 257, 260
Wayne, John, 260, 266
Weil, Cynthia, 143
Welch, Raquel, 159, 271
Welles, Orson, 201–2, 267
Werner, Fred, 278
West, Mae, 211
Western Union, 146
West Side Story, 171

Westwood Village Memorial Cemetery, 137
Wexler, Jodi, 147, 275
Wiig, Kristen, 269
The Wild Angels, 222
The Wild Bunch, 141, 200, 203
Wild Hogs, 175
Wiley & Sons Inc, 140, 280
Wilhelmina Cooper, 240
William Morris Agency, 195, 265
Williams, Albert, 118–19, 121–22, 255
Williams, Andy, 119
Williams, Barry, 237
Williams, Robin, 263
Williams, Susan, 278
Williamson, 188–89, 280
Williamson, Albert, 280
Williamson, Bruce, 187–89, 240
Willis, Bruce, 263
Willy & Scratch, 182
Wilson, Lenora, 278
Wilson, Woodrow, 155, 162, 208–9, 248
Winwood, Steve, 196
Wonder, Stevie, 214
Wonder Woman, 196, 237, 263
Wood, Grant, 113
Wood, Natalie, 254
Wood, Ronnie, 208
Woodrow Wilson Drive, Bobby and Claudia's house on , 155, 189, 192, 250
Woodward, Morgan, 203–4, 278
Woolf, Virginia, 171
World War II, 153
Woronov, Mary, 222

Y

Young, Neil, 166

Z

Zieff, Howard, 193
Zi

About the Author

Eric Karell is a writer and professional chef who resides in the north Atlanta suburbs. Originally from New York City, he attended the University of Michigan before graduating with honors from the Culinary Institute of America. Eric has 20 years' experience writing for various culinary magazines and journals, and contributes a monthly column to *The Restaurant Informer*, the magazine of the Georgia Restaurant Association.

Eric reviews films for *Attack from Planet B*, a website dedicated to cult, horror and science fiction movies. He has also written blogs on film, particularly the horror genre. Once a year, Eric posts a genre-specific Top-10 list, which includes seven areas of horror films and his top 10 movies of all time.

Eric is a serious student of the world of horror and cult films. He has researched both international and domestic titles, from the blasphemous films of José Mojica Marins and the infamous *pinku eiga* of Japan, to such underappreciated masterpieces as Michele Soavi's *Dellamorte Dellamore*.

Eric has one self-published work, *Mimi*, which he describes as an erotic paranormal romance novel. He is a member of the Romance Writers of America, the Georgia Romance Writers, the International Association of Culinary Professionals and the American Culinary Federation.

Before writing full-time, he was a successful chef, having spent 30 years working in some of the top private clubs, hotels and restaurants in the United States.

John Steinbeck, Kurt Vonnegut, and John Farris are some of the authors that he draws inspiration from.

For a catalog of Midnight Marquee titles
visit our website at www.midmar.com or
send $2 for a catalog
Midnight Marquee Press, Inc.
9721 Baltimore, MD 21234

410-665-1198

www.ingramcontent.com/pod-product-compliance
Lightning Source LLC
Chambersburg PA
CBHW071303110526
44591CB00010B/760